The Struggle for Mexico

The Struggle for Mexico

State Corporatism and Popular Opposition

DEBRA D. CHAPMAN

McFarland & Company, Inc., Publishers
Jefferson, North Carolina, and London

LIBRARY OF CONGRESS CATALOGUING-IN-PUBLICATION DATA

Chapman, Debra D., 1957–
The struggle for Mexico : state corporatism and
popular opposition / Debra D. Chapman.
        p.   cm.
Includes bibliographical references and index.

ISBN 978-0-7864-6583-5
softcover : acid free paper ∞

1. Mexico — Politics and government — 2000–   2.   Corporate state — Mexico.   3. Political
participation — Mexico.   4. Opposition (Political science) — Mexico.   5. Democracy — Mexico.
    6. Representative government and representation — Mexico.   7. Globalization — Political
aspects — Mexico.   8. Ejército Zapatista de Liberación National (Mexico).   I. Title.
        JL1281.C53 2012   320.972 — dc23   2012002928

British Library cataloguing data are available

Front cover design by David K. Landis (Shake It Loose Graphics)

Manufactured in the United States of America

*McFarland & Company, Inc., Publishers
Box 611, Jefferson, North Carolina 28640
www.mcfarlandpub.com*

To Peter for his encouragement, support and
patience through this long process.

To Cytlalli and Tania for understanding what
it takes to complete a task of such magnitude.

Contents

Acknowledgments

My biggest debt is to my friends in Mexico with whom I shared many hours protesting in the streets, attending meetings, selling newspapers and learning about the political, economic, cultural and social reality of Mexico, not to mention the frequent social gatherings to keep our spirits up in a world rife with conflict, injustice and hardship. It was their persistent questioning and discussing of how to bring about a more just and equitable world that continues to drive me today. Their support and understanding following the political repression I suffered at the hands of the government of Chiapas in 1977 is what gave me the courage to continue the struggle for the subsequent twelve years. The heaviest burdens I carry today as a result of this truly enlightening experience are the unease I feel trying to live with the contradictions of a privileged life in Canada and the sadness I feel every time I leave my friends behind as they struggle to support their families and continue their search for justice. It was this twelve-year experience that brought me to think about the issues taken up here.

I would like to give a special thanks to Dinorah for always opening her door for me whenever I've needed a place to stay, to Champiñion for his hospitality and for my cultural edification, to Rogelio, Patotas, Carlos L., Carlos B., Memotas, Alicia, Arturo, Rosario, Oso, Magda, Mercedes, Irma, JJ, Virginia, José B. and Rolando for keeping my political thoughts straight and for always being open to discussion. A heartfelt thank-you goes to Marilu, Luis, Gustavo, Estela and Vita and the clan for providing an escape from the political turmoil of everyday life.

The academic writings and political commentary of Arturo Anguiano also inspired this work.

Doug Long has been there since the beginning of the writing of the dissertation on which this book is based. I am grateful for his detailed editing of my work, and for picking up the pieces at a most crucial moment. As a friend and colleague his support has been indispensable. I would also like to thank Andrés Pérez for his help in getting me started and helping me frame my research question. His encouragement and support will be forever appreciated.

The completion of this research project would have been impossible without the support of the University of Western Ontario which provided office and library space to me as well as financial support for my fieldwork and funding to attend conferences. Wilfrid Laurier University's financial support was also very instrumental in making this a fait accompli. The inspiring music of Silvio Rodríguez, Pablo Milanes, Victor Jara, Mercedes Sosa and Atahualpa Yupanqui, just to mention a few, also helped to keep me engaged.

I would also like to thank Brian Griffith for the detailed index.

And finally, but by no means lastly, I will be forever indebted to Peter Eglin for his patience, encouragement and loving support. He never gave up on me and always said the right things when I felt overwhelmed. Cytlalli and Tania were also model children who celebrated my academic achievements along the way and whose own accomplishments I celebrate in return. A last special thanks goes to my parents and siblings for their moral support and encouragement.

Abbreviations of Organizations and Interviewees

Translations of organizations' names are provided. Interviewee information is in *italics*. An * indicates interviews that are cited in the text.

AC   Alianza Cívica [Civic Alliance].

AD   Acuerdo por la Democracia [Accord for Democracy].

AD(a)   Alianza Democrática [The Democratic Alliance].

ALBA   Alternativa Bolivariana para las Américas [Bolivarian Alternative for the Americas].

AMDH   Academia Mexicana de Derechos Humanos [Mexican Academy of Human Rights].

ANECAP Acuerdo Nacional para la Elevación de la Productividad y la Calidad [National Accord for Raising Productivity and Quality].

APPO   Alianza Popular del Pueblo de Oaxaca [Popular Assembly of the Peoples of Oaxaca].

ASE   Asamblea por el Sufragio Efectivo [Assembly for Effective Suffrage].

ASM   Alianza Sindical Mexicana [Mexican Union Alliance].

ATE   Alianza de Trabajadores de la Educacion [Educational Workers Alliance].

BTD   Bloque de Trabajadores Democráticos [Democratic Workers' Block].

BUO   Bloque de Unidad Obrera [Worker Unity Block].

CAFTA   Central American Free Trade Agreement.

CAM   El Campo no Aguanta Mas [The Countryside Cannot Bear It Anymore].

CARICOM Caribbean Community.

CBI   Confederation of British Industries.

CCE   Consejo Coordinador Empresarial [Business Coordinating Council].

CCL   Consejo Central de Lucha [Central Council of Struggle].

CD   Corriente Democrática [Democratic Current].

CDHFBC* Centro de Derechos Humanos Fray Bartolomé de Las Casas [Fray Bartolomé de las Casas Human Rights Center] *(Alejandro Aldana. Area of Diffusion and Analyses. May 25, 2004).*

CENEVAL Centro Nacional de Evaluaciones [National Evaluation Center].

CGH   Comité General de Huelga [Strike General Committee].

CGOCM   Confederación General de Obreros y Campesinos de México [General Confederation of Mexican Workers and Peasants].

CGT   Confederación General de Trabajadores [General Confederation of Workers].

CIDHM* Comisión Independiente de Derechos Humanos de Morelos [Independent Human

Rights Commission of Morelos] *(Juliana G. Quintanilla. General coordinator. February 20, 2004).*

CILAS*   Centro de Investigación Laboral y Asesoría Sindical [Resource Center for Labor Advice] *(Héctor de la Cueva. General coordinator. February 12, 2004).*

CIM   Centros Integrales de la Mujer [Centers for the Integration of Women].

CIPM   Coordinadora Intersindical Primero de Mayo [May First Interunion Coordinating Committee].

CJS   Coordinadora de Jóvenes Socialistas [Socialist Youth Coordinating Committee].

CMC   Consejo Mexicano de Café [Mexican Coffee Council].

CMD*   Ciudadanas en Movimiento por la Democracia [Women Struggling for Democracy] *(Josefina Chavez. General coordinator. February 5, 2004).*

CNC   Confederación Nacional Campesina [National Peasant Confederation].

CND   Convención Nacional Democrática [National Democratic Convention].

CNDPI   Comisión Nacional para el Desarrollo de los Pueblos Indígenas [National Commission for the Development of Indigenous Peoples] *(Arnulfo Embriz Osorio. Consultant to the general director. April 2, 2004).*

CNH   Consejo Nacional de Huelga [National Strike Council].

CNI   Congreso Nacional Indígena [National Indigenous Congress].

CNOC*   Coordinadora Nacional de Organizaciones Cafetaleras [National Coalition of Coffee Organizations] *(Fernando Celis. General coordinator. February 16, 2004).*

CNOP   Confederación Nacional de Organizaciones Populares [National Confederation of Popular Organizations].

CNT   Central Nacional de Trabajadores [National Workers Center].

CNTE*   Coordinadora Nacional de Trabajadores de la Educación [National Coordinator of Education Workers] *(José Basurto. Founder of Comité Central de Lucha in Morelos, member of CNTE. January 25, 2004).*

COCD   Convergencia de Organismos Civiles por la Democracia [Convergence of Civil Organizations for Democracy].

COCM   Confederación de Obreros y Campesinos de México [Mexican Workers and Peasants Confederation].

COCOPA   Comisión de Concordia y Pacificación [Commission for Peace and Reconciliation].

CONAIE   Confederación de Nacionalidades Indígenas del Ecuador [Confederation of Indigenous Nationalities of Ecuador].

COPARMEX   Confederación Patronal de la República Mexicana [Confederation of Mexican Employers.].

COSACI*   Comisión de Salud para la Atención de Comunidades Indígenas [Commission on Health Care Services for Indigenous Communities] *(Irma de la Cruz and three other members of COSACI. January 17, 2004).*

COSEVER   Comisión de Seguimiento y Verificación [Commission for Follow-up and Verification].

CROC   Confederación Revolucionario de Obreros y Campesinos [Revolutionary Confederation of Worker and Peasants].

CROM   Confederación Regional Obrera Mexicana [Regional Confedcration of Mexican Workers].

CSUM   Confederación Sindical Unitaria de México [Unitary Confederation of Mexican Unions].

CT   Congreso del Trabajo [The Congress of Labor].

CTM   Confederación de Trabajadores de México [Confederation of Mexican Workers].

CU   Ciudad Universitaria [University City].

DESMI*   Desarrollo Económico y Social de los Mexicanos Indígenas [Social and Economic Development for Indigenous People in Mexico] *(Jorge Santiago Santiago. Member and coordinator of Operations Team. May 15, 2004).*

EEC   European Economic Community.

EPR   Ejército Popular Revolucionario [Popular Revolutionary Army].

Eureka*   *(Rosario Ibarra de Piedra. Coordinator. December 12, 2003).*

EZLN   Ejército Zapatista de Liberación Nacional [Zapatista National Liberation Army].

FAR   Fundación Arturo Rosenblueth [Arturo Rosenblueth Foundation].

FARC   Fuerzas Armadas Revolucionarias de Colombia [Revolutionary Armed Forces of Colombia].

FASUES   Frente Amplio de Sindicatos Universitarios y de la Educación Superior [Wide Front of University and Higher Education Unions].

FAT   Frente Auténtico del Trabajo [Authentic Labor Front].

FC   Frente por el Cambio [Front for Change].

FDN   Frente Democrática Nacional [National Democratic Front].

FESEBS   Federación de Sindicatos de Empresas de Bienes y Servicios [Federation of Goods and Services Companies].

FESIUAL   Federación de Sindicatos Universitarios de América Latina [Federation of University Syndicates of Latin America].

FLN   Fuerzas de la Liberación Nacional [Forces of National Liberation].

FNCR   Frente Nacional Contra la Represión [National Front Against the Repression].

FNCRDDH   Frente Nacional Contra la Represión y en Defensa de Los Derechos Humanos [National Front Against the Repression and in Defense of Human Rights].

FNR   Frente Nacional de Resistencia (Frente de Resistencia Contra la Privatización de la Industria Eléctrica) [National Resistance Front Against the Privatization of the Electrical Industry].

FNSU   Federación Nacional de Sindicatos Universitarios [National Federation of University Workers' Unions].

FPFV   Frente Popular Francisco Villa [Francisco Villa Popular Front].

FRAYBA   Centro de Derechos Humanos Fray Bartolomé de las Casas [Human Rights Center Fray Bartolomé de las Casas].

FSM   Federación Sindical Mundial [World Federation of Trade Unions].

FSM(a)   Frente Sindical Mexicano [Mexican Labor Front].

FSTSE   Federación de Sindicatos de Trabajadores al Servicio del Estado [Federation of Unions of Workers at the Service of the State].

FTAA   Free Trade Area of the Americas.

FZLN*   Frente Zapatista de Liberación Nacional [Zapatista National Liberation Front] *(Numerous militants. April 24, 2004).*

GATT   General Agreement on Tariffs and Trade.

Granito de Café*   *(María Eugenia Santilla Ramírez. Member. November 26, 2003).*

IDB   Inter-American Development Bank.

IET   Instituto de Estudios del Trabajo [Institute for Labor Studies].

IFE   Instituto Federal Electoral [Federal Electoral Institute].

IFI   international financial institution.

IMF   International Monetary Fund.

INEGI   Instituto Nacional de Estadística, Geografía e Informática [National Institute of Statistics, Geography and Data Processing].

INI   Instituto Nacional Indigenista [National Indigenist Institute].

INMECAFE   Instituto Mexicano del Café [Mexican Coffee Institute].

INMUJERES   Instituto Nacional de las Mujeres [National Women's Institute].

ISCD   Instituto Superior de la Cultura Democrática [Superior Institute of Democratic Culture].

ISI   import substitution industrialization.

ISSSTE   Instituto de Seguridad y Servicios Sociales de los Trabajadores del Estado [Institute of Security and Social Services for State Workers].

IVA   Impuesto al Valor Agregado [Value added tax].

JBG   Junta de Buen Gobierno [Councils of Good Government].

K'inal Antsetik*   *(Nellys Paloma. Coordinator of organization in Mexico City. February 6, 2004).*

LFT   Ley Federal del Trabajo [Federal Labor Law].

LOM   Liga Obrera Marxista [Marxist Workers' League].

LUS*   Liga de Unidad Socialista [Socialist Unity League] *(Manuel Aguilar Mora. Member of the Central Coordinating Committee. May 5, 2004).*

MCD   Movimiento Ciudadana para la Democracia [Citizens' Movement for Democracy].

Mercosur   Mercado Común del Sur [South American Common Market].

MRM   Movimiento Revolucionario del Magisterio [Revolutionary Teachers' Movement].

MSD   Movimiento Sindical Democrático [Democratic Union Movement].

MST   Movimento dos Trabalhadores Rurais Sem Terra [Landless Workers' Movement].

NAFTA   North American Free Trade Agreement.

NGO   nongovernmental organization.

NSM   new social movement.

OC   La Otra Campaña [The Other Campaign].

OECD   Organisation for Economic Co-operation and Development.

OST*   Organización Socialista de los Trabajadores [Workers' Socialist Organization] *(Luís Vázquez. Director. June 1, 2004).*

PAN   Partido Acción Nacional [National Action Party] *(Luís Hernández Álvarez. Ex-president of the party, senator. February 3, 2004).*

PASC   Partido Alternativa Socialdemócrata y Campesina [Social-democratic and Peasant Alternative Party].

PCM   Partido Comunista Mexicano [Mexican Communist Party].

PD   La Planilla Democrática [The Democratic Slate].

PDRP-EPR   Partido Democrático Popular Revolucionario–Ejército Popular Revolucionario [Popular Revolutionary Democratic Party–Popular Revolutionary Army].

PEMEX   Petróleos Mexicanos [Mexican Petroleum].

PFP   Policía Federal Preventiva [Federal Preventive Police].

PMT   Partido Mexicano de los Trabajadores [Mexican Workers' Party].

PNA   Partido Nueva Alianza [New Alliance Party].

PNR   Partido Nacional Revolucionario [Revolutionary National Party].

POS   Partido Obrero Socialista [Socialist Workers' Party] *(Enrique Gómez. Executive Committee. April 22, 2004).*

PPP   Plan Puebla Panamá [Puebla Panama Plan].

PPS   Partido Popular Socialista de México [Socialist People's Party of Mexico].

PRD   Partido de la Revolución Democrática [Democratic Revolutionary Party].

PRI*   Partido Revolucionario Institucional [Institutional Revolutionary Party] *(Samuel Palma. Coordinator of the Editorial Committee. May 10, 2004).*

PRM   Partido de la Revolución Mexicana [Party of the Mexican Revolution].

PROCEDE   Programa de Certificación de Derechos Ejidales y Titulación de Solares Urbanos [Program for Certification of Ejido Rights and Urban Land Titles].

PRS   Partido de la Revolución Socialista [Socialist Revolutionary Party].

PRT   Partido Revolucionario de los Trabajadores [Revolutionary Workers Party] *(Edgard Sánchez. Member of the Political Committee of the party. February 3, 2004).*

PRUS   Planilla Roja Unidad Sindical [The Red United Union Slate].

PSN   Partido de la Sociedad Nacionalista [Nationalist Society Party].

PST   Partido Socialista de los Trabajadores [Socialist Workers' Party].

PT   Partido del Trabajo [Labor Party].

PVEM   Partido Verde Ecologista de México [Green Ecological Party of Mexico].

RCMDCI   Reformas Constitucionales en Materia de Derechos y Cultura Indígena [Constitutional Reforms on Indigenous Rights and Culture].

RMALC   Red Mexicana de Acción Frente al Libre Comercio [Mexican Network for Action Against Free Trade].

SAPs   structural adjustment programs.

SEDUE   Secretaría de Desarrollo Urbano y Ecología [Secretariat for Urban and Ecological Development].

SENER   Secretaría de Energía de México [Mexican Federal Secretariat of Energy].

SEOUAM   Sindicato de Empleados y Obreros de la Universidad Autónoma de México [Union of Workers and Employees of the Autonomous University of Mexico].

SEP   Secretaría de Educación Pública [Secretariat of Public Education].

SINTCB*   Sindicato Independiente Nacional de Trabajadores del Colegio de Bachilleres [National Independent Union of Workers of the Colegio de Bachilleres] *(Severo Escudero Carillo, Javier Carasco Ruiz, Arturo Ballarron Carapia. Members of the executive. November 14, 2003).*

SIPAZ*   Servicio Internacional para la Paz [International Service for Peace] *(Volunteer Recruitment. May 15, 2004).*

SITUAM   Sindicato Independiente de Trabajadores de la Universidad Autónoma Metropolitana [Independent Union of Workers of the Metropolitan Autonomous University].

SME*   Sindicato Mexicano de Electricistas [Mexican Electricians' Union] *(Ex-secretary of the exterior, unofficial spokesperson. October 14, 2003).*

SMO   social movement organization.

SNESCRM   Sindicato Nacional de Electricistas Similares y Conexos de la República Mexicana [National Union of Electricians and Related Industries of the Mexican Republic].

SNTE   Sindicato Nacional de Trabajadores de la Educación [National Educational Workers' Union].

SNTSS   Sindicato Nacional de Trabajadores del Instituto Mexicano del Seguro Social [Union of Social Security Workers of Mexico].

STPRM   Sindicato de Trabajadores Petroleros de la República Mexicana [Mexican Oil Workers' Union].

STRM   Sindicato de Telefonistas de la República Mexicana [Mexican Telephone Workers' Union].

STUNAM*   Sindicato de Trabajadores de la Universidad Nacional Autónoma de México [Union of Workers of the National Autonomous University of Mexico] *(Carlos Galindo Galindo. Secretary of External Relations. December 9, 2003).*

SUTERM   Sindicato Único de Trabajadores Electricistas de la República Mexicana [Sole Union of Electricity Workers of the Mexican Republic].

TC   transnationalized corporatism.

TNC   transnational corporation.

TRIFE   Tribunal Federal Electoral [Federal Electoral Tribunal].

TRIPS   Trade-Related Aspects of Intellectual Property Rights.

TUC   Trades Union Congress.

UD   Unidad Democrática [Democratic Unit].

UEUNA   Unión de Empleados de la Universidad Nacional Autónoma [Union of Employees of the National Autonomous University].

UISTE   Unión Internacional de Sindicatos de Trabajadores de la Energía [International United Electrical Workers Unions].

UNAM   Universidad Nacional Autónoma de México [National Autonomous University of Mexico].

UNIOS*   Unidad Obrera y Socialista [Socialist Workers' Unity] *(Alejandro Varas. General secretary of the Executive Committee. April 27, 2004).*

UNT   Unión Nacional de Trabajadores [National Union of Workers].

UOE   Unidad de Observación Electoral [The Electoral Observation Unit].

UTRND   Unidad de Trabajadores por el Rescate de Nuestros Derechos [Workers United for the Recovery of Our Rights].

WTO   World Trade Organization.

Preface

My subject is the struggle for Mexico between corporatist capitalism and the organizations and movements of the people who oppose and resist it. Rather than being the epic of a failed state threatened by a new feudalism of fiefdoms ruled by drug lords (Grayson 2010), or of a modernizing state with a burgeoning market economy and a pluralist, liberal-democratic polity (Xelhuantzi López 2004), it is the story of a remarkable form of state rule, namely corporatism, that has not only dominated Mexico in the twentieth century but persists, albeit modified to accommodate a globalizing economy, into the twenty-first. The "globalization" that is generally acknowledged to have emerged as a consequence of political-economic changes to world order in the 1970s is often credited with affording at least two major political consequences. One is the ceding of state sovereignty to what has been called a "de facto world government" of international financial institutions (IFIs) like the World Bank and the IMF, trading structures like NAFTA and the WTO (before 1995 the GATT) and executive meetings like the G7 and G20, all ruled over by transnational corporations and international banks (Chomsky 1993: 7, citing the U.S. business press). The second is the antiglobalization movement that arose to counter it.

Without gainsaying the undoubted importance of both of these consequences, not least in the form of the Zapatista movement that inspired so much of the antiglobalization movement, what is significant about the case of Mexico in this context is the continuing salience of the *national* unit in the form of the state both as a ruling apparatus (just as it is the chief vehicle of globalization [Albo, Gindin and Panitch 2010: 10, 17–23]) and as the object and target of organized, nonstate, political opposition (as indeed it has been for the Zapatistas). Moreover, what is especially striking is the persistence of *corporatism* as the characteristic form of state rule despite the transformation of the economy from a state-capitalist to a neoliberal-capitalist form, despite a degree of democratization in the electoral process and despite the anticorporatist efforts of oppositional movements. In fact, I go so far as to argue that much anticorporatist maneuvering has, in classical functionalist fashion, the unintended, latent consequence of integrating oppositional conflict groups into the prevailing order (Merton 1967; Coser 1964). In this way the argument presented herein is a cautionary, not to say revisionist, one in relation to the view that the combined forces of neoliberalism and democratization have swept away "all fixed, fast-frozen relations, with their train of ancient and venerable prejudices and opinions," to borrow a famous phrase used to characterize an earlier transition (Marx and Engels 1987 [1848]: 24). On the contrary, it is the thesis of this work that corporatism, albeit somewhat diminished and in "transnationalized" form, continues to hold sway in Mexico.

1

Since corporatism is a particular form of what political scientists call state-society relations — that is, the relations between state institutions, chiefly the government, on the one hand and the political, economic and voluntary organizations that make up civil society on the other — attention is focused here on the interaction between governments and such organizations as unions, oppositional political parties, nongovernmental organizations (NGOs) and a selection of social movements, most prominently the Zapatistas. Since neoliberalism is generally held to have taken hold in Mexico from 1982 I have limited the scope of the inquiry to the period from that date to the present, but in the context of a general description of the state corporatism that prevailed in the country in the preceding decades. To investigate this thesis I carried out fieldwork in Mexico in 2003–2004 and have continued to do so at various times in the years since. What I hope distinguishes the case made here, and lends it whatever persuasive force it has, is its ethnographic grounding in the author's close familiarity with at least some of the oppositional movements in question, in the interviews with leading figures in the various organizations and in the archival research of their documents that are the sources of this study's empirical data.

It would be wrong, however, to leave the reader with the impression that the origin, means and motivation of this study were simply intellectual curiosity arising from a good education at the hands of good teachers at good universities in the discipline of political science. On the contrary, it was the experience of encountering the agents of the state while accompanying activists in an oppositional organization that awakened my interest, to put it mildly. It was life in Mexico within a network of friends and comrades in opposition that, by educating me in the language and politics of the country, furnished the indispensable means for my inquiry. And it has been the revelation of poverty, inequality and repression from living in both Mexico and Canada that motivated it.

In northern countries like Canada where basic economic needs are looked after through employment or through state-run programs (renewed neoliberal assaults on the public domain notwithstanding), public attention is often focused on such issues as the local impact of road construction, pesticide contamination, obesity, the price of gasoline, wait times at the emergency ward, the welfare of pets, and public safety, including crime. But beyond this world of relative wealth and prosperity, where "the country ranks at or near the top in many of 11 well-being indicators in a new quality of life index" such that "Canadians are a pretty comfortable and happy lot" (D'Aliesio 2011), there is a whole other world in the South, whose people do not enjoy material well-being supported by substantial, relatively well-paid employment, social welfare programs, unemployment insurance, old-age pensions, and publicly funded housing. This is notably true of the third (until recently overlooked) partner in NAFTA, Mexico. Not only are there chronic and dire employment issues that the poor confront on a daily basis — "only 13 per cent of the Mexican population has a regular salary; the rest are precarious workers" (Roman and Arregui 2007: 250) — but with the introduction of neoliberalism in the past thirty years they have also had to contend with such things as "the real wages of the best-paid workers, those with a collective contract, [falling] by 18 per cent between 1995 and 2007" (ibid.), being driven off the small plots of land passed down from generation to generation, getting caught in the cross fire of a drug war, and watching funding for basic health-care services and public education be depleted under the assault of privatization. The average minimum wage in Mexico today is $5 a day, which is not enough to live on. Since public funding for the unemployed and the handicapped does not exist, people are forced to depend on family members, or leave, or live and beg in the streets.

The poor, whether working or without work, continue to protest in those same streets, demanding employment, housing and justice while the dispossessed rebel in the name of basic human rights. Women denounce political repression and take to the streets demanding the reappearance of their loved ones. Campesinos fight for the right to keep their land from being expropriated for an airport (Atenco 2002). Some types of protest are clearly economically based while others focus on more geographically or culturally specific issues. None of this is new. What is new are the political and economic policies forced on national states by bodies that in turn modify the central demands and actions of the different oppositional groups that are directly affected. It is the changing relationships among these actors that are of most interest here.

For example, since the inception of structural adjustment programs (SAPs) in the early 1980s, there has been ongoing privatization of state corporations and social programs, while nonstate actors have, in many cases, sought nontraditional ways to confront the government's readiness to ignore societal needs. Fearing the privatization of the state corporations, workers have taken to the streets in opposition. Opposed to the increase in tuition fees at the Universidad Nacional Autónoma de México (UNAM) in 1999, students and their parents shut it down and demanded respect for public education. Rejecting the election results, citizens took over the Zócalo in Mexico City in 2006 in an effort to be heard. What is a departure from tradition here are the organizational actors (including some that are middle class, multiclass or culturally based), their relationship to the state and state institutions, the interrelationships among the opposition forces themselves, and their chosen means of responding to the changing economic environment. The constraining influence that the IFIs and the global market economy have had on Mexican state-society relations has brought new challenges to nonstate actors in their struggle for improved political-economic and social conditions.

Parallel to the ongoing political struggles and modifications to state-society relations in Mexico are the drug wars. Dating back to the 1980s, cocaine and marijuana drug trafficking, territorial gang confrontations, kidnappings, turf wars and car thefts have left tens of thousands of people dead. Since Felipe Calderón took over the presidency in 2006 the bloodshed has increased. It is estimated that over 50,000 people have been killed since 2006. The United States has maintained close ties with the Mexican government over the years and in 2007, under the Mérida Initiative, approved $400 million with an expected $1.4 billion contribution to the Mexico government by 2010. The purpose of the money is to "carry out counter-narcotics, anti-terrorism, and border security measures" (Grayson 2010: 238). Neither the legitimacy nor effectiveness of U.S. involvement in Mexican affairs will be discussed here, but it cannot be ignored if only as a backdrop to state-society relations in Mexico. When this was written there were two peace marches taking place, one in the state of Morelos and the other in the state of Chiapas, calling on the government to find a peaceful solution to the violence spreading through Mexico. In the meantime, there is no quick fix or solution on the horizon. This is owing not least to the fact, supported by what evidence there is, that such state institutions as the security forces, whether police or army, are themselves heavily implicated in the drug industry.

In relation to oppositional nonstate actors, while it is difficult to make generalizations about state-society relations in Mexico at this point, there is evidence of a change in focus from gremial[1] to more general demands in some movements. This is not to suggest that these movements have become transnational, as Keck and Sikkink (1998) would have it, but rather that their demands have come to address more general, systemic issues. Broadening of demands has brought different movements into contact with each other working on joint projects. Although there was some cross-border solidarity work among unions, environmentalists and peace activists during the period leading up to the signing of NAFTA (Hathaway 2000: 3), most social movements have remained within national borders and direct their discontent against their national governments rather than international institutions such as the World Trade Organization (WTO), the International Monetary Fund (IMF) or the World Bank, all of which play a central role in the "new world order." The antiglobalization movement of the late 1990s has been an exception to this norm as activists throughout the world denounced the role of these international institutions. The shift from the gremial to the general or the local to the international is not characteristic of all social movements, but where it does occur it can perhaps be explained as a response to the emergence of new power structures.

When it comes to understanding the nature of these oppositional movements and explaining their actions, academic commentators have asked a number of different question reflecting differences in theoretical point of view. A fundamental prerequisite of the position adopted here is that political and social scientists need to be cognizant of the central characteristics and concerns of a movement and not overlook the actual actions and intentions of the social actors themselves. Do political activists look for opportunities and then engage in contentious action based on what they consider to be the chance of succeeding? Has social action gone beyond economic demands and become culturally based? Are class divisions a thing of the past? These are all difficult questions to answer, and the particular cases taken up here may not appear to fit exactly the criteria of one model or another. It is true that social-economic differences between northern developed countries and southern underdeveloped countries make it difficult to apply northern theories to the South (see Centeno 2002). That said, it appears that Marxist theory, a northern theory after all, has been set aside by a majority of both political actors and theorists in the North. Part of the reason for this is the fact that in the North, social/political activists continue to try to work within the established framework of liberal democracy and take advantage of the provisions that are in place to assure a somewhat safe environment for contentious action (although we must not forget Ipperwash, 1995; Seattle, 1999; and Caledonia, 2006). Another explanation for this is that the basic economic needs of most of the people in the North have been met and Marxist theory has come to be seen as something that was left behind with the end of the Cold War and deemed irrelevant.

However, economic issues continue to be of fundamental importance in the South (which is not to ignore the fact that they have come to have increased salience in the North in the wake of the Great Recession of 2008–2009). The fact that they have been minimized in McAdam et al.'s (2001) work, for example, is not a simple oversight but an attempt to force us to look beyond the Marxist framework in search of something "new." It is precisely the political-economic reality of southern, underdeveloped countries that I argue makes Marxism relevant today.

Does democratization provide a more protest-friendly environment? Possibly. But does this mean that people will not protest or that protest will be more sporadic if democracy has not been reached? Innumerable Latin American protests seem to contradict the assertion that democracy is a prerequisite for social actions because it provides safety. The case of Jean-Bertrand Aristide's rise to power in Haiti thanks to the Lavalas movement is an outstanding (and astounding) example of the willingness of the most impoverished people to organize and be organized under the most severe and brutal state repression and in the absence of effective liberal-democratic institutions. The "Arab Spring" spreading from Tunisia and Egypt across North Africa and the Middle East (and beyond?) is another striking case of revolutionary uprisings against more or less brutal dictatorships. Political repression is not a desirable outcome for any social movement but it is a known possible outcome of all movements. This is unquestionably true of the Mexican case. Although there is progress toward liberal democracy, the country is still eons away from becoming a consolidated democracy capable of representing the majority of the population.

Whether through reformist or revolutionary antisystemic movements, Aguirre Rojas (2005: 27) holds that it is thanks to a combination of many different types of resistance that the only party to rule Mexico to 1988, the Partido Revolucionario Institucional (PRI), was finally "defeated" in that year.[2] It is the actions of subaltern groups in society that force change and not the goodwill of those in power. Furthermore, Rojas argues (2005: 67) that the birth of politically, economically and socially aggressive governments in Latin America (including that of Felipe Calderón in Mexico) is a reflection of the "terminal crisis of the capitalist historical system" which has caused a political and social polarization. The analysis of Aguirre Rojas is an attempt to draw on the idea that the development of capitalism will produce the conditions of its own demise (Marx and Engels 1978b [1848]: 478). However, the demise of a particular political party, in this case the PRI, is one thing, and the demise of a mode of production, capitalism, is another. The Partido Acción Nacional (PAN) is as capitalist as its predecessor. While there is continued polarization of the classes in Mexico there appears to be no sign of a waning capitalism (though it is tempting to view the global economic crisis of 2008–2009 as indicative of such). One of the few obvious changes that have emerged over the last thirty years is the increased salience of international institutions that have come to shape the forms of interaction between the state and nonstate actors in Mexico.

There are five general categories, and one special case, of nonstate actors that need considering in the analysis of Mexican contentious politics. The general categories are unions, political parties, nongovernmental organizations (NGOs), the groups forming electoral movements, and the groups forming gremial, sometimes cultural, social movements. The one special case is the indigenous movement that took to the streets in 1994 in the state of Chiapas, known as the Zapatista movement. Notwithstanding that such social movements as the electoral movement, and political organizations such as the teachers' union, are constantly changing their demands and tactics, there *is* a difference in the way that the different categories or groups have responded to the new neoliberal world order and to the changes in state-society relations brought about by this new world order.

As is historically expected, movements within a given society appear and then subside in such a way that they will take center stage at certain times and slide into the background at other times. They may be said to develop in waves (see Petras 1999: 18–19). These waves may occur in response to such things as international events (such as the end of the Cold War), national economic crises, political repression, the vicissitudes of funding, changing political mandates, burnout of leaders, or an internal leadership crisis of a particular group or movement. Some organizations or movements will emerge not in response to something new but in response to the leadership's awareness of a particular issue that may have existed for an extended period but that has created intolerable consequences. Political action may also arise from the refining of an organization's tactics or identity. Many social movements emerge on the public scene in response to government actions or the introduction of an undesirable policy or bill, but most social movements take years to develop. Although not caught on mainstream media radar until they actually engage in "noteworthy" public action, they work behind the scenes trying to grow their support base, to modify and clarify their raison d'être and strategically to determine their next move.

Yashar (2007: 175–176) holds that when

> we look comparatively at collective action, it is apparent that the international arena does not simply shape social movements. Nor does globalization help to explain the timing or intensity of movements that emerge, with some prior to the heyday of globalization..., others following on the heels of globalization conjunctures..., and yet others emerging several years later.... Even though changes are taking place in the international economy, networks, and norms, one should not be too quick to assume that these descriptive developments have causal significance. For it is neither clear why, when, and where these changes do or do not generate collective action nor which form collective action is likely to take.

That is, many of the movements that are in the spotlight today either predate or postdate the emergence of neoliberalism and globalization. Yashar (2007) emphasizes the role that *changing state-society relations* have in shaping collective action. "Collective action is not universal; it remains an outcome that requires us to explain variation across and within cases ... it is this variation that becomes a tool for discerning and substantiating arguments about when and where movements [or organizations] emerge" (ibid. 172).

Although the categories of nonstate actors proposed here are not exclusive but in fact overlap and interact, they allow me to examine the varied responses to the changing political, economic and social environment in the past thirty years in Mexico. While corporatism — the incorporation of nonstate actors into the state system of decision making (see introduction) — is less salient today than it was in the mid–1900s, its presence cannot be ignored. Changes to political and economic policies under neoliberalism and during this latest period of market expansion have brought some gremial social movements — for example, the indigenous movement and some unions — to respond by enlarging their scope to include antisystemic demands as they struggle to survive. NGOs have taken over responsibilities from the government as state responsibilities have shifted from a primarily economic focus to a more political, managing role. As the state's connection to international institutions has augmented in recent years, so political parties appear to have modified their focus from simply meeting the demands of their constituents to also aligning their policies, discourse and practices with the "common sense" imposed by neoliberalism. Others, for example the electoral movement, persist with their time/event-specific demands in their continuing struggle to bring liberal democracy to Mexico. Rather than a strictly action/reaction relationship between the state and nonstate actors, there exists a range of social movements that draw on government-led reforms to grow their own movement and call on dormant sectors of society that they hope to attract. In other words, they not only respond to the new limitations imposed by the state but also try to take advantage of the new conditions to create new political opportunities.

There is no one set pattern for all social movements and political organizations. Some have shifted to encompass more generalized demands that respond to the changes in state-society relations, while others remain fixed within their gremial struggles. To anticipate the position adopted and developed throughout this book, it is fair to say that some organizations maintain their corporatist relationships with the state, others fight against corporatism while working within the neoliberal framework and still others have limited engagement with the state and can best be understood as noncorporatist. Democratic reforms influence different movements in different ways and in some cases have no influence on the way that a given organization engages in political activity. I agree with Yashar (1999: 75–76) when she asserts that new democratic institutions in Latin America "rather than securing democratic consolidation across the board, have in fact had a more checkered effect — as evidenced by the incomplete reach of the state, the survival of authoritarian enclaves, the uneven incorporation of social sectors, and the emergence of opposing social forces" (see also Migdal 1988; O'Donnell 1993; and Migdal et al. 1994). While this study critically assesses the organizational strategies and tactics of different organizations and movements, it does not for one moment deny the positive work and intentions of the many people who struggle and organize in their attempts to improve the lives of the many.

Nevertheless, some things have hardly changed for the better over the past thirty years. Indeed, the gap between the rich and the poor has increased rather than decreased as was once promised. Political repression has not subsided, although, it could be argued, it is more selective. It has come to be termed "low-intensity warfare," which characteristically targets the leaders of specific organizations rather than intervening indiscriminately.[3] Both of these factors — growing inequality and persisting repression — contradict the common belief that democratic reforms and a globalized, free-market economy would address the negative effects of capitalism. On the contrary, one of the primary driving forces behind social movements in Mexico continues to be the worsening of economic disparities.

Against this background, and seemingly out of nowhere, the world awoke on January 1, 1994 to the sight of a ragtag "army" of indigenous people, with a charismatic spokesperson called Marcos, emerging from the Lacandón jungle of Chiapas to challenge the Mexican state. Gaining unprecedented international support, the Zapatistas put their name on the political map of Mexico and of the world. Eighteen years later they are still at it. But now their political strategy has evolved into an attempt to disconnect themselves entirely from the Mexican state. In this, they have gone far beyond what other social movements have attempted to do in Mexico.

Whether we are examining privileged countries of the North or the economically marginalized countries of the South, territorial states, as Meiksins Wood (2003: 5–6) explains, are "more essential than ever to capital, even, or especially, in its global form. The political form of globalization is not a global state but a global system of multiple states." Furthermore, "capitalists ultimately depend on coercion by the state to underpin their economic powers and their hold on property, to maintain social order and conditions favourable to accumulation" (ibid.: 10).

Everything points to the need to change a system that has proven incapable of addressing the economic needs of the majority of the population. In the case of Mexico, electoral reform has been tried as have other approaches. This book is an attempt to specify how state-society relations have been modified under the current political-economic model by examining the different strategies adopted by nonstate actors in response to such things as economic inequality, job insecurity, and privatization, all of which have been intensified under neoliberalism. My many years as a political activist in Mexico have drawn me to search for an understanding of how political actors interact and how opposition forces organize in their struggle to effect change. One of the most important realizations I have come to through this project is that change is slow, and often what appears to signify change is not what we perceive or what we want to perceive. Two clear examples of this are first the realization that while there have been many electoral reforms in Mexico this does not equate with democratization, and second that the defeat of a seventy-one-year-old one-party authoritarian regime does not leave Mexico with a pluralist polity. Change requires far more than superficial, administrative modifications.

If the force of the argument proposed herein is on the staying power of the "incorporating" hand of corporatism in its old and new guises, it is not to the disparagement of the brave movements struggling to cast it off or of the incipient possibilities for positive change they embody. Rather, the emphasis is put there out of what I hope is a realistic appreciation of power's seemingly endless capacity to accommodate its rule to the changing strategies of all types of resistance short of revolution.

All translations from Spanish to English throughout the text are those of the author.

Introduction

Thesis

The thesis of this work is that the advent of neoliberal globalization has modified state-society relations in Mexico from a state-corporatist to a "transnationalized-corporatist" model, producing corresponding changes in the character of social movements and political and nongovernmental organizations. After a review of relevant theory, substantive chapters are devoted to a discussion of corporatism and contentious politics in the period of global neoliberal capitalism's growing ascendancy in Mexico since 1982. This is followed with a particular focus on the relationship between the Zapatista movement and the state in an effort to understand and evaluate the movement's partial "delinking" strategy, adopted as a nonviolent means of defending human rights and opposing capitalism in the context of transnationalized corporatism (TC). These contemporary developments in Mexican state-society relations are examined through the lens of Marxist political economy in an effort to explicate them in terms of the consolidation of capitalist relations of production. This introduction presents the shape, content and terms of the argument, describes the methodology used in the fieldwork component of the study, and gives a brief historical account of the political and economic changes experienced by the Mexican state in the period in question that form the context of this inquiry.

The conceptual innovation here, namely the idea of transnationalized corporatism is a model of state-society relations characterized by the increasing power of transnational forces to define the role, organization and functions of the state, and by the decreasing capacity of civil society's nonstate actors to influence state decisions through established legal channels of political participation. The concept's utility resides in its capacity to provide both a faithful and rational account of the diversity of oppositional strategies and actions that characterize the recent period of changing state-society relations in Mexico. While there are similarities across the range of strategies used by different groups and organizations, there is by no means a set pattern into which all actions fit.

The eclectic pool of strategies examined herein exhibits the paradoxical nature of TC itself. The responses by civil society to the changing role of the state in Mexico may be classified using the following typology of strategies: corporatist, anticorporatist and noncorporatist (or postcorporatist). That not all groups follow the same path or reach the same result is characteristic of the complicated relationships that exist among the different political and social actors in Mexico under TC. Nevertheless, the diversity itself is intelligible in terms of the changing face and place of corporatism. The concept's paradoxical

9

character is intended. It is meant to capture the persistence of corporatist relationships in Mexico alongside both neoliberal, anticorporatist, democratic reforms and postcorporatist movements seeking autonomy in relation to the state. Under TC the role of the state has changed in relation to international organizations and institutions, and civil society has responded in not one but a variety of ways. Corporatism has itself changed. For example, the state's ability to co-opt workers' organizations — which is the principal characteristic of *state* corporatism — has diminished as state corporations have been privatized, as international institutions have become predominant players, and as workers have organized independently of the state.

Since the mid–1970s, as the global capitalist political economy has expanded and taken on an increasingly neoliberal form, international institutions such as the World Bank, the International Monetary Fund (IMF), the World Trade Organization (WTO) and the Organisation for Economic Co-operation and Development (OECD) have come to play a more significant and somewhat changed role in international economic regulation. With the proliferation of international trade negotiations and agreements, and through the vehicle of structural adjustment programs (SAPs), these international institutions have increasingly come to shape the internal economic and political dealings of the countries involved. While these institutions do not remove from the state its principal function of "establishing and maintaining an economic and social order" (Williamson 1985: 10), they do constrain it and add a new dimension to the political process with new political actors. The Mexican state has found new ways to maintain economic and social order through intermediary regulatory agents, although it is an order that is precarious.

In other words, in what I refer to as TC, national states are increasingly "embedded in wider or prior structures of power and meaning" (Meyer 1999: 123). To be more specific, in TC, national states operate within a power structure that represents the interests of global capital while balancing them against the interests of their own national capitalist class. According to Kohout (2008: 135), the Mexican economic and political elites have consolidated persisting corporatist relationships "by shifting power to government bureaucracies that contro[l] the economy such as the treasury, budgeting and programming, and commerce and industrial development."

The nature of this structure increasingly shapes the order that states and societies maintain. That is to say it conditions the nature of state-society relations that are considered legal and legitimate, including the identity of the actors that are allowed to participate in the national system of representation. The behavior of these actors — their demands and the ways in which these demands are presented — is thus conditioned by the power structures within which national states operate today. Mexican societal responses have been modified accordingly in that some sectors of society maintain corporatist relationships with the state, others engage in anticorporatist actions, and still others adopt noncorporatist or postcorporatist strategies.

Corporatism refers to the way in which the state deals with the main constituent units of society. It refers to the integration and incorporation of nonstate actors into the state system of decision making dominated by the government itself (see Wiarda 1997; Grayson 2007). Along with changes to the traditional corporatist structures established under state corporatism, new state-controlled institutions have emerged which pose as autonomous bodies advocating the interests and rights of particular groups. It will be argued that in the Mexican case, democratization — that is, reforming the electoral system and including a greater number of political parties in the electoral process — has *not* resulted in the *wholesale* transformation of the model of state-society relations from one of corporatism to one of pluralism. *Pluralism* refers here to a relationship where the state manages or addresses the demands and interests of civil society's nonstate actors (individuals, groups, classes) in a relatively free marketplace of political competition where the actors are more or less equal. The view that Mexico has moved from an authoritarian to a liberal-democratic and pluralist polity is regarded as only partially true at best, and at worst as a misleading, not to say ideological, account of recent history. It is more correct to say that while some sectors continue to be incorporated into the operations of the state, large sectors of society are effectively *excluded* from any participation in the policy-making process, including some actors who exclude themselves. In the light of these facts it will be argued that TC is the most faithful and rational model for furthering our understanding of current state-society relations in Mexico and their recent development.

The topic is approached from a Marxist point of view as it provides the most reliable analytic tool to explain how these relationships have come to be by relating them to developments in Mexico's political-economic mode of production. The great value of the Marxist approach derives less from the theoretical claims it stipulates than from its methodological stance or practices. As Marx and Engels put it in *The German Ideology* (1970 [1845/46]: 46), "Empirical observation must in each separate instance bring out empirically, and without any mystification and speculation, the connection of the social and political structure with production." When the development of the relationships between the state and society are viewed from a political-economic perspective, it becomes clear that the efficacy of different social actors is contingent on their position in the capitalist system of production.

Transnationalized corporatist relationships can best be understood, then, as a reflection of the global expansion of the international capitalist economy and the neoliberal controls or impositions that have come to bear on "less" or "under-" developed countries accordingly. Financial and political constraints imposed on such nations by external forces have been augmented as neoliberal policies have been implemented. This is not to suggest that states have lost their sovereignty or that they are controlled from above. It simply means that the economy, one of the primary functions of the state, is negotiated with international (and their corresponding national) elites, with resulting policies being adopted and implemented nationally. After all, capitalist states represent the interests of their national elites, while advancing the implementation of neoliberal reforms as required by international institutions. In turn, state-society relations are influenced by these exogenous forces, but in a variety of ways. These are reflected in the strategies adopted by some nonstate actors that have sought to take advantage of these changes to further their struggle to break away from the state as it engages in its own transformation.

The state has come to manage its own affairs differently under the transnationalized corporatist model. Oszlak's definition of the state provides a useful framework within which the state can be understood in this model. He (1981: 5) holds that, "on the one hand, in an ideal abstract sense, the state is a social relationship, a political medium through which a system of social domination is articulated. On the other, its concrete manifestation is an independent group of institutions that form the apparatus in which the power and resources of political domination are concentrated." Governments manage state institutions and will attempt to modify aspects of these institutions as they see fit during their tenure in office. Petras and Veltmeyer (2003: 158) refer to the Latin American state as being "essential to the operation of markets and the defence or transformation of the dominant social relations of production," the new, so-called "leftist" governments of Chavez, Morales and others notwithstanding. The mechanisms adopted by the state to integrate these material forces will determine which model of state-society relations is being implemented. The concept "state" can only be understood in the context of its historical reality, other interacting external components, and the relations that develop within a particular nation or between the state and external actors.

Certainly, in economic terms the capitalist state represents primarily the interests of its national elites, principally the capitalist class, the owners of the means of production, what Williamson (1985) refers to as "private capital." In the *Communist Manifesto* [1848], Marx and Engels famously refer to "the modern state ... [as] a committee for managing the common affairs of the whole bourgeoisie." Without subscribing fully to this instrumentalist view of the role of the state, it will be argued here that there is a significant degree of cooperation or mutual interaction between the international institutions and the national state representatives just as there is a significant degree of cooperation between the national capitalist class and the state. In TC the international institutions and the transnational corporate interests that drive them, as well as the corporate elites in the countries that submit to the preestablished conditions, benefit the most. In the case of both state corporatism and TC the majority of the population, whether employed or unemployed, that is to say the nonelites, are the ones who suffer the most from the economic and political consequences of such arrangements. This phenomenon is repeated throughout all Latin American states that have adopted the capitalist mode of production. Under TC, the argument is that corporatist relationships persist, even though it would be naive to assume that they exist in just the way they did under state corporatism. Just as certain labor unions maintained a direct affiliation with the Mexican state prior to the introduction of neoliberal and electoral reforms, so some of the most important trade unions in Mexico today continue to uphold corporatist relationships with the state. By using TC's trichotomous classification of societal responses, one can account for the persistent, although somewhat antiquated, corporatist relationships in Mexico while also providing a means with which to identify and analyze the anti- and noncorporatist actions of other nonstate actors.

Societal responses to the repositioning of the state under neoliberal globalization have varied, then, depending on the type of organization involved, whether a union, an NGO, a political party, a middle-class organization or a grassroots social movement. There is no unitary pattern of response across this range of nonstate actors. Rather, there are three broad, prevailing categories of response. The first is, indeed, a *corporatist* response, a continuation of the corporatist relationships that existed under state corporatism. This is evidenced in state-run unions such as the Sindicato Nacional de Trabajadores de la Educación (SNTE) and the Sindicato de Trabajadores Petroleros de la República Mexicana (STPRM) where the leadership elites maintain corporatist relationships with the state regardless of the wishes of their memberships. The second strategic response is *anticorporatist*. Unions such as the Sindicato Independiente Nacional de Trabajadores del Colegio de Bachilleres (SINTCB) or the Sindicato Mexicano de Electricistas (SME), as it existed prior to 2009, fall into this category. They struggle to democratize their internal structures while maintaining close relationships with the state. Their stance is essentially reformist.

They do not denounce the capitalist mode of production. Rather, in keeping with Luxembourg (2006 [1899]), it can be argued that their actions are incapable of suppressing capitalist exploitation and thus indirectly and unintendedly further the agenda of the elites. The third strategy employed by a small minority of nonstate actors is *noncorporatist* (or *postcorporatist*). Organizations or movements adopting this stance work outside of corporatist relationships with the state altogether. The most radical example of this strategy is that adopted by the Ejército Zapatista de Liberación Nacional (EZLN) since it ended negotiations with the government and turned inward. It has created services and political structures parallel to government structures and developed an anticapitalist, anti-neoliberal discourse. These actions, which will be further discussed in chapters 5 and 6, approximate those that Samir Amin (1990) calls "delinking."

To emphasize the radical nature of the departure from conventional state-society relations constituted by the noncorporatist strategy, and to highlight an important theoretical point, the trichotomy of divergent societal responses is presented as a *dichotomy*, in which corporatist and anticorporatist strategies are combined as one category under the title "integrative," where the other category is occupied by the noncorporatist strategy under the title "delinking" (that is, nonintegrative). The integrative responses are those that work within the system in an attempt to maintain or reform it in line with actors' demands. All but one of the organizations examined in this book fall into the integrative category. In sharp contrast, the nonintegrative response examined through the Zapatista movement is an approach characterized by turning inward and rejecting conventional relationships with the state. While the EZLN continues to maintain a small degree of connectedness to the Mexican state, it is attempting to rely mostly on its own means. Surely there has never before been as radical an attempt in Mexico to disconnect from the state as that being made by the EZLN. Although there have been attempts by different indigenous groups to establish their own autonomous structures, there has never been a severing of relationships as advanced as that which the Zapatistas are currently practicing.

The case of the Zapatista movement invites comparison with Amin's (1990) argument that while delinking will not on its own lead to substantive structural change, in theory it has the potential of laying the foundation for the development of socialism. Communities that delink both fall back on and develop their own economic and political resources, in contrast to conventional struggles for autonomy in Mexico that have always maintained a close economic relationship with the state while distancing themselves politically or culturally from it. The EZLN falls short of full delinking because it continues to depend on state-run-and-financed medical facilities for its most gravely ill patients. Furthermore, its new dependency on NGOs calls into question the extent to which it is willing to sever all relationships with institutions that depend on capitalism to survive. That said, it is evident that the indigenous organizations and communities in the Zapatista zone have come to have a noncorporatist or postcorporatist relationship with the Mexican state, that is to say a relationship that is virtually void of content.

It is unclear whether the current strategies being practiced by the EZLN have been adopted to put pressure on the state to fulfill its obligations as detailed in the peace accords or whether its end goal is in fact socialism. When the Zapatistas went public in 1994 they received the support of tens of thousands of Mexicans who rallied to their cause. Yet when the "Other Campaign" emerged in 2006, the support it received as it traveled around the country was significantly less. What distinguishes the current campaign is its anticapitalist, anti-neoliberal slogans. The eclectically radical strategies adopted by the movement have transitioned from first claiming the geographical regions in Chiapas (the uprising), to negotiating a workable agreement with the government (San Andrés Accords), to creating autonomous municipalities (Caracoles), to its current strategy of searching for a new path (the Other Campaign).

Under TC, the responses of nonstate actors have ranged from the very minor to the very dramatic. Most organizations have sought ways to unite with other organizations behind common demands as they try to make sense of the new model of state-society relations. Also under TC, new organizations, namely NGOs, have proliferated throughout the country offering services and material goods to help the plight of the oppressed.

While a strong argument has been made that Mexican society is divided along "reconstituted" class lines (Petras and Veltmeyer 2001), among the social movements and organizations examined here are some which cross over class lines. A justification for their inclusion can be found in chapter 1. Because Mexico's working class is too fragmented to examine as a unity, social movements and established organizations are examined in their own right to determine how they have responded to the emergence of TC.

In the larger context, the transition from state corporatism to transnationalized corporatism in Mexico has resulted in "incorporating" different actors and a different distribution of power. Under state corporatism, the primary actors were the state, organized labor, the peasantry and the popular sectors (including the middle class). Under one-party rule, the Mexican state held the sole political-economic power in the country. It was through its corporatist relationships with nonstate actors and its military might that it exercised this control. Official unions with appointed leaders were created to organize the workers in the state-owned corporations. The protectionist characteristics of the import substitution industrialization (ISI) economic model allowed the Mexican bourgeoisie to flourish and to work with the state to set the minimum wage, set prices for basic food items and determine the labor laws that in the end would benefit the capitalist class. Social programs such as Pronasol would occasionally emerge in response to social unrest and extreme poverty yet usually failed to meet their preestablished goals. Often replete with corruption, these programs were underfunded and services were often misdirected. The organization of socioeconomic relationships under state corporatism was very much in keeping with Schmitter's definition of corporatism (which will be introduced in chapter 1). To adopt the language of positivism one could say that under state corporatism the state's rule is the "independent variable" and civil society's response the "dependent variable."

Following the economic crisis of the 1970s and the accrual of a huge financial debt, the Mexican government turned to neoliberal reforms in the 1980s as it struggled to turn the economy around. This marked the beginning of the transition to transnationalized corporatism. Under TC the corporatist relationships among the government, labor, the peasantry and the popular sectors have been modified as neoliberal policies have been implemented and as new actors have emerged. For example, the IFIs and the WTO, both of which are directly influenced by transnational corporations, have come to shape the political-economic path of the government by insisting on such things as the privatization of state-owned corporations, constitutional reforms to facilitate the free movement of capital and the reduction of social spending. The Business Coordinating Council (CCE,

Consejo Coordinador Empresarial) has become a dominant actor in the current political-economic model.[1] In this clientelist relationship, the state's policies are the dependent variable, and the actions of the transnational corporations and the IFIs become the independent variables (mediated by the "intervening variable" of such bodies as the CCE). The state has also established institutions to manage the mandate of different "interest" groups such as women and indigenous people. NGOs have also emerged during this period and serve as a means to keep society content. Of particular importance, and characteristic of neoliberalism, hundreds of state corporations have been privatized, the domestic market has been "liberated" as the economy has integrated into the international market, and the state's role has come to focus more on the political task of maintaining "stability" and instituting new policies and regulations to meet the requirements of the new world order. These changes have resulted in the partial dissolution of the state's corporatist relationships with workers. In many cases, those that used to be organized in official unions have lost all organizational structures as their workplaces have been bought out by the private sector, while others have struggled to set up independent unions and still others have joined the reserve army of unemployed. Those that remain affiliated with the government and its corporatist structures have not changed much (see chapter 3). Beyond unions, many other social actors have sought innovative ways to fight against corporatist arrangements. These organizations and their strategies will be examined in chapter 4.

Transnationalized corporatism is a reflection, then, of the emergent stage of capitalism known as neoliberalism where the basic structural arrangement of the capitalist mode of production has not changed. Meiksins Wood (2003: 9) describes capitalism as

> a system in which all economic actors — producers and appropriators — depend upon the market for their most basic needs. It is a system in which class relations between producers and appropriators, and specifically the relation between capitalists and wage labourers, are also mediated by the market.... In capitalism, the market dependence of both appropriators and producers means that they are subject to the imperatives of competition, accumulation and increasing labour productivity; and the whole system, in which competitive production is a fundamental condition of existence, is driven by these imperatives.

There are those who own the means of production and those who must sell their labor power. The basic components of the means of production continue to be land (natural resources), labor, capital and technology. While the basic structure of the relations of production has remained the same under neoliberal capitalism, the identity of the owners of the means of production and the role of the state have changed. With some notable exceptions, not least the Mexican entrepreneur who vies to be the richest man in the world, Carlos Slim, the national capitalist class has been largely supplanted by the international capitalist class. The state in turn has experienced a transformation of power in which it no longer solely or primarily determines economic policy in the interest of its national capitalist class, but instead serves as a conduit to implement and institutionalize the economic policies that have been determined by international capitalist interests. Its function as legitimator and enforcer of capitalist hegemony remains, however, largely the same as before. It continues to strive to win the consent of civil society through corporatist means backed up by the use of force to keep extracorporatist opposition in line.

Institutional actors that serve as state-corporatist agents under TC are organizations such as the Comisión Nacional para el Desarrollo de los Pueblos Indígenas (CNDPI) and the Instituto Nacional de las Mujeres (INMUJERES). The CNC Azul is a contemporary creation designed to draw agrarian workers closer to the Partido Acción Nacional (PAN) and to counteract the Partido Revolucionario Institucional (PRI) and PAN stronghold in rural areas (Reveles 2006: 43, 67). These bodies serve as means to centralize political constituencies and to feign concern for the dispossessed sectors of society. The directors of these institutions are appointed by the government in power. Service-sector employees and those of the remaining state corporations continue to maintain corporatist relationships with the state—a state that has succumbed to the demands of the IFIs and the WTO, and whose actions are reflective of those demands.

Clearly, as state corporatism has given way to TC, fewer unions maintain corporatist relationships with the state. Yet the unions and the workers that continue to do so remain hierarchically structured. In relation to them, "decisions made by the state officials depend on what concessions they see as valid and/or necessary, and to what extent they should be satisfied according to their estimation of the prevailing correlation of social forces" (MacKinlay and Otero 2004: 76). There are also many organizations and sectors of society that interact outside of the traditional corporatist model. These organizations flourish under TC because of the changed role of the state regarding economic policies. National and international NGOs are examples of such organizations. They have come to fulfill roles that would otherwise be the responsibility of the state. NGOs do everything from building schools and providing building supplies to organizing microfinancing programs. NGOs could not have flourished in the same way under state corporatism because of the need the state had to control its economy and all of the corporations it owned and operated. However, according to López Monjardin and Sandoval Álvarez, the Mexican state has introduced what they call a "new system of social corporatist control" (2003: 45). Under this new model the traditional state-corporatist arrangement is replaced with a model that benefits the state by keeping different social forces distant from each other by allowing NGOs to work directly with communities. NGO work has in part taken over work that in the previous model would have been done by workers in official unions. Other workers from defunct state corporations that are now in the hands of the private sector have come to be controlled by what are referred to as Sindicatos Blancos.[2] These unions are a form of control used in the private sector. It may be argued that they are themselves a form of corporatism between the owners of the means of production and the workers, replacing the nexus between the state and official unions. These organizations, along with the independent unions, which are also popular under TC, do not have a direct corporatist relationship with the state, yet they function quite comfortably under TC. Theoretically speaking, they have the unintended consequence of sustaining corporatist state-society relations.

Method

To study the "integrative" (corporatist and anticorporatist) responses of the organized Mexican political opposition, data was collected on a range of different groups. Of primary concern was whether their approach to dealing with the state changed in any way in this new context of TC. Purposive sampling (Berg 1998: 229; Trochim 2006) of a range of social movement organizations (SMOs) (consisting of four "independent" unions, eight political parties, three social movements, seven NGOs, and the EZLN) and of their elected or employed representatives was carried out. The data were collected from three sources: interviews, review of political documents and academic literature.

Cases that emerged prior to neoliberalism and cases that have emerged under the sway of neoliberalism were both selected. Both established SMOs and smaller, more obscure organizations were purposely chosen in an attempt to draw on examples that are representative of the range of organized nonstate actors in Mexico. For example, both official political parties and unregistered smaller parties were included. NGOs that receive national and/or international funding as well as grassroots, volunteer-based organizations were also examined. Three contemporary social movements that cross class lines, namely the electoral movement, the Barzón and the student movement, were included. While El Barzón is primarily a middle-class organization comprising "small and midsize farmers, urban mortgage holders, and credit cardholders" (Olvera 2004: 425), people who were victimized by high interest rates in 1993 and the subsequent economic collapse in 1995, it is nonetheless important to consider for this analysis given the fact that it emerged during the period of TC. Observations of the Barzón and student movements are drawn from the literature.

"Independent" unions refer to those that are not affiliated with the Confederación de Trabajadores de México (CTM). However, the concept has also come to be used to describe unions that see themselves as independent even though the official affiliation may exist or may exist by default where the union works under the auspices of an official union. Although restructuring in union organization went on before, and has gone on since, the elections of 2000, ones that were considered "independent" before the establishment of neoliberalism were studied first. Representatives from the Sindicato de Trabajadores de La Universidad Nacional Autónoma de México (STUNAM, founded in 1977), the Coordinadora Nacional de Trabajadores de la Educación (CNTE, founded in 1979), the Sindicato Independiente Nacional de Trabajadores del Colegio de Bachilleres (SINTCB, founded in 1976), and the Sindicato Mexicano de Electricistas (SME) which was formed in 1914 during the time of the Mexican Revolution, were interviewed. While attempts were made to schedule an interview with a representative from the Sindicato Nacional de Trabajadores de la Educación (SNTE), the official teachers' union, nobody was available.

As stated above, both official and unregistered political parties were included in the study. In particular, representatives from the PRT (Partido Revolucionario de los Trabajadores), the Liga de Unidad Socialista (LUS), the Organización Socialista de los Trabajadores (OST)[3] and the Unidad Obrera y Socialista (UNIOS) were interviewed, along with a representative from the Partido Obrero Socialista[4] (POS).

The author was unsuccessful in arranging an appointment with a Partido de la Revolución Democrática (PRD) representative, but was able to review their documents. The PRD was experiencing an internal crisis at the time that divided the party into two competing camps. The divisions made it difficult to know which faction represented the official party line, if such a party line existed at all at the time. This should come as no surprise given the origins of the party. The PRD emerged from the Frente Democrático Nacional (FDN) following the 1988 elections and comprised organizations and representatives whose political tendencies ranged from very left-wing ideological stances to center-left positions.

As a partial control, representatives from the PAN and the PRI were interviewed. The PAN spokesperson was Luis Hernández Álvarez. He mediated the negotiations between the government and the EZLN from 1994 to 1996. He was a former leader of the PAN but at the time of the interview was more involved in keeping peace with the indigenous people in Chiapas than leading a political party. He qualified his comments by stating that they were not official PAN positions but his own, as someone who happened to be a member of the PAN and was actively involved in the Chiapas issue.

The grassroots organizations that were examined included ones that date back to the 1970s and continue to exist today, and others that emerged following the Zapatista uprising in 1994. One of the most prominent pre–1994 organizations is Eureka led by Rosario Ibarra de Piedra, a political figure who emerged in the 1970s following the disappearance of her politically active son. "La Senora," as she is known in left-wing political circles, founded the Frente Nacional Contra la Represión y Por la Aparición de los Presos Políticos y Desaparecidos (FNCR). She came to represent the PRT as their presidential candidate in the 1982 federal elections and then again in 1988. Although she was unsuccessful in her electoral attempts, she has continued to be well respected on the left and represents, for many, a symbol of unity and persistence. In 2007 the FNCR was revived. She was president of Eureka when interviewed in the living room of her main-floor apartment not far from the Parque de Chapultepec. Her living room was lined with photographs of her political career and of course her missing son, Jesus Piedra Ibarra. Among the photos were ones with Subcomandante Marcos, John F. Kennedy and Fidel Castro.

Other pre–1994 organizations, the representatives of which were interviewed, are Desarrollo Económico y Social de los Mexicanos Indígenas (DESMI), K'inal Antsetik, Centro de Derechos Humanos Fray Bartolomé de las Casas (FRAYBA), Centro de Investigación Laboral y Asesoría Sindical (CILAS), the Comisión Independiente de Derechos Humanos (CIDHM) de Morelos, and the Coordinadora Nacional de Organizaciones Cafetaleras (CNOC). As for NGOs that emerged after the Zapatista uprising, the Granito de Café, Comisión de Salud para la Atención de Comunidades Indígenas (COSACI), Ciudadanas en Movimiento por la Democracia (CMD) and Servicio Internacional para la Paz (SIPAZ) were examined.

To study the "delinking" response, attention was focused on the Zapatista movement in the southern state of Chiapas. The movement provides a useful framework for the discussion because of how it has deviated from the familiar model of state-society relations in the Mexican case by reducing its interaction with the Mexican government and turning to NGOs and other grassroots organizations for support. The Zapatista case shows that TC is incapable of organizing the constituent units of society in such a way that the varying demands are addressed appropriately. This is an example of how TC presents new challenges to all groups in society as they struggle to get an effective political response from the state to their demands.

Mexico After 1982: Neoliberal Globalization and Corporatism

The onset of *economic* neoliberalism in Mexico can be traced to the large-scale privatization of state-owned industries, policies encouraging foreign investment (via, for example, tariff reduction) and the 1986 entry into the General Agreement on Tariffs and Trade (GATT). All were carried out under the presidential *sexenio* of Miguel de Madrid from 1982 to 1988. Garza Toledo (1994: 196–197) refers to the Mexican state's governing practices in the pre–1982 period as "social-authoritarian development style" and the post–1982 period as "neoliberal-authoritarian development style." Under the social-authoritarian model, the state intervened directly in the market economy, and state corporatism best described the state's relationship with labor. In the 1980s the state began to reduce public spending in favor of greater capital accumulation through private and foreign investment. The extent of the corporatist relationship between the state and labor was also modified during this period due to the privatization of state corporations. For Valdez Ugalde (1994: 240), the earlier period was characterized by a "public enterprise system, economic protectionism, and corporatist arrangements," in contrast to the more recent period characterized by "a state that privileges regulatory mechanisms, opens Mexico to international competition, and selectively distributes 'solidarity' resources" through government-run social programs. He acknowledges significant changes in state-society relations in the post–1982 period of transition, holding that "the mechanisms that permit the federal executive to exercise its concentrated power are stronger now [in 1994] than at most other times in Mexico's history" (ibid.).

The prelude to the de la Madrid period was one of economic crisis. According to the Nacional Financiera (see Ramírez 1989: 86, table 4.5) real GDP growth fell from 7.9 percent in 1981 to -0.5 percent in 1982, industrial output fell from 7.0 to -2.9 during this same period while the public sector deficit rose from 14.7 percent of GDP to 17.9 percent. In 1980 the public sector deficit was 7.9 percent. The rate of inflation reached 98.2 percent, up from 26.7 percent in 1981, and the real minimum wage fell by 9.6 percent. The Mexican government turned to external financing, leaving Mexico with a debt of over U.S. $60 billion. "In 1984 the World Bank, for the first time in its history, granted a loan to a country in return for structural neoliberal reforms" (Harvey 2007: 100).

In an attempt to stabilize the economy, Miguel de la Madrid first authorized the sale of 34 percent of the assets of the banks which his predecessor, López Portillo, had nationalized (ibid.: 99). His second move was to abandon the Global Development Plan and adopt the IMF austerity program. The economic adjustments that came along with this program were as follows:

> (1) a reduction in the public-sector deficit to 8.5 percent of GDP in 1983, 5.5 percent in 1984, and 3.5 percent in 1985; (2) an increase in the prices charged for a wide range of goods and services provided by such government agencies...; (3) a move toward opening the economy to international competition...; (4) a concerted effort by both the private and the public sectors to promote nonpetroleum exports via the further development of maquiladoras...; (5) a more flexible interpretation of the 1973 Foreign Investment Law to encourage foreign investment and technology; and (6) ...reduction by more than 40 percent of the number of public-sector firms[ibid.: 99–100]..

Mexico's entry into the GATT in 1986 was actually the reversal of a decision made by López Portillo six years earlier. When it was first contemplated, it drew opposition from the working class and the small and medium-sized firms that benefited from the protectionist policies under ISI. De la Madrid's austerity measures most affected the working class and the poor (ibid.: 106), causing real wages to plummet. Mexico's inability to pay back its foreign debt throughout the 1980s resulted in its acceptance of neoliberal reforms.

During the period leading up to the signing of the North American Free Trade Agreement in 1993 the Mexican state sought new approaches to solving its chronic economic hardships. "Policy makers believed that a debt-reduction agreement with commercial banks was essential to reduce net resource transfers and enhance the business sector's confidence" (Lustig 1998: 56). This resulted in the signing of the Brady Plan in 1989, a plan that would regulate the debt and institute a debt repayment schedule amenable to the current economic situation in the country. Two years later, President Salinas de Gortari announced his intention to seek a free-trade agreement with the United States. This announcement boosted business confidence and opened investment opportunities for the rich while promising little change for the majority of the population. The consequences were drastic. Not only did

> more than 2 million Mexicans [lose] their jobs during the first two years of the implementation of NAFTA ... [but m]ore than 28,000 Mexican businesses went bankrupt. Banks failed, while consumer debt reached astronomical proportions [and] [t]he minimum wage plummeted to levels below those of 1981 [Cockcroft 1998: 295].

Since 1988 there have been many attempts to stabilize the economy through a variety of neoliberal reforms and the emergence of new international relationships. The period beginning in 1988 was also characterized, however, by significant changes in the *political* evolution of the country: (1) 1988 witnessed the first time since the founding of the PRI that opposition forces came within a very narrow margin of defeating the ruling party. During the vote counting the computer system crashed and all ballots were subsequently destroyed, eliminating all traces of possible electoral fraud. To this day the official results of the election are widely disputed. (2) 1989 marked the first time in Mexican history that the election monitoring process became autonomous when the Instituto Federal Electoral (IFE) was separated from the ruling PRI party.[5] (3) The 1994 Zapatista uprising marked the first time in Mexican history that an indigenous movement received such overwhelming support from international and national communities and such extensive media coverage. In fact it was the first time that an indigenous movement turned national. (4) 2000 marked the first time, since the founding of the modern state as we know it today, that a non–PRI president was elected in Mexico. (5) The mobilization generated against the *desafuero* of López Obrador in 2004–2005 was one of the largest social movements ever recorded in Mexican history. (6) September 1, 2006, marked the first time that a president was stopped from presenting his annual report to congress as opposition leaders descended onto the congressional platform. In the end President Vincente Fox was forced to submit a hard copy of his report to the legislative assembly. (7) September 15, 2006, marked the first time since Mexico's independence that the president was forced to give the "grito de la independencia"[6] in a location other than the Zócalo in Mexico City. It was also the first time in Mexican history that the independence "grito" in the Zócalo was presided over by the Jefe de Gobernación (Carlos Abascal Carranza) and the acting mayor (Alejandro Encinas Rodríguez). They were joined by the personage referred to above, the left-wing female senator, twice presidential candidate for a left-wing Trotskyist organization and founder of Eureka, Rosario Ibarra de Piedra (Doña Rosario). Curiously, this event was not televised, yet the celebration conducted by the president in Dolores, Hidalgo, and similar Mexican independence celebrations in Spain, New York and Paris were closely followed by the media. (8) November 20, 2006, marked the first time since the Mexican Revolution that the president of the republic did not preside over the revolutionary commemorative march of athletic teams in the Zócalo. In its place there was what was referred to as the "people's revolutionary march" that brought people dressed in revolutionary attire, many on horseback, to celebrate the triumph of the Mexican Revolution. There was also an athletic contingent but on a much smaller scale than is customary. (9) Since 2007, relationships between the Mexican government and the United States government have become solidified with the war against drug trafficking, a relationship that many would argue compromises Mexico's sovereignty. The peace march held on May 8, 2011, demonstrates the exhaustion felt by the people after over six years of bloodshed and uncertainty. All of these events reflect changes in state-society relations as the country transitions into a model of TC. They demonstrate new expressions of disapproval of the current relationships.

Although there are many firsts, there are also many constants. Political repression has continued to be used against opposition forces; economic inequality continues, if indeed it has not increased; political corruption is systemic[7]; corporatism remains widespread; and racism and the subordination of women are characteristic of everyday life. Addressing these issues requires much more than introducing liberal-democratic policies and institutions that we are all too familiar with in the North.

Synopsis

Following this introduction, the book proceeds by locating its argument in the theoretical literature on corporatism, Marxism and social movements. It first discusses the recognized types of corporatism before turning to address in detail this work's central concept, transnationalized corporatism, and its relationship to other theories of corporatism. Secondly, it discusses the relevant theoretical and, most importantly, methodological components of Marxist political economy that will be used to comprehend state-society relations. Thirdly, it critically examines the conceptualization of nonstate actors in contemporary social movement theory from this Marxist position. Fourthly, it reviews the theories of "delinking" and "deglobalization" as articulations of Marxist thought useful for understanding the Zapatista strategy in particular. Together these ideas provide a fruitful theoretical framework for understanding the development of societal responses, in the Mexican case, to TC.

Chapter 2 then turns to a detailed consideration of the emergence, institutionalization and transformation of state corporatism in Mexico. It also examines how the state itself has been transformed during this period. This account draws from a review of the relevant literature, official data, mainstream press reports and interview results. State corporatism of the 1930s laid the foundation for the TC of today. This historical grounding of state-society relations in Mexico can be modified but not easily eliminated. In fact, it will be argued that there are aspects of corporatism that are entrenched and continue to be found across a range of organizations.

Drawing from case studies and fieldwork undertaken in Mexico in 2003–2004, chapters 3 and 4 discuss the integrative approach adopted by the preponderance of nonstate actors in response to the consolidation of transnationalized corporatism. They examine how different political and social organizations and groups have engaged in political interaction with the state as they attempted to push for new policies or reforms to address their needs. Chapter 5 examines the historical developments within the EZLN that have led to its partial delinking strategy in response to TC in Mexico. The dramatic severing of the relationship between the EZLN and the state demonstrates a clear example of how TC is incapable of maintaining control of all constituent units of society. Chapter 6 broadens the scope of the argument to consider other cases of partial delinking or deglobalization found in Latin America today. This chapter provides the basis of my claim that the partial delinking strategies adopted by the EZLN are, in the end, sustainable but not transformative. I then offer conclusions about the evolving state-society relationships involved in the struggle for Mexico.

1

Theoretical Framework

The purpose of this chapter is to discuss the different theoretical perspectives that are drawn on in the course of the analytic-descriptive chapters of this study. While there is a degree of heterogeneity among the different sections of the chapter, this is because there are four interrelated aspects to the overall research problem, and dealing with them requires engaging the various theoretical literatures with which they are associated. Recall that the overall problem is to describe and explain the particular form of state-society relations that characterizes contemporary Mexico. It is the argument of the study that current state-society relations (1) can be represented as modifications of and departures from a previous, long-standing and seemingly stable form of state-society relations captured by the phrase "state corporatism," (2) have come about in the wake of the onset of neoliberal globalization, (3) are not homogeneous but diverse in character, and (4) include, in particular, one form of response that seeks to remove the actors from the state in toto. The term "transnationalized corporatism" is intended to characterize these interrelated aspects in one pregnant phrase. In order to address these aspects of the overall problem it is necessary (1) to show how the corporatist model of state-society relations has changed from the state form to the transnationalized form, (2) to account for this transition in the context of neoliberal globalization, (3) to show how these changes in turn are related to further, diverse responses on the part of nonstate actors making up civil society, and (4) to account in particular for noncorporatist or postcorporatist response strategies.

In view of this complexity of the overall problem in its various aspects it is necessary to draw on several bodies of theory that deal respectively with (1) the nature of corporatism, (2) political economy, (3) social movements (or nonstate actors) in general and (4) the delinking response in particular. These theories can then provide an analytic description of the transition from state to transnationalized corporatism, an explanation of the transition in terms of the political-economic context, a means of locating nonstate actors (movements or organizations) in a framework that will explicate how they have developed and responded to TC under neoliberal capitalism, and an understanding in particular of the noncorporatist strategy adopted by the Zapatistas.

Since the principal theoretical part of the argument being advanced in these pages is played by the concept of TC, this chapter will begin by placing TC in relation to the considerable literature on corporatism in general and in Latin America in particular. It will then turn to deriving a theoretical perspective on the phenomena of corporatism and oppositional politics in Mexico from the corpus of Marxist political-economic thought from a Latin American perspective. This will provide the tools for critically appraising the capacity of current theories of social movements to illuminate the changing strategies and tactics of contemporary social movements and political organizations in Mexico, notably the partial delinking strategy of the Zapatistas, about whom much has been written. Accordingly, the chapter is divided into four sections. The first section undertakes a conceptual analysis of what is meant by corporatism and examines its varying theoretical models; chapter 2 will further develop corporatist theory and examine its applicability in Mexico. The second section expounds Marxist theory and methodology in terms of its utility for understanding the political-economic relations of production in Mexico. Its objective is to provide the tools to determine the places that the different actors and their action strategies occupy in relation to the mode of production — whether as owners of the means of production or "others." Given that Mexico is a Latin American society, not a European one, and given that there is a tradition of adapting Marxist thought to the political-economic circumstances of Latin America, some space will be taken to relate the author's position to that tradition. The third section critically discusses contemporary theories of social movements in terms of their ability to account for the fact, detailed in the case studies of chapters 3, 4 and 5, that the strategies adopted by the nonstate actors under examination here are not homogeneous but diverse in character. The fourth section reviews the neo–Marxist theories of Amin and Bello as interpretive resources for locating and assessing the Zapatistas' partial delinking strategy. The eclectic strategies used by the Zapatista movement have aspects approximating the delinking and deglobalization theories of Amin and Bello, respectively. This section will explicate the usefulness of these theories for understanding the noncorporatist or postcorporatist relationship that the movement has with the Mexican state.

Corporatism

While corporatism *in Mexico* is discussed at length in chapter 2, this section considers the theoretical foundations of TC starting with the conventional understanding of corporatism. According to many European analysts (see, for example, Grahl and Teague 1997; Schmitter and Streeck 1991), the explanatory power of the concept of corporatism is said to have declined with the decline of the Keynesian welfare state and the Fordist industrial model, and indeed the phenomenon itself is said to have been replaced with a neoliberal political-economic system of reduced state involvement and a more expansive international market economy. It is argued that if the political-economic structures on which a corporatist state are founded are eroded, then so too are the corporatist relationships. The relationships become unsustainable.

At the dawn of neoliberalism, according to Schmitter (1979: 7), "for a while, the concept itself was virtually retired from the active lexicon of politics, although it was left on behavioral exhibit ... in such museums of atavistic political practice as Portugal and Spain.... Lately ... the spectre is back amongst us ... haunting the concerns of contemporary social scientists" (see also Wiarda 1997). Like many theories that originated in Europe, the corporatist model soon came to be applied in Latin America.

Schmitter (1979: 13) provides us with an interest-driven, analytical definition of state corporatism. He sees state corporatism as an alternative to the pluralism that dominated political theory throughout the 1970s.

Corporatism can be defined as a system of interest representation in which the constituent units are organized into a limited number of singular, compulsory, noncompetitive, hierarchically ordered and functionally differentiated categories, recognized or licensed (if not created) by the state and granted a deliberate representational monopoly within their respective categories in exchange for observing certain controls on their selection of leaders and articulation of demands and supports.

Williamson (1985: 10) uses table 1 to highlight the four dimensions of corporatism:

Table 1. The Four Dimensions of Corporatism

1. The state has a principal function of establishing and maintaining an economic and social order. Such an order is not compatible with an essentially market-based economy. The performance of this function must override any conflicting popular or particular demands; the state is dominant in the economic and social sphere.
2. The economy is predominantly constituted of private ownership of the means of production and wage labor.
3. There is at least a circumscription upon the role of liberal-democratic institutions in authoritative decision-making. Indeed, liberal-democratic institutions may not exist at all.
4. Organizations of producers undertake an intermediary role between the state and societal actors, performing not only a representative function but also operating as a regulatory agency on behalf of the state.

The reader is encouraged to keep in mind that corporatist relations were created in the first place to maintain "class harmony and organic unity" (Panitch 1979: 119). They are a means, used by the state, to "incorporate," and thereby control and pacify, opposition (Ramírez Saiz 2003: 159). According to Hermanson and de la Garza Toledo (2005: 184), corporatism has come to form part of the "workers' culture." Although the term was originally used to describe state-society relations in fascist states, there are many more recent examples of corporatism in liberal-democratic and authoritarian regimes. Central to this argument is the claim that, as political-economic arrangements in capitalist modes of production have been modified over the years, so too have corporatist relationships. Developments in the global market economy and the consolidation of the WTO and the IFIs, principally the IMF and the World Bank, have come to influence state-society relations within defined geopolitical regions all over the world (see Woods and Narlikar 2001). With the spread of international trade negotiations and agreements, these IFIs and the WTO increasingly influence the internal economic and political dealings of the countries involved. As stated in the introduction, these relationships do not eliminate the view that the principal function of the state is "establishing and maintaining an economic and social order" (Williamson 1985, 10), but they do add a new dimension to the political process. Governments have been pressured by international forces to introduce reforms that will facilitate the free movement of capital and the investment rights of transnational corporations. On the basis of the questionable, not to say discredited, theory that capitalism needs liberal democracy to flourish, some political theorists hold that state corporatism has been replaced by pluralist state-society relations as democratizing reforms have been introduced.

Pluralism, according to Schmitter (1979: 15), is best

defined as a system of interest representation in which the constituent units are organized into an unspecified number of multiple, voluntary, competitive, nonhierarchically ordered and self determined (as to type or scope of interest) categories which are not specially licensed, recognized, subsidized, created or otherwise controlled in leadership selection or interest articulation by the state and which do not exercise a monopoly of representational activity within their respective categories.

Pluralism is most commonly found in liberal democracies and is premised on the inclusion of varying interests and the dispersion of power. Zeigler (1988: 3) adds that "pluralism is best understood as the belief that advanced industrial democracies ... generate a system of multiple, competing elites (including interest groups) that determine public policy through bargaining and compromise." This assumes but does not ensure that political resources and power are equally distributed. It gives voice to many otherwise silenced sectors of society. Without being dismissive of the pluralist model, it will be argued that in this case study of Mexico, state-society relations moved from state corporatism to transnationalized corporatism (in which there is a degree of pluralism in some sectors) rather than to a wholesale or thoroughgoing pluralist model of state-society relations.

Returning to Schmitter's definition of corporatism, Williamson (1985: 138) adds that the corporatist state "sustains a particular socio-economic order and overrides any popular or particular demands which conflict with the maintenance of that order." Schmitter distinguishes what he calls his analytical definition from Manoïlesco's ideological definition (see Schmitter 1979: 44n22.): Manoïlesco holds that

> the corporation is a collective and public organization composed of the totality of persons (physical or judicial) fulfilling together the same national function and having as its goal that of assuring the exercise of that function by rules of law imposed at least upon its members.

Nedelmann and Meier (1979: 96–97) raise concerns about the descriptive nature of Schmitter's definition. They argue that "it is unclear whether it should contain only two basic dimensions, namely, the associational organizations and the state, or whether it should also include a third one, namely, the socioeconomic structure or, more specifically the nature and extent of the unorganized population." Throughout this study all three dimensions discussed by Nedelmann and Meier will be drawn on, with particular interest in the socioeconomic structure in the context of the international market economy (thus the category "transnationalized corporatism") while acknowledging that corporatism can coexist with different types of economic arrangements.

More in keeping with corporatism in Mexico in the twenty-first century, Ramírez Saiz (2003: 158–159) argues that there are three conditions that characterize the corporatist stronghold. The first condition is manifested in the inability to liberate union associations from the regime in power. The second condition is continuous state intervention in the official registration of unions and farmer and professional associations. The third condition is the continued lack of transparency within the unions and the fact that many decisions are made without the participation of the membership. All of these conditions create obstacles for the democratization process and undermine any attempts at creating a pluralist organization of state-society relationships. In addition, Bizberg argues (2003: 226), the changes implemented throughout the 1980s and 1990s which led to the defeat of the PRI in 2000 were electoral reforms and not social reforms, thus leaving state-society relations intact. The parameters or conditions detailed by Ramírez Saiz above are of primary interest to the argument here.

When the corporatist model was reintroduced into political theory, it was in response to excessive claims made on behalf of the pluralist interpretation of state-society relations. The pluralist model did not provide the tools to examine the particularities of regions such as Latin America. It is argued that in a pluralist society, even though decision making is realized by the elites of society, influence is widely (although not necessarily evenly) extended throughout society (see Williamson 1989: 53). One of the primary differences between the corporatist state and the pluralist state according to Schmitter is that of ordering. Corporatism is hierarchical and pluralism is not. "Under pluralism, corporate groups are free and unfettered; but under corporatism the groups are integrated into, and sometimes even created by, the state" (Wiarda 1997: 160). Nonstate actors maintain a much greater degree of autonomy in a pluralist arrangement, and their demands are heard and addressed, sometimes favorably, sometimes not (although, in actual fact, they are frequently left with only the illusion of being heard). The electoral process is at the center of a pluralist society, and it is argued that by taking societal demands seriously, a political party could expect to fare well in an election. Pluralism focuses more on individualism whereas corporatism employs a group-based organizational model.

From a functionalist perspective (see Parsons and Smelser 1956), any political resistance that emerges in a pluralist society is considered as not against the functioning of the system as a whole, but only against a particular social or economic policy; in fact, opposition can be regarded as functional for the system. The distinction between manifest and latent functions (Merton 1967) will be applied to the theoretical interpretation of anticorporatist strategies in subsequent chapters.

Gobeyn (1993: 20) argues that corporatism is no longer necessary under the current political-economic realities of advanced capitalist societies, but he neglects to examine its application in underdeveloped countries. Martens (2001: 395) argues that "corporatism expresses the view that societal participation in the political process is not diffuse and partial, but well shaped and durable." From the perspective of mainstream liberal ideology, pluralism is a much more desirable political arrangement than corporatism. (This debate will be revisited in the third section of this chapter and in the last section of chapter 2.)

Political theorists distinguish among such different forms of corporatism as, for example, state corporatism, neocorporatism and international corporatism. State or "authoritarian-licensed" corporatism (Williamson 1985: 11) is "top-down" and lacks the negotiation process common to neocorporatist arrangements. State corporatism is the more authoritarian style of corporatism classically found in fascist Italy but evident in Mexico since the early twentieth century. Under such state corporatism, government representatives lead societal organizations in a way that benefits the party in power or the interests of the state by maintaining a complacent environment, but one in which subjects have a sense of being collected together and heard. Polities that have not consolidated liberal democracy are usually organized under some form of state corporatism. Under this arrangement the state organizes society hierarchically by creating state-run organizations to control citizens' actions. Unions, for example, are led by government authorities and controlled from above (for example the CTM in Mexico). Affiliation is mandatory and these structures are run noncompetitively. That is, mandatory affiliation in state-organized groups prevents workers from choosing their own representative bodies unless they create independent organizations parallel to the government organizations. Independent union organizing appears to be a manageable alternative yet it often leads to repression. Lehmbruch (1979: 150–151) describes the essential features of what he refers to as liberal corporatism as cooperation and negotiation. Liberal corporatism is a softened version of classical state corporatism approximating the societal corporatist mode. There is a fine line between liberal corporatism and pluralism. Yet Panitch (1980) views state corporatism of all varieties as just another tool used by capitalists to exploit the workers. Thus, even ostensible pluralism could be such a tool.

Neocorporatism is considered a sort of corporatism from below. Germany is an example of neocorporatism where workers are represented by a workers' federation that then negotiates with the government. Businesses also have their national federation to defend their interests. In the UK, the Trades Union Congress (TUC) represents unionized workers and the Confederation of British Industries (CBI) represents owners. Representatives of these organizations regularly sit down with government to plan the British economy. The primary relationships are between such groups and the state. For example, the CBI-TUC Productivity Group was founded in October 2001 to assess "the reasons behind the productivity gap between the UK and its major competitors" (European Industrial Relations Observatory On-line 2001). The government in turn consults this group on policy development. Likewise on September 5, 2005, the UK government, CBI and the TUC "issued a joint statement declaring how each will help the immigration system to best aid UK interests" (Millar 2005). In neocorporatist relations there is autonomous interaction among individuals, groups and organizations which counterbalances the otherwise dominant actions of the state. Williamson reserves neocorporatism for Western industrialized nations. He (Williamson 1985: 11) describes the three central characteristics of this type of corporatism as listed in table 2.

Table 2. Neocorporatism: Three Characteristics

1. State achieves domination by securing favorable "contracts" or exchanges with producer groups through bargaining. Producer group leaders in turn secure compliance of their members to terms of contract by various means (sometimes aided by state); weaker means employed may display tendency to breakdown.
2. There is a general consensus in support of existing order, but particularistic demands and conflict threaten stability of the order.
3. Corporatist structures are so established as to generate a high degree of voluntary consent to authoritative decisions. In consequence corporatist structures are institutionally less formal.

Wiarda (1997: 119) refers to neocorporatism as "inclusionary, societal, participatory, and democratic." He also refers to it as "social justice oriented." Neocorporatism tends to exist in industrially developed countries where the economic situation of the majority of the population is resolved. Different interest groups are often subsidized by the government in an attempt to keep them on side. Business and labor, he argues (ibid.: 121; see also Molina and Rhodes 2002), "are no longer just private interest associations ... rather they ... become quasi-public or even fully public agencies." As public agencies they come to have much greater input in the political process than did nonstate actors under authoritarian or state corporatism. Gatica Lara (2007: 79) refers to social corporatism as a form of neocorporatism. He holds that some analysts differentiate between state corporatism as an arrangement under authoritarian regimes and social corporatism as that which can be found under liberal pluralism.

International corporatism is referred to by Wiarda (1997: 124–125) as a possible successor of neocorporatism or as "the next stage of corporatism." He refers specifically to the establishment of agencies under NAFTA and the European Economic Community (EEC) which regulate such areas as "pollution and environmental controls, enforcement of labour laws, and business practices" (125). Representatives from government and the private sector are appointed to manage these institutions. Wiarda (124) holds that in the EEC many of the regulatory boards and agencies that exist already function in a corporatist manner with representation from many sectors of society. That said, Wiarda (168) also asserts that corporatism "is still largely national in its regulatory scope and reach," even though business is becoming more international, and downsizing, deregulation, and privatization have resulted in a "further pillar ... [being] removed from the foundation of corporatism" (171). The primary differences between Wiarda's international corporatism and the proposed transnationalized corporatism explicated here are the actors involved and the international dimension of the model. International corporatism includes the active participation of nonstate actors (beyond corporate representatives) on "regulatory boards and agencies" (124) which participate in the elaboration and enforcement of laws and policies, whereas in transnationalized corporatism these voices are absent. In TC, the IFIs, the WTO, nation-states and the transnational and national corporate sector work together to determine policies. Under this model, while the IFIs may influence the relationships between nonstate actors and the state, they do not themselves maintain corporatist relationships with the nonstate actors.

While Schmitter's definition of corporatism emphasizes the hierarchical ordering of society and the controls that are implemented to establish social order, Wiarda's neocorporatism and international corporatism provide the tools to understand developments in democratic industrial countries where state-society relations are perceived as horizontally structured. In fact many have questioned how neocorporatism differs from pluralism because of the close similarities found in the two models.

The various forms and interpretations of corporatism reviewed above view state-society dynamics from slightly different angles. Whether it is the international interaction between states, or the cultural or ideological domination of states over society, or the relations between the state and labor that are emphasized, corporatism provides a useful explanatory model for examining state-society relations. To remain relevant today, however, corporatism as an explanatory model for understanding state-society relations must consider current international political and economic developments. Transnationalized corporatism, as a model, allows for the influence that these developments have on internal state-society relations while also providing the tools to account for the varying strategies used to resist corporatism. The international institutions and the transnational corporations that dominate the global economy have become increasingly influential actors in the international arena. They have coerced or pressured national states to adopt neoliberal policies and to reform specific economic and political policies to accommodate their interests. In turn, these changes directly affect the dynamics between the state and society.

In TC, the normative framework that states create to define, regulate and reproduce the dominant system of representation is directly shaped by the instrumental rationale of global capital as expressed in the policy frameworks and models of state-market-society relations formulated and disseminated by institutions like the IFIs, including the Inter-American Development Bank (IDB), and the WTO. Therefore, the main "constituent" units of the system of representation in TC are predominantly those that belong to the sectors of the economy that participate in the global market, nonstate organizations and the state itself. Moreover, those constituent units that maintain their status in the system of representation or that emerge as new actors in that system must operate — that is, modulate their demands — in congruence with the values and norms that are part of the instrumental rationale of the global economy.

While this model is paradoxical in nature, the virtue of TC is that it acknowledges the changed relationship between the state and the international institutions and organizations, and between the state and the strategies adopted by nonstate actors. Therefore, TC is not just "transnational," nor is it just "corporatist"; it is a model that embodies and expresses changes at the national and extra-national level. To refer only to the transnational relationship of the state with the international institutions would assume that the state has somehow integrated into the international realm of global governance independently of its role or the consequences of its actions in a particular geopolitical region. In the Mexican case it would be misleading to refer to state-society relations as being wholly pluralist or democratic because of the persistent corporatist relationships that exist among the public sector workers and the state and because of the many aspects of democracy that the Mexican state has not instituted. While it is true that from the perspective of many workers this corporatist relationship has become ineffectual, it cannot be denied that the state holds the upper hand in the organizational structures of public-sector unions as will be seen in chapter 3.

A greater understanding of corporatist relations will help us understand the role nonstate actors play in the policy-making process, if any, and how this has changed over the years. It will also enhance our understanding of the logistics of power in neoliberal capitalist society. With such an understanding it is easier to appreciate the interaction among nonstate actors and where they fit into the power equation. That is, as new political and economic arrangements emerge, as external forces come to have a greater influence on the existing power structures, and as the state's managing methods change, variation in how nonstate actors interact among themselves and in relation to the state as they attempt to have their demands heard and acted upon may be expected. Wiarda's (1997: 162) assertion that corporatism as a model "should be viewed as offering important insights into state-society relations as well as helping to fill the gaps in comparative analysis for which other explanations are inadequate," seems most convincing.

The transnationalized corporatist model provides an explanation for the most significant aspects of state-society relations in Mexico and serves as a useful tool for understanding the persistent corporatist relationships that date back to the postrevolutionary period. Although it is true that corporations have extended their reach beyond national borders and that international institutions and trade agreements have come to impose structural adjustment programs that have resulted in the reduction of the number of manufacturing trade unions in underdeveloped countries, and while neoliberalism has meant a theoretical reduction in the role of the state in the market economy, there has been a simultaneous increase in the unionized public-service sector in many countries around the globe and a greater political role for states. This increased political role is often expressed through the tightening of labor laws, increased security measures and new forms of repression and management techniques. Therefore, to address the issue of corporatism in a country like Mexico in the late twentieth and early twenty-first centuries it is useful to take note of the roles of the many different actors that have come to hold positions of power or influence at the national level which supersede or complement the previous corporatist actors. In the case of Mexico, it is evident that the emergent, state-society, transnationalized, corporatist relations that are predominant as we move toward the second decade of the 21st century undermine the democratic reforms that have been introduced since the late 1980s.

Marxist Political-Economic Theory and Method

Corporatism is not exclusive to any particular political arrangement. It can exist under an authoritarian regime or one with a liberal-democratic veneer. As several formulations in the preceding section intimate, the conceptualization of transnationalized corporatism (and attendant criticism of liberal-democratic pluralism as a description of contemporary Mexican state-society relations) is grounded in a Marxist approach. Marxist theory and methodology provide an indispensable analytical tool with which to make sense of the role of political, economic and social actors in any state, including how such state-society relations as what I am calling TC can be sustained in a neoliberal, capitalist society. A Marxist perspective provides the most incisive and realistic analysis of the political-economic model that has been developing in Mexico since the early 1980s. This section will examine the history of Marxist theory in Latin America and then highlight the aspects of it that are most relevant to the Mexican case.

While there are those who consider Marxist theory irrelevant today, Marx himself acknowledged the need to constantly renew his works to account for historical changes. "Marxism is not a dogma but a living theory that has grown and been substantially modified" over time (Boron 1995: 227). Just as such figures as Lenin and Trotsky, Luxemburg and Gramsci sought to understand and transform into socialism the modes of production they confronted in such disparate situations as revolutionary Russia, imperial Germany and fascist Italy, so many political activists today continue to view Marxism as "a guide to action, an ethical and political project pointing toward a superior form of social organization, as well as a scientific theory that allows one to understand some vital aspects of the structure and functioning of contemporary societies" (224).

The varying and overlapping applications of Marxism nevertheless "preserve the main theoretical and methodological premises of Marxist thought," according to Boron (Boron: 233). Issues that were underevaluated by Marx such as the role of women, the environment, peasants and indigenous people (the marginalized) have come to be an integral part of all nondogmatic Marxist analyses. Whether we refer to Marx's own class analysis in terms of bourgeoisie and proletariat, the reconstituted class analysis of Petras and Veltmeyer (2001) or Mariátegui's integration of indigenism, the basic tenets of Marxist theory interpreted methodologically continue to be as relevant in Latin America today as are the basic tenets of capitalism, namely the exploitative social relations of production.

There are many different interpretations and applications of Marxist theory in the history of Latin America (see Aguilar 1978; Riddell 2008). Whether from a theoretical or practical perspective there have always been disagreements on how best to understand and apply Marx's theories. However, the fact that Marxism is still even considered and debated in Latin America today demonstrates that capitalism has not been capable of addressing the needs of the majority of the people.

Juan Bautista Justo was the first serious Latin American intellectual to study Marxism. He approached politics from a humanist perspective; that is, he emphasized human agency and subjectivity. For example, his 1915 *Theory and Practice of History* "treated the diverse social aspects of work and developed a general theory of human activity" (Liss 1984: 42; see also Justo 1984). Social inequality, the capitalist monopoly of the means of production and the impact that the capitalist mode of production had on workers' lives were central to his analyses. He sought practical ways to address social inequalities while rejecting revolution and the dictatorship of the proletariat. "We have managed to break away from the simple formula and the schematic doctrine, and we are developing a popular method of historic action, vast and complex enough to meet the demands of circumstances," he argued (1920 [1978]: 114). Justo's contributions were adopted by socialist organizations throughout Latin America (Aguilar 1978: 7).

Following the Russian Revolution of 1917, communist parties emerged throughout Latin America. The 1920s relied heavily on orthodox Marxism. There were, on the one hand, the orthodox Marxists like Luis Emilio Recabarren of Chile and Julio Antonio Mella of Cuba, and, on the other hand, the more populist leaders such as Víctor Paz Estensorro, Juan José Arévalo of Colombia and Rómulo Betancourt of Guatemala, not to mention the anarchist organizations that created a challenge for all parties involved.

One of the most influential theorists of "Latin American Marxism" (see Munck 2007: 157) during the 1920s was José Carlos Mariátegui from Peru. Mariátegui is considered the founder of this school of thought. Two of his most important contributions to Latin American political theory were the integration of indigenism and his focus on national rather than international issues. The indigenous question was ignored by orthodox and Eurocentric Marxists, who were more concerned about the industrial working classes. In Latin America, Mariátegui's Marxism concentrated on land distribution and cultural issues that were reflective of national realities. He was accused of being a populist by the Leninist and Trotskyite organizations in Latin America.

Carlos B. Baliño and Jorge Antonio Mella founded the Cuban Communist Party in 1925. They held both U.S. imperialism and the Cuban bourgeoisie responsible for the dreadful living conditions of the majority of Cuban people. According to Liss (1984: 241), "Baliño struggled for socialism until his death." Mella supported Baliño's views and admired his determination. He believed that in order to effect change in Cuba the first step was to reform the university by organizing students who would then coordinate their efforts with the working class to overthrow the government. He took the praxis component of Marxist theory very seriously.

Castro's nationalistic approach to the Cuban Revolution led to its triumph as the first successful Marxist revolutionary victory in Latin America. While Marxist in theory, it was unique in that what drove the movement was armed guerrilla warfare rather than class struggle. This approach was mirrored in 1979 with the Sandinista uprising in Nicaragua and by the Zapatista movement in Mexico on the eve of January 1, 1994. Che Guevara and Fidel Castro were the makers of the Cuban revolution in its tactical, strategic, and at times dogmatic approaches. While Castro ultimately adopted a Marxist communist revolutionary doctrine, his discourse focused on the "pueblo" and its needs. One of Che's most important contributions to Marxist theory in Latin America was his contention that it was not necessary to have reached a fully "ripened" stage of capitalism for there to be satisfactory conditions to effect revolutionary change. According to Fernández Nadal and David Silnik (2001: 127–128), Che held and demonstrated that underdeveloped marginal countries such as Cuba were in fact more likely to work toward a socialist mode of production.

Not all Marxist theorists in Latin America during this period were as wedded to Russian ideology as those mentioned above. For example Caio Prado from Brazil was also more of a humanist who believed "that given a chance, socialism [would] prevail in the minds of men and women" (Liss 1984: 116). His analyses were always economically backed. Chilean Marcello Segall was another Marxist who came to reject dogmatic Marxist tendencies in his later works (Lowy 1992: 143).

Following the Cuban Revolution there continued to be differences of emphasis between intellectual Marxists like Carlos Rafael Rodríguez and Lombardo Toledano (1967) and what Liss (1984: 254) referred to as the Stalinists, such as Blas Roca. Rodríguez insisted that a real Marxist had to look beyond an economic analysis of a country and examine social relations through a historical materialist analysis. Like Che Guevara, Rodríguez rejected sectarian attitudes among the revolutionary forces and leaders of the movement. While Lombardo Toledano (1967: 49) adopted a nationalist, humanist, Marxist approach in his promotion of a Mexico free of exploitation, he dismissed working-class revolutionary change in favor of working-class collaboration with other sectors of society. He supported the drive for industrialization, which he believed would benefit all.

Dependency theory became popular in the 1960s and 1970s throughout Latin America. It served as a means to explain the circumstance of nation-states that were politically independent yet economically dependent. Dependency theory concerns itself with the division of society into classes and with marginality in postcolonial countries. It is a counter to modernization theory, which it tends to criticize as little more than a rationale for U.S. imperialism. It premises its thesis on a political-economic analysis of global development. Dependency theorists claim to study the real history made by real people, to study countries within their global context, and to consider inequality as the primary ground for state intervention (Rist 1997: 110–111).

Prominent dependency theorists like Gunder Frank, Baran, Sweezy, Faletto, Dos Santos and Cardoso all sought to determine what effect the economic dependency of underdeveloped countries had on their social structures. Dependency theorists "attributed development problems to the consequences of integration into the international capitalist economy and to exploitation by foreign economic and political interests" (Geddes 1991: 50). They believed that by analyzing the relationship between developed countries and underdeveloped countries they could demonstrate how this relationship explained the characteristic class structure of the latter. They believed it would be almost impossible for many of the poorest countries to become modern and prosperous under the existent world order.

The fall of the Berlin Wall transformed Marxist theory for many in Latin America. While Vasconi (1990) concentrates on a shift from an emphasis on revolution and socialism to an emphasis on democracy and socialism, Chilcote (2003) argues that the "crisis of Marxist political thought" in Latin America today is in part a consequence of "external intellectual influences" brought back by those who studied on the European continent.

One of the early transformations of Marxist thought preceding the end of the Cold War was Laclau and Mouffe's (1985) theory of radical democracy, a theory that resonated in Latin America among some theorists yet was damned by others. Laclau (1990) broke with orthodox Marxism and held that "socialism is no longer a blueprint for society, and comes to be part of a radical democratisation of social organization" (xv). In their article titled "Post-Marxism without Apologies," Laclau and Mouffe (1987: 80) refer to a series of historical transformations that precipitated their rejection of orthodox Marxism. These transformations are

> structural transformations of capitalism that have led to the decline of the classical working class in the post-industrial countries; the increasingly profound penetration of capitalist relations of production in areas of social life, whose dislocatory effects ... have generated new forms of social protest; the emergence of mass mobilizations in Third World countries which do not follow the classical pattern of class struggle; the crisis and discrediting of the model of society put into effect in the countries of so-called actually existing socialism, including the exposure of new forms of domination established in the name of the dictatorship of the proletariat.

Laclau and Mouffe's (1985) theory of radical democracy eliminates the idea of class division and replaces it with "agonistic pluralism." Radical democracy adds "difference" to the main tenets of liberal democracy, namely freedom and equality. They hold that liberal democracy's attempt to build consensus in fact suppresses the particular needs and demands that exist along class, race and gender divides. While Boron (2003: 88) dismisses Laclau and Mouffe's theories as *discursive reductionism*, Moulian (1981) and Nun (1981) support the concept of radical democracy.

Petras, whom Munck (2007: 165) refers to as a "revivalist," argues that the left is coming back to challenge the dominance of the free market. Electoral politics and reformist tactics, he argues, are incapable of responding to such a challenge. Boron is another political theorist who draws on more traditional aspects of Marxism to understand political-economic and social developments in Latin America today. In particular he praises the value of Marxist theory for its utility in making sense of exploitation, marginalization, and oppression found in modern capitalist societies. The relationship between theory and practice is also an element of classical Marxist theory that Boron considers relevant today (Boron 2006: 36; Amadeo 2006: 95). Given the current political-economic situation of the world, Boron, Petras and Amadeo, among others, consider the reintroduction of Marxism in contemporary political philosophy and into the agenda of current social movements to be indispensable. While all three theorists return to a classical Marxist beginning, they all adapt their interpretation of Marxist theory to current political, economic and social developments. Petras and Veltmeyer's (2001) theory of reconstituted class analysis[1] is an example of this adaptation.

John Holloway's thesis of "changing the world without taking power," according to Munck (2007: 168), distinguishes "between 'power over' (characteristic of private property, under capitalism) and 'power to' (which needs to be appropriated by those seeking to transform the world)." Rather than speak of the working class, Holloway (2002: 5) speaks of the "antagonistic 'we' grown from an antagonistic society." He rejects the notion of the state as the center point of social transformation or as a sovereign body confined to geographical boundaries. Instead, he argues that the state is "embedded ... in the web of capitalist social relations" (ibid.), which transcend national boundaries. His analysis rejects the nationalist approach of many contemporary Latin American Marxists. Changing the world or a particular country by taking power, according to Holloway (18) negates the struggle against power because in the end it only reproduces power, the very thing we are struggling against. In fact, contrary to Marxist theory, "the world cannot be changed through the state" (19).

The Zapatista movement in Mexico has grown its own unique forms of resistance and dialogue, many of which are in keeping with aspects of Holloway's analysis and to a degree with Laclau and Mouffe's radical democracy. Drawing on the experience of the Zapatista movement, Anguiano (2006b: 4) argues that Marx's concept of the proletariat must be understood today as one that includes all oppressed people, not only those who fall into the original category of "industrial workers." This interpretation of the working class includes the exploited, those who are discriminated against, the excluded sectors of society, peasants, indigenous people, women, the unemployed, migrants, and so on. By grouping all of these people in one category, Anguiano is able to include all the oppressed sectors in society in one grouping. The struggle he proposes differs from Marx's revolutionary approach and focuses on the organizing and regrouping of sectors of society into equalitarian, democratic, nonmercantile alternatives to capitalism.

Indigenous struggles are often directed at the preservation of their cultural, linguistic and religious background, concepts that go against Marx's classical vision of a world culture as a precondition for revolutionary action. Muga (1988), for example, recognizes the indigenous struggle in Latin America as an effort to achieve self-determination in the struggle against "the power of capital." "Both the proletariat and the Aboriginal peoples are oppressed by trans-national capital in their efforts at achieving self-determination.... The aboriginal peoples [are oppressed] by the control exercised over their land" (quoted in Bedford 1994). In fact, the extensive, ongoing, indigenous struggles in Latin America are indicative of the importance of considering Marxist analysis when examining political, economic and social aspects of the region.

At the risk of sounding dogmatic, this analysis will detail the aspects of traditional Marxist thought that help to explicate the political, economic and social arrangements in Mexico. In the preface to *A Contribution to the Critique of Political Economy*, Marx (1978b [1859]: 4) asserts that

> In the social production of their existence, men inevitably enter into definite relations, which are independent of their will, namely relations of production appropriate to a given stage in the development of their material forces of production. The totality of these relations of production constitutes the economic structure of society, the real foundation, on which arises a legal and political superstructure and to which correspond definite forms of social consciousness. The mode of production of material life conditions the general process of social, political and intellectual life. It is not the consciousness of men that determines their existence, but their social existence that determines their consciousness.

Marxist theory is based on a political-economic interpretation of society in which all political, economic and social processes, relationships and institutions are founded on a particular mode of production. Whether in feudal or capitalist society, it is the class that owns the forces or means of production, such as the land, labor, capital, raw materials, machines and technology, which takes on political power, while it is the nonowning class which is exploited for its labor and dominated politically.

When discussing political power and the role of the state there are two distinct interpretations of Marx's theory: the instrumentalist and the structuralist. The instrumentalist interpretation, favored by Miliband (1969), states that the capitalist class is the ruling class by virtue of its economic power. The state is run by and reflective of the capitalist class's interests. It will always rule in favor of the elites.

Poulantzas (1975) rejects the notion of the state as an instrument controlled by the capitalist class. His structuralist approach conceptualizes the state as an organizer or mediator between capital and labor. Here the state creates conditions that will ensure accumulation of capital while engaging in activities that will win the consent of the working class or the nonelites, thus legitimizing the state as a representative body. This can involve making concessions to the subordinate classes through such things as social programs and human rights legislation, as well as propaganda exercises in population thought control via state and corporate media of communication.

Mexico can best be understood from the structuralist perspective. While authoritarian in many of its political practices, the state's corporatist nature and its social programs, albeit lacking in substance and scope, serve as means to effect legitimacy. This study provides examples of how the state goes beyond merely servicing the interests of the elites.

In a capitalist mode of production, such as that in Mexico, the two principal contending forces are the class of owners of capital (and land) and the class of nonowners of capital (and land). Of course, within the class of owners of capital there are the billionaire capitalists like Carlos Slim on the one extreme and smaller family corporations on the other extreme, just as there are large landowners and peasants that own and work the land for their own subsistence. Since the onset of neoliberalism, there has been an indisputable transformation of the capitalist class's composition as transnational corporations move in and the national capitalist class struggles to survive. The worker or the nonowner of capital in this relation of production — whether in the primary, secondary or tertiary sectors — represents nothing more than a commodity.

> We have shown that the worker sinks to the level of a commodity and becomes indeed the most wretched of commodities; that the wretchedness of the worker is in inverse proportion to the power and magnitude of his production; that the necessary result of competition is the accumulation of capital in a few hands, and thus the restoration of monopoly in a more terrible form; that finally the distinction between capitalist and land-rentier, like that between the tiller of the soil and the factory-worker, disappears and the whole of society must fall apart into the two classes — the property *owners* and the propertyless *workers* [Marx 1978a (1844): 70].

While keeping in mind that this two-pronged class divide is not as simple as Marx describes it here, it continues to be the case that workers or nonowners of capital are at the disposition of the owners of the means of production. They own only their labor power. Their "labour is therefore not voluntary, but coerced; it is forced labour. It is therefore not the satisfaction of a need; it is merely a means to satisfy needs external to it. Its alien character emerges clearly in the fact that as soon as no physical or other compulsion exists, labour is shunned like the plague" (ibid.: 74). In keeping with the characteristics of the current labor market and of the nonowners of capital in Mexico, one must include the vast number of people working in the informal sector, the peasantry, the indigenous people[2] and the many workers that have migrated north and who send remittances to their families in Mexico, all of whom are victims of the economic arrangements of neoliberal capitalism. The capitalist class has also changed in that its constituency now transcends national borders. While these groupings are not the traditional proletariat and capitalist classes that Marx described, they continue to stand in essentially the same relationship to ownership of private property in the means of production: a few own virtually everything; the mass of the people own virtually nothing. When considering the division of society into social classes, it is important to understand the *methodological* interpretation of Marxist theory being adopted here. While classes are the most significant relation of production for Marx they are nowhere defined explicitly in his work. However, Giddens (1971: 37) asserts that it is

> relatively easy to infer from the many scattered references which Marx makes in the course of different works [that] classes are constituted by the relationship of groupings of individuals to the ownership of private property in the means of production. This yields a model of class relations which is basically dichotomous: all class societies are built around a primary line of division between two antagonistic classes, one dominant and the other subordinate. In Marx's usage, class of necessity involves a conflict relation.

What is critical here, then, is not to reproduce some nineteenth century historically-geographically located division of classes but to approach the analysis of the resistance activities of civil-society, social-movement organizations in terms of their relationship to "ownership of private property in the means of production" mediated by the state and the contemporary nature of social consciousness.

The forces of production and the relations of production are what constitute the mode of production, in this case capitalism, neoliberalism being simply a form of capitalism (distinct from, say, welfare or state capitalism). The legal and political superstructure that exists atop a given mode of production comprises such things as the state, the legal and education systems, and the prevailing ideology informing social consciousness. The state represents primarily the interests of the elites, whether national or international, namely those who own the factories, the land, the capital and technology. According to Mandel (1994: 25; see also Wood 1995: 33),

> the state is the product of the division of society into classes, an instrument for the consolidation, maintenance, and reproduction of the rule of a given class.... State institutions ... include both coercive elements (the army, repressive bodies and the judicial system) and integrative elements used to persuade the productive classes to accept the class exploitation and oppression they suffer, to mask and "legitimate" the exploitative and oppressive nature of these institutions.

The class-divided society that Marx refers to effectively describes how capitalist societies are divided into those who have a direct input into the economic and political process and those who are marginalized, excluded or simply victims of these arrangements. Wood (1995: 33) reminds us that historically "the existence of a state has always implied the existence of classes." Mexico is no exception. The Mexican state's involvement in international institutions and the protection it provides for its national elites and international corporate elites is in keeping with neoliberal capitalist expectations. Those who do not possess political or economic power will often seek ways to eliminate the alienation and oppression they experience. This is not to suggest that people's working conditions will necessarily heighten their political consciousness or that all working people in the world will unite to overthrow their oppressors. However, what it does suggest is that some people *will* act against oppression, dispossession, human rights violations, inequality, corruption and poverty, and in a variety of ways. Most often it is the state which becomes the target of social movements either seeking to reform its practices or struggling to overthrow it. Katz (2007) rejects the assertion that "no subject exists to undertake socialism in Latin America." Instead, he reminds us that the current anticapitalist forces include workers of the informal sector and agrarian or peasant communities. While we might agree that the "working classes" have been hit hard by neoliberal restructuring, there can be no doubt that struggle and organizing has persisted under new banners. Katz points out that the countries in Latin America have fewer resources to solve the problems of nutrition, education and sanitation and that it is in response to these conditions that people organize and rebel. Moreover, he argues, in Latin America,

> the great differences between the current period and that of 1960–80 lie more in the area of political consciousness than in the realm of relationships of force or in the changes in civil society. It is not the intensity of the social conflict, the willingness of the oppressed to struggle, or the capacity of the oppressors to control that has substantially changed, but the visibility of— and confidence in — a socialist model [Kate 2007].

This lack of confidence in the socialist model is due to a number of factors. First came the fall of the Soviet Union and the authoritarian ways of its government. Second has been a sense of betrayal caused by governments and political parties that identify themselves with the left but once in power reveal themselves as ready to accommodate neoliberal prescriptions (for example, Lula in Brazil, Ortega in Nicaragua and the PRD in Mexico City). Third, the massive repression suffered by revolutionary forces in the 1960s and 1970s as they fought to overthrow corrupt, illegitimate governments has had a lasting impact on opposition movements in Latin America.

The emergent "left-wing" governments in the region cannot be considered anticap-italist, Marxist, social movements but are more in keeping with social-democratic, electoral movements which work within the capitalist constitutional framework to effect change. The value of left-leaning electoral triumphs and political struggles of all sorts is that they serve to enhance people's political consciousness through organization. They will not in themselves lead to the overthrow of capitalism (assuming that is the desired goal). While there are various social-democratic governments in power in Latin America, there are no cases of socialist governments in Latin America that have come to power through electoral processes.

The debate over how society is divided and how "working class" is actually defined becomes less important when discussing transnationalized corporatist relationships in the current context of a global market economy where transnational corporations and inter-national institutions come to shape the economic and political policies of nation-states. Suffice it to say that those sectors of civil society that exist as subordinate entities, excluded from the decision-making process, those nonowners of capital, are best described as the victims of the political-economic arrangements found in capitalism. This is not to say that civil society is all of one piece. Its varying, not to say contradictory, elements have been the subject of considerable theorizing, which will become apparent in the following sections.

Many current theoretical approaches seek to understand the relationships among the multiple political actors in the twenty-first century. These include Samir Amin (delinking theory), I. Wallerstein (world systems theory), E. O. Wright (inequality, socialism in the future), Toni Negri (empire and the multitude), John Holloway (changing the world without taking power), and González Casanova (the new left), not to mention Boron and Petras and Veltmeyer who are referenced throughout this book. None of them would be considered dogmatic Marxists, yet all of them refer to Marxist theory as they clarify their own political interpretations of the world. Marx's political-economic analyses provide a methodological model through which to examine such recalcitrant economic facts as the ever-increasing gap between the rich and the poor and such political facts as the disproportionately large influence of the owners of the means of production on the state.

Unemployment, income differentiation, regional differentiation, class differentiation, and penetration by foreign capital are all concepts that many use as a means to make sense of contemporary capitalist societies. Marx's economic theories and his historical materialist perspective are fundamental to the "praxis" component of his political thought. He argued that capitalism was proving to be such a destructive mode of production that there was no option but to supersede it by eliminating rights to private property in the means of production, to produce a classless society through a revolutionary struggle led by a communist party. Most current social movements throughout Latin America are not led by communist parties. In fact, while many nonstate actors have organized along class lines, others organize along ethnic lines, while still others organize in response to environmental degradation, privatization and corruption. The most common denominator among social movements is the identification of the government and its policies as the enemy. At the same time, it has also become more common to hear anticapitalist discourse among peasant organizations such as the Movimento dos Trabalhadores Rurais Sem Terra (MST) in Brazil, the EZLN in Mexico and the Confederación de Nacionalidades Indígenas del Ecuador (CONAIE) in Ecuador.

At various points throughout this study reference will be made to a number of organizations which during different stages of their development have claimed or currently claim to be antisystemic or anticapitalist. To be antisystemic or anticapitalist, according to Marxist theory, implies the desire to replace the existing mode of production with something different. With the exception of the unregistered political parties that will be examined in chapter 4, none of the other nonstate actors that express antisystemic sentiments describe what would replace capitalism or organize against capitalism. In fact, it may be argued that an organization that considers itself antisystemic, yet whose existence depends on the preservation of capitalism, embodies a serious contradiction. Unions would fall into this category. It is hardly surprising that Marxism has long debated when and to what extent unions serve to "incorporate" workers into capitalism or move them toward a revolutionary consciousness and praxis (Hyman 1971).

González Casanova detailed the seven essential characteristics of the "new left" in Latin America in a letter to Subcomandante Marcos in *La Jornada* on March 9, 2000. According to González Casanova (2000), these characteristics must be considered by "new left" organizations which emerged in the 1960s if they have any hope of surviving. The list includes the following: the reevaluation of the political, economic and social structures and of imperialism; an examination of the contradictions of capitalism, social democracy, socialism, and communism; a reassessment of the class struggle and the new role of transnational corporations; a reevaluation of universal democracy and its relation to socialism; a conversion of personal struggles to national and international struggles; the need to overcome the dilemma between reform and revolution; and the inclusion of cultural-political ethics and historical, scientific and technical knowledge in the publicly funded universal education system.

Attending to these issues does not contradict the drive behind Marxist revolutionary movements of the twentieth century. González Casanova's seven points are reflective of his concern about the direction of current social movements and his attempt to contribute to the development of the Zapatista movement while remaining faithful to Marxist premises. The "Zapatista question" will be examined in chapter 5.

Social Movement Theories and Marxist Critique

Mexico's long history of corporatist state-society relations has meant the "incorporation" of leaders of unions, companies and other major civil society organizations. But "extra corporate" resistance and opposition have never been absent. This section will serve as a theoretical precursor for chapters 3 and 4 which discuss the development of a sample of social movements and political organizations in Mexico. This introduction is intended to facilitate the understanding of the changes in political strategy that may or may not have occurred during the transition from state corporatism to transnationalized corporatism.

The historical development of social movements demonstrates how state-society relations have changed over the years. Traditional social organizations, modern social movements and new social movements are three categories that have come to be used to define historical periods of heightened political contention. The three categories emerged and have been adopted in developed countries throughout Europe and North America. According to Tilly (1995), the first period of traditional social organizations prevailed until the mid–1700s. The state was not the only or the primary target of the opposition forces in their search to effect change. Violent acts were often directed against bosses; smugglers confronted each other, and child molesters were attacked. It was a period of people making claims against other people unlike later eras when people acted primarily against the state. These acts of contention were not organized but episodic. Following a violent confrontation the participants would return to the activities of their everyday lives and might never again engage in a similar act against the same political actor. The three key characteristics of contentious actions during this period are that they were parochial, apolitical and decentralized. The state was not seen as directly relevant, and the social actors did not see their actions as stepping-stones to a bigger movement. Their actions were often violent and episodic. In his comparable analysis of Europe during this period, Te Brake (1998) emphasizes popular political action. He reminds us that not all political action during this period was a reaction to state actions.

The second stage of contentious politics referred to by Tilly is that of modern social movements, which is what we are most familiar with today. This period began in the mid-eighteenth century around the time of the formation of the nation-state in Europe (Tilly 1995). This type of contention is more organized and has long-term goals most often directed against the state apparatus. Contentious activities during this period moved from violent sporadic confrontations to peaceful protests, hunger strikes and long-term strategizing. According to Tilly, these changes resulted from a greater concentration of capital, greater power afforded to the nation-state and the response of the contenders to the more centralized power structure we know as the nation-state. Common demands became more frequent, public meetings were held and factory strikes ensued. Public collective action came to be a viable means to influence the political process, such as the struggle for the extension of the suffrage in the early 1830s. People also sought to influence the taxation process, the role of religion in the political process, corruption, and the treatment of the poor through popular collective action. The process of democratization and the creation of a central state defined a clear target and a relatively friendly environment. Discontent was no longer an act of individual reaction but collective action.

The third type of political contention is referred to as "new social movements" (NSMs). According to Melucci (1989), Laclau (1985), and Touraine (2002) it has become necessary to examine social movements from a cultural perspective. They claim that the development of communications technology, the disappearance of traditional historical and political cleavages, and the cultural differences within and across nations justify this new theoretical approach to examining contentious actions. This type of social movement analysis downplays the organizational structures of modern movements and instead highlights the identity politics of "affinity groups" constituting "postmodern" social movements. These identity groups might come together because of geographical origins, gender, cultural origins or for religious reasons. NSM theories reject the idea that people group together because of economic or class affinities. Identities become the basis for collective action. The struggle becomes one of reformation or autonomy rather than gaining control of the state (see Holloway 2002: 11). Movement activists are seen to be primarily involved in advancing decentralized, egalitarian and participatory organizational forms. This said, Melucci (1996) in particular acknowledges the existence of class divisions while arguing that NSMs no longer develop on class lines.

The concept of NSM has come to be applied to any movement that can be seen as neither labor related nor class related. This classification emerged in the 1970s and focuses on the cultural aspects of social movements. Even Tilly's more recent works (2004) consider culture to be an important "causal mechanism," as he puts it. There is still much debate as to whether there is such a thing as a *new* social movement or whether the concept is simply a new way for political theorists to examine social movements. NSM theorists criticize Marxism for reducing all political phenomena to economic events and seeing all social action as driven by class interests. Laclau (1985: 29), for example, argues that

> categories such as "working class," "petit-bourgeois," etc., become less and less meaningful as ways of understanding the overall identity of social agents. The concept of "class struggle," for example, is neither correct nor incorrect — it is, simply, totally insufficient as a way of accounting for contemporary social conflicts.

Thus NSM theorists argue that collective action today is not based on class identity or class consciousness as Marx would have it, but rather on nonclass factors such as gender, ethnicity, environment, and so forth. (see also Touraine 1971; Evers 1985; Laclau and Mouffe 1985a). Let us consider this argument as it applies to Mexico.

It is true that Mexico's socioeconomic divisions are interlaced with vast ethnic-cultural diversity. Accordingly, there is continuing debate regarding where the emphasis should be placed when discussing social movements in Mexico. Ethnic-cultural approaches to understanding civil society tend to be agency specific and focus on why individuals get involved in collective action rather than examining the collectivities themselves. Such arguments (see Álvarez, Dagnino and Escobar 1998; Brysk 2000) overlook the relevant class, economic distribution and structural referents, and instead focus on the creation of countercultures, criticizing prevailing values and presenting new ones.

Other categories or identities that are commonly invoked are "indigenous," "Black," "feminist" and "gay." It is argued that social movements or parts of civil society coalesce into organizations with which individuals can personally identify. The Zapatista uprising, for example, would be considered an indigenous movement because the participants are indigenous, live in indigenous communities and have indigenous demands. A feminist movement, therefore, is not an indigenous movement but a feminist movement because it comprises feminists asserting feminist demands.

A serious shortcoming of this approach is that it places all members of a particular identity in the same package. Let us take the feminist example. Women within a given society are considered all part of the same struggle because, after all, they are women. Yet, a working-class, single mother would not feel a kinship with a female CEO of a transnational corporation, just as an indigenous, landless peasant would not sympathize with indigenous large landowners. In fact, within the indigenous communities in the state of Chiapas, there is a history of conflict between different sectors of the same communities where the primary contentious issue is land ownership and power.

From a Marxist perspective, the confrontation between the EZLN and the government would be defined along class lines. The conflicts within the communities themselves can also be explained in class terms. According to Marx, as the subordinate class becomes more aware of its role in society it acquires a conscious desire to change its own political and social conditions. Class, remember, is a matter of the social relations of production. In defense of such class analysis, Wood (1995:270) argues that

> capitalism could survive the eradication of all oppression specific to women as women [or indigenous people as indigenous people] — while it would not, by definition, survive the eradication of class exploitation ... struggles conceived in purely extra-economic terms — as purely against racism or gender oppression, for example — are not in themselves fatally dangerous to capitalism.

Building on a Marxist foundation Petras and Veltmeyer suggest a means to integrate the particularities of a given movement. For example, they want to integrate the indigenous component of the EZLN while preserving the identity of the movement as a class fraction to be distinguished from the state, and from the owners of the means of production. They (2001: 91–92)

> see the peasantry in class terms: that is, actors the agency of whom is affected as much by the economic and political structures which constrain them, as by the forms of their own consciousness.... Both these processes are regarded by [them] as inseparable, as a dialectical unity.... The peasantry are viewed ... as a highly modern social class, a catalyst for antisystemic change and a dynamic force in an ongoing modernization process.

This revised definition of social class thus provides a neo–Marxist category for contemporary political analyses.[3] Petras and Veltmeyer, as well as Gramsci, would expect the Zapatista movement to have direct influence on other social movements in their search for systemic change. Within this larger movement, they would expect to see the integration of the economically and politically underprivileged sectors of society and enhanced consciousness of the participants.

Petras and Veltmeyer refer to their approach as "reconstituted class analysis." They modify the Marxian concept of the proletariat to focus on the potential of the rural peasantry and its transformative capabilities, while nevertheless validating class analysis. They claim that peasant movements like the EZLN resist the neoliberal agenda and provide a vehicle for the participation of other opposition forces such as those organized around gender, ethnic or development issues. To make their case they draw on movements throughout Latin America, such as the MST, the Revolutionary Armed Forces of Colombia (FARC), the CONAIE in Ecuador as well as the EZLN in Mexico. Petras and Veltmeyer (2002: 60) argue further that the recent peasant/indigenous-led movements in Latin America comprise the primary opposition force to neoliberalism in the region.

In his analysis of the peasant movements in Latin America, Veltmeyer (1997: 154) argues that "in many contexts peasants are of indigenous origin, giving their struggle a national and ethnic character, but the cause of the struggle can be found in their relationships to the means of production and to the State." He highlights the fact that these movements are independent of political parties and that their tactics include such things as "land invasions, the blocking of highways, marches and demonstrations, and the occupation of public buildings" (155); negotiations with the state could be added to this list. Veltmeyer acknowledges the characteristics of the peasant movements of the 1990s that distinguish them from previous peasant movements. He argues that the "new peasant movements"[4] are very aware of the new world order, within the context of neoliberalism and globalization, and the manner in which these economic policies directly affect the living conditions of the indigenous people and the rest of the population. This understanding draws the indigenous and peasant populations together with other sectors that oppose the neoliberal agenda in the creation of common fronts or coalitions (156). Of particular importance is the fact that these new peasant movements function independently of political parties and established urban politicians, while at the same time seeking out alliances nationwide and in some cases globally (for example, the practices of the EZLN [see chapter 6]). According to Petras and Veltmeyer (2002: 60) the leadership of these movements is unique in that they "are not part of [or] subordinated to a bureaucratic apparatus, but are the product of grassroots debates and accountable to popular assemblies." They are similar to other social movements as they adopt new means of struggle to confront the neoliberal state and the globalizing political powers, which influence the state's actions. This approach to NSMs can be directly tied to the transnationalized, corporatist, state-society relations model that will be discussed in detail in chapter 2. What Petras and Veltmeyer are observing are changes in the forms of resistance used by the peasants and the indigenous communities in response to current, global, economic power structures. That said, upon further examination it will become apparent that unlike other social movements, the Zapatista movement has distanced itself from the Mexican state. This places it in a unique situation in relation to the state.

Critique of Liberal-Democratic Pluralism

According to McAdam et al. (2001) the development of social movements is based on "opportunity." They argue that the democratic expansion of the electorate with a more centralized government bureaucracy increases political opportunities by giving voice to the voiceless through voting but also through contentious actions that are more tolerated under a democratic system. Democracy, they say, provides a friendlier environment for political action because the state is considered a representative of the needs of all the people and its protective qualities provide a safe environment for political action. Coalitions are formed as opportunities open up. (It must also be said, surely, that a fragmented, weakened state also provides opportunities for contentious action.) However, as Boron (1995) argues, liberal democracy may advance civil and political rights, but it generally fails to address the social and economic rights which provide the material foundation for the effective exercise of civil and political rights by the majority of the population. As the model that is being promoted throughout the underdeveloped world, liberal democracy may pretend to address the economic inequalities that exist, but that pretense has long been exposed as a fraud. In structural Marxist terms, the individualism underlying liberal-democratic pluralism is a legitimating ideology. As Poulantzas puts it, one of the central functions of the capitalist nation-state is to disorganize the opposition forces through the representation of the individual. He holds that

> the state presents itself as the incarnation of the popular will of the people/nation. The people/nation is institutionally fixed as the ensemble of "citizens" or "individuals" whose unity is represented by the capitalist state: its real substratum is precisely this isolating effect manifested by the CMP's [capitalist mode of production's] socioeconomic relations [Poulantzas 1975: 133].

Liberal-democratic governments managing a neoliberal agenda in undeveloped countries have shown themselves incapable of addressing the most basic economic needs of the majority of their populations. It is an activist's truism that engagement by an organization in contentious action tends to follow from the political-historical trajectory of the organization and the agenda of the leadership more than from the opportunities that may or may not emerge at a given time. As can be seen throughout Latin America, contentious action predates the emergence of liberal democracy. In fact, it dates back to the colonial period when indigenous populations confronted their conquerors. The liberal-democratic model has introduced a form of electoral representation that, if it were effective in representing all sectors of society, as the model claims to be, would eliminate the need for further contention.

In keeping with the TC model, nonstate actors fit into this discussion not only as social movements seeking ways to effect change but also as actors either integrated into the corporatist state-society relations model, fighting against it or on the margins. This will be discussed further in chapters 3, 4 and 5.

Delinking and Deglobalization

From a world systems perspective (see Wallerstein 1987, 2004; Hopkins and Wallerstein 1996) the Egyptian political philosopher Samir Amin (1990) examines what he calls the "delinking" of national governments from the international political arena as the only means to set the stage for socialism. The United States and the international institutions it backs are, he argues, the biggest obstacles to political, economic and social development in underdeveloped countries. The U.S. (Amin 2003: 18–19) "lives parasitically to the detriment of its partners in the world system.... The world produces, and the United States, which has practically no funds in reserve, consumes. The U.S. advantage is that of a predator whose deficit is covered by loans from others, whether obtained by consent or force." This has never been more true of the United States than in the wake of the Great Recession of 2008–2009.

Amin is careful to state that delinking will not always lead to socialism but rather is a process or a transition that over an extended period could *potentially* lead to socialism (Amin 1990: 55, 67). He emphasizes the need for underdeveloped countries to adopt new market strategies and values different from northern developed countries. Delinking, he explains, does not mean "autarky but refusal to bow to the dominant logic of the world capitalist system" (Amin 2006: 27). This is in contrast to the neoliberal push in the North for political, economic and social "integration" (read, capitalist domination) through "international laws and institutions" (read, transnationalized corporatism). The integration concept has provided a means for the "industrialized countries" (read, Northern ruling classes) to benefit from the natural resources, labor force and accrued interest on the debt payments of the underdeveloped countries. It is not a process of equal integration where all benefit. It is expected that the underdeveloped countries of Latin America will submit to international laws, conditions and structural adjustment programs.

This international integration emerged with capitalism and has become more institutionalized in the last two decades. Underdeveloped countries like Mexico are linked to the international market and to the dominant countries at the center. "Capitalist expansion," argues Amin (1990: 56), "disintegrates the societ[ies in the periphery], fragments [them], alienates [them] and eventually destroys the nation[s] or destroys [their] potential." Unlike autarky, which is "the withdrawal from external commercial, financial and technological exchanges," delinking is the "pursuit of a system of rational criteria for economic options founded on a law of value on a national basis with popular relevance, independent of such criteria of economic rationality as flow from the dominance of the capitalist law of value operating on a world scale" (62). Delinking does not necessarily reject foreign technological developments. It is a process of transition that puts less emphasis on comparative advantage and gives more attention to introducing economic, social and political reforms in the national interests of southern countries. Delinking implies a transfer of political hegemony to new "centers." Delinking is a form of selectively cutting oneself off, "a kind of active anti-globalization which is in dialectical relationship with globalization itself" (Hannerz 1996: 18).

There are four components to Amin's (1990: xiv) thesis of delinking. He explains them in the following way:

> First, the necessity of delinking is the logical political outcome of the unequal character of the development of capitalism.... Unequal development, in this sense, is the origin of essential social, political and ideological evolutions.... Second, delinking is a necessary condition of any socialist advance, in the North and in the South. This proposition is, in our view, essential for a reading of Marxism that genuinely takes into account the unequal character of capitalist development. Third, the potential advances that become available through delinking will not "guarantee" certainty of further evolution toward a pre-defined "socialism." Socialism is a future that must be built. [And f]ourth, the option for delinking must be discussed in political terms. This proposition derives from a reading according to which economic constraints are absolute only for those who accept the commodity alienation intrinsic to capitalism, and turn it into an historical system of eternal validity.

Amin and Gunder Frank agreed that the "centre grew at the expense of the periphery" (Velasco 2002: 44). It was in this context that Amin argued that the only way for the third world to prosper would be through the process of delinking. Contrary to Amin's position, Gunder Frank eventually came to the conclusion that delinking was not "a very viable or fruitful policy" (ibid.: 45). Sandbrook et al. (2006: 76) refer to delinking as a "utopian project.... [Amin] call[s] for an unrealistic future: self-contained communities and the reduction or even elimination of long distance trade." The study of the Zapatistas in chapter 5 and the review of similar cases in chapter 6 are intended to contribute to this debate.

Bello's theory of "deglobalization" is similar to Amin's delinking theory in that it refers to a severing of conventional relationships. Bello (2004: 107) considers "the current crisis of global economic governance [as] a systemic one." In that vein, he promotes the idea of "reorienting economies from the emphasis on production for export to production for the local market" (ibid.: 113). Bello sees the central target as the WTO whose mandate needs to be halted or reversed (ibid.: 109). The constructing of a new pluralist system of global governance would follow his deconstruction of WTO hegemony. The central components of Bello's deglobalization model involve the implementation of the following processes (ibid.: 113–114):

- drawing most of a country's financial resources for development from within rather than becoming dependent on foreign investment and foreign financial markets;
- carrying out the long-postponed measures of income redistribution and land redistribution to create a vibrant internal market that would be the anchor of the economy and create the financial resources for investment;
- de-emphasizing growth and maximizing equity in order radically to reduce environmental disequilibrium;
- not leaving strategic economic decisions to the market but making them subject to democratic choice;
- subjecting the private sector and the state to constant monitoring by civil society;
- creating a new production and exchange complex that includes community cooperatives, private enterprises and state enterprises, and excludes TNCs [transnational corporations];
- enshrining the principle of subsidiarity in economic life by encouraging production of goods to take place at the community and national level if it can be done at reasonable cost in order to preserve community.

Amin's and Bello's theories both accentuate the role of nation states while calling for the destruction of the current economic model of global governance. They discuss the relationship between the state and international institutions and how it can be resisted, rejected or modified. Bond warns that "the hope of attracting potential allies from a (mainly mythical) "national patriotic bourgeoisie" still exists in some formulations of delinking and coincides with reformist tendencies among state-aligned intelligentsia and trade unions." In some cases such reforms, he continues, "tend to legitimize, strengthen and deepen existing state control and capital accumulation functions, while doing nothing to shift the balance of forces towards the oppressed" (2005: 4).

Before examining how these theories best explain the actions of different political and social movements, the development of corporatism in Mexico will first be discussed.

2

The Mexican Corporatist State

Recall that the argument put forth in this study is that because of the advent of the neoliberal, globalized form of capitalism beginning generally in the mid–1970s and taking effect in Mexico in the 1980s, state-society relations in Mexico have changed from a form best described as state corporatist to one exhibiting transnationalized corporatism. Accordingly, this chapter is divided into three sections. The first examines the development of state corporatism in Mexico in the twentieth century under the PRI regime. The political, economic and social aspects of this development that warrant the title state corporatist will be highlighted. The section includes an overview of nonstate actors and their relation to the state, and it draws on the theoretical literature of the state-corporatist model reviewed in the previous chapter. The second section then traces the transformation in Mexican state-society relations from a traditional state-corporatist model to a transnationalized corporatist model. Hermanson and Garza Toledo's (2005) model of corporatist development under neoliberalism will be used to highlight the changes during the transitional periods. In the third section, the nature and significance of the changes in state-society relations that have emerged under transnationalized corporatism will be discussed, and an assessment of the explanatory value of the aforementioned theoretical concepts when applied to the Mexican case will be made. Keep in mind that the transition has been a slow, drawn-out process that is likely to undergo further change in the future. While neoliberal economic "reforms" were adopted quickly and were the spur to the transition to TC, the latter emerged gradually and "incompletely," as the concept itself is meant to convey.

The argument of the chapter is as follows: the hierarchically structured state-society relationships dating back to the period of the Spanish conquest were consolidated by Lázaro Cárdenas in the postcolonial and postrevolutionary Mexico of the 1930s, in the context of the Great Depression, as state corporatism, a new social contract; from the early 1980s, however, as capitalism developed into its current neoliberal stage, state corporatism has been transformed into transnationalized corporatism.

The overall shape of the argument is informed by Marxist political economy as set out in chapter 1. Over the course of the twentieth century and into the twenty-first century, the capitalist class in Mexico has come to dominate both the economy and the politics of the country. Inherent in the capitalist mode of production is the close relationship between the capitalist class as the owners of the means of production and the state, Mexico being no exception. The Mexican state's adoption, since the 1980s, of neoliberal policies to facilitate global market expansion to benefit the (now increasingly transnational) owners of the means of production demonstrates this dynamic.

In addition, however, it is important to note the following elements of Mexico's political history and culture. Mexico did not experience the postwar, Keynesian, welfare state as known in the North, yet the PRI managed to maintain power through corrupt electoral processes and corporatist relationships with key sectors of society, and by repressing opposition forces. Although Mexico is a federal state officially known as the United States of Mexico, and although there was an attempt to decentralize in the mid–1980s, the political and economic center of the country has always been Mexico City (see Reyna and Wienert 1977; Centeno 1997). This high degree of centralization has contributed significantly to the development of corporatist relations. Furthermore, during the seventy-one years of one-party, authoritarian rule, the state and the PRI (the governing party) were one and the same. The party ruled the country and the president of the country was the president of the party (see Anguiano 2010). In fact, the national flag was the flag of the party.[1] These conditions also facilitated the emergence and the sustainability of corporatist relationships in Mexico. Thus, the corporatist relationships that existed between the state and the nonstate actors under the PRI government continue in a somewhat modified way today under the PAN regime. How then did corporatism come to be in Mexico?

State Corporatism in Mexico under the PRI

Lázaro Cárdenas instituted state corporatism in Mexico in the 1930s in the context of the Great Depression and in the wake of previous failed attempts in the postrevolutionary period to "incorporate" workers and their organizations into the state. In October 1929 the U.S. stock market crashed, marking the beginning of the economic depression of the 1930s. International commerce was affected throughout the world as factories shut down and millions became unemployed. Latin America was hit hard because of its dependency on foreign markets, in particular the U.S. market (see Anguiano 1975: 11). The export industrialization model was directly affected by this global economic crisis. Mexico experienced a reduction in oil production, a fall in the price of silver and a general downturn in the metallurgical industry. Although these industries were foreign owned, they were still considered the most important support to the Mexican economy during this period because they connected the national economy to the world market as a provider of raw materials. Export taxes accruing from these resources were one of the Mexican government's primary sources of income (12). As the international economy took a downward swing, it was inevitable that the Mexican economy and workers would suffer. Mexico also had the misfortune of being subject to natural disasters that drove the agricultural industry into crisis. The year 1929 was replete with flooding, drought and frost that reduced the production of corn and beans to levels so low that the government was forced to open the borders to the importation of these products. According to Anguiano (13), in 1929 "629 thousand tons of corn and 73 thousand tons of beans were lost" in relation to what the harvest was expected to produce, and "20 thousand agricultural labourers became unemployed." The high rates of unemployment, the low incomes and the increase in the cost of living crippled consumption of the overpriced agricultural products and general commodities. The interconnectedness of industries within the national and international capitalist markets caused a domino effect around the globe and throughout Mexican society. The international crisis and the inability of foreign markets to import Mexican products forced Mexico to turn inward and expand its national industry. This moment is generally considered the beginning of the import substitution economic model and the emergence of a renewed labor force.

The first postrevolutionary workers' confederation had been founded by the state in 1920 in an attempt to protect and control the workers and their engagement in the economic development projects of the nation. The Confederación Regional Obrera Mexicana (CROM) was led by the government-appointed Luis Morones who fought tirelessly against all attempts to form independent unions. This led to bloody confrontations between the state and the independently organizing labor force. Although the "red" [communist] workers were defeated, state-society relations remained unstable. This instability and the international and national economic crisis discussed above led to the fall of the CROM in the late 1920s. This left the workers in a state of demoralization, dispersion and disorganization. Following the decline of the CROM there were numerous failed attempts[2] to create a vinculum between the workers and the state.

When Lázaro Cárdenas came to power in 1934, he was determined to win the support of the workers, reorganize them and draw them into the political process. As a strong supporter of the Revolutionary State (see Córdova 1979: 37–39), he sought solutions to problems of production, distribution, and communications. He was also on a mission to rescue the natural resources, primarily petroleum, which were in the hands of foreign capitalists (Córdova 1974: 90). He was cognizant of the fact that the agricultural industry did not meet the needs of the population and that important industries such as mining and oil were in the hands of foreign corporations that exploited the Mexican labor market and invested their profits elsewhere. He also noted the divisions within the working class, which he saw as a consequence of corrupt politicians and opportunistic leaders. In response to this situation, Cárdenas called for a Common Front which would draw in all of the segregated groups of society and unite and organize them under the auspices of the Revolutionary State. He claimed to want the workers to manage themselves rather than be managed. He wanted the workers to *feel* dignified in their struggle and in their victory over the enemy class. It was in this vein that he promoted corporatism. He believed that it was the most viable means to manage the existing political and economic inequities of the time. Córdova (1979: 63) points out that while Cárdenas continually reiterated his position that the working class should play an active and direct role in national politics, the president himself appointed the workers' representatives. This was very different from authentic worker representation in the political process.

Corporatist relations in Mexico were consolidated by the Cárdenas government in 1939.[3] This was the year that Fidel Velázquez was appointed leader of the CTM. Velázquez was to remain in that position until his death in 1997. Throughout his fifty-eight years as leader of the CTM, Velázquez "generally discouraged strikes, supported presidential initiatives, backed PRI candidates, and behaved like an advocate of 'responsible syndicalism'" (Grayson 1998: 31). When the CTM was founded, the government insisted that all workers' unions and organizations be affiliated with it. There were to be no exceptions. Labor disputes were negotiated by the Labor Ministry, local union representatives and Fidel Velázquez. Yet repression was a quick solution to any unresolved dispute.

Keeler (in Cook 1996: 35) defines

> official unions [as] those to which the state grants competitive advantage over other
> labor organizations through such supports as monetary subsidies, the indirect or direct

repression of rival unions or of dissent groups within these unions, and sometimes partial authority for formulating or implementing aspects of public policy, as well as access
to the decision-making centers of the state.

Official unions were those affiliated with the Congreso del Trabajo or the CTM.

Local, regional and state federations were formed to increase government control.
In 1939 there were 3,000 worker and peasant groups, totaling over 600,000 members that
were affiliated with the confederation. Two years later numbers had increased to 3,594
groups and over 945,000 members. Within the ranks of the CTM the government workers
were the first to reconcile their autonomy with the founding of the Federación de Sindicatos de Trabajadores al Servicio del Estado (FSTSE). Although marginalized from the
CTM, the FSTSE continued to be directly controlled and linked to the government.
Beyond this, Cárdenas used the CTM to generate support and to give the illusion of
working with the people through *their* organizations.

When we think of corporatist relations in Mexico, manufacturing industry and public
services are the first things that come to mind. However, other sectors of society have
also been corporatized. Such corporatist organizations include the Confederación Nacional
Campesina (CNC), which was founded in 1938; the FSTSE, founded in 1938; the Confederación de Obreros y Campesinos de México (COCM), founded in 1942; and the
Confederación Nacional de Organizaciones Populares (CNOP), which was founded in
1943. The indigenous population, the women's movement and the environmental movement have also been co-opted by the state (see below). One of the clearest consequences
of state corporatism was the divide it created among the different sectors of society. For
example, unions tended to focus on their immediate, gremial demands, which resulted
in a labor landscape littered with dispersed, fragmented and unintegrated unions. The state
was successful in dividing industries into sectors; the government employees belonged to
one union, peasants joined a separate confederation, and employees of state corporations
were affiliated with the CTM; each sector mobilized separately (see Xelhuantzi López 2004).
There was very little solidarity work among the different unions. The Partido de la Revolución Mexicana[4] (PRM, subsequently known as the PRI), the party in power in the
late 1930s, was itself a party of "*corporations*"[5] comprising the organized sectors of society
(Córdova 1974: 148). Workers would become affiliated with the party not as individuals
but, by default, as members of a group. This implies that although confederations were
created to distance the different groups from each other, they were simultaneously the
foundation of the party, a foundation that gave legitimacy to the party. The role of the
party was to administer or coordinate the corporations, ensure that each group remained
autonomous and isolated, resolve the disputes and difficulties that emerged within a given
group, and maintain a unified supportive body during election time (Córdova 1974: 165).

One of the biggest movements that the CTM organized was an orchestrated struggle
against foreign oil and gas monopolies that culminated in the nationalization of the oil
industry (see Anguiano 1975: 61–63). Lombardo Toledano, the principal organizer of the
movement, called for a national protest on March 23, 1938. He called for all affiliated groups
and members and local vendors to attend the protest and to suspend all of their work
activities on that day. He also called on students, teachers, women, peasants and leaders
of the Communist Party to support the government in its nationalization activities. They
were able to draw a record-breaking crowd of over 200,000 people to the Zócalo to support
the government. The mass movement triumphed, and the oil industry was expropriated.

The government, through the CTM, advocated the creation of cooperatives in failed factories and in areas of scant resources. What was made out to be an attempt to "give back to the community" came to be another means of control when the government stepped in and led the cooperatives in conjunction with the previous owners. The results were disastrous for the workers who were underpaid, overworked and many times not paid at all (see Anguiano 1975: 86–92). Not surprisingly this arrangement was short-lived.

The 1960s and 1970s experienced strong opposition from Marxist-Leninist-Trotskyist-Maoist organizations advocating socialist, revolutionary transformations and clandestine guerrilla movements seeking alternative modes of production throughout Latin America. The Soviet and Cuban socialist models served as a backdrop to these antisystemic movements. National governments responded by killing, torturing, and disappearing participants and perceived supporters, detaining them as political prisoners, supporting paramilitary forces and infiltrating those political and social organizations by which they felt threatened. Throughout all of Latin America there was widespread unrest. U.S.-backed, authoritarian dictatorships were the predominant form of rule. There was a generalized, communist/socialist phobia expressed by national leaders and their U.S. counterparts. Corporatist structures persisted as a means to manage and control many sectors of society by giving them the illusion that they were somehow participating in the political process.

The economy during this period appeared to be flourishing under the ISI economic model thanks to persistent borrowing. This resulted in greater state involvement in the economic process and an abandonment of laissez-faire principles (see Cammack et al. 1993). In particular, the ISI model "emphasized the erection of trade barriers to reduce the volume of foreign-manufactured imports. Mexican leaders sought to keep out products from abroad, while fostering their nation's industrialization" (Grayson 1998: 26). Products that were produced nationally were protected from international competition, which served to boost the national labor force and the availability of jobs. While there is no doubt it provided a useful tool to cope with the economic effects of the Great Depression, the adoption of ISI was, as Grayson (2004: 243) described it, "a godsend to Mexican corporatism." ISI led to an important increase in the number of state-owned corporations and thus to an increase in CTM-affiliated workers. Some of the benefits that went along with some of the state-organized unions were "low-cost housing, short-term loans, generous pensions and broad health care coverage" (Grayson 1998: 30). The nationalist characteristics of the ISI economic model defended Mexican producers against their "foreign enemies," while simultaneously supporting and legitimizing the authoritarian regime (see Herzog Márquez 1999: 20).

Mexico continued with its one-party authoritarian regime under the PRI, which maintained strong corporatist control over the majority of organized labor. Being an oil-producing country, Mexico reaped the benefits of the oil crisis in 1973 as prices increased dramatically and the state shifted its focus to "oil-export-based development" (Cockcroft 1998: 143). At the same time, large amounts of money at low interest rates were borrowed in an attempt to further boost the economy. According to Weisbrot and Sandoval (2006: 1), "Mexico experienced healthy economic growth [from 1960 to 1980], and GDP (or income) per person grew by 99 percent." The protectionist policies were reflected in high tariff rates that shielded national industries from foreign takeovers and competition.

Exportation in the 1960s was minimal throughout most of the country, with the exception of the northern border area where the first maquiladora factories were opened. Although in macroeconomic terms the Mexican economy in the 1960s and 1970s may be technically described as healthy, this did not translate into an equalitarian distribution of wealth or the elimination of poverty. As quoted in Edwards (1995: 1), "by the late 1970s, the region [Latin America] had, by far, the most unequal distribution of income in the world." According to a 1977 survey of income and expenditures, 22 million Mexicans were living below the poverty line as defined by the World Bank (Aspe and Sigmund 1984: 4). From 1975 to 1986, the lowest 40 percent of income earners in Mexico received 10 percent of the national income. During this period, the top 20 percent of income earners received 19.6 times more income than the lowest 20 percent of income earners (United Nations 1990: 159).

Aziz Nassif and Sánchez (2003b: 52–53) describe the pre–1968 government in Mexico as stable while undemocratic. They describe the political order of the time as one with

> hierarchical institutions, headed by the executive powers.... It was governed by a party ... which was spread out over the country, [the party] held all of the elected positions and covered just about all social spaces; there was a Congress of the Union which provided a place to manage presidential initiatives ... and a judicial power which was controlled by the executive.... The budget was completely centered and managed by the federation and the states and the municipalities.... This organization functioned within a scheme of stability, its actions were very predictable, it had the support of a growing economy, the borders were closed and the economic strategy was to substitute importations; there was agrarian distribution, basic free education for all, a network of medical services which was expanding and the possibility to acquire subsidized housing through one's employment.

The emphasis of Aziz Nassif and Sánchez here is on governability, control and the stability of the political powers, but they also detail the injustices and violence that marred the pre–1968 period. What they seem to ignore is that during this period of stability and effective governing there was great economic inequality.

Table 3. Income Distribution and Poverty: 1963 –1968

	1963	1968
Percentage of Disposable Household Income Received by:		
Lowest 40%	10.3%	10.5%
41– 80%	30.8%	31.2%
Highest 20%	58.9%	58.3%
Measures of Inequality:		
Share of Highest 20%/Share of Lowest 20%	16.8%	17.1%
Gini index (calculated from decile distributions)	.527	.522
Theil index (calculated from decile distributions)	.494	.488
Households with Real Incomes Less Than 1977 Min. Wage:		
Number of households (millions)	4.2	3.7
Percent of all Households	57.1%	44.7%
Average Real Income of Lowest 40 Percent (1977 dollars per year per household)	$565	$742

Author's estimates from household budget surveys. Source: Joel Bergsman, Table 6: Summary Measures of Income Distribution and Poverty; Unadjusted (1980: 19).

The percentage of disposable household income changed little over the five-year period, 1963–1968. Yet the lowest 40 percent of income earners received only 10 percent of the national disposable household income while the highest 20 percent received almost 60 percent of the national disposable household income. While there was a slight increase in average real income from 1963 to 1968, the lowest 40 percent of the population made less than $742 per household in 1968. This amounted to barely $2 per day (see table 3).

During this period of economic hardship, the Congreso del Trabajo (CT) was founded in February 1966. The CT served as a centralizing body of corporatist activity. It comprised more than 85 percent of the unionized labor force in Mexico. By the early 1990s, this amounted to over 9 million workers, down from a previous high of 22 million. Some of the long-standing members of the CT are the teachers' union (SNTE) and the Sindicato de Trabajadores Petroleros de la República Mexicana (STPRM). These unions continue to maintain corporatist relationships with the Mexican state, and their strategies will be referred to as corporatist under the TC model. Independent unions were founded in many sectors, either parallel to the official unions or instead of official unions, as workers sought democratic means to choose their representatives and to manage their own affairs. These unions acted within the neoliberal structures in an anticorporatist way. They fought to democratize the unions without engaging in postcorporatist actions. They did not take over the factories or delink from the established governmental procedures. Another modified and somewhat more relaxed form of unionism was that exhibited by such organizations as the SME or the Sindicato de Telefonistas de la República Mexicana (STRM). These unions maintained a degree of independence while still being linked directly to the government, through the CT. While their actions were also anticorporatist they continued to enjoy a close relationship with the government. They maintained internal democratic structures and a degree of autonomy. Throughout the 1970s and 1980s they were referred to as independent unions, although many today question the reality of their independence (see Patroni 2001). The 1970s were referred to as a period of historical transition which debilitated and changed the look of state corporatism in Mexico (Anguiano 2010: 55)

In 1978 the CTM took unprecedented liberties when the government introduced its political reforms.

> It now appears to be the champion of revolutionary reformism, ... while obscuring the fact that [its actions] were nothing more than an emergency response to the political reforms and [an attempt] to conserve the privileges of corporatism ... [In this manner] the CTM again adopted the ideology and the program of the Mexican Revolution [Córdova 1989: 43].

The CTM during this period took to fighting for a more equitable distribution of wealth, greater buying power for the working classes, the elimination of large monopolies, an expansion of social programs, protection against privatization, and a reduction in unemployment (ibid.). These are clearly demands that went beyond the gremial demands of earlier periods. But one should not be fooled by their appearance given that behind these "progressive" demands was a leadership struggling to survive; it was an attempt to preserve the sectoral structures of the party. This marked the beginning stage of transnationalized corporatism and a weakening of the postrevolutionary state-corporatist relations. González Casanova (1993) says of the transnationalization of the state starting at this time, that it is a process that transfers "important parts of power in terms of finances, currency, public and private property, markets, fiscal and tax policies, investment and spending, technology of production, consumption, modernization, 'reconversion' and 'structural change'" (54) over to the IMF and the U.S. government. It is in this context that transnationalized corporatism can best be understood.

From State Corporatism to Transnationalized Corporatism

The 1980s began with an economic crisis arising from the huge debts accrued during the previous period, an increase in international interest rates and a fall in oil prices. All sectors of Mexican society were implicated in the crisis. The Mexican rich responded to the economic crisis by withdrawing their money and investing it in foreign banks, which resulted in a 300 percent devaluation of the peso (Girón González 2001: 38) over a ten-month period. The Mexican government responded to the economic crisis by first declaring bankruptcy. It then devalued the peso (three times during 1982) and subsequently nationalized the private banks, a move that increased the friction between the private sector and the state. These dramatic measures resulted in a deterioration of real salaries, a decrease in investments, promotion of exports, an increase in the informal economy, higher rates of unemployment and restructuring of the state (see Ramos Sánchez 2000). Mexico subsequently joined the GATT in 1986 under the dictates of its creditors (see Cockcroft 1998: 143), a move which demonstrates the influence of international institutions on the internal economy of Mexico.

The 1980s are often referred to as the "lost decade" by Latin American scholars. In response to the economic crisis, governments in Latin America were forced to find alternative sources of revenue to balance the books. Economic deregulation, fiscal reform, and the privatization of state corporations were measures taken in an attempt to stimulate the economy. At the same time, the state sought to increase exports which in turn would increase foreign exchange and create the revenue needed to service the debt (see Lustig 1998: 1–13). Neoliberalism became the new economic model to follow. Cockcroft (1998: 143) describes this model as "market-driven, private sector led, export-based ... [requiring] privatization of state sectors of the economy, reduced social spending and 'opening up' ... to foreign investment." The changed role of the state in neoliberalism facilitated, indeed was itself part of, the transition from state corporatism to transnationalized corporatism.

Hermanson and Garza Toledo divide the transition from state corporatism to what I refer to as TC into four periods. While they focus primarily on manufacturing industry, their analysis is also useful for understanding public-sector unions in the context of these changes. The first period ran from 1982 to 1992 and was one during which laws relating to collective agreements and terms of employment were relaxed. The second, short period from 1992 to 1994 was one in which there was an attempt to restructure corporatist relationships in Mexico. The third period, from 1994 to 2000, was one of renegotiation following the failed attempt to convert the existing terms of production into a new pact between the workers and the factory owners. The last period, which began in 2001, is one in which further retrenchment of corporatism has occurred (Hermanson and Garza Toledo 2005: 186). Let us now turn to the particular developments in each of these periods.

1982–1992: Economic Crisis Weakens Corporatist Bonds

The first period under the new economic model of neoliberalism began with the aforementioned economic crisis, which had dire consequences for labor: real wages were diminished, collective agreements became a source of competition among corporations and social security fell as the government tried to boost public finances (Hermanson and Garza Toledo 2005: 184). Corporatist relationships suffered as the leaders of the official unions experienced a reduction in their ability to influence political and economic outcomes. This period experienced a unilateral relaxation of the laws relating to labor regulations, which benefited the owners of the means of production over the workers. Many state corporations were being privatized during this period, which made it easier for the new owners to play the game their way. In response to these changes and the reduction of real wages, many workers engaged in strike action. According to Hermanson and Garza Toledo (187), 1983 was a year of widespread social unrest during which unions organized in their fight for higher wages. Most of these strikes ended in defeat, and it took over two years for the CTM to mend its relationships with the state. Many unions took advantage of the debilitated condition of corporatism at this time and announced their independence. Independent unions adopted anticorporatist strategies. They sought alternative ways to organize that invoked greater worker participation and a democratization of internal processes. The state responded with increased corruption and repression.

At the same time, some corporations sought new ways to increase productivity by shifting away from the traditional Taylor-Ford production assembly line model to a Toyota style of manufacturing. Called the "Toyota Production System," it is often referred to as "lean manufacturing." Under the Toyota model, the organization of labor was modified such that the workers worked in groups rather than individually, and the production process itself was designed to reduce overproduction, eliminate waste and enhance lines of communication between the workers and the company. The Toyota approach was quite successful in the corporations that had been privatized. In many cases, traditional state-corporatist relationships were terminated in companies that were privatized, while in other cases, union leaders were co-opted by the companies to head corporate "*sindicatos blancos*" (see introduction).

After the PRI regime privatized some seven hundred state corporations in the 1980s under Miguel de la Madrid (a trend continued by his successor Carlos Salinas de Gortari), the antiprivatization movements emerged (La Botz 2005). The most important sectors to survive this period were the workers in the petroleum industry, the electrical workers, and the workers in service industries such as health-care workers and teachers. Parts of all of these industries have since been privatized and funding cut, yet most of them continue to organize under the auspices of the CT that is controlled by the ruling party. As state corporations were privatized, many of the corporations were replaced by nonunion shops owned by foreigners, many of which moved to remote areas. However, corporatist relations continued to predominate in the remaining state-owned corporations and throughout the public-service sector.

During the privatization process, many manufacturing plants relocated to northern areas along the Mexico-U.S. border. This period of adjustment brought massive layoffs due to corporate downsizing and the termination of collective agreements as unions were destroyed. The relocation of manufacturing industries also brought the relocation of large sectors of the service industry into areas that were geographically distant from the political and economic infrastructure in Mexico City. Of the roughly nine hundred state-owned corporations that were privatized from 1982 to 1994, most are now owned by transnational corporations. Indeed, "the terms of privatization were increasingly set to encourage foreign ownership" (Harvey 2007: 101). The transnational corporations destroyed preexisting labor structures, either replacing them with sindicatos blancos or prohibiting union organizing altogether.

The greater recourse to sindicatos blancos and management-run unions under the new transnationalized corporatist model exemplifies how corporatist state-society relations in Mexico have been replaced in these cases by corporatist-style relations between owners and workers. This is still not pluralism. That is to say, on the one hand we have a reduction of state-run manufacturing corporations and thus a reduction in official union affiliates, yet on the other hand we have an increase in the overall population and a relocated workforce of people in the maquiladora areas and other industrial sites, requiring new infrastructure and employees in the service sector. The impact of these changes was compounded by a decrease in the remuneration of real wages by 50 percent from 1988 to 1998 (Velasco Arregui and Morales Valladares 2005: 59–60). It was in the context of the privatization of so many state corporations and the increased competition facing the resultant businesses that (nonstate) "incorporated" labor relations were established to ensure the survival of the corporations.

The 1980s also marked a period when electoral democratic reforms were introduced in many countries in Latin America. Authoritarian rule in Argentina, Chile, Peru, Bolivia, Brazil, Ecuador and Uruguay ended, replaced by elected governments. While some argue (see Córdova 1989: 40; Brachet-Márquez 2007) that "corporatism is incompatible with democratic forms of organization," all evidence shows that the democratization process in Mexico has not interfered with the staying power of corporatist relationships. The many electoral reforms that have been introduced since the mid–1980s have not been capable of eliminating the culturally based corporatist relationships in Mexico. Electoral reforms successfully cleared the way for the registration of a variety of new oppositional political parties and what in 1988 appeared to be the first (if unofficial) defeat of the then sixty-year-old PRI regime.[6] The PRD under Cuauhtémoc Cárdenas was met with repression, yet its presence on the electoral scene instilled a new sense of hope in the population that change was possible.

Corporatist relationships did not go unchallenged by nonstate actors in Mexico during this period. Many workers organized independently of the state-led syndicates and engaged in anticorporatist action. For example, there is the "official" teachers union, the SNTE, and an independent union, comprising teachers who distrust the motives of the state-run union, known as the CNTE. Another example is the teachers at the Colegio de Bachilleres who have formed their own independent union, called the SINTCB. These cases are discussed in detail in chapter 3.

In conclusion, the initial stage of neoliberalism, which began in the early 1980s, forced labor leaders and the state to negotiate more "flexible" labor agreements to compensate for the loss of state-owned corporations, the increased competition and the decrease in real wages. The workers' strategic responses varied from efforts to maintain close corporatist relationships with the state to anticorporatist strategies through independent union organizations. These changes marked the beginning stage of transnationalized corporatism in a world that was turning to international institutions and organizations to set the guidelines for the neoliberal free-market economy.

1992–1994: ANECAP and Free Trade Restructure Corporatism

The second stage is defined as a period of restructuring of corporatist relationships. Before this time, corporatist unions in Mexico were not much concerned with problems in manufacturing or the production process itself (Hermanson and Garza Toledo 2005: 188). Union leaders confined themselves to maintaining relationships of negotiation with the state and fulfilling their role as protector of workers' interests. This changed during the pre–NAFTA period as union leaders had to consider production issues in order to survive in the open market. According to Aguilar García (1990), the government adopted production criteria (productivity, etc.) as the most effective means by which to determine the value of labor. This in turn heightened labor's involvement and interest in participating in determining the guidelines for production. When Salinas de Gortari came to power in 1988, he was determined to transform the corporatist relationships in an attempt to weaken or destroy the power of unions. His target was the petroleum workers' union and the teachers' union, the two most powerful unions in the country. His efforts culminated in the signing in 1992 of the Acuerdo Nacional para la Elevación de la Productividad y la Calidad (ANECAP; the National Accord for Raising Productivity and Quality). This agreement was signed by government, business leaders and labor representatives. It called for "federal and state governments and businesses to underwrite increased worker training and investment in return for union flexibility on work rules and quality and productivity issues" (Nolan 1994: 236). While labor signed onto the agreement, the latter has been criticized for benefiting business by facilitating work rule changes that went against the interests of labor.

NAFTA negotiations were going on during this period. In order to accommodate labor concerns, a side agreement was signed which incorporated guidelines for "transition periods,[7] rules of origin and safeguards"[8] (Nolan 1994: 236). In a bid for more manufacturing jobs, labor supported NAFTA in hopes that it would benefit from the migration of transnational corporations to Mexico where labor costs were much lower than in the North. While these negotiations were taking place, the government proposed a salary increase equal to the rate of inflation. This was against the backdrop of labor conflicts as corporations were privatized and national industries were shutting down, unable to compete with the transnational corporations. The CTM was the driving force behind most of these labor disputes. Workers were also beginning to feel the impact of the weakening of labor laws from the late 1980s and early 1990s.

Throughout the 1990s, the state's focus continued to be on remodeling the economy to open the market to world economic forces. A consequence of this remodeling was an increase in service-sector employees from approximately 2.4 million people in 1990 to over 3.5 million in 1996 (Velasco Arregui and Morales Valladares 2005: 56–57). Of these, 1.6 million worked for the public education system, 300,000 in higher education, 500,000 worked in public health and 280,000 worked in the communications industry. The 1990s also experienced an increase in employment in manufacturing industry. In 1990 there were 4.5 million people working in manufacturing, and this number increased to around 5.8 million in 1996 (ibid.). Cross-border trade agreements were signed among Latin Amer-

ican countries and with non–Latin American countries. Trade barriers were all but eliminated, resulting in an increase in trade. "Between 1990 and 1996, the region's exports
expanded by 73 percent...; imports grew even faster, at 127 percent" (Devlin and Ffrench-
Davis 1999: 263). U.S. and European leaders saw the fall of the Soviet Union in 1989 as
the start of a new world order where neoliberal capitalism ruled without the constant
external threat of communism. Francis Fukuyama (1992) hailed the "end of history."
"Underdeveloped" countries were sold on the idea that democratic and economic reforms
would bring them in line with the developed world.

A primary expression of the neoliberal trend during this period was the introduction
of NAFTA in 1994. Cockcroft (1998: 310) explains that "NAFTA promised to phase out
trade barriers over the next fifteen years.... [It] augured a $6 trillion market for 363 million
consumers ... and a corresponding rise in workers' wages and jobs." However, not all sectors of society bought into this economic "miracle" jargon; after all, this was the year that
the Zapatista movement emerged from the jungle denouncing the political-economic
policies of the government. The promised boom from this "bill of rights" for investors
was not reflected in the buying power of the majority of the population or in the levels
of poverty in Mexico, as most of the profit was either exported or remained in the coffers
of the corporations (see Ángel Barrios and Mariña Flores 2003).

In conclusion, dramatic changes to the traditional, state-corporatist form of state-
society relations in Mexico emerged with the introduction of neoliberal policies in the
1980s and more notably in the 1990s as the effect of these policies became evident (see
Aguilar García 2006: 77). The period from 1992 to 1994 was one in which labor, government and business signed agreements such as the ANECAP, which restructured the
power relations that existed under state corporatism. The workers' "incorporation" was
now mediated to a greater degree by business, and workers were drawn into areas of production that in the past were of little concern to them. The confrontations between labor
and business often left the workers at a loss. During this period, the large official labor
conglomerates (CTM and CROC) worked hard to attract different labor unions into their
fold.

1994–2000 Corporatist Crisis: Using Culture to
Manage Changing Industrial Relations

In December 1994 the Mexican economy entered a deep crisis. GDP growth decreased
by 6.2 percent in real terms, inflation rose to 50 percent, while salaries rose by a mere 1.4
percent (Hermanson and Garza Toledo 2005: 190). The divide between the rich and the
poor increased dramatically during this period. "In 1996, the country's richest ten percent
of families accounted for an estimated 42.8 percent of income, while the poorest twenty
percent of families received only 4.5 percent [while at the same time] Mexico ranked
fourth in the world for the number of billionaires (in dollars)" (Cockcroft 1998: 156).
Corporations and the state addressed this economic crisis by depressing real wages in an
attempt to control inflation. These measures were approved by the labor unions. Production bonuses were increased by a mere 2.2 percent in 1996 and eventually were replaced
with the reduction of real wages. (Hermanson and Garza Toledo 2005: 190). Ernesto
Zedillo's presidency (1994–2000) is notable for its socioeconomic and political instability,
and its embrace of "dirty war" repressive tactics (Anguiano 2010: 308).

Industrial relations in Mexico during this period changed in three ways. First, in mid–1995 the CTM and the Confederación Patronal de la República Mexicana (COPARMEX) engaged in unprecedented negotiations to draft a document that would serve to change labor culture in Mexico. The final document recognized the globalization process, global economic integration and the need for corporations to be able to compete in order to survive. It proposed that worker-owner relationships should focus on such things as "good faith, loyalty, justice, veracity, responsibility, equality, dialogue [and] coordination of labor relations" (Hermanson and Garza Toledo 2005: 191). What it proposed was that a new labor culture replace conflict with collaboration; as in Bill Clinton's "campaign propaganda you've got workers and their firms, but not owners and investors" (Chomsky 1996: 84), contra Marx. By buying into the need for cultural transformation, the CTM and the CT fell into a crisis of credibility, as they proved unable to meet the basic demands for a dignified salary and standard of living for their members. A crisis in corporatist relationships between the union leaders and the state best described this period, a crisis that would not be resolved through the modification of cultural norms.

The second change during this period was the creation of the Intersindical Primero de Mayo (the May 1st Inter-Union Organization). This was a coalition of independent unions that, for its time, signified a very radical move. Its mandate was to organize the workers nationally against corporatism and the corrupt labor practices of the government and the corporations. A very militant organization, it was dissolved in 1999 because of internal ideological differences between the Marxist and non–Marxist members.

The third development during this period was the convocation of a national forum, the first of its kind, to discuss the economic crisis caused by neoliberalism and the crisis of state-society relations. The forum was convened by the leaders of the largest unions in Mexico. It culminated in 1997 with the creation of the Unión Nacional de Trabajadores (UNT). Shortly after its founding, the UNT engaged in negotiations to modify cultural practices with the owners of the means of production. They did not officially affiliate with any political party yet many of its members allied behind the PRD. This was contrary to the CT and the CTM, which maintained close corporatist ties with the PRI. According to Hermanson and Garza Toledo (2005: 193), even with its alternative discourse, the UNT has been unsuccessful at transforming state-society relations in Mexico. This, they argue, is due to the unrelenting *caudillismo* of the leaders and the indifference expressed by the workers themselves toward overthrowing the corporatist structures in their entirety. Gatica Lara (2007: 77–78) refers to the UNT as a new "side of union corporatism ... [also referred to as] neocorporatism." Although state corporatism continued to flourish under the PRI regime during this decade, independent unions were organizing, as they had in the 1970s, in an attempt to maintain a sense of dignity and control in their workplace.

A reflection of this impact was visible on May 1, 1995, when for the first time since the founding of the corporatist state in Mexico, the CT did not convoke its members to the annual May Day parade in the Zócalo.[9] The May Day march had come to be a symbol of the political-economic power of the state. This was reflected by the marching of the workers by sector, in uniform, past the president and Fidel Velázquez who stood high above the marchers on a balcony in the national palace that overlooked the massive civic square below. Workers were given the day off with pay to attend the march and were reprimanded and had the day's pay deducted from their salary if they did not attend. In 1995 the Coordinadora Intersindical Primero de Mayo (CIPM) led an independent march through the Zócalo which took over five hours to complete and from start to finish covered over twelve kilometers. This historic day marked the return of Labour Day to the workers out from under the grip of the corporatist state.

The most important transformation during this period was the state's attempt to use cultural means to maintain worker incorporation. It was an attempt to get the workers "on side" and to make them feel like they were active participants in their own destiny, while continuing to function within the hierarchical structures of corporatism.

Since 2001: Corporatist Retrenchment under the PAN

The late 1990s saw a dramatic economic downturn, and by March of 2001 the U.S. economy was officially declared to be in a recession. It dragged the rest of the world economy down with it (see Mariña Flores 2003: 21–25). The manufacturing industry in Mexico was hit very hard by this recession. Fourteen percent of the maquiladora industries were shut down, which meant that the employees of over 520 factories became unemployed by September 2002 (Ángel Barrios and Mariña Flores 2003: 41). Many other sectors of society[10] also suffered during this period because of the recession, the decrease in funding to the public health-care system and public education and other political reforms that were introduced as a direct response to economic globalization and neoliberalism. In preparation for Mexico's integration in NAFTA, constitutional and legislative reforms had been implemented.[11] From the presidential elections in 1994 to those in 2000 the PRI had lost 828 municipalities, the PAN had won 219 and the PRD had won 12 (see Aziz Nassif and Alonso Sánchez 2003a: 29). These results reflected the opening up of the electoral process and an electorate in search of change.

The year 2000 marked Mexico's most important turning point since the Mexican Revolution in 1910, when the PRI was defeated after seventy-one years of one-party rule. Incoming president Vicente Fox promised he would put an end to corporatist relationships in Mexico. His declared intentions lost credibility very early on when he appointed Carlos Abascal as his Labour Minister. Abascal was a former corporate executive who had drafted the new cultural labor document in 1995 in an attempt to strengthen corporatist relationships. Quiroz Trejo holds that Fox's government, which claimed to reject the traditional PRI corporatist practices, "was as corporatist as his predecessors" (2007: 37–38) with one variation: it was held up by the business sector which formally criticized the regime rather than the workers (see also *La Jornada* 2009). He considered Fox's model to be corporate-centric with strong corporatist ties to the conservative sectors of the church, Grupo Monterrey,[12] higher education institutions such as the Tecnológico de Monterrey, as well as with the CT and the CTM (56).

Hermanson and Garza Toledo (2005: 194) describe corporatism under Fox as "Christian Corporatism."[13] They argue that Fox's renewed labor relations were nothing short of "a continuation of the antique labor regimen" (ibid.) which now had the support of the business leaders, a group of self-interested actors who were not interested in democratizing the existing labor relations. The corporate leaders were also quite concerned about potential labor disputes in response to the economic situation in the country, another motivator to promote cultural transformation. The corporate and governmental leaders have adopted this so-called "Christian cultural" approach, which was initiated in the mid–1990s as an attempt to replace the traditional worker/owner dichotomy by a discourse of human dignity and resolution through modified cultural practices. Hermanson and Garza Toledo (ibid.) hold that given the current labor relations and the economic situation in Mexico this model is ineffectual. They criticize the fact that even the 2001 proposed revisions to the New Federal Labour Law are said to be based on Christian principles.

Discussions around the new labor law accentuate the ideological differences among the many interested parties. For example, the UNT seeks a democratic, anticorporatist alternative; the union leaders within the CT are willing to continue with the "flexible" labor relations but want to preserve their ability to influence the decision-making processes; the independent unions in the Coordinadora Primer de Mayo are against all changes to the current labor laws; the sindicatos blancos have no interest in participating in the process; President Calderón (2006–2012) is willing to work with the relaxation of the labor laws and is willing to discuss possible democratic reforms; the corporate leaders reject the idea of democratization for fear of giving the workers more power; the PAN supports Calderón; the PRD rejects anything coming from the labor minister and instead is working on its own alternative labor law; and finally the PRI continues to work within the corporatist structures (Hermanson and Garza Toledo 2005: 195). When the PRI attempted to introduce a bill to reform labor laws in 2011, with the support of Calderón's government and the CT, they were met with resistance. The reforms would have

> allowed new categories of temporary and casual employment, such as 60-day training periods, 30-day probationary periods, seasonal employment and other forms of temporary work. It would have allowed subcontracting, reduced the legally required severance payments to laid-off workers, and opened workers to retaliation by forcing them to provide lists of workers voting to strike [La Botz 2011].

Such reforms would have undermined the labor laws adopted in the 1917 constitution which legally gave workers certain protections, rights and benefits.

It is in this context that Hermanson and Garza Toledo (2005: 195) affirm that while unions have lost strength under neoliberalism, corporatism has not disappeared in Mexico. Corporatism today is propped up not only by the government but also by the owners of the means of production, who have a vested interest in seeing corporatist relationships maintained. They see the empowerment of the workers as an undesirable alternative. The interconnection between the labor leaders, the government and the corporations has in many ways strengthened corporatist relationships in Mexico. Under corporatism, labor leaders benefit from political and economic perquisites, while corporate leaders and the government benefit from a controlled working class. Sánchez Fernandez (2004) argues that while the number of occasions on which unions were in a legal position to strike decreased from 8,282 in 2000 to 2,762 in 2004, this is not a reflection of calm and satisfaction on the part of labor but rather a greater effort by the labor leaders to appease the business owners through negotiations and compromise.

Regarding public-service union organizing, by the first quarter of 2007 the number of people employed in the service industry increased to 4.2 million people (INEGI 2007). All of these workers were integral parts of transnationalized corporatism. Their unions were directly affiliated with the state, and their leaders were appointed by the state. The first quarter of 2007 showed an even greater increase to over 7 million people working in manufacturing industry (INEGI 2007). However, the state-corporatist structures were not strengthened by the increases in the manufacturing industries as might be expected, because many of these increases were in the private sector. On the service-sector end of things the increased numbers were a reflection of the restructuring and relocating of public-sector services. This aided in the transformation of state-corporatist relations to transnationalized corporatist relationships.

Under the PAN government, whether led by Vicente Fox or Felipe Calderón, little changed in the economic landscape for the majority of the population. Elizondo (2003: 46) warns that, "without more public resources, the inequalities of Mexican society, where a relatively low GDP per capita implies that significant numbers of Mexicans live in poverty, will persist even under the most optimistic growth scenario." Lustig and Szekely (Elizondo 2003: 53n) argue that "even with an annual growth rate of 5 percent extreme poverty will not be completely eradicated until the year 2033."[14] According to a United Nations Human Development Index report (2006), the annual GDP per capita growth rate in Mexico from 1990 to 2004 was 1.3 percent, well below the 5 percent suggested by Lustig and Szekely.

The persistent impoverishment of most Mexican people carries us into the twenty-first century with continued political unrest. The elites maintain close ties with their international counterparts, while the gap between the rich and the poor has augmented since 1984.

Table 4. Distribution of Current Monetary Income of Households According to Their Per Capita Income and Measures of Inequality, 1984–2004.

Deciles of Households	1984	1989	1992	1994	1996	1998	2000	2002	2004
Total	100.0	100.0	100.0	100.0	100.0	100.0	100.0	100.0	100.0
I	1.2	1.0	0.9	0.9	1.1	0.8	1.0	1.2	1.1
II	2.4	2.2	2.0	2.0	2.2	1.9	2.1	2.3	2.4
III	3.3	3.2	3.0	2.8	3.1	2.9	3.0	3.3	3.4
IV	4.3	4.2	3.8	3.7	4.0	3.8	3.9	4.2	4.2
V	5.6	5.2	4.9	4.8	5.1	4.9	5.0	5.3	5.3
VI	7.1	6.5	6.1	6.1	6.4	6.2	6.3	6.5	6.6
VII	9.0	8.3	7.9	7.8	8.2	7.9	7.9	8.3	8.3
VIII	11.8	10.9	10.8	10.5	10.8	10.7	10.5	11.1	10.9
IX	17.0	15.9	16.1	16.2	16.1	15.9	16.0	16.3	16.0
X	38.3	42.6	44.6	45.3	43.1	45.0	44.4	41.7	41.8
Gini Coefficient	0.495	0.522	0.545	0.550	0.528	0.548	0.540	0.516	0.512
Theil Indicator	0.185	0.214	0.235	0.241	0.219	0.238	0.231	0.207	0.206
10% richest/ 10% poorest	31.9	41.7	51.3	48.7	40.2	54.8	44.9	36.3	36.7
20% richest/ 20% poorest	15.4	18.0	21.3	21.3	18.2	22.4	19.9	16.9	16.2
10% richest/ 40% poorest	3.4	4.0	4.6	4.8	4.2	4.8	4.5	3.8	3.8

Source: Consejo Nacional de Población (2005).

Whether in terms of percentage distribution of per capita income by household deciles or Gini coefficient or Theil index, over a twenty-year period from 1984 to 2004, during which neoliberal policies were consolidated in Mexico, the overall degree of income inequality remained high and increased (see table 4). While seemingly irrelevant to the analysis of state-society relations, the economic situation in Mexico has a direct impact on how nonstate actors respond to such things as job losses, underemployment and the reduction in social services, which in turn are reflected in their relationship with the state and with the owners of the means of production.

It was anticipated by many that the death of Fidel Velázquez in 1997, the subsequent defeat of the PRI in the 2000 presidential elections and the democratic reforms that have been adopted in the past twenty-five years would result in the demise of corporatism in Mexico. But this is not what has happened. As Samstad (2002: 2) argues, "The relationship between democratization and corporatist change can be reciprocal: not only can democratization reshape corporatist practice, but changes in corporatist structures can have a critical impact on democratic consolidation." This is not to suggest that relationships have not changed, but as we have seen throughout this chapter, they have displayed a remarkable capacity for persistence. Velázquez's legacy greatly benefited the ruling class in Mexico, and while the Mexican government has maintained a strong relationship with international institutions, it continues to use available national resources to keep nonstate actors in line. For example, the PAN maintains such practices as the "*toma de nota.*" Introduced by the PRI, this is a practice that gives the government the authority to reject democratically elected union leaders.[15] Basurto (1997) criticizes this practice in his discussion of the roles played by the Ley Federal del Trabajo and the Junta Federal de Conciliación y Arbitraje. Furthermore, in a study by Alcalde Justiniani (2006a: 39), workers in Mexico said that "there was no improvement [in wages, working conditions or democracy], the old habits [of corporatist practices] continue, and the network of interests that place the workers in a state of defencelessness has not changed [under PAN rule]." Even the PRD has been accused of engaging in traditional corporatist practices (Grayson 2007: 279).

Samstad (2002: 8) provides a useful account of the argument that democratization heralds the demise of corporatism. In summary, democratization is held to bring into existence new nonstate actors (including new political parties), new channels of participation (including worker representation), new forms of resistance and increased influence of the new actors in the political process (including shifts in power). However, what he observes in fact is that "Mexican corporatism has demonstrated a remarkable staying power over the years and has managed to operate successfully through a variety of historical circumstances" (ibid.). Roman and Velasco Arregui (2006: 99) concur with this observation when they assert, "The Mexican transition from one party rule to electoral alternation led to a deeper fragmentation of union organizations but not to a breakdown of the fundamental structures of autocracy within unions and union federations." Garza Toledo (n.d.) went further by arguing that new forms of worker representation actually acted in ways that preserved corporatism.

The democratic reforms that led to the demise of the PRI in 2000 have aided in transforming the *state* component of corporatism without removing the corporatism. Some of the interpretations of these transformations are as follows: Castañeda (2003: 1),[16] for example, holds that the results of the July 2, 2000, elections "marked the end of an era of authoritarianism and corporate politics." Middlebrook (1995) insists that the Mexican state, not the PRI, retained the ability to rule over the workers through state regulations (see also Bennett 1995). Córdova (1989: 40) rejects this assessment, asserting that "Mexican corporatism is not fascist, not because it is not repressive, but because it operates within the realm of the official party, not in that of the state and much less in the economic sphere; it is ... exclusively party based." The implications of these assertions could bring into question the traditional understanding of corporatism and the current state-society relations in Mexico. The unique relationship between the party (PRI) and the state complicates the analysis even further. Under PRI rule, the party and the state were one and the same. The clarification of where corporatist relations reside came in 2000 when the PRI was defeated in the federal elections. If corporatism rested on the PRI, in keeping with Córdova, then one might expect it to dissolve after the PAN took possession of the presidency and would conclude that Mexico has advanced to a pluralist state-society arrangement, as Castañeda (2003) would have it. However, if the corporatist relations persisted beyond the PRI, then one would have to conclude that the corporatist relations are grounded in the state (see Middlebrook 1995). This is not an attempt at a causal examination of state versus party but rather an attempt to understand the shape of corporatism in Mexico in the twenty-first century. What actually seems to be the case in Mexico under TC is a persistent corporatist relationship between the Mexican state and nonstate actors. Rearranging and shifting of power dynamics have occurred, yet the "interest representation in which the constituent units are organized" has remained largely the same. This will be further discussed in chapters 3 and 4 with reference to case studies.

That said, there are also corporatist-like relationships that persist between the PRI and different labor organizations such as the Confederación Campesina Mexicana and the Confederación Nacional Agronómica that are affiliated with the party.[17] This begs the question whether corporatism cannot be considered a feature of Mexico's political culture as a whole, a state of affairs that goes beyond either party-electorate or state-society relations. However, this is a discussion that will not be taken up here.

Every six years a newly elected president is inaugurated in Mexico. Invariably accompanying the new president are newly appointed directors of the departments of the government bureaucracy. The upper echelons of the bureaucracy are appointed by the incoming president. This creates a degree of instability as old programs are discarded, new projects are introduced and new appointees struggle to understand the system. "Permanent amateurism" is the phrase used by Herzog Márquez (1999: 32) to describe the transition from one president to the next in Mexico. This arrangement complicates state-society relations because not all "teams"[18] function in the same way. When the PAN was elected in 2000, and as state governorships have been won by non–PRI candidates throughout the country, the appointment of new directors and their teams has resulted in laborious learning curves and uncertainty for many nonstate actors as relationships with the state have been restructured. Castañeda (1994: 20) refers to this period of transition as a "stalled system" and one in which progress has been lost.

In Mexico, corporatism is as established a way of doing politics as is corruption. Neither a change in government nor the implementation of electoral reforms is likely to change such long-standing historical practice. In fact, in a recent interview with *La Jornada* newspaper, Loaeza (Vargas 2008) argued that one of Mexico's biggest problems is the fact that the PAN government under Calderón has maintained the corporatist structures and relationships that were initiated by the PRI many years ago. It is too early to determine whether transnationalized corporatism is merely a transitional stage in the phasing out of corporatism or whether it is here to stay. Given the 2008 world economic crisis, it is most probable that we will see a strengthening of corporatist relationships throughout Latin America as states struggle to maintain control and national businesses struggle to survive.

Given the foregoing description of the changing face of corporatism in Mexico, it is useful perhaps to try and formulate the import of the observed changes. What do they amount to and what is their significance in the context of an expanding market economy and a democratizing polity?

The Nature and Significance of the Change: A Modified Version of the Same

The argument found throughout this study is not uncontroversial, given the widespread subscription among Mexican (and more broadly North American) intellectuals to the view that corporatism has been, or is being increasingly, supplanted by both liberal-economic and liberal-democratic reforms. This section will take up the debates, introduced in chapter 1, that have emerged around the characterization of current Mexican state-society relationships. The issue of the role of democracy in state-society relations will be discussed and whether in this context Mexico has developed into a pluralist state-society arrangement or whether it is bound by that modified version of corporatism called transnationalized corporatism. Furthermore, the explanatory value of different theoretical positions when applied to the Mexican case will be assessed.

In Williamson's (1985: 10) four dimensions of corporatism, it is clear that the majority of these characteristics have remained a constant at the national level in Mexico even under transnationalized corporatism.[19] Recall that his first point states, "The state has a principal function of establishing and maintaining an economic and social order. Such an order is not compatible with an essentially market-based economy. The performance of this function must override any conflicting popular or particular demands; the state is dominant in the economic and social sphere." While neoliberalism is (theoretically, though not necessarily in practice)[20] characterized by a reduction in the role of the state in the economy, its political role to maintain order while overriding popular demands is found in its response to the waves of contentious action initiated by nonstate actors. Repression in the indigenous villages and against peasant and political movements is currently a common practice. Examples include the repression suffered by the teachers' movement in Oaxaca and the political repression in San Salvador Atenco. Because of these state aggressions, the Frente Nacional Contra la Represion reemerged in 2007 after over fifteen years of fragmented efforts.

Williamson's second point is that "the economy is predominantly constituted of private ownership of the means of production and wage labour" (1985: 10); in other words, it is capitalist. Mexico's economic arrangements, while still capitalist, have changed under neoliberalism as transnational corporations have come to dominate the scene and as the national capital class struggles to survive. The middle class continues to waffle somewhere in the middle as some ascend to the upper class and others are driven into poverty. By fostering the conditions for greater accumulation, the Mexican state continues to represent primarily the interest of the capitalist class, whether the national or international variety, while creating rudimentary social programs to placate the opposition.

Williamson describes his third dimension of corporatism as follows: "There is at least a circumscription upon the role of liberal-democratic institutions in authoritative decision-making. Indeed, liberal-democratic institutions may not exist at all" (1985: 10). This characteristic is more in keeping with state corporatism, which flourishes under authoritarian regimes. While there are examples of continued authoritarian practices under the PAN, similar to those characteristic of the PRI, there have been some liberal-democratic reforms introduced since the early 1980s. However, it would be difficult to consider the PAN liberal-democratic because of the inconsistencies in the electoral process, the persistent corrupt political practices and the clientelist patronage practices found throughout the political system. Moreover, the international actors (WTO, etc.) do not require that a state function as an established liberal democracy in order to do business with it. In fact, TC has many of the characteristics illustrated by Williamson (11) in his description of "authoritarian-licensed" corporatism[21] such that decisions, especially economic decisions, are ultimately imposed on states by international institutions.[22]

Williamson's (1985: 10) fourth point is that "organizations of producers undertake an intermediary role between the state and societal actors, performing not only a representative function but also operating as a regulatory agency on behalf of the state." Since the 1980s, the number of state-run corporations has diminished substantially due to the privatization practices of neoliberalism. However, public-service sector employees continue to be integrated into the state structures through state-controlled unions that serve as regulatory agencies of the state. There is also a plethora of intermediary organizations that exist between the state and societal actors at the *national* level. These include institutions such as the Comisión Nacional para el Desarrollo de los Pueblos Indígenas (CNDPI), which works with the government to determine state policy around indigenous issues and helps to market indigenous artifacts. The CNDPI was originally called the Instituto Nacional Indigenista (INI), founded by the PRI in the 1960s, but was renamed in 2001 by the PAN.[23] According to presidential decree (Fox 2003), the CNDPI is an autonomous decentralized body whose role it is to "orient, coordinate, promote, support, foment, give follow up and evaluation to their programs, projects, public strategies and actions for the integral, sustainable development of the indigenous towns and communities" in Mexico.

Similarly, the PAN government created the Instituto Nacional de las Mujeres in January 2001 as a means to maintain corporatist relations with women. Another example is the Consejo Mexicano de Café (CMC) which replaced the Instituto Mexicano del Café (INMECAFE) in 1994 and serves as a means to centralize the coffee industry. The autonomy of all these organizations is seriously in doubt insofar as, for example, their directors or presidents were appointed by the president of the republic. These new social actors, which have emerged under TC, allow the state to maintain a hierarchically structured relationship with key sectors of society.

Internationally there are also important intermediary agencies. While there may not be a *corporatist* relationship between these agencies and the states, any relationship that does exist comes to influence the development of state-society relations within that nation. The G20[24] is one such body. It was founded in 1999 and provides a "forum [for industrialized countries] to discuss, study and review policy issues among industrialized countries and emerging markets with a view to promoting international finance and economic stability" (Department of Finance, Canada 2002). The G20 for developing countries, which is most relevant to Mexico, is a forum of finance ministers and central bank governors.

Both G20 groups function as intermediary agencies between the states and the international institutions, which in turn cater to the interests of multinational corporations. As Morales-Moreno (n.d.) explains, "Mexico ... joined the G20 club of developing countries ... [where it was successful in placing] the issue of the abatement of subsidies and domestic supports at the forefront of the Doha negotiations." Mexico's involvement in international organizations such as the G20 is another example of extrastate dealings that come to influence internal state-society relations. Agreements that are struck within the G20 are eventually introduced at the national level, while at the same time "unions must be able to assure business and government that their members will comply with the terms of the 'social contract'" (Zeigler 1988: 71). These two levels of governing are interconnected, and the relationships of all parties involved will necessarily be modified to make things work.

Another significant change that has emerged under transnationalized corporatism is that new responsibilities have shifted to corporations and NGOs. These power shifts can be understood as what Molina and Rhodes (2002: 326) refer to as "new types of corporatist concertation [which] should be understood in terms of networks," or what Wiarda (2004: vii) refers to as a "new, mixed, often transmuted form" of corporatism. However, rather than refer to these NGO relationships as corporatist, as Molina and Rhodes, and Wiarda do, they will be considered "power relations" here so as to preserve the concept "corporatist" for relationships that the government or the *state* has with other social and political actors, while acknowledging the fact that these power relations have emerged in response to transnationalized corporatist relations and neoliberal policies. That is, NGOs do not have the function of a state to "establish and maintain an economic and social order." On the contrary, they "have a short-term agenda, and their contribution is often piecemeal, curative, limited and dependent on the agenda of donors" (Mojab 2007: 15; see Veltmeyer 2007b). They do not maintain corporatist relationships with the state or the communities they come into close proximity with, even if, on occasion, they do negotiate with the state to fulfill their own needs. In most cases, the power relations that exist between NGOs on the one hand and civil society on the other are independent of the government in power.[25] It does, of course, work in the state's favor to have these extrastate bodies take on responsibilities that would otherwise be fulfilled by the state, as long as they don't interfere with the policy-making process.

The factor most germane and central to the debate over the contemporary persistence of corporatism is, of course, democratization. Democratization throughout Latin America has not gone beyond formal or electoral democracy in most cases. The conceptual understanding of "democracy" has undergone many modifications since Aristotle's ancient use of the term. Aristotle (1981: 362) held that in democracies "the poor have more sovereign power than the rich; for they are more numerous, and the decisions of the majority are sovereign." This is democracy in the sense of rule by the common people, which for the Greeks also meant direct democracy — full public participation in political decision making. Today, representative democracy is the type of democracy most commonly used to describe current political arrangements in developed societies. Dahl (in Wiarda 2004: 6) defines representative democracy as

> [1] a system of organized contestation through regular, free, and fair elections; [2] the right of virtually all adults to vote and contest for office; ... [3] freedom of the press, assembly, speech, petition, and organization; ... [4] freedom to form and join organizations; [5] freedom of expression; [6] alternative and diverse sources of information...

Boron (1995: 7) cautions that, historically,

> the essential content of democracy — that egalitarian kernel found in Aristotle's and Rousseau's writings... — was abandoned and replaced by a formalistic argumentation that favours the procedural aspects of the political process and of the governmental apparatus at the expense of the substantive attributes of citizenship. In this way, a point is reached where the egalitarian and "subversive" character of democracy is dissolved into a lukewarm and unappealing doctrinal proposal rightly called elitist democracy.

Throughout Latin America in the past fifteen years there has been a drop in support for institutional or representative democracy from a high of 80–90 percent to a low of 30 percent in regions such as Brazil and Ecuador (Wiarda 2004: 18). This drop is a reflection of the inability of institutional democratic reforms to solve the economic and social issues that exist throughout the region.

In their lengthy discussion of the transitional period from an authoritarian regime to an alternative political arrangement (liberal democracy), O'Donnell and Schmitter (1986) assert that replacement or incoming regimes "justify themselves in political terms only as transitional powers, while attempting to shift attention to their immediate substantive accomplishments — typically, the achievement of 'social peace' or economic development" (15). In the Mexican case, the transition from the PRI regime to the PAN has lacked the social peace and the economic development that O'Donnell and Schmitter refer to, yet the PAN repeatedly justifies its actions in just these terms. Rather than supporting these assertions with empirical data or statistics, PAN leaders take their truth to be self-evident.[26] They consider them nondebatable outcomes of the neoliberal model of development in which neoliberal policies and democratization are believed to have left authoritarianism behind (see Montalvo Ortega 2003). Regarding corporatism in this period of transition, Wiarda states (2004: vii), "If authoritarianism was disappearing in Latin America as democracy advanced, corporatism, with which authoritarianism was often closely associated would disappear as well."

There are two sides to the debate about whether the Mexican state continues to maintain corporatist relations. Firstly, there are those who argue that corporatism has been on a downturn since the early 1980s, when neoliberalism was introduced and democratic reforms were initiated, and that corporatist relations finally ended with the defeat of the PRI in 2000 and were replaced with pluralism. As discussed in chapter 1, pluralism acknowledges the existence of different political views and ideologies and provides the means for all sectors to be heard. Pluralism is found in multiparty systems where political power is diffused among different groups in society. Pluralism "focuses on the dynamics of group politics and ... the relationship between electoral competition and the activities of organized interests" (Chilcote 2000: 258). It is focused on bargaining and confrontation between groups, regulated by the agencies of the state and generally found in countries where democracy prevails. For pluralism to be meaningfully applied, however, there cannot be a marked disparity in the distribution of power in the society in question.

Vite Pérez (2002: 220) contends that although clientelist practices persist in Mexico, they exist within a pluralist arrangement as defined by Chilcote (2000: 258). To defend his argument he examined the events of 1997 when for the first time in Mexico City the head of government (the mayor) was elected. (Before 1997 the Representative Assembly of Mexico City comprised sixty-six PRI-appointed members.) Vite Pérez (2002) also celebrates the opening up of legal registration to opposition parties in the 1980s, the elimination of electoral fraud and the technical evolution of the electoral process. However, contrary to Vite Pérez's assertions, the 2000 and 2006 elections demonstrate that the electoral reforms introduced since 1979 have not won the confidence of the electorate. The 2006 presidential election results were widely considered controversial and unreliable, and came close to precipitating a "democratic coup." The popular contestation of the results led to the formation of the Convención Democrático led by Manuel López Obrador. The Federal Electoral Court confirmed that there was reliable evidence of irregularities in about 9 percent of the polling stations, which amounted to approximately 70,000 stations (Martínez Heredia 2006: 1). All of these developments lend little credence to Vite Pérez's belief that Mexico is or has a functioning pluralist polity.

Yet, in keeping with Vite Pérez, Xelhuantzi López (2004) holds that pluralism is the desired outcome of twenty-first century union organizers in Mexico. She commends the founding of the independent Unión Nacional de Trabajadores (UNT) in 1997 and its unification mandate as a reflection of pluralist relations. The UNT has approximately 477,000 workers from thirty different unions affiliated with it. The largest representation is from the telephone workers union which numbered 54,466 members in 2005 (Aguilar García 2006: 78). The UNT comprises unions that are affiliated with the CT and those that are not. Not everybody agrees with Xelhuantzi López's and Vite Pérez's optimism. Grayson (2004: 248), for example, challenges López's claims and argues that the UNT is an organization that practices "secrecy, authoritarianism and dubious financial operations" (see also Gatica Lara 2007). Furthermore, the corporatist relationships that interest us here are between the affiliated unions in the CTM and the CT and the state with which many UNT unions are affiliated.

Secondly, many analysts hold that, although corporatism has been on the decline as old unionized corporations have closed and new, nonunion, transnational corporations have saturated the national market, nevertheless it continues to be the predominant paradigm for understanding state-society relations in Mexico (Anguiano 2010; Velasco Arregui and Morales Valladares 2005; Wiarda 2004; Vergara 2005; Zapata 2006; Loaeza in Vargas 2008; Garza Toledano, n.d.). Molina and Rhodes (2002) consider the corporatist paradigm a necessary tool for understanding policy-making processes and state-society relations. These views are in keeping with the findings of historical analysis which plainly show that the most important forms of political action and the relationships between the state and society in Mexico are systemically entrenched and do not disappear with the changing of one political party to another or as the result of minor modifications to economic arrangements or electoral procedures. As Wiarda (2004: 19) puts it,

> While Latin America has in recent decades made significant strides toward democracy, it has retained various authoritarian and corporatist structures and features that were deeply ingrained within the culture and the social structure.

That is, these "corporatist structures and features" that are "deeply ingrained within the culture and the social structure" have *not* disappeared as liberal democracy has (re-) appeared. Zapata (2006: 447) holds that Fox "confirmed his commitment to the institutions that administer corporatism, in spite of the economic restrictions on spending that derived from the 2001–2003 recession." Similarly, following a meeting with Fox on August

1, 2000, Leonardo Rodríguez Alcaine, leader of the CTM, declared that the CTM and its affiliates would maintain a close relationship with the president for the betterment of the nation and the workers (see Montalvo Ortega 2003: 118). A further expression of these close-knit relationships is that there have been many good intentions to modify the federal labor law to remove the antiquated clauses that protect the corporatist model, yet none of these good intentions have ever been realized. Aziz Nassif (2003: 20) holds a slightly different version of this argument, maintaining that corporatism has been overcome in the electoral terrain but continues to exist between unions and the state (see also Ramírez Saiz 2003).

Aquilar García's (2006: 89) table puts affiliation numbers into perspective. According to this table, groups that belong to the official unions total 3,367 and have over 4 million affiliated members.[27] The unofficial unions total 77 groups and 1.7 million members. The corporatist relationships that exist among the official unions and the state continue to predominate, although, as has been pointed out, the numbers of persons directly involved have diminished over the years. That said, the persistence of official unions is what legitimizes the argument that corporatist-style relationships continue in Mexico. While the numbers may have decreased under TC, they are still substantial and need to be taken at face value. Recall that TC is not based solely on quantitative data but also on the strategies adopted by nonstate actors and the extranational relationships that the state has. Some nonstate actors maintain close corporatist relationships with the state while others engage in anticorporatist actions. In both cases the neoliberal model is upheld, yet corporatist state-society relations continue. This is, of course, not the case with the noncorporatist or postcorporatist strategic approaches.

Table 5. Mexico: Primary national unions, 2005, Apartado A and B

Organization	Apartado	# of Associations	# of Members
CT	Ap. A	1923	951,538
CTM	Ap. A	1351	754,286
FSTSE	Ap. B	74	746,000
FDSSP	Ap. B	19	1,646,688
UNT	Ap. A	30	477,755
FESEBS	Ap. A	13	138,336
STRM	Ap. A	1	54,466
FSM	Ap. A and B	28	90,000
SME	Ap. A	1	56,990

Source: DGRA, STPS, Base de Datos, August 25, 2005 (in Aguilar García 2006: 89).

Table 6 gives an overview of affiliation trends within the official unions from 1997 to 2005 (Aguilar García 2006: 87). In some cases the number of official unions has increased while the number of affiliated members has decreased, but overall there are fewer people engaged in corporatist relationships with the Mexican state than during the peak periods under the PRI. Again, while the decreased membership is a reflection of the privatization of state corporations, the state continues to use corporatist structures to maintain control of state employees. It would be irresponsible to ignore the staying power of corporatist relationships under transnationalized corporatism while thousands of unions continue to be affiliated with the official unions with millions of members.

Table 6. Mexico: Centralized organizations: CT, CTM, CROC, CROM, groups found under Apartado A. 1997–2005.

Organization	1997 Unions	1997 Members	2000 Unions	2000 Members	2005 Unions	2005 Members
STPS	1,726	2,246,970	2,155	2,352,005	2,585	1,964,204
CT	1,353	1,964,690	1,686	1,250,878	1,923	951,538
Not in CT	373	282,280	469	1,101,127	658	1,012,666
CTM	581	926,455	706	896,678	1,351	754,286
CROC	328	166,708	401	176,355	210	81,083
CROM	277	47,427	315	51,744	171	30,895
Others: COR, CGT...	127	33,838	179	49,322	89	15,827

Source: DGRA, STPS, Base de Datos, Aug. 25, 2005 (in Aguilar García 2006: 87).

Corporatist relations in Mexico have changed as the economy has become privatized and restrictive policies have been introduced which interfere with traditional union organizing. A restructuring of the labor market has led to an increase in small businesses and privately owned corporations, a rise in the number of people who have become part of the informal sector and an increase in independent union organizing. In fact, power is being redistributed as transnational corporations and NGOs come to fulfill roles previously performed by the Mexican state. These organizations work alongside the corporatist relationships being discussed here and play an important role in the political and social relationships within the country.

State-society relations continue to be hierarchically ordered to a persistently significant degree, such that the Mexican state continues to impose its will on the many groups of nonstate actors around the country. This control is manifested through the policy-making process and is directly influenced by the more intense relations of subordination of the Mexican state to the global market and international institutions. The primary benefactors of TC are the economic elites found in the national and international arenas. As the national government has attempted to decentralize responsibilities by giving state governments greater control over their local jurisdictions, a more localized corporatism has emerged as well,[28] not to mention the emergence of national, somewhat independent unions such as the UNT and the Alianza Sindical Mexicana (ASM).

These shifts in economic, political and social organizing have had a direct influence on the ways nation-states interact with nonstate actors. In the particular case of Mexico, transnationalized corporatist relations have made it harder for workers to organize and to participate in internal labor relations. Morales-Moreno (n.d.) holds for example that the role of the state within the WTO is to "[maintain] an equilibrium between domestic constraints and international imperatives." This desired outcome is rarely met. The changes brought about as a result of the transnationalized character of the corporate capitalist (and corporatist!) state have resulted in underpaid employment, privatized pension benefits, part-time contractual positions, and the inability to form autonomous labor organizations within the corporations' jurisdiction. Contrary to Grayson's (1998: 86) assertion that the CTM is not interested in organizing service workers in the agricultural and manufacturing sectors because the workers "might rebel against authoritarian rule if brought into the official fold," it seems more accurate to point out that when workers have attempted to organize they have been killed, disappeared or fired for their efforts. For example, according to Gates (1994), "in Chihuahua twenty Honeywell workers were fired for leading a union organization drive to form a union affiliated with the Frente Auténtico del Trabajo (FAT)." A General Electric plant in Ciudad Juárez fired eleven workers who participated in a cross-border organizing effort. In June 2001, Pung Kook fired the president of the local union, Raquel Espinoza, for organizing the workers (see Americas Program 2005). This followed threats against his person. On April 20, 2006 (La Botz 2006), two mine workers were killed when police attacked striking workers in Lázaro Cárdenas. As mentioned above, about a year later Napoleón Gómez Urrutia (United Electrical International 2007), the head of the Mexican Miners Union, was dismissed by the Mexican government because of his political activity (and took refuge in British Columbia). All of these incidents reflect the difficulty workers have in organizing to defend their interests in the context of TC where the relationship between the state and society continues to be hierarchically ordered.

To justify referring to state-society relations in Mexico as TC requires a closer examination of the various nonstate actors and their recent evolution in relation to the consolidation of neoliberal capitalism. The last part of this section will be used to address briefly what is discussed at length in chapter 3, namely some examples of transnationalized corporatist relations in Mexico between the ruling party and unions in this context. Middlebrook's (2004: 31) assertion captures the importance of the economic context very well:

> Whereas political factors such as increased partisan competition and media opening have been the main sources of change in intergovernmental and civil-military relations, economic forces (especially the combination of financial crisis, prolonged economic stagnation and market-oriented reforms) have been the principal elements producing major shifts in the state's relations with rural producers, urban and industrial workers, and the private sector.

One of the most important things that kept the working classes in conformity with the PRI following the revolution was the PRI's ability to offer the workers the possibility of a better life. As long as organizations like the CTM provided the tools to negotiate increased wages, minimal job security and social benefits, the corporatist relationships were successful in keeping things relatively under control. As state corporations were privatized, numbers of affiliates were dramatically reduced. However, in the many cases where state corporations have survived, so too have corporatist relationships. Moreover, in other cases the state, corporations and labor leaders have worked together to establish workable guidelines, at the expense of the workers. For example, Petróleos Mexicanos (PEMEX) and the Sindicato Único de Trabajadores Electricistas de la República Mexicana (SUTERM), which are mostly state-owned-and-run corporations, continue to be affiliated with the CTM. Álvarez Béjar (2006: 25; see also Loaeza in Vargas 2008) describes these arrangements as consistent with the "worst vices and traditions" of PRI corporatist relations.

Corporatist relationships were evident from the beginning of Fox's term in power, especially in the state of Guanajuato where Fox originated (see Grayson 2004: 248). Most of the groups that were co-opted by the PAN came from already established PRI-supported groups. In June 2001, the PAN co-opted the taxi and bus drivers, construction workers, workers in the petroleum industry and market vendors in the state of Guanajuato (Delgado and Espinosa 2002). This is just one example of many in which unions and organizations transferred allegiances to the PAN after the 2000 presidential elections. The union leaders did not necessarily change, but their loyalties were transferred to the incoming regime.

During his presidency, Fox managed to accomplish a realignment of many of the CTM unions whose leaders hung up their tricolor flag only to replace it with a blue and white one.[29] The railway workers union (Sindicato Ferrocarrilero), which is affiliated with the CT, and the ASM have both expressed their support for Fox and for his successor, Felipe Calderón. The ASM is itself a very interesting case. It comprises dissenters from the CT, the CTM and the CROC. Enrique de la Garza[30] describes this as a "poorly designed [corporatist] manoeuvre" by the PAN (see Vergara 2006). The founding of the ASM has caused a divide in the corporatist organizational structures in Mexico. De la Garza holds that there are approximately 70,000 workers affiliated with the ASM, yet many of them do not even realize that they are members.

The official teachers' union, the SNTE,[31] continues to be directly linked to government institutions and is led by Elba Esther Gordillo. Gordillo has been a member of the SNTE since 1960 and became leader in 1989 when Salinas de Gotari came to power. She attempted to reorganize the SNTE by including the CNTE (see Guevara Niebla 2002). Her efforts failed and the SNTE continues with its hierarchical, undemocratic practices. On September 20, 2005, Gordillo resigned her post as general secretary of the PRI (Peréz-Silva, September 20, 2005), yet concerns about her loyalty to the PRI date back to July 2003 (Mendez, July 17, 2003). By September 2007, her intentions became quite clear as she engaged in direct, political, corporatist-style relationships with the PAN where she received power within the union in exchange for her political support of the PAN in national politics (see Muñoz, September 4, 2007).

Because of the decentralization of certain administrative responsibilities in the early 1990s, some negotiating powers were transferred to state educational authorities. This gave state actors the ability to negotiate with local union sections found in their state rather than leaving all negotiations in the hands of the federal government. An example of the consequences of this decentralization occurred when Section (Local) 22 of the teachers' movement in the state of Oaxaca took to the street in May 2006. Although the movement grew to extend beyond the boundaries of the SNTE, becoming a popular movement called the Alianza Popular del Pueblo de Oaxaca (APPO), its initial demands were education based. Its demands included but were not limited to breakfast programs, school supplies, and adequate funding. The fact that a particular section acted autonomously is a reflection of the reorganization of responsibilities within the government. In the past, the teachers of Section 22 of the SNTE in Oaxaca would have received the unconditional support of the national union and acted as a whole, but given the segmentation of the union, it was more or less forced to turn to the surrounding community to increase its numbers and expand its demands. The primary target became the governor of the state rather than a federal representative in far-off Mexico City.

This is not to suggest that the union's leadership suddenly saw virtue in community participation at the local level, because, as Góngora Soberanes et al. (2005: 104–105) point out, the internal structures of the SNTE are not democratic, and the hierarchical corporatist structures persist. On October 28, 2006, the Policía Federal Preventiva (PFP) entered the City of Oaxaca and proceeded with force to drive the protesters out of the Zócalo. The corporatist relationship that used to exist between the federal state and the union representatives has come to lie between the Oaxaca state representatives and the SNTE leaders. This is an example of what could be referred to as "decentralized corporatism" where some of the federal state's relations with society are transferred to the state level.[32] One of the historical roles of the SNTE is to defend public, free, secular education. This task has become more difficult, however, as Mexico's expanded integration into the international market economy has meant opening up its education sector to more private institutions, many of which are owned and operated by foreign investors, while coping with reduced public school funding to comply with structural adjustment programs (Torres 1995). Private education is not new in Mexico, but it has grown exponentially over the past fifteen years.[33]

These are just a few concrete examples of transnationalized corporatism at work where state-society relations have been influenced by the changing economic policies deriving from the international arena.

Summary and Conclusions

In this chapter (a) Mexico has been described in terms of the model of state corporatism that, it is generally agreed, has characterized its state-society relations from the 1930s to approximately the early 1980s; (b) the changes in said relations from 1982 to 2006 have been analyzed in terms of a four-stage transition from state corporatism to transnationalized corporatism; and (c) the claim that corporatist relations persist in the form of TC has been defended against the view that they have been supplanted by the pluralist relations characteristic of liberal democracy.

In keeping with a general theoretical approach based in Marxist political economy, the importance of the onset of neoliberal globalization in the 1970s and its impact on the Mexican state, economy and polity have been highlighted. Above all, perhaps, neoliberalism has reduced the number of state-owned corporations, which has resulted in fewer unions and fewer workers organized directly under the state. This has undoubtedly weakened traditional state corporatism. However, the Mexican state has found ways to maintain economic and social order in a variety of ways (although it is an order that is precarious), and nonstate actors have adjusted likewise.

The state's response has been to introduce political reforms to improve the electoral system and to protect its own legitimacy, to protect the interests of its national elites, to work closely with corporations, to introduce new intermediary regulatory agents and to allow for a relaxation in the interpretation of labor laws. Although many aspects of Cárdenas's original design have been modified, transnationalized corporatist state-society relations in Mexico continue to shape economic and social order today. For example, policies, such as those found in the Ley Federal del Trabajo, have been maintained to help control the actions of the workers and society in general at the national level.

Internationally, the Mexican state maintains close relationships with the international institutions, the economic agenda of which is determined by transnational corporate interests. Mexico not only submits to WTO policies but is also a "founding member of the WTO ... and an important player in the negotiations aimed at establishing the Free Trade Area of the Americas" (Ortiz Mena and Rodríguez 2005: 430). Mexico is part of the decision-making process within the organization, a process established principally to benefit U.S. corporate interests through its trade liberalization measures. The structural adjustment programs that have been handed down by these institutions have been readily adopted by Mexican governments. These reforms included such things as the privatization of government institutions, reduction in tariffs, the protection of intellectual property under the Trade-Related Aspects of Intellectual Property Rights (TRIPS) agreement, and reforms to fiscal and tax policies. The reduction in tariffs and many of the economic reforms of the time were measures created to pave the road to NAFTA. "From 1983 onward the Mexican government divested hundreds of state-owned enterprises, deregulated dozens of economic sectors, and transformed the economy from a highly protected to a much more open one" (M. E. Williams 2001: 3).

Two principal features differentiate TC from state corporatism. The first feature is the influence that international institutions have on the internal state-society relations, as seen above. The second feature is the adoption of varying strategic responses by nonstate actors to the persistent corporatist relationships, whether those responses be corporatist, anticorporatist or noncorporatist. These responses have evolved parallel to the weakening of labor laws, the bringing of corporate leaders to the negotiating table and the attempts at introducing cultural alternatives. They are taken up in the following chapters.

As for the future, widening gaps in the economic distribution of wealth, high levels of unemployment, job insecurity, inequality and poverty are likely to worsen under neoliberal capitalist rule. The transnationalized corporatist state-society relations model will be limited in its ability to control completely nonstate actors as long as these realities of everyday life remain unresolved. One can expect further alliances between labor leaders, corporate leaders and the state. Insofar as TC presents an obstacle to further development of the democratic process, there will be more examples of repression and violations of people's basic rights as external policies continue to be adopted by national governments. The IMF austerity programs that were promoted globally in response to the 1982 debt crisis highlight this external influence. According to Morton (2003: 638), the IMF policies introduced by the Mexican government "involved reductions in government subsidies for foodstuffs and basic consumer items, increases in taxes on consumption, and tight wage controls targeted to control inflation." In 1992 the Mexican government adopted the IMF accumulation strategy when it reformed Article 27 of the constitution to pave the way for NAFTA (ibid.) and facilitate corporate expansion. The widespread popular resistance to these reforms was met with repression and violence.[34]

In chapters 3 and 4, the response of nonstate actors to transnationalized corporatism is discussed in terms of the following questions: Have political oppositional forces confined themselves to legal channels to express their demands? Has government repression subsided? Have new corporatist actors been successful in managing and controlling ("pacifying") the actions of the nonstate actors that fall within their jurisdiction? A range of such actors are examined — unions (official and independent), political parties, indigenous organizations and NGOs — to observe how these responses have developed.

3

Integrative Oppositional
Strategies I

Chapters 3 and 4 report, analyze and discuss an extensive study of "integrative" strategies employed by Mexican nonstate actors in response to changes in the state under TC. Chapter 3 considers union responses, while chapter 4 examines the variety of strategies adopted by a sample of social movements, political organizations, political parties and NGOs in their dealings with the government in the changing political context brought about by the increased influence of transnational forces on the state's role, organization and function. This change in the state has direct consequences for state-society relations in Mexico. TC has resulted in nonstate actors engaging in new forms of political resistance and interaction that are tied to the political-economic developments in the capitalist mode of production sketched in previous chapters. The remainder of this opening section serves as a general introduction to chapters 3 and 4 and, indeed, to chapter 5.

In keeping with the position outlined theoretically in chapter 2, the discussion in these chapters is framed, and the organizations examined are classified, in terms of the tripartite typology of strategies — corporatist, anticorporatist, and noncorporatist or postcorporatist — conceived as ideal types. The ideally corporatist organization is one that continues to have corporatist relationships with the state. The ideal anticorporatist organization is one that adopts strategies to terminate corporatist relationships; within this category, numerous strategies may be utilized, and varying degrees of independence can, in actuality, be found. The ideal noncorporatist or postcorporatist organization is one that has successfully terminated corporatist relationships with the state or, indeed, is independent of the state altogether.

As may be expected, actual nonstate actors vary in the degree to which they resemble the "pure" types. Not all of the organizations or movements that are examined here follow the same sequential path. In fact, no one strategy has been used by all organizations. Within the organizations themselves, there is often a division between the leadership and the membership. In some cases, the leadership maintains corporatist relationships with the state while the membership acts independently of the leadership. In other cases, the membership goes so far as to adopt anticorporatist strategies against its own leadership. In still other cases, the leadership of the nonstate organization is totally removed from the corporatist structures. In yet other cases, organizations sustain transnationalized corporatist relationships by fulfilling state obligations (which the state itself has abandoned) or by attempting to reform aspects of state-society relations through political action. This last class of cases is anomalous in relation to the traditional corporatist relationships: while not necessarily maintaining such relationships with the state, they do not necessarily sever them either. Hence, their actions contribute, largely as an unintended consequence, to maintaining transnationalized state-corporatist relationships. In any case, how the different nonstate actors have responded to the transnationalizing state is what interests us here. While the typology of strategies is a heuristic guide to help sort through the variety of responses actors have made, and not a fixed set of categories to be imposed on the data, it does turn out to be theoretically fruitful.

Moreover, the purpose of the study of these social movements and political organizations is not to determine the effectiveness of their actions, which would require another research project, but to examine whether and how they have changed their course of action under TC, and to discover what new strategies (if not organizations) have emerged in this changed political environment. In each case, the historical particulars of the movement or organization, the stance of the Mexican state or other corporatist actors in relation to their activities and the strategies adopted by the nonstate actors under TC are examined. Chapter 5 is an extended examination of the "nonintegrative," noncorporatist EZLN as it relates to the other opposition forces and organizations examined in chapters 3 and 4 and in relation to the state under TC.

What then are the different nonstate actors that this theoretical approach recognizes? In the transnationalized corporatist model there are the following classes of organizational actors: those that hold formal power *in* the state (the agencies of the state, including leaders of official unions); those that may and do bring their substantive (often formalized) power to bear *on* the state (the international institutions, national employers' associations, business lobbies and large corporations, largely representing transnational or national corporate and financial interests); those that struggle against the structures of power (independent unions, opposition parties and "civil-society" social movements); and those that bring relief or immediate amelioration of existing conditions to impoverished communities (NGOs, whether national or international).

While it is conventional to refer to this collection of actors (other than those in and of the state) as "civil society," the label "nonstate actors" is preferred just because it is plural and useful for looking at particular cases. For Hegel, "civil society" was a concept used to differentiate society from the state. It is that part of society that lies between the private sphere of the family and the state. Foweraker et al. (2003: 50) assert more precisely, "Civil society is composed of voluntary associations and organizations that represent a variety of interests not directly related to economic production or governmental activities." Keep in mind that Marx emphasized the class component of civil society which was absent in Hegel's and Foweraker et al.'s interpretation of the concept.

A combination of these interpretations of "civil society" is adopted here and the term *nonstate actors* is used to refer to those parts of society that do not possess "state-based" powers. Although corporations are generally considered nonstate actors, they will not be examined in their own right, or examined to determine whether they may or may not have changed their strategies over the years. They will only figure into this analysis in the same way that Hermanson and Garza Toledo (2005) see them, as accessories of the state. Their exclusion as case studies is justified because of the control they have over the actions of the workers through the state, the role they have played in establishing and implementing neoliberal state policies, the link they have to state power and the class interests they represent. Borrowing from Otero (2004: 1), *nonstate actors* include "the peasantry, the working class, and middle classes in rural and urban Mexico ... [those] from the subordinate groups, classes and communities." The power structures thereby excluded from the nonstate actors category are the government, the ruling political parties (the PRI, the PAN) and the transnational and national corporations and their representative bodies. Of course, the category "nonstate actor" is not a homogeneous grouping. As well as unions and opposition political parties, there are middle-class movements like El Barzón, which emerged in rural Mexico in the mid–1990s, national and international non-government organizations and the electoral movements of 1988 and 2006, the composition of which tends to cross class lines.

Under TC the division between the state and nonstate actors can become blurred when the leaders among the nonstate actors themselves become indistinguishable from the state, or when the state creates pseudo-independent institutions that centralize and control the policy-making process at the expense of the sectors they are claiming to represent. Such institutions include the Instituto Nacional de las Mujeres (INMUJERES) and the CNDPI (see chapter 2). Many nonstate actors continue their struggle through established legal channels of political participation (corporatist) while others have established independent structures (anticorporatist or noncorporatist) as they search for ways to influence the political process. The nature of their demands and the way they present them in the political arena have been altered by the changed power structures conditioning the way in which the state operates today.

The division between the state and the international institutions is also somewhat blurred, as the Mexican state directly participates in the international institutions that set the guidelines and policies for trade agreements such as NAFTA and neoliberal policies such as privatization and tariff reductions. Pressure is put on the state by international institutions, such as the IMF, the WTO and the World Bank, to implement the policies of the hegemonic economic model that have been determined by a combination of corporate and financial interests and the interests of dominant states. This relationship is one of interdependence where the international institutions require reforms by member states, which in turn receive financial support to realize their "development" and security programs.

This chapter, then, takes up the subject of unions. It considers the strategies adopted by the electrical workers union (SME), the university employees union (STUNAM), the teachers' unions (SNTE and CNTE), and the Bachilleres high school union (SINTCB). It reveals how the different unions have adopted new strategies to respond to transnationalized corporatism such as denouncing the neoliberal privatization initiatives and in some cases expanding their outreach practices. Because of the historical relationship between unions and the state, more space is devoted to examining these relationships than is given to the other nonstate actors, some of which did not even exist prior to the advent of TC.

Union Organizing

Unions have the longest-standing corporatist relationships with the state. In the context of TC, different unions have responded in different ways. Some have maintained close corporatist relationships with the state while others have gone independent. For example, although there have been some changes to the dynamics of these corporatist relationships, unions such as the petroleum workers' union (STPRM) and the teachers' union (SNTE) have maintained strong ties with the state, and the membership, for the most part, has legitimized the leadership (see Hermanson and Garza Toledo 2005). That is, the strategies used by the leaders of these unions are corporatist, and the membership has supported them. In other cases, official unions have fragmented as internal groups have turned on the leadership, broken away and organized themselves as independent, parallel unions.[1] The CNTE, an independent teachers' union is a good example of this. The CNTE has come to have a strong voice within the teachers' movement, yet all teachers' collective agreements are nevertheless bargained between the official union, the SNTE, and the government. The strategies used by organizations such as the CNTE are categorized here as anticorporatist.

Whether corporatist or anticorporatist, union organizing has been modified under TC in response to neoliberal economic reforms. Even the corporatist relationships that continue to exist do not have the same capacity to "control" the actions of union memberships as was afforded union leaders under state corporatism. Beyond concerns about how to exist within the corporatist structures, many unions have modified their standard gremial struggles to engage in antiprivatization struggles as they fight to preserve their jobs and their bargaining power. In many cases factory closures, downsizing and privatization policies have brought unions closer together, as will be demonstrated below.

Under state corporatism, the relationship between the state and the large industrial unions provided the clearest indicator of the hierarchical order of Mexican society. Under TC, it is the public-service sector workers who are most representative of traditional corporatist relationships in Mexico. Their leaders continue to be appointed by the ruling party, and the membership is excluded from the decision-making process. The CTM and the CT continue to serve as means to organize unionized public-service workers in Mexico. They have the largest number of members of any such organization in Mexico (Quiroz Trejo 2004: 7). According to 2003 statistics, under transnationalized corporatism there were approximately 3,367 groups comprising over 4 million workers (or 5 million according to Rodríguez Alcaine [in Muñoz Ríos 2003]) affiliated with the CT (Aguilar García 2006: 89), numbers that cannot be ignored.[2] While large industrial union membership in the CTM declined substantially throughout the 1990s, membership within the public-service sector unions increased between 1970 and 1998 "from 48 to 96 thousand" (Roman and Velasco Arregui 2001: 57). Such quantitative data are important. Nevertheless, it is necessary to look beyond numbers in order to examine how union leaders interact with the state, how executive leaders have come to fit into this equation and where the membership fits in.

An important development in state-society relations in Mexico came in 1996 with the signing of the New Labour Culture Pact between the CTM and the COPARMEX, Mexico's most powerful employers association (Kohout 2008: 135). It was the first time in Mexican history that a labor agreement was negotiated between these two parties with the exclusion of the state. However, shortly after the signing of the agreement the Mexican state was invited to join as sponsor and administrator of the pact. This, according to Kohout (ibid.),

> incorporated the New Labour Culture into the state structures of labour-capital relations, reinforcing the government's role in constructing consensus between workers and employers and strengthening its ultimate decision-making authority in any dispute

between the two. The pact did nothing to alter the corporatist framework whereby government-sponsored labour unions, employers' associations, and the government decide social and economic policy and present the so-called consensus to the Mexican people as the state's solution to social and economic problems.

Far from restructuring state-society relations in Mexico in a democratic pluralist manner, the incorporation of employers at the negotiating table strengthened the corporatist relationships and weakened the bargaining power of the unions. It served as a means to control the CTM by effectively ending any attempts by the confederation to resist labor law reforms (ibid.).

Six years later, following the election of Vicente Fox, the labor reform issue resurfaced. Over the years, there have been many attempts to reform the Ley Federal de Trabajo (LFT). The most recent of these was the Ley Abascal[3] which imposes a number of limitations on the right to freedom of association, the right to strike, the right to negotiate a collective agreement (see Alcalde Justiniani 2006b: 171; Robles et al. 2007) and the protection of women's rights (Brickner 2006: 66). The Ley Abascal was first presented by the Ministry of Labour to the Chamber of Deputies in December 2002 and was greatly criticized by labor activists for its role in advancing state-corporatist relationships (see Alexander and La Botz 2003; Ochoa Camposeco 2003). The drafting of such a proposal was a clear reflection of the government's attempt to protect its power structures. Regardless of how labor activists perceived the government's intentions, according to Roman and Velasco Arregui (2006: 96–97), "the Fox administration ... collaborated with the unions' authoritarian and antidemocratic practices, and, though representing a very small portion of the labour force, they [were successful in] represent[ing] and control[ling] workers in the key private and public sectors of the economy."

In response to the Ley Abascal, the UNT and the PRD elaborated parallel reform projects that stalled the government's initiatives (Villegas Rojas 2006). According to Zapata (2006: 446), "In spite of the fact that many good intentions of reform were expressed so as to make [the labour law] compatible with the new economic model, nothing substantial has happened given the political costs that those reforms would imply for any Mexican president." This suggests that interests on both sides, labor and government, need to be considered carefully in the process. On the one hand, the federal government seeks to reform the labor law to "attract investments, increase production, make the law more flexible and modernize the law" (Villegas Rojas 2006: 348–349). On the other hand, the UNT and the PRD seek to "democratize the work environment, link the modernization process and the competition among the corporations to the appreciation and professionalization of the workers, and to promote autonomous, representative unions" (ibid.). Although the original LFT of 1931 was reformed in 1970, and then again in 1980, the process begun in the late 1990s that culminated in the reforms of 2002 was an unconventional one. Nonstate actors were initially called to the table to see if they agreed with reforming the existing law or not and then to help draft a list of reforms. The organizations that contributed to this consultation process were all affiliated with the (corporatist) CT. The UNT rejected the process and in the end drafted a parallel document.

The methods adopted by the government in the consultation process demonstrate a transnationalized corporatist approach to policy change in Mexico, giving voice to the employers. Those closest to the government (such as government union leaders and corporate leaders) were called to the table to participate. In this case, the negotiation process was controlled by the government and left to the unions and corporate elites to rubber-stamp. According to Kohout (2008: 136), the Mexican economic and political elites have managed to consolidate corporatist relationships in this manner ever since the economic crisis in the early 1980s. This consolidation was achieved through the shifting of power to "government bureaucracies that controlled the economy such as the treasury, budgeting and programming, and commerce and industrial development" (ibid). This is another indication of the evolution of transnationalized corporatism, which incorporates new functions for old actors.

Unlike the consultation process in 2002, in 2011 the PRI,[4] with the support of the PAN and the CT, drafted a bill to reform Mexican labor laws. La Botz (2011) refers to it as a "union-busting bill." According to Spook World: Independent Media (2011), "The bill was drawn up without consulting the social partners," namely the employers and the labor representatives. When the PRI attempted to introduce the bill they were met with resistance from tens of thousands of protesters. The reforms would have

> allowed new categories of temporary and casual employment, such as 60-day training periods, 30-day probationary periods, seasonal employment and other forms of temporary work. It would have allowed subcontracting, reduced the legally required severance payments to laid-off workers, and opened workers to retaliation by forcing them to provide lists of workers voting to strike [La Botz 2011].

When this was written the passing of the reforms had been put on hold. The government's approach to these reforms is corporatist in nature and an attempt to make the Mexican market more amenable to international corporations, a true example of TC and the influence of international pressure. Under the Calderón regime there have also been oppositional responses to the rampant contracting-out initiatives which have become common practice. The passing of the PRI bill would legislate this practice.

Romero (2008) pointedly observes that when reforms to labor laws have been discussed there has been a chronic absence of strong, clear oppositional voices. Historically, few speak out about the limitations and restrictions these reforms place on union members and few push for viable alternatives. The areas that most concern Romero (ibid.) are the nature of the negotiation process of the collective agreement, the exclusion clause,[5] the union registration protocol, the determination of the legality of a strike and the ability of the government to overturn democratically elected union leaders ("*toma de nota*"). All of these practices have continued since the original corporatist framework was established by the PRI, and have been adopted by the PAN.

Unions typically engage in political struggles that focus on local issues affecting the well-being of their members. Most of their traditional demands (improved wages, benefits and working conditions) are dealt with through union-specific, collective bargaining. The bargaining by the teachers, for example, is quite distinct from that of the electrical workers or that of the people living in a particular community or village. Traditionally, the workers in one factory are not much interested in the struggles that emerge in neighboring factories or communities. However, this has changed under TC: there are now many cases of unions banding together to form common fronts of different sorts to better address the issues that are common to all, while continuing to address the immediate concerns of those affected in their own jurisdiction. Yet, for the most part, the strategies they adopt continue to support the corporatist relationships. Transnational corporatist relationships have had a direct effect on how union organizations negotiate with the government and how they have, in more recent years, come to address issues that reach beyond the local; in fact, some of their demands have become antisystemic and in some cases anticorporatist in nature. The particulars of the changes for each case are discussed below. Aguilar García (2006: 70–71) considers international union organizing to be indispensable in this global market economy where the transnational corporations seek to eliminate all forms of organized labor around the globe. International union organizing is the only hope for workers to be able to respond globally to a global phenomenon, he argues. Unfortunately, such international union organizations have not been consolidated, and where there have been attempts to organize internationally the result has remained a relationship of dialogue and exchange rather than action.[6]

Let us move now to the first case to be examined, that of the electrical workers union.

Sindicato Mexicano de Electricistas (SME)

The SME case is very interesting in that the union's existence has changed dramatically from when this study began until now. It has been considered by many to be a clear example of a democratically structured union, affiliated within the official structures, yet acting independently. It has been one of the strongest unions in Mexico and one of the most supportive of other labor and social movements. It was founded in 1914. Its actions have evolved from negotiating annual revisions of the collective agreement and addressing gremial demands to leading the most important antiprivatization movement in the country, until, that is, it was shut down in 2009.

Since it became affiliated with the CTM in 1936, the year the latter was founded, the SME has had an inconsistent relationship with the official unions. This was first manifested in 1947 when the electrical workers left the CTM along with workers from the petroleum and mining industries in an act of anticorporatism. When Fidel Velázquez attempted to create a new centralized union organization in the mid–1950s called the Bloque de Unidad Obrera (BUO), the SME was busy denouncing the corrupt practices of its general secretary, Juan José Rivera Rojas (Gutiérrez Castro 2006). Some years later, in 1960, the Central Nacional de Trabajadores (CNT) was founded, of which the SME was an integral part. In a further attempt to centralize union forces in Mexico, the BUO and the CNT were unified in 1966 to form the CT, a manifestation of corporatist strategizing.

Despite many transformations in the electrical industry over the years, the SME remained a consistent element of it until 2009. Sánchez Sánchez (1989: 110) highlights the regular general assembly meetings that were held every month since its founding in 1914, its ability to communicate with its members and its ability to keep the membership informed of the union's activities. Bensusán (2005: 548) commends the union's ability to provide an environment of belonging and voluntary enrollment, yet she reminds us that SME's primary source of power came from institutional practices such as "the exclusion clause, the exclusive ownership of the collective agreement, the centralized managing of loans and the support it received from the government." All of these practices, according to Bensusán, served to maintain corporatist relationships, which in turn interfered with the modernization of the company.

Throughout the 1960s and 1970s, the electrical workers were organized in various unions, namely the SME, the Sindicato Nacional de Electricistas Similares y Conexos de la República Mexicana (SNESCRM) and the Sindicato Único de Trabajadores Electricistas de la República Mexicana (SUTERM).[7] While their primary focus during this period was on their gremial demands, they also came to perceive socialism as an alternative to capitalism. For example, the August 31, 1972, edition of the union's newspaper (*Solidaridad* 1972: 4) states that

> The revolutionary nationalist state is not a finished form of restructured state but a capitalist state still, though deeply influenced by the Revolution ... in which the measures of the state, even without proletarian direction, weaken the capitalist system through nationalization, stratifications, land reforms, etc.... All these conquests must be defended by the workers ... in order to finally realize fully their own historic interests by arriving at socialism. The condition for all this, of course, is the political, ideological, and organizational independence of the working class.

This antisystemic sentiment did not filter through to other labor organizations and, in fact, SME did not join forces with left-wing revolutionary political parties, which would have been in keeping with their "revolutionary" assertions. They instead remained affiliated with the official political apparatus as members of the CT and maintained corporatist relationships with the PRI while many of the workers fought to end corruption within the union. Their primary demands during this period were for salary increases and better working conditions. Samstad (2002: 5) defines the SME's relationship with the state as one of "plural clientelist unionism." This arrangement is one of "interest intermediation ... [where] informal, personalistic ties to individual officeholders" (ibid.) are maintained. While not as closely tied to the state as some official unions, the SME's relationship with the state was not as autonomous as that of the independent unions either. Roman and Velasco Arregui (2006: 100) refer to the SME as a "dissenting union." Whereas the SME joined other dissenting unions in the Frente Sindical Mexicano (FSM[a]), the SUTERM, as the "official" electrical workers union, holds very close corporatist ties with the state. Dissenters from the SUTERM affiliated with the SME. SME opportunistically waffled between corporatist and anticorporatist strategies. Its antiprivatization initiative, while denouncing neoliberal policies, did not propose noncorporatist alternative strategies. The SME's "core goal was protecting jobs of its workers through continued public ownership of the energy sector; it sought to pressure the government but avoided confrontation" (Roman and Velasco Arregui 2006: 100).

Until 2009, SME continued to be one of the largest unions in the country with over 55,000 members, and was the most vocal opponent of the privatization policies of the state. SME was antisystemic only insofar as it denounced the government's privatization agenda; it fell short of promoting a socialist alternative or severing ties with the government altogether. It was because of the introduction of neoliberal policies and the government's privatization campaign that there was a reawakening of antisystemic and anticorporatist sentiment within the electrical workers' movement. "The actions of the leaders of the UNT and the FSM (of which the SME was a member) were not consistent with their rhetoric about challenging the neoliberal program" (Roman and Velasco Arregui 2006: 100).

The electrical industry, like all state-owned industries, was directly threatened by the state's neoliberal agenda. It was not until SME called for a Frente Nacional de Resistencia (FNR) in 1999 of all those organizations that opposed the privatization of state corporations that it gave support to and received support from organizations other than organized labor. The previous organizational structures under state corporatism were such that unions like SME focused on their own gremial demands independently of other unions or nonstate organizations. Interestingly, many of the issues that have come to be discussed at the FNR are not, in fact, labor issues at all but rather issues that went beyond the electrical workers' collective agreement to include working-class demands such as strengthening state corporations rather than privatizing them.

According to an unofficial spokesperson (interview October 14, 2003), it was in 1999[8] that SME modified its strategies and sought new national and international relationships. Before 1999, the union focused on maintaining its membership and fighting for increased wages; although there were antiprivatization slogans iterated as early as 1991 (see *LUX* [SME official newspaper/magazine] February–March 1991, nos. 400–401), there was little action along these lines. In contrast, at the thirty-seventh anniversary celebrations of the nationalization of the electrical industry, SME reached out to parliamentary groups from the PAN, PRI and the PRD (*LUX* October–December 1997, nos. 463–465). This was uncharacteristic of the union and was justified as an act to protect the electrical industry and national sovereignty against world capital and international corporations. As uncharacteristic as it may seem, Roman and Velasco Arregui (2006: 101) hold that

> both the union federations and the political parties have viewed the working class as a base for winning elections, for intra-elite bargaining, or as a way of leveraging bureaucratic union negotiations.... The unions ... carry out a policy of lobbying among parties and running candidates in various parties, often competing against each other, with the idea of maintaining sufficient union representation to give them leverage in their dealings with the state and the capitalists.

The leadership of the union justified its actions by claiming that it had a kinship with the national political actors against foreign interests. By 2002, this sentiment had disappeared as the SME returned to denouncing the government's antilabor politics (*LUX*, January–February 2002, nos. 515–516). In 1999, the SME created its first website and reached out to international unions that were also struggling against privatization. In that year, they began traveling to international forums and seminars. They joined the Federación Sindical Mundial (FSM) and the Unión Internacional de Sindicatos de Trabajadores de la Energía (UISTE). They also came to use the print media more frequently in 1999, to disseminate their message to other sectors of society. In that same year, they participated in a number of forums organized by the Chamber of Deputies where they presented their positions on the initiation of constitutional reforms to Articles 27 and 28. At the turn of the century, the union turned to the televised media to educate people about the dangers of privatization. It seems clearly the case that while the SME opposed corruption and corporatism, it was not willing to assume noncorporatist strategies because it would lead to its own demise. In the end, even these precautionary tactics did not save the union from the government's heavy-handedness.

Although neoliberal policies were implemented as early as 1982, and the promulgation of NAFTA took place in 1994, it was not until February 1999 that the Secretaría de Energía de México (SENER) submitted a bill to amend Articles 27 and 28 of the Mexican constitution. These amendments would come to modify the national electricity industry and open the door to private investment. Together with the university students' strike, the "anti-globalization" protest in Seattle, and the preelectoral euphoria of 1999, these proposed amendments may well have been instrumental in bringing about changes in the political tactics of the electrical workers. As asserted by an unofficial spokesperson (interview), "The union is quite clear that right now it is more important to defend the electrical industry and other public corporations because that is where the life of the union rests.... Without the student struggle in 1999, the electricians would not have been able to defeat the Zedillo government's [privatization policies]." Despite these amendments to the constitution, intended to give the government the official license to privatize state services, union and public resistance have limited the amount of privatization that the government has actually been able to carry out to this point.

A number of important organizational developments within the SME are worth noting. In 1990, under a plan which President Salinas de Gortari called the "new unionism," the SME formed the Federación de Sindicatos de Empresas de Bienes y Servicios (FESEBS) with the Sindicato Nacional de Trabajadores del Instituto Mexicano del Seguro Social (STRM). "The new federation linked a number of unions whose relationship with the state had been closer to that of plural clientelism than officialism or pure independence" (Samstad 2002: 11). This does not indicate that corporatism had waned, but rather it suggests that some unions, while still affiliated with the CT, were seeking ways to organize outside of their membership to form broader alliances to put more pressure on the government in opposition to its new neoliberal economic policies. In 1995, FESEBS joined with other unions (such as the SNTE, STUNAM and the SNTSS) to form the Foro (El Sindicalismo ante la Nación), which, according to Martínez and Vázquez (1997), sought to become an alternative voice for labor, while continuing to be a member of the CT. In 1997, the Foro divided into two groups, those who wanted to sever relationships with the CT (anticorporatist) and those who wanted to remain in the CT (corporatist). In the end the SNTE and eight other union organizations comprising about 84 percent of the Foro's membership, including the SME, decided to remain in the CT (see Samstad 2002: 13). The other group, which was led by the telephone workers, founded the UNT in 1997. By the end of 1997, the UNT had approximately 1.5 million members (ibid.) and advocated the termination of traditional corporatist relationships with the state by democratizing the internal structures of the union and holding true to its membership. At the same time that many of the workers were advocating the severance of relations with the state, Rosendo Flores Flores, the general secretary of SME, emphasized the importance of "establishing relations with different government functionaries particularly with those who ha[d] direct contact with the administration of the electrical industry" (*LUX* 1997: 4). He held that the new political environment in Mexico required the union to work more closely with the parliamentary bodies and the corporate executives in order to assure the preservation of quality electrical services (ibid.). Subsequently, in 1998 the FSM was founded and led by the SME and the Sindicato Independiente de Trabajadores de la Universidad Autónoma Metropolitana (SITUAM) to denounce neoliberal policies.

The union appeared to have difficulty defining its relationship with the state during this period. On the one hand, its membership sought to distance itself from the government (anticorporatist) and turn inward, while on the other hand its leadership sought relationships with the government (corporatist) to guide it through the economic difficulties of the time. This is indicative of a stage of transition from state corporatism to TC where the actors, in this case the union leadership and its members, were trying to determine their relationship with the state, itself under pressure from the international institutions.

SME came to be considered one of the most radical unions in Mexico as it struggled against the imposition of neoliberal policies, particularly the privatization of state corporations, and against the Ley Abascal (see Leyva Pina 2006: 157). While their struggle managed to help unify many sectors of society under a common demand, there were many political developments that the government was careful to keep from the public, out of fear of a greater backlash. Breceda-Lapeyre (2002: 12) explains that,

- Regardless of the debate on the market structure that Mexico's power industry will take, a *silent*[9] process of mounting private investment in generation facilities is taking place and, by the end of this decade, private generation could constitute almost half of total installed capacity in Mexico.
- Foreign direct investment in the power generation sector has increased consistently in the last eight years.... The overall goal of reaching over 32 thousand MW of additional capacity during this decade, of which 90% would be private, seems to be feasible.
- In the near future, the SENER ... will be concentrating its efforts on addressing local demand and practically withdrawing from export market niches, allowing practically free access to the private sector.

These assertions offer a completely different picture from what the government disclosed to the public as the antiprivatization movement expanded. In conversations the author had with many members of the public in Mexico in 2004, it was clear that many were unaware of the fact that *any* services had been privatized and that more investment from the private sector was on its way. The SME worked hard at limiting the privatization process, yet its ties to the state and its struggle for self-preservation limited its ability to act independently of the Mexican state.[10]

In October 2009 the Mexican government under Felipe Calderón seized the state-owned electrical plants of the Central Light and Power Company (Luz y Fuerza). This meant the liquidation of the company and the firing of over 45,000 workers, and in turn the end of SME. According to La Botz (2009; see also Carlsen 2009), "20,000 retirees are also now severed from their former employer and their union. The government's action directly affects at least 250,000 workers and their families." The primary motivation behind the government's takeover was privatization. Accordingly, the government had to get rid of the SME and take control of the electrical industry. Luz y Fuerza was just one of two electrical companies in Mexico. The other one, the Federal Electrical Commission, maintained close corporatist relationships with the government. The delivery of electricity would now be controlled by the government, but rather than a move to protect a state-run corporation, many predict that it is a move to prepare for the privatization of the same.

Many workers have taken severance packages while others continue the struggle to win back their jobs and to obstruct the privatization plans of the state. For six days in February 2011, "over 40 countries on five continents took action demanding trade union rights in Mexico" (International Federation of Chemical, Energy, Mine and General Worker's Union 2011). This collective action was in response to the SME shutdown and to a mining explosion in 2006 that killed sixty-five miners, for which nobody has been held accountable.

In conclusion, the SME was a union that promoted member participation and had the confidence of its membership. Its actions were dictated by the desire to survive the economic and political turmoil characteristic of neoliberalism. Its strategies are best described as anticorporatist. However, its leadership was known to capitulate to corporate and government demands, and in that way upheld transnationalized corporatist state-society relations. While the government has eliminated the SME, the struggle for many of the workers continues, in a way that can best be described as non-corporatist. Let us now turn to the university union.

Sindicato de Trabajadores de la Universidad Nacional Autónoma de México (STUNAM)

The university professors' union and the university workers' union are very important public-sector unions in the Mexican landscape. STUNAM, the largest of the many university unions, has approximately 23,000 affiliated members. STUNAM members are employees of the Universidad Nacional Autonóma de México (UNAM) at Ciudad Universitario (CU) in Mexico City and at its campuses around the country. Because STUNAM is not affiliated with the CT or the CTM, it escapes the grip of corporatist state-society relationships. Nevertheless, UNAM campuses are government-funded, public institutions, the administrations of which maintain corporatist relationships with the state. Strategies used by the STUNAM are for the most part anticorporatist. Internally, segments of the membership are known to struggle against the union leadership when it is perceived to be working too closely with the administration on policies that are not in the best interests of the membership. While the union itself is organized independently of the official unions, basic corporatist political links between the state and the university are maintained through professional organizations and associations, such as the National Medical Association (Gilberto Guevara Niebla, in Basurto 2006: 27).

Under neoliberalism the university has modified its philosophy from one of quality to one emphasizing quantity. Its existing programs have been modified and new programs created to meet the needs of corporations and professional associations. The introduction of performance indicators for evaluating the productivity of faculty members has resulted in creating a competitive atmosphere that, according to Basurto (2006: 28), does not enhance the quality or the quantity of work but in fact causes animosity among union members. Neoliberalism has also altered the decision-making process relating to salary scales and promotions. These are now being left up to the discretion of the administration, which has led to a weakening of the union and a strengthening of the relationship between the state and the administration.

The standard demands for money, benefits, job security, better working conditions and transparent rules and regulations negotiated in the collective agreement have formed the union's mandate since 1929 when the university was founded and granted its autonomy.[11] In keeping with Ramírez Saiz (2003), Basurto (1997: 15–16) argues, in his discussion about the STUNAM, that the apparent innocuous creation of the Ley Federal del Trabajo in 1931 and the Junta Federal de Conciliación y Arbitraje in 1927, have been the crux of corporatist relationships. The corporatist regime, he argues, has remained unscarred because the official registration and recognition of unions is determined at the discretion and under the control of the political system itself. While the STUNAM represents workers of an autonomous institution (UNAM), its members reap the benefits of the state employee health-care system, and their wages come from the public purse. The union membership receives the same benefits as the corporatist unions yet has maintained a greater degree of independence since its founding. According to Basurto (2006: 274), the leadership regularly finds excuses to hobnob with the university administration and often conforms to its norms. This causes division within the union, as not all of the membership support this type of interaction.

The union is an eclectic mix of "left-wing" political ideologies the adherents of which organize in *planillas* (election slates)[12] every three years to elect the executive committee of the union. While procedures are democratic, there is some concern about the staying power of the elected representatives. There are no limits to terms served, and the smaller *planillas* find it hard to break into the power structures of the union.

Over the years, the political struggles of the STUNAM have been to a great degree focused on the refining and preservation of their collective agreement. However, according to Carlos Galindo Galindo, the secretary of public relations (interview on December 9, 2003), the current primary demand of the union is "that the public university be financially accessible to the poorest people in Mexico." Galindo acknowledges the importance of struggling for dignified wages, but he argues, "Things have changed and now the public education patrimony is in danger." The biggest change in recent years has been the government's threat to increase tuition fees, which are currently almost fully subsidized by the state, to a level that far exceeds the financial abilities of most of the students. These measures are in keeping with the privatization mandate of neoliberalism.

Benefits are another concern under the current neoliberal dispensation in which the union pension plan held by the Instituto de Seguridad y Servicios Sociales de los Trabajadores del Estado (ISSSTE) was modified by the new and controversial Ley del ISSSTE in March 2007. The workers (Guerrero Santos 2007) object to the higher premiums and the longer years of service required to qualify for a retirement pension, while the government justifies the reforms in the name of saving the plan (Calderón Hinojosa 2007). These are just some of the central demands that will continue to feature in the annual collective agreement negotiations.

The autonomous nature of the UNAM and its union has kept the STUNAM from affiliating with or participating in party politics. This changed for the first time in 1988 when the union had its first contact with the world of electoral politics. On May 26 of that year, Cuauhtémoc Cárdenas of the PRD held a political meeting at the university before tens of thousands of university staff, students and academics. Subsequently, at the Ninth Congress of the STUNAM, a motion was passed that "the union would support the left-wing party candidates and the real democratic opposition" (*Unión*, June 6, 1988: 2). While this event marked an important change on the university campus, there is no indication that similar events were held during the subsequent electoral campaigns. This could be because the 1988 election was unique — it was the first time in over sixty years that a presidential election was contested so strongly. There was generalized mobilization throughout the country as people organized against the PRI strongholds.

During the transition from state corporatism to transnationalized corporatism, that is throughout the late 1980s and the 1990s, there were many political pronouncements that reached beyond campus concerns and the demands of earlier years. The nature of their demands changed little, but the issues of concern reached beyond the gremial demands of the union. For example, the STUNAM denounced the payment of the foreign debt (*Unión*, June 26, 1989: 5) and they supported non-higher educational movements such as the Cananea copper workers' strike, the miners at Sicarsa, the workers at the Ford automobile plant, musicians and the teachers (*Unión*, October 16, 1989: 8). In the January

8, 1990, issue of their newspaper (*Unión*: 8) they expressed their concern about funding for postsecondary institutions. As early as June 3, 1991 (*Unión*: 8), they began their struggle against NAFTA which they saw as a threat to university funding. These strategic changes highlight the perceived need for organizations to reach beyond local demands and align with other organizations that were and are suffering similar consequences brought about by neoliberal reforms in this period of transnationalized corporatism. As the union reached out to support the struggles of other unions, it was engaging in anticorporatist strategizing. This is particularly evident in the support it gave to the teachers' union, a union that has a long-standing, traditional, corporatist relationship with the state.

In July 1992, the Inter-American meeting of university and postsecondary unions was held at the UNAM. There were representatives from twenty countries in attendance. Elba Esther Gordillo, as representative of the SNTE, inaugurated the event. Gordillo, it may be said, was an unlikely spokesperson for an event that was held at a venue that took pride in housing an independent democratic union given that she herself maintained a corporatist relationship with the Mexican state (see the third section of chapter 2 above, and the "SNTE" section below).

As TC advances, unions have sought new ways to organize against the state's neoliberal policies. In 1997, there was a shift from basic gremial demands to more general national and international demands. This shift coincided with the advances of transnationalized corporatism. It also coincided with the founding of the UNT, which was designed to replace the CT and the CTM with a national union that would "fight against privatization, labour law reform, Fox, and neoliberalism" (La Botz 2005). During this period, the STUNAM joined the FSM and the Federación Nacional de Sindicatos Universitarios (FNSU) and reached out to other university syndicates throughout Latin America. It attended the first meeting of the Federación de Sindicatos Universitarios de América Latina (FESIUAL) in 1998. In keeping with the trend to form coalitions or national fronts, the STUNAM was also instrumental in forming the Frente Amplio de Sindicatos Universitarios y de la Educación Superior (FASUES) in 1998 (*Unión*: June 17, 1998: 4). According to Galindo (interview 2003), the union broadened its scope in response to globalization and the "new order." He held that the only way to contest these developments was to unite with other organizations that shared the same concerns. Although he defended the autonomy and the independent nature of the union and the fact that it has internal democratic structures, he made reference to the fact that before the Salinas government (1988), the STUNAM was run by "caudillos," that is, by top-down, authoritarian-type leaders often described as "politicians backed by military force."[13] Salinas, he claimed, dismissed Peréz Arreola, who was the STUNAM caudillo at the time, because he saw him as a threat (Peréz Arreola was the president of the union from 1977 to 1988). This was in keeping with Salinas's "new unionism" policies[14] that required greater communication and cooperation between the union and management, and greater autonomy and representation for the union. Galindo holds that the union has become much more democratic since that time. He stopped short of calling the union corporatist under Peréz Arreola. When asked what was special about 1997–1998 that brought about the changes to the union, he responded, in an excusatory manner, that they were just a bit slow in restructuring to meet the changes of the time and that these changes were well overdue. From 1976 to 1981, the union executive was made up entirely of Planilla Roja Unidad Sindical (PRUS) members. In the 1981 election, Bloque de Trabajadores Democráticos (BTD) sympathizers were elected.

In summary, the main strategic adjustments adopted by the STUNAM to confront neoliberal challenges were reaching out to other national and international educational union organizations and expanding their demands to include political-economic demands that went beyond their place of work, which brought them into contact with workers affiliated with corporatist unions.

Sindicato Nacional de Trabajadores de la Educación (SNTE)

Like the university workers' organizations, the teachers' movement has existed in Mexico for many years. It is considered one of the largest union organizations in all of Latin America with over 1.3 million members. While it has had close corporatist ties with the Mexican state since its founding, it is also one of the most combative unions in Mexico (see Pelaez Ramos 1999). The SNTE was founded in 1943 as part of the FSTSE. It functioned under the corporatist, bureaucratic control of the ruling party, the PRI. Its strategies are corporatist in nature, yet, as will be highlighted throughout this section, within the union there have been various anticorporatist factions. The most notable case was the partial severing of relationships with the SNTE by a group of "radical" teachers who formed the CNTE.

An early example of the division within the union came during the mid–1950s, when the leadership of the union became more corrupt and compromised. It was in response to this that a group of disgruntled teachers began to organize in an effort to democratize the union, moves that are best described as anticorporatist. They formed El Movimiento Revolucionario del Magisterio (MRM) in Mexico City and took to the streets in 1958 demanding salary increases of 40 percent, improved bonuses, and travel expenses to get to work (see Hodges and Gandy 2002: 58–69). The movement was repressed but came back even stronger months later when it called for a general strike. The government considered the movement illegal and refused to negotiate with the leaders. Eventually the government offices were taken over by the teachers and support poured in from community-based organizations, parents of schoolchildren and other unions. The teachers drew on Article 7 of the constitution, which states that

> Public functionaries and employees will respect the exercise of the right of petition, provided that it is formulated in writing and presented in a peaceful and respectful manner.... Every petition must receive an answer from the authority to which it has been directed, and said authority is required to make it known within a short time [Hodges and Gandy 2002: 64].

The leaders of the Secretaría de Educación Pública (SEP) eventually agreed to negotiate with the leaders of the MRM. While the negotiations were under way, the president announced a 17 percent wage increase for all SNTE members, an indication that the negotiations were little more than a charade. Repression followed against all remaining MRM protesters, and the principal leader was arrested and imprisoned. In the end, the union, in corporatist fashion, came to a negotiated compromise with the government. The MRM continued to organize but on a much smaller scale.

As the preceding account shows, the teachers' union was able to maintain strong corporatist relationships with the state during this period, but within the union itself it was not uncommon for members to organize and rebel against the leadership. Such internal rebellions occurred between 1979 and 1989 when the standard demands for better wages and improved benefit packages were transformed to include democratization within the union and a rejection of corporatism as some members sought to turn the SNTE into a more 'authentic' organization (see Pelaez Ramos 1999: 9). The result of this anticorporatist struggle was the creation of the CNTE, which now functions in parallel to the official SNTE union while reaping the benefits of SNTE's negotiated collective agreements. The biggest struggle throughout this whole period was for control of their work conditions and negotiating procedures. Some sections of the union were more combative than others were and managed to form their somewhat autonomous structures sooner than others did. The teachers' movement has developed in waves (see Petras 1999: 18–19), which are closely tied to the renewal of their collective agreements. Over the years, the teachers have suffered brutal repression, cutbacks and job losses.

The more conservative wing of the union was heavily influenced over the years by Elba Esther Gordillo, often referred to as "La Maestra" (the Teacher). She entered the SNTE in 1960 as a primary school history teacher. In 1970, she began her political career in the SNTE and the PRI when she replaced Carlos Jonguitud Barrios. He had led the union for over fifteen years before being finally forced to resign (Pelaez Ramos 1999: 146). Throughout her more than forty years in the SNTE, Gordillo was instrumental in maintaining corporatist relationships between the state and the teachers, whether under PRI or PAN governments. She managed to endure political upsets, national strikes, restructuring and ridicule. As Quiroz Trejo (2004: 7) explains, silence and inconsistency in one's discourse and actions both contribute to maintaining corporatist relationships.

Following the founding of the UNT in 1997, Gordillo announced that the SNTE needed to democratize, modernize and terminate the corporatist relationship with the state, yet her actions contradicted this discourse. She has since resisted unification with other organizations, has refused to abandon the CT and the CTM, has attempted to form her own political party and has continued to maintain a close relationship with the government in power. She is most criticized for remaining silent in response to the government's proposal to implement a new tax, Impuesto al Valor Agregado (IVA); for neglecting to respond to the privatization of the electrical industry; and for having nothing to say about the proposed reforms to the LFT.

In May 1992, the Mexican government signed the Acuerdo Nacional para la Modernización de la Educación Básica (National Agreement for the Modernization of Basic Education) with the SNTE, which decentralized education and transferred some responsibilities to the thirty-one states. The Ley General de Educación (General Law of Education) was approved in 1993 and Article 3 of the constitution was reformed to legalize the decentralization process (see Ornelas 2000: 427). All negotiating was done behind closed doors and spanned a period of about ten years. According to Ornelas (ibid.), there is

> no information to suggest that the 31 states were preparing themselves at the time to take control of the education system. This fact suggests that the transfer of education was a part of federal policy alone rather than policy of the 31 states. In addition, at the time political and social demands for decentralization were not evident. Nor was the teachers' union demanding such a policy change.

The "why" of the decentralization process has been an issue of contention among Mexican commentators. Some argue that decentralization resulted from the government's desire to create a strong federation of smaller, more manageable units, a move that would inevitably strengthen corporatist relations (see Reyes-Heroles 1985: 74). Others (McGinn and Street 1986) argue that decentralizing education would make the decision-making process more efficient. There are also those (Benavides and Velasco 1993) who argue that it was an attempt to dismantle the teachers' union or to decentralize the rising conflict that existed between the teachers and the government (see O. Fuentes 1983). Whatever the motives behind the decentralization, the central government has not devolved all decision-making powers to the states.

> It is a model in which the central state maintains the power to dictate general, nation-wide norms for the overall system. This power covers the elaboration of the national curriculum and the approval of regional curricula, the evaluation of the system, and the channelling of compensatory and extraordinary resources to poor states. The states assume responsibility for labor relations, school management and the administration of other reforms decided in the SEP [Ornelas 2000: 427].

It is in this context of partial decentralization that the most recent teachers' movement can be understood.[15] It began in May of 2006 when over 70,000 teachers in the state of Oaxaca went on strike. The initial demands of the movement "included legal recognition of Radio Planton[16] ... improvements to educational infrastructure (construction of class-rooms, laboratories and workshops; free student breakfasts; uniforms and more funding for scholarships and staff hiring) and salary increases" (Cuevas Fuentes and Windhager 2006: 22). Following a police raid on June 14, the movement quickly grew into a statewide movement heavily backed by the population in Oaxaca. The growth of the movement dramatically changed the initial direction and demands. The movement proclaimed a strong political position when it demanded the resignation of the governor of the state, Ulises Ruiz Ortiz. "Oaxaca is one of the three poorest states in the country and has the highest percentage of indigenous people of any state in Mexico" (ibid.). Whereas the national average of indigenous people is 10.5 percent, the proportion of indigenous people in Oaxaca is 47.9 percent (CNDPI 2000a). Similarly, the national average proportion of working people without an income is 25.8 percent, while the proportion of working people in Oaxaca without an income is 40.4 percent (CNDPI 2000b). Given the fertile agricultural lands in the state, Oaxaca has experienced vast foreign investment and land takeovers. The people are all too familiar with repression, injustice, exploitation, and with organized political responses to them.

The name of the popular organization that emerged to back the teachers' movement was the APPO. Its primary demand was the resignation of PRI governor Ulises Ruiz Ortiz. The APPO adopted anticorporatist strategies in its struggle to save public education and democratize the electoral process. It engaged in many different forms of political protest including sit-ins, a caravan to Mexico City, a hunger strike and the occupation of state-owned radio and TV stations. During the movement there were many political disappearances (a tactic common in the 1960s and 1970s), and many protesters were arrested and beaten, with a few being killed. In October 2006, the teachers agreed to go back to work, and the APPO continued its struggle.

The consequences of the decentralization of the public education system were played out in this movement. In particular, the debilitation of the national SNTE leadership was exposed when Section 22 went on strike with the backing of an important popular contingent. When things got out of hand, Gordillo contacted President Vicente Fox and insisted that any issues to do with any local of the teachers union had to be negotiated through the union's national bureaucracy and not at the state level, in this case Oaxaca

(Azul 2007). The teachers in Oaxaca maintained an anticorporatist struggle until Gordillo stepped in and facilitated a back-to-work order.

Thus, what started as a teachers' movement expressing very gremial demands evolved into a popular political movement when the population jumped to the defense of the teachers who were being repressed by state authorities. There was speculation that the APPO movement would end on December 1, 2006, when Calderón was elevated to office, and that Ulises Ruiz would resign to allow for the end of the conflict, but this did not happen. In fact, the repression increased as one of the key leaders of the APPO, Flavio Sosa, was arrested in Mexico City on December 4, 2006 (Mendez et al. 2006), on his way to speak to government officials in an attempt to negotiate a solution to the crisis. It is understandable that the government would be reluctant to order Ulises Ruiz to resign because this would call into question the legitimacy of the electoral process and set a precedent that could weaken Calderón's staying power in the presidential seat. Ulises Ruiz was in power from 2004 to 2010, and at all of his public appearances he was accompanied by heavy security personnel. His speeches alluded to a peaceful state that was under control while ignoring the prevailing conflict.

The movement's actions originated as a response to the consequences of neoliberal policies that have reduced funding to education in all its dimensions, yet its demands are attempts to reform these policies rather than to transform the political-economic system. Unlike other union movements, the very nature of the workplace brings teachers into close contact with parents and the surrounding neighborhood. By capitalizing on these relationships, the teachers have received support that has helped to strengthen their position at the negotiating table and, in the case of Oaxaca, grow the movement into one that was community based.

The strategies adopted in Oaxaca by the teachers are best understood in the context of transnationalized corporatism where nonstate actors seek alliances with other nonstate actors to denounce the imposition of policies legislated and administered by the national state but originating in directives from the international institutions (the WTO, the IMF and the World Bank). The transnational corporatist relationship between the leadership of the SNTE and the Mexican government is a classic example of how it is that corporatism continues to exist. This is most clearly demonstrated through the examination of the relationship between Gordillo and the state, a relationship that dates back to the 1970s and one that was rejected by the CNTE.

The CNTE emerged in 1979 as a left-wing teachers' organization parallel to the SNTE. It rejected the state corporatist relationship that existed between the official union, the SNTE, and the state ministry, the SEP. Its emergence predates the transitional period when transnationalized corporatism and transformations in the state corporatist relationships were in the works. According to José Basurto[17] (interview January 25, 2004), there are approximately 500,000 members of the CNTE who take pride in the union's democratic structures and processes. They reject all forms of corporatism, corruption and antidemocratic policies and actions within their ranks. Their strategies fit those of the anticorporatist category. Their primary objectives are to improve the lives of the teachers and their communities, and to improve the quality of public education in Mexico. The decentralization of the education system has brought new challenges to the CNTE, as they too have had to decentralize their activities to meet the particular needs of each state. From an organizational perspective, this is not necessarily a bad thing because it allows each group to work closely with the local communities, as we saw with the teachers in Oaxaca. The annual demands for increased wages persist. For example, in 2004 the CNTE was calling for a 100 percent wage increase. However, according to Basurto (2004) the teachers are now protesting against the privatization of education, calling for better medical services for all state employees, for an increase in financial resources for the education sector and for democracy within the SNTE. The addition of these more global, politically radical demands is a reflection of the modified state-society relations in Mexico.

Since the Zapatista uprising in 1994, political networking between the CNTE and other political and social struggles in Mexico has increased. It was the Zapatista movement and the neoliberal agenda, according to Basurto (2004), that made the CNTE realize that it was not good enough simply to engage in annual struggles for wage increases.

Independent unions may escape the grip of state corporatism, yet transnationalized corporatist relationships indirectly affect all sectors of society. In the case of the CNTE, their struggle against the privatization of social services and for increased funding for public education and their inevitable connection to the SNTE are reflections of this. The SNTE continues to engage in direct transnationalized corporatist relationships with the state, which sees no alternative but to respond with force to the contentious actions initiated by the teachers. Leyva Piña (2007: 102) agrees that the SNTE continues to maintain corporatist relationships with the state but argues that the way of doing politics has changed under the PAN. While the leadership of the SNTE is a notable example of state corporatism in Mexico, there have been many attempts to democratize the union. The establishment of the CNTE is the best expression of worker discontent. It is clear that the SNTE leadership has lost a lot of power over its membership under TC, yet its staying power cannot be ignored.

Let us now turn to the SINTCB, an "independent union."

Sindicato Independiente Nacional de Trabajadores del Colegio Bachilleres (SINTCB)

The SINTCB has an interesting history as an independent union since its founding in 1976. The Colegio de Bachilleres was founded by presidential decree in September 1973 in the state of Chihuahua. By 1987 there were twenty campuses around the country. From the beginning, SINTCB has worked in close proximity with other higher-education unions such as the STUNAM and SITUAM. This is evident in the newspaper clippings of their first strike, which lasted for sixty-seven days in 1976–1977. The demands of the union throughout the 1980s were "50 percent wage increase,[18] 100 percent increase in daycare and the basic food hamper, improved retirement and pension plans, the right to retire voluntarily, and a review of the job descriptions" (*Boletín Informativo*, no. 3, November 6, 1989).

However, this changed at the Third Academic Forum of the SINTCB on January 11 and 12, 1990, when a document was drafted that addressed issues that went beyond the college workers' immediate demands. The document denounced the role of the CTM at the Ford plant. It denounced the U.S. invasion in Panama and the harassment of the Cuban, Nicaraguan and Peruvian embassies, and it called for respect for the sovereignty of these countries. It called for solidarity with the indigenous people in Mexico, and it called for support for their colleagues at other Colegios de Bachilleres around the country.

While always cognizant of the national and international struggles, it was during the period of transition from state corporatism to transnationalized corporatism that they mobilized their membership to support objectives beyond the gremial.

The SINTCB is one of the few unions that continue to consider themselves independent. However, what the union considers itself is one thing, and how it is registered in law is another thing. The union takes pride in its democratic structures and procedures, yet its official registration ties it to the state through the different apartados. Although in 1976 it was regulated under Apartado B, the government eventually changed its position regarding the apartado registration of the SINTCB and granted it entry into Apartado A in 1999. This gave the union greater negotiation powers, their first collective agreement, and the legal right to strike for increased wages and better working conditions (see *Gaceta Académica* 2001). Under strict state corporatism this switch from one apartado to another might not have been granted because under Apartado B the corporatist relationship was easier to sustain. Under TC, the move to Apartado A reflected a weakening of the state's power to maintain tight control of all public unions and the strength of the union to fight for this change. The SINTCB engaged in anticorporatist action while under both apartados as it struggled for greater independence.

While still officially registered under Apartado B, in 1998 it declared itself independent of both Apartado A and B. According to Severo Escudo Carillo (interview November 14, 2003), the SINTCB considered "Apartado A and B of Article 123 of the Mexican constitution to limit union and political liberties, and serve as a means for the government to control the workers.... [Instead he held that they prefer to be] independent of the bosses ... [by forming] a distinct entity." This is a demonstration of how corporatism exists at all levels of engagement with the Mexican state. Even though they considered themselves independent from the beginning their ties to the state are undeniable, hence the need to continue with anticorporatist strategies. Their struggle for independence, Escudo Carillo argued, involved "defend[ing] the[ir] right to meet, to manifest, organize and strike as ... [they saw] necessary" (*Estatutos*, 1998, Declaración de Principios: paragraph 9, p. 2). Since its founding the SINTCB's focus has been on the collective agreement, a mostly gremial approach to politics. Their approach to doing politics has changed little under TC, but this can be explained because of the SINTCB's small size and its ability to maintain a degree of independence, or at least internal democracy. Its approach is successful in that it has survived as a union and not been crushed or absorbed by a larger union or coalition.

The SINTCB has a long history of struggling for the workers and teachers of the colleges, and is recognized for the support it gives to other political struggles in Mexico. As well as being affiliated under Apartado A within the CT, it is also affiliated with the FSTSE, which holds close corporatist relationships with the Mexican government and has about 1.5 million members. So, while they consider themselves to be an independent union the umbrella organization under which they fall has direct corporatist relationships with the state. It is only through its constant anticorporatist struggle that the SINTCB has escaped being more absorbed by the state apparatus. In keeping with Ramírez Saiz (2003), regardless of how it might choose to consider itself it continues to contribute to corporatist relationships in Mexico, and more precisely to transnationalized corporatism, because of its affiliations.

Because of the size of the union much of what they do and accomplish is a reflection of other unions and organizations in the country. For example, the outcome of their annual collective agreement negotiations, according to Severo Escudero Carillo (interview November 14, 2003), is predetermined by the outcome of the negotiations of the STU-NAM, which come before those of all other higher-education unions. Its strength also rests in the fact that it has a history of democratically electing its representatives. Its independent nature, its internal democratic arrangements and its willingness to work with other organizations and unions in Mexico will inevitably aid in its survival under transnationalized corporatism.

Conclusion

In conclusion, union movements such as those examined above can come across as unifocal most of the time, yet as things change in the political arena, and as state-society relations take on transnationalized corporatist characteristics and neoliberal initiatives take hold, demands also change. In the context of globalization and TC, these demands have become more general. Because of their direct connections to the political system as a provider of employment, most cases of these movements do not become anticapitalist, although they might struggle against particular systemic policies that directly affect them. Union struggles have not changed in response to democratic electoral reforms. That is, the leadership of the unions that have close ties to the government in power will announce their support for that party, whereas the more independent unions will assert their support for opposition leaders or leave it up to the membership to vote as they please.

The negative consequences of transnationalized corporatist relations and neoliberal policies have brought unions to the point of having to struggle against policies that threaten the well-being and even survival of the institutions that they service. Nevertheless, the reaction to TC by the different unions, whether dependent or pseudo-independent, is not homogeneous. Many internal and external factors inevitably intervene to determine just what issues are taken up and how they are responded to. The memberships of particular unions quite often engage in anticorporatist actions against their leaderships. The power of the leadership has also suffered a decline in many unions as TC has taken hold. Despite all of the changes that have been discussed above, one factor that seems constant among all the unions examined is that the period from 1997 to 1999 was one of outreach, expansion and transition. Throughout the 1990s and to date there has also been a search for partnerships with other organizations. Common fronts, coalitions and national organizational structures of varying types provide unions with greater resources to confront the consequences of globalization and its "de facto world government." Outreach of this sort was not common under state corporatism where demands focused on internal needs. Although, because of the privatization of whole industries or segments of industries and the regrouping of labor unions, the decrease in membership in the official unions is indisputable, the staying power of corporatist relationships is a phenomenon of Mexican political culture. Corporatism has long been, and remains, the institutionalized way of governing in Mexico.

4

Integrative Oppositional Strategies II

This chapter is divided into four sections corresponding to the remaining groups of nonstate actors (save for the EZLN) that are the subject of the study. The first section reports how small, left-wing political parties have responded to transnationalized corporatism. Although these parties escape incorporation by the state, their strategies fall short of the attempted postcorporatist actions of the Zapatista movement. They have not been able to avoid having to adapt to the political changes brought about by the changing state-society relations under TC. The parties considered here are the PRT, POS, OST, LUS, and UNIOS.

The second section discusses the different responses by NGOs to the changing state-society relations. Three of the NGOs, DESMI, Eureka and CIDHM, were founded before the consolidation of TC. These three cases serve as a means to study the different responses to the transition from state corporatism to TC. Their varying sources of funding, their mandates and their relationship with the state are among the issues covered in this section. Briefer consideration is accorded the remaining eight NGOs, namely the Centro de Derechos Humanos Fray Bartolemé de Las Casas (CDHFBC), CNOC, CILAS, K'inal Antsetik, COSACI, CMD, Granito de Café and SIPAZ.

The third section traces the unprecedented emergence of an organized electoral movement in Mexico in 1988, and then again in 2006. Although Mexico has an extensive history of electoral fraud and voter resistance, the 1988 and 2006 mobilizations emerged during the period of TC. The electoral reforms introduced following the popular manifestation of disapproval in 1988 set a precedent for the popular response to the 2006 elections. While some explain the popular response as a reflection of democratic reforms, this section makes sense of the electoral movement as a struggle to capture the state for democracy in the context of TC.

The final section of the chapter focuses on the response of two gremial social movements, namely the student movement and the Barzón movement, to changing, transnationalized corporatist state-society relations. Of particular interest in the student movement are the developments from 1968 to 1999. Through a comparison of the 1968 and the 1999 student movements, the changes incurred under TC become more apparent. The Barzón movement that emerged in response to neoliberalism captures the impact of the changing state-society relations on middle-class small landowners.

Political Opposition Parties

As expressed by Samuel Palma, coordinator of the editorial committee of the PRI (interview May 10, 2004), the "obvious" objectives of any political party are to "seek political power, win the presidential elections, have a majority in congress and maintain a political project that is directly associated with the slogan of democracy and social justice." To this list, one may add growing the party by increasing its membership. None of these objectives conflicts with either TC or the current social relations of production. Even the more progressive parties, such as the PRD, have shown themselves to be, once in power, followers of the neoliberal agenda and users of corporatist relationships (see Grayson 2007). While political parties of all stripes generally share the objectives of gaining power, winning elections and obtaining a majority in congress, their interpretations of democracy and social justice can be quite different. For some, the concept of democracy refers to the right to participate in the electoral process, while for others it refers to equal participation in political and economic decision making, equal distribution of wealth, the right to live a dignified life and the right not to feel threatened by the hegemonic powers in the country. The political opposition parties considered here waffle between these two positions. On the one hand, they promote conventional electoral democracy because it is a means with which to pave the road for their own political aspirations, while on the other hand, those without official recognition promote democracy in terms of economic and social equality and justice.

The contemporary state of political opposition in Mexico has been shaped by electoral reforms in the context of neoliberal globalization. In 1977, for example, reforms were introduced which brought about the adoption of the proportional representation model used in the country today. The results of these reforms were reflected in the push for opposition parties to get official registration status and participate in the electoral process. Leading up to the presidential elections in 1988 there was an unprecedented unification of opposition forces in support of Cuauhtémoc Cárdenas. As well as drawing large numbers of people and organizations together, the opposition movement also attracted people and groups with a variety of different ideological convictions, from the PRI to small Trotskyist parties. Across the political spectrum, a large, enthusiastic portion of the electorate saw Cárdenas as a potential way out of the historical grip of corporatism. As noted in the preface and introduction, the results of the 1988 election were effectively stolen and the PRI was reelected. Nevertheless, many opposition parties subsequently registered in order to gain official status and to participate in future elections. These parties include the PRD (1989), el Partido del Trabajo (PT—1990), el Partido Verde Ecologista de México (PVEM—1991), Convergencia (Convergence—1997), Alternativa Socialdemócrata y Campesina (PASC—2005) and Partido Nueva Alianza (PNA—2005). Of these, the Trotskyist party, PRT (1979), has run candidates on two occasions. The socialist party, the communist party and the social-democratic party, PRD, have also emerged as potential threats to the PRI and now PAN strongholds.

While some of the many small opposition parties in Mexico[1] have come to have official party status, others are not registered. In many cases they are simply too small to meet the registration requirements as defined by the IFE. Consequently, they have opted to engage in protest politics in their struggle for an alternative to capitalism. Of the parties examined hereinafter, none has been in a position of power where it could potentially effect change. This is due in large part to the divisiveness of their own internal politics. What has most stunted the growth of these parties is the ideological discussions that rage within and among them, resulting in a fractured left. Whether to run a presidential candidate, whether to support the EZLN, whether to accept money from the government or how to define the current political situation in Mexico are just some of the many issues that have led to divisions. Chronic sectarianism notwithstanding, there are many issues in recent years, under TC, that have brought the opposition parties to the street in solidarity with such movements as the antiprivatization and the antirepression struggle.

All of the left-wing political parties interviewed — UNIOS, PRT, POS, OST and LUS — have at one time or another negotiated unification among some or all of themselves. For example, POS and LUS militants once militated within the PRT and then separated, POS and OST (then LOM) attempted unification in the late 1970s but failed, the POS and the LUS formed the Coalición Socialista (Socialist Coalition) in 1997, and more recently there have been negotiations between UNIOS, PRT, and LUS to form a united party. All of these parties have a very anti-neoliberal discourse. This is what differentiates them from the mainstream parties and captures the attention of the citizens that do not want to conform to neoliberal politics and that no longer trust the old-school politics practiced by the three larger parties. They all maintain their socialist convictions and, although they may support the Zapatista movement, they will not dissolve into such a movement.[2] Manuel Aguilar Mora, member of the Central Coordinating Committee of the LUS (interview May 5, 2004), sums up the objectives of his party in the following way: "democracy, the emancipation of the working class, socialism ... free education independent of all religious affiliations or convictions, ... liberation of women ... abortion." These demands are shared with the other parties mentioned above. Their socialist convictions sum up their anticapitalist, anti-neoliberal approaches to politics in Mexico.

While the mainstream parties (PAN, PRI and PRD) support the capitalist system and propose reforms that will pacify opposition forces, the small parties of the left reject this moderate approach and recognize that the problems of social inequality, poverty, unemployment, and injustice are all inherent to capitalism. Accordingly, they hold that the only way to solve the problems brought about by capitalism is to eliminate it and introduce an alternative mode of production. How to accomplish this very tall order is, of course, problematic. These parties have not modified their way of doing politics or their relationships within the political realm as state-society relations have been modified. Their refusal to adapt to the changing relationships has left them marginalized. Often considered very sectarian, their attempts at working effectively in coalitions or fronts or to unite their parties have for the most part failed.[3] While their anticapitalist approach to politics is inherent in their ideological convictions, they have been forced more recently to reach beyond conventional Marxist doctrine to address such issues as the environment, culture, indigenous struggles and the position of women.

These smaller parties are also known for the rigid centrality of their leadership. In most of the parties examined, the "maximum" leader of the organization has held that position since the founding of the party. Their internal structures are very hierarchical and corporatist-like. Given the systemic nature of corporatism, this should be no surprise. It is not uncommon for members to be expelled from the party for speaking out against the leadership. The case that the author can best speak about is that of the LOM/OST. The LOM was founded in 1970 and the OST in 1989. Luis Vázquez was the founding leader of both of these organizations. While it is unclear why the LOM folded and why the OST emerged, it is clear that the leadership did not change. Furthermore, the offices of the OST are the same as those used by the LOM, the archives kept by the OST include the LOM archives and, although many of the old LOM militants have left the party, the two main leaders, Luis Vázquez and Humberto Ramírez, are a constant. They control what gets published in their newspaper, which events they will participate in, what the party line is, what organizations they will work with, which coalitions they will participate in and who is in and who is out. While militating in the LOM, the author notes that there were three members of the organization who were expelled and accused of being "petit-bourgeoisie" because they opposed the political analyses being made by the leaders. The party comprised a number of levels, namely the executive committee, the cell leaders, the cell members, the pre-cell leaders and the pre-cell members. Each level was privy to different amounts of information and held varying responsibilities specific to that level within the party. Group leaders were responsible for controlling the actions of their members. In exchange for being willing to donate a portion of their salary to the party, approving of the party's political platform, achieving high newspaper sales and being a regular participant in public events, the party would promote said member to a higher level.

Despite the centrality of the leadership, the strength of ideological conviction and the rigidity of internal organization, the actual focus of the small parties at any time has much to do with the nature of their membership and the prevailing political economic context. For example, throughout the 1980s the LOM was influential in the teachers' movement as many of its members were teachers. The POS, by contrast, worked at influencing the Euzkadi (a tire plant) workers, many of its members being drawn from that industry. According to Alejandro Varas, general secretary of the Executive Committee of UNIOS (interview April 27, 2004), when UNIOS was founded it concentrated its efforts on helping members organize their own neighborhood committees and social groups rather than concentrating on the organization of the party. In this way their constituency came to comprise many sectors of society beyond their disciplined militants. They were very active in the early years of the EZLN and subsequently worked in solidarity with the Frente Zapatista de Liberción Nacional (FZLN). In fact all of the parties examined acknowledged growth following the Zapatista uprising. They "jumped on the bandwagon," so to speak, and benefited from the political "boom."

Political parties have more to lose than social movements do if they stray from their principles. They are in the game for the long term and will reach out to all sectors of society in their search for approval and support. They pride themselves on what they consider to be their internal democratic structures, and differentiate themselves from NGOs. For example, Luis Vázquez, director of the OST (interview July 1, 2004), criticizes NGOs for obliterating the concept of social class in their discourse. As long as capitalism exists, so too will Marxism and the struggle of classes, he argues.

It is safe to say that the smaller left-wing parties will continue on the margins unless they are co-opted by the social-democratic PRD. Although they will always lack legislative power, they arguably fulfill an important role at the grassroots level in organizing people against neoliberal policies, corruption and social injustice. They tend to work outside of the existing labor structures and outside of the government institutions. Looking at the larger picture, they are the organizations that have the longest history of fighting against capitalism. What is important for them is not necessarily effectiveness or success but rather what they perceive as the historical responsibility of a particular group of social actors to keep the Marxist, anticapitalist agenda on the table and the revolutionary discourse present, as long as the prevailing political economy continues to reproduce unconscionable economic inequality and political subjection. The practices of these left-wing opposition parties — not least the practice of organizing vulnerable sectors of society — have changed little under transnationalized corporatism because their approach to politics is to reject the capitalist system, including the international institutions that influence internal state-society relations in Mexico.

Where then do they stand in relation to our theoretical analysis of TC? While the nature of oppositional political parties does not tie them to the state along corporatist lines, they move within a society where corporatist structures continue to dictate political interaction. Insofar as electoral democratization since the late 1970s has occurred in the context of neoliberal globalization, corporatism has not been overcome. Rather it has shifted from a state to a transnationalized form. Consequently, though opposition has grown and broadened, with both new official parties and new fronts or coalitions, important elements of political organization remain corporatist in character. The current role of the economic and political elites under the New Labor Culture pact requires political parties to engage directly with the state bureaucracy if they want to proceed through legal channels to lobby the government. Many of the parties discussed above prefer to organize society directly in their quest for change while some consider the electoral route as the desired approach. In either case, their willingness to exist in the political space afforded by the status quo, but to go no further, means that their actions do not transgress the limits of anti-corporatism. By affirming the existing political structures of the country, even as they engage in oppositional politics, their praxis has the unintended consequence of helping to sustain the very corporatism they reject.

Nongovernmental Organizations (NGOs)

A crucial feature of TC is the part played by another group of nonstate actors, NGOs. NGOs of both the grassroots and international types have flourished under TC as they attempt to meet basic needs of communities that have been neglected by the state as the latter has withdrawn from social welfare provision under neoliberal imperatives. NGOs are, in general, not-for-profit advocacy groups that perform a wide variety of service-oriented tasks. Some are major relief organizations. Some are simply lobby groups that negotiate with government officials to advance a particular concern. Others serve as organizing groups, centers of information and research, educators or project managers, or they provide support services of varying types. Funding for NGOs can come from many different sources. International NGOs solicit funding from municipal, state and federal governments for projects they seek to realize abroad while grassroots NGOs depend on their own finances or the fund-raising activities they do in their communities or at public events. Religious organizations are a substantial source of funding. Some development projects are even funded by corporations. The largest of NGOs are familiar with the corridors of power (and the stages of celebrity).

> Powerful international NGOs are often funded by the UN, which itself is dominated by U.S. policy makers. Governments, banks, the Vatican, and industrial giants all get into

> the funding act.... These funding sources are not neutral actors ... they are pillars of capitalism and demand loyalty from those whose fancy salaries they pay [Hoddersen 2006: 55]

Most striking about these interconnections is how well they fit into the transnationalized corporatist model where the key political actors serve and defend the interests of the masters. One thing NGOs all have in common is that although they may be fulfilling what was once considered a government responsibility, they are not elected representatives and they are not accountable to the population. Their presence in one community rather than another is a matter that is decided internally or mandated by the funding bodies. Shefner (2007: 188) explains how

> some of these civil society groups [NGOs] are held in favor by the state, as their work facilitates state thinning, on one hand, and provides rationale for the commercialization — or marketization — of social welfare on the other. In contrast are some of the human rights or civic NGOs that often challenge state prerogatives. In further contrast are still other NGOs, which may first challenge the state to become more formally democratic and later work with the state in their acceptance of neoliberal politics that limit the role of the state.

As governments privatize state-owned corporations, withdraw funding from public services and otherwise shape their economic agenda in line with transnational neoliberal priorities, NGOs have emerged to fill in where governments have stepped aside. Projects such as the construction of day-care centers, orphanages, schools, electrical plants, water wells, and so forth abound. TC facilitates and welcomes the integration of NGOs into Mexican society. In fact, it was during the transition to TC that NGOs proliferated on the national scene. When state corporatism held sway, NGOs were neither welcome nor required, though they did exist on a much smaller scale and under stricter controls. Under the current model NGOs paradoxically help to maintain corporatism. While anticorporatist by disposition, their strategies do not promote alternative arrangements from those that currently prevail. Even the NGOs that have aided the Zapatista communities in Chiapas have not themselves delinked from the state.

The NGOs are anticorporatist insofar as they fulfill roles properly performed by the state and thereby uphold transnationalized corporatism rather than "delinking" from it. With whom and how NGOs act is often determined by the source of their funding. If it is a grassroots local NGO with little or no salaried staff, working off a limited budget and with a limited infrastructure, the organization has greater autonomy than do larger national or international NGOs. However, it does not follow that grassroots NGOs are noncorporatist, because to be so they would have to be working with the population to terminate contact with the state, whereas, in the typical case, they work within the existing structures and uphold the prevailing dynamics between the state and nonstate actors. Many of these organizations also work directly with other anticorporatist organizations. For example, the Centro de Investigación Laboral y Asesoría Sindical (CILAS) supports the anticorporatist strategies of various union organizations. It is true that grassroots NGOs appear to work independently of the state, directing their energies to the communities they are servicing. Moreover, the government is not interested in managing or controlling grassroots NGOs because they do not depend on the government for financing and they tend not to organize against government policies. However, what they do is perform tasks that were historically considered the responsibility of the government, whether building a bridge or running an orphanage. This is what makes them anticorporatist. One might say that grassroots NGOs live in harmony with the state and for the most are unregulated. Larger national and international NGOs are likely to maintain more clearly defined corporatist-style relationships with a government or corporate sponsor. In these cases, the sponsors dictate the actions of the NGOs, the projects they engage in and where the projects will be realized.

By addressing or resolving immediate problems, NGOs are favored by the Mexican state as a reliable resource. For example, in examining an NGO in Mexico City that works with street children and poor families, Magazine (2003: 248) found that

> the NGO workers conceive of the problem[4] in a way that puts the blame on neoliberal policy, but that involves the actions of family members. Thus, even though they cannot bring about large-scale economic changes, they feel that they can still do something to resolve the problem in an immediate sense.

NGOs find funding beyond the state to build sewage systems, day-cares or provide basic food supplies to whole communities. NGOs by nature do not seek to modify the mode of production they work within, but rather to mend some of the small wounds caused by the system — a system that continues, inevitably, to cast off and marginalize the "superfluous" sectors of society (Christie 1994: 60–61; Chomsky 2000: 81).

There is much debate about the role of NGOs and their place in the social relations of production. While some applaud them for the benefits accruing from their development projects, others criticize them for their role in facilitating the neoliberal project. For example, according to Cockcroft (1998: 283), NGOs not only alter the role of the state but also interfere with the organizational success of opposition forces.

> NGOs serve ... the interests of the World Bank, US imperialism, and national elites by atomizing social movements, placing "outsiders" in command of budgets and planning, and reducing political/economic struggle to the local level where resources remained scarce. NGOs in Mexico undermine ... the earlier national networking and collectivizing of Mexico's social movements. They also divide ... movements into competing political camps, as some Mexican NGOs even backed the conservative PAN.

More succinctly, Hardt and Negri (2000: 36) describe NGOs as "some of the most powerful pacific weapons of the new world order." Nagar and Raju (2003: 3) refer to them as "an arm of the government," while others, like Smillie and Hailey (2001: 173), hold that NGOs "offer something new and important." Regardless of one's interpretation of the role or effectiveness of NGOs, they clearly represent a phenomenon that has flourished under transnationalized corporatism in México where the state has come to depend on the services provided by NGOs to help keep people divided and pacified. This in turn gives the state the space in which to concentrate on maintaining its existing corporatist relationships. Of course, one must differentiate between grassroots NGOs, internationally funded NGOs and everything in between. While the sample of NGOs examined below is indicative of this range, I have also chosen cases based on their degree of contact with the indigenous communities in Chiapas. This is because of the impact that the Zapatista uprising has had on NGO work in Mexico.

This section is divided into NGOs that emerged before TC and those that emerged under TC. Consistently throughout the sample, it is evident that while most NGOs do not have corporatist relationships with the state, the strategies they adopt are at best anticorporatist because they do nothing to sever ties with the government, a move that would demonstrate a noncorporatist position. In fact, to be noncorporatist would mean ceasing to exist given the role that NGOs play in supporting government actions and, as Petras and Veltmeyer (2005) argue, in pacifying nonstate actors. NGOs serve as "the glue" that is applied to bind the society together since something needed to come into the political arena to cover for the reduced role of the (welfare) state under neoliberalism. The only other alternative that I can think of would be the state's increased use of militarization to control the response of nonstate actors to the reduction of services, increasing instability of employment, growing inequality and increasingly severe economic recessions caused by the neoliberal policies.

NGOs Originating before TC

One of the oldest NGOs in Mexico, DESMI, was founded in 1969. According to Jorge Santiago Santiago (interview May 15, 2004), director of DESMI, they are currently working with approximately seventeen mainly Tzotzil municipalities. This brings them in contact with over two hundred projects. The justification of their work is based on a detailed analysis of the political-economic situation in the country. Their analysis (see DESMI 2007) examines such things as the following: the impact of Plan Puebla Panamá, the fraudulent electoral processes, the replacement of native agricultural products with products that serve the interests of the transnationals, and the Programa de Certificación de Derechos Ejidales y Titulación de Solares Urbanos (PROCEDE), not to mention the approximately 150,000 people from Chiapas that migrate to the United States each year in search of a dignified standard of living. They also critically examine how NAFTA has changed rural living (ibid.):

> The farmers and producers live in an agricultural crisis, which is caused mainly by the structural reforms introduced to facilitate the commercial liberalization impelled by NAFTA: that is, reforms to eliminate price controls; constitutional reforms regarding land possession; reforms to eliminate restrictions on, and the private use of, ejidal and communal lands. Also reforms to reduce subsidies to farmers.

It is in response to this assessment that DESMI supports local projects through loans, consultation and development initiatives. DESMI receives its funding from international sources such as Oxfam or Development and Peace (a Canadian-based Catholic organization). They attempt to help communities become self-sufficient through the implementation of local, sustainable agricultural practices, cooperative job-generating projects and support in their struggles for autonomy. Santiago (interview May 15, 2004) explained how the struggle for autonomy of many communities in Chiapas began in 1992, prior to the EZLN uprising in 1994, but that the concept of "autonomy" has come to mean "the right to self-determination, the right to preserve their language, identity, local organization, the right to elect their own representatives and the political right to rule their own communities." All of these rights have come to be threatened by the neoliberal agenda of the Mexican government. That said, Santiago explained how the organizations which support them now have supported them in some cases for over 30 years. What has changed, he asserts, is not which organizations they can count on for support but rather the projects that are being undertaken. This may be directly linked to the funding sources, as Hoddersen (2006) would have it, a reflection of the changed political and economic needs of the populations or possibly the exacerbation of these needs as the state withdraws services.

According to Santiago (interview 2004), the previous fifteen years had seen an increase in the number of NGOs in the region. One of the determining factors throughout the 1980s was the migration of political refugees from Guatemala and El Salvador to southern Mexico, in particular Chiapas and Oaxaca, which brought international NGO support to the area.

More recently, DESMI has coordinated projects with the autonomous municipal governments, the Juntas de Buen Gobierno (JBG), which were founded in 2003 by the Zapatistas. According to Santiago, one of DESMI's primary disadvantages is that their staff do not speak the native languages in the areas that they have been working in for the past thirty-five years. They consider their work to be anti-neoliberal. It is by means of local projects that undermine transnational interests that they work toward the creation of an alternative to neoliberalism. Note that this is not the same as an alternative to capitalism. They are not proposing a new mode of production but rather economic reforms to the existing model that will address the needs of the indigenous people. They are promoting what has been called "capitalism with a human face."

While DESMI predates TC, it has been required to adapt to the changing world order. The primary changes it has introduced are in the nature of the projects that it realizes. While initially working with the migrant refugees, it has now come to focus on the indigenous populations in the Lacandon Jungle in Chiapas. Otherwise, TC has not modified its organizational structure or influenced its overall mandate. There is no evidence that its dealings with the government have changed, hence the classification anticorporatist.

Another NGO that predates TC is the FNCR, formerly Eureka. The FNCR has undergone numerous transformations, but it continues to hold Rosario Ibarra de Piedra as its primary spokesperson and national coordinator. While Eureka, like various other national fronts against repression and disappearances, is not what we think of as a typical NGO that goes into a community to provide a service, it is not a political party either. By gathering information from government and other sources about the disappearance or arrest of loved ones, it seeks to end these practices. In that way it works with and within the existing state-society relations model, not outside of it. The organization was founded in 1977 after Ibarra de Piedra's son was disappeared and over five hundred other political activists had either gone missing or been arrested. The organization was known as the Comité Eureka de Desaparecidos in 1977. In 1979 it changed its name to FNCR. Its biggest achievement was the liberation of 148 of approximately 557 political prisoners following a hunger strike in 1979. Ibarra de Piedra (interview December 12, 2003) declares that their "minimum demand is the maximum and their maximum demand is the minimum." The life and liberty of all political prisoners are not negotiable. They have given up discussing with government officials because "they are all the same." The response of Vicente Fox of the PAN is no different from that of PRI presidents. Their struggle has not changed under neoliberalism or during the recent period of market expansion. Although they offer their support to anti-neoliberal struggles, and struggles of all sorts for that matter, their primary struggle is unifocal — liberty to all political prisoners and the reappearance of the disappeared. When asked about the process of democratization in Mexico, Ibarra de Piedra responded that "there can not be democracy in a country where there are disappearances, where there are clandestine jails, where there is political repression, where indigenous people who protest against the devastation of the forests are arrested.... Those who participate in political parties need to realize that there cannot be democracy until popular demands are met."[5] Because of their unifocal mandate, Eureka has changed little with the changing political and economic context. The most recent development is the founding of the Frente Nacional Contra la Represión y en Defensa de Los Derechos Humanos (FNCRDDH) in September 2007 by Ibarra de Piedra. This is a revival of the FNCR that she founded during the period of state corporatism. It was unclear at the time of writing this chapter whether there were any substantial changes to the strategies of the original Frente.

The CIDHM is another NGO that emerged in 1977. As its name implies, its primary focus has been to denounce human rights violations and provide legal support for the violated. Its founding, according to Juliana Quintanilla (interview February 20, 2004), was directly linked to the struggles of Rosario Ibarra de Piedra and the violation that many families had suffered from the disappearance of their loved ones. In Morelos, in 1977, it calculated that there were at least twenty-nine political prisoners. It sees its job as educating the public to speak out when violations occur, to make them known and to denounce them. It was also very instrumental in defending the right to land in a community called Xoxocotla in 1979 when the government threatened to build an international airport there, and again in 1983 in Tepetzingo. The CIDHM considers the defense of native languages and culture to be of primary concern as they serve as a means to defend the rights and identity of the people and the villages. Its central demands at the time of the interview were an end to political repression in the indigenous communities and an end to violence against women. In the fall of 2008 it played a central role in denouncing human rights violations against the teachers in the state of Morelos who were on strike against the privatization of public education. In this context, it adopted anticorporatist strategies to reform the system in an effort to make it more humane.

Both Eureka and the CIDHM have worked independently of the government in power. As a matter of empirical fact, they have both avoided direct corporatist relationships with the state. Nevertheless, theoretically speaking their actions facilitate the corporatist strategies of the state. They both have a narrow focus and grassroots character and they see the PRI and PAN governments as violators of human rights. They do not receive money from the national government, and although they may engage in negotiations with them, their relationship with the government in power does not go beyond their tacit support of corporatism. Both organizations draw on the rule of law to make their point and demand justice. Their relationship with the government is primarily one of denunciation. Quintanilla (interview) stated that the "government doesn't like human rights groups like theirs because they are always denouncing the neoliberal politics of the government."[6] Because they are unwilling to delink from the status quo, however, little has changed in their struggle for justice. Most of their work is done for the benefit of people whose basic rights have been violated. They also spend much time educating people about the injustices in Mexican society. While they do not pose a threat to the survival of the Mexican state, they do call into question its integrity. Their mandates have not changed since their founding. The services they provide are those which the state has no interest in, or intention of, providing. They are not services that were at one time supplied by the state and are now taken over by NGOs. On the contrary, the fact that NGOs have come to take up such human rights issues exposes the government's deep unwillingness to address them.

NGOs Originating under TC

Two grassroots NGOs which emerged during the transitional phase of transnationalized corporatism are the Centro de Derechos Humanos Fray Bartolomé de Las Casas (CDHFBC, 1988) and the Coordinadora Nacional de Organizaciones Cafetaleras (CNOC, 1989). Both of these organizations serve as umbrella groups that draw existing, isolated groups into one central body with a common agenda.

The founding of the CDHFBC was an initiative of Bishop Samuel Ruiz[7] of the diocese in San Cristobal de las Casas in Chiapas. Samuel Ruiz was a liberation theologian who sought to resolve the persistent conflicts between the *caciques*[8] and the indigenous people. (He detected a degree of "autonomy" which had been adopted by the caciques and which superseded the law, resulting in human rights abuses.) His center functions as a nonpartisan information, education and legal resource. It stations observers in the different indigenous communities throughout the state who help to monitor human rights violations and the movements of the military. It also has a group of researchers who write analyses of the political and economic situation in Chiapas. It strives to influence political parties in power while simultaneously accompanying civil society in its denunciation of social injustices. According to Aldana (interview May 24, 2004), the center's knowledge and information comes from its many years of work with the indigenous communities.

The indigenous people have taught the center's members to be cognizant of cultural and social issues and to take account of the already existing community organizations. This contact and sharing of information predates the Zapatista uprising and emerges with the development of the neoliberal economic model. The center views the Zapatistas as just another indigenous group living and working within the communities in which it also has a presence. What has changed over the years is its sensitivity to the society and culture of the indigenous people. As Aldana (interview) explains, it used to see the communities with the same lenses used by the government, but today it sees the communities through the lenses of the indigenous people themselves. He acknowledges that the Zapatista uprising clarified both the demands of the indigenous people and their way of life. Its work continues to denounce human rights violations in the state of Chiapas, violations that in some regions occur under political parties other than the PRI. Given the international economic support it receives to keep the center functioning, it has been forced to modify its practices as TC has taken hold. For example, the international funding maintains it as a resources center rather than a center of political action. Its enforced inaction can be considered a means by which its paymasters channel people's energy toward theoretical and empirical research ends, ends that may result in a pacifying of those involved. This is an outcome that Hardt and Negri (2000: 36) warn us about. Its inaction also serves to support the argument that NGOs can engage only in anticorporatist activity and that noncorporatist strategies would lead to their ruin.

The founding of CNOC also came during the transitional phase of corporatism where state corporatism was being replaced with transnationalized corporatism. It emerged in response to the changing role of the Mexican government in the international economic arena. CNOC sought to unite coffee growers around the country in response to the coffee crisis in the late 1980s. It has affiliated organizations in the states of Chiapas, Oaxaca, Guerrero, Hidalgo, Puebla, Veracruz and San Luis Potosí. As a gremial organization, CNOC focuses its attention on issues directly related to coffee growers while supporting more general struggles as they arise. According to Fernando Celis (interview), the primary demands of the CNOC are (1) the creation of a public organization to deal with coffee-related issues, (2) the introduction of mechanisms to improve the price of coffee and (3) public resources and subsidies for coffee producers so that they can improve their crops and be more competitive in the neoliberal market. All of this preserves the status quo. It rejects neoliberal policies that interfere with its demands. It negotiates with the government through dialogue and only in extreme cases pressures the government through mobilizations. When the government began to pull out of the economic dealings of the coffee industry and left the market to its own resources, the national producers were directly impacted. This drew the rural farmers closer to the urban antiprivatization struggles. This rural-urban collaboration was not a common mix prior to the neoliberal reforms and TC. Just as unions have been searching for alliances and seeking to expand their mandates to better respond to TC, and just as left political parties have been trying to unite, so has CNOC been searching for ways to unite the rural and urban coffee industry workers. It seems that organizations of all sorts have become willing to enact common platforms to which all parties involved can consent. However, this does not necessarily result in a more effective or powerful organization. In fact, the platforms themselves tend to be watered down as they capture only the agreed-upon demands.

Celis (interview) points out that "CNOC is not a very centralized organization," as is often the case with umbrella NGOs. It serves as a coordinating body, which exchanges information and experiences, and approaches the government to negotiate common demands. The organizations that make up the CNOC have their own internal autonomous structures. He also points out that one of the most successful mobilizations occurred in February 1994 during a pricing crisis. It was the first time that the government willingly engaged with the organization and negotiated a workable deal. This, he figures, was a direct consequence of the Zapatista uprising which obliged the government to take indigenous demands more seriously. In this case, rather than social movements always reacting to government actions, as many social movement theorists would have it, the government has been forced to modify *its* reactions to indigenous people in general so as to avoid further confrontation. What is ironic about this is that while the government groups all rural struggles with indigenous struggles, the CNOC is very critical of the political tactics of the EZLN. Celis (interview) mentioned that when the "El Campo no Aguanta Mas" (CAM) movement organized in 2003, the Zapatistas did not declare their support for the movement even though many of the organizations within the CAM had supported the Zapatista movement. Celis referred to the Zapatistas as sectarian. Many organizations on the left consider the Zapatista movement to be sectarian for the same reason. Of course, this criticism could be an expression of resistance by these organizations to engage in the radical delinking strategies of the Zapatista movement. They prefer to conform to strategies that, whether they intend to or not, sustain corporatist relationships in Mexico and protect their own survival. Celis continues that it is a false proposition to assert that the Zapatistas are the only organization that can lead a general social movement in Mexico and bring about change. On the contrary, he argues, they will isolate themselves further if they do not modify their way of doing politics.[9] It does not follow from this assertion that CNOC has the ability to be that leading force, but it does highlight their emphasis on the need to unify forces in order to respond effectively to neoliberal policies. The discourse endorsing the unification of forces has appeared repeatedly as a necessary requirement of social action under TC. It is held that in order to confront international alliances between the state and the international institutions, opposition forces must make their own internal alliances united on common demands or issues. Most often the biggest obstacle to such alliances or fronts is the question of under which organization and which platform such a unified body would mobilize. Those who classify the Zapatista movement as sectarian neglect to acknowledge its call for unification along noncorporatist lines.

CILAS is a grassroots NGO founded in Mexico City in 1990 when TC was well under way. It serves as a center that does research, training and consultation for labor unions. As Héctor de la Cueva, general coordinator of CILAS (interview February 12, 2004), explained, although it is nonpartisan, it "has a vision to create an alternative to globalization." It works with international organizations with the same agenda. He described the center as part consultation, part NGO and part support projects for workers. The center also seeks to educate unions about corporatism and encourages them to do their part to end these relationships with the state. This is a task that he believes can be accomplished by organizing the membership of the unions themselves. However, the very actions of CILAS serve to uphold corporatism as it works within the very structures it claims to want to destroy. A more consequent approach would be to affiliate with the Zapatistas or adopt similar noncorporatist strategies. The center has been working with the UNT[10] since its founding in 1997 and is a member of the Red Mexicana de Acción Frente al Libre Comercio (RMALC). Although not a union, CILAS engages in similar activities while pushing for the "internationalization of union vision" (the organizing of unions in international alliances against neoliberalism) in Mexico and for the unionization of those workers who remain unorganized.

CILAS provides a good example of an organization that emerged in response to the globalization process and neoliberal reforms. It is an organization that appreciates the importance of breaking with corporatist relationships, yet it is unclear how far it is willing to go. The divided and dispersed labor movement, and the difficulty that workers have in organizing under transnationalized corporatism, gave the founding members, Héctor de la Cueva, Luis Bueno Rodríguez and Jorge Sánchez Rodríguez, a reason to create a center that would analyze and work toward improving the organization of labor in Mexico. The changing economic and political circumstances in the country were also ideal for creating such a research and education center. CILAS has also worked hard to consolidate relationships with international union organizations as they, too, struggle against neoliberal policies.

Many national and international NGOs gravitated to Chiapas following the Zapatista uprising and the promulgation of NAFTA on January 1, 1994. Some of these NGOs are grassroots, depending on their own resources, while governing bodies such as municipal, state or federal governments fund others. K'inal Antsetik and the COSACI are two grassroots organizations that already existed prior to January 1, 1994. What makes these cases worth mentioning is that both NGOs set their preestablished agendas aside and put all of their energy into supporting the cause of the indigenous people in Chiapas following the uprising. In both cases it can be argued that the redirection of these organizations was directly linked to the Zapatista movement and the desire of people to help the indigenous people in their struggle, rather than in response to TC. However, it can also be argued that the uprising was in itself a response to transnationalized corporatism. It can be further argued that while these organizations have offered support to the indigenous communities they have not themselves jumped on the noncorporatist partial-delinking bandwagon. They still maintain close ties to the prevailing state-society relations model. González Figueroa (2004: 3) reminds us that the "increase in civil organizations [following the 1994 uprising] ... has a direct relationship to the economic, social and political conditions which have characterized poor, rural, [predominantly] indigenous states such as Chiapas." The pressures placed on the Mexican government by the IFIs and the WTO to adopt the neoliberal agenda have had a very negative impact on the people of many rural, indigenous communities.

As Nellys Paloma[11] (interview February 6, 2004) explains, K'inal Antsetik was founded in 1988[12] by a group of feminists, lesbians and indigenous women. The five founding members worked independently with indigenous women around the country as consultants, artisans and in some cases political organizers. Following the Zapatista uprising they decided to work together as a unit. They changed their name, and sought legal registration, an act of incorporation rather than exclusion. The organization has grown to over thirty members, and they currently have a coordinating team in Mexico City, with another one in Chiapas. Their work is divided into the areas of commercialization, production, education, and conflict resolution. Their goal is to work with indigenous women as they develop projects and organizational structures that will empower them and allow them to develop a political conscience to carry them forward in their struggles. Their biggest project has been the creation of a cooperative of artisans with a storefront in San Cristobal de las Casas. Since 1994 they have openly supported the Zapatista initiatives, participated in international forums, pushed for the legalization of abortion in Chiapas, and more recently supported the struggle for autonomy of the indigenous communities. While they support the Other Campaign, they do not themselves delink from the state. They have openly denounced the Plan Puebla Panamá (PPP) because of its anticipated impact on women's lives and livelihoods. Paloma (interview) emphasized the positive impact the Zapatista movement had on the rethinking of political strategies and tactics of the left in Mexico. It has induced left-wing organizations to look beyond their immediate surroundings and to support the indigenous struggle as a worthwhile struggle that goes beyond "class" struggle. Intellectuals, she said, have also had to reassess the importance of identity and cultural politics.

COSACI has followed a similar path to that of K'inal Antsetik. Although formally registered as an NGO in 1996, the members of the Comisión had been doing work with indigenous people around Mexico as early as 1968. In 1994 they joined together to coordinate work in the Zapatista zone in Chiapas. All of the members of COSACI are either doctors or nurses. They support communities with medical supplies, free consultation, vaccinations and training programs for members of the "*promotoras de la salud*" (Irma de la Cruz, interview 2004). Typical of all small, grassroots, nongovernmental efforts, COSACI is faced with the problem of its own inability to remain in the Zapatista area all year long; its volunteers or members make trips to the region three to four times a year. This is, of course, an inadequate substitute for proper health-care services that, if Article 12 of the International Covenant on Economic, Social and Cultural Rights (ratified by Mexico in 1981) were actually taken seriously, would be provided by the government. Three considerations deserve mention. First, necessary medical services have never been provided to the indigenous communities in Chiapas by the state. Consequently, any support from nonstate actors has been welcomed. Second, COSACI's support in the Zapatista area predates the Other Campaign. The importance of the timing is that during the period before the Other Campaign began, any services that were entering the area were in keeping with the anticorporatist strategies of the EZLN at the time. Third, and probably most importantly, the services being provided by COSACI following the initiation of the Other Campaign in 2006 contradict the noncorporatist partial delinking strategies of the EZLN. COSACI and its affiliates all reap the benefits of the current Mexican state-society relations model. Their implicit involvement in the system upholds the model.

Their training programs are an attempt to pass on minimum knowledge to the local "promotoras de la salud" who in turn fill in when external support is unavailable. Health-care has always been of concern in rural Mexico, and although organizations like COSACI and the promotoras themselves provide a bit of a reprieve, many people continue to die of curable diseases. COSACI's projects since 1994 are responding, not to neoliberal reforms, but to the outcry of the Zapatista communities. While their actions have decent, humanitarian intentions, they do not solve the health-care issues in the Zapatista communities. In fact, they could be accused of placating people by offering them band-aid solutions to potentially larger health-care problems (see Petras and Veltmeyer 2005; Kamat 2003). They do not concern themselves with seeking solutions to the lack of infrastructure, namely hospitals, in the region because they do not have the resources to solve these bigger issues.

The biggest wave of NGOs in Mexico emerged under TC.[13] According to the Philanthropic Center in Mexico, there were over 5,000 NGOs working in Mexico in 1998 (in Olvera 2003b: 57). The growth in international funding for these organizations contributed to their increased numbers. A survey conducted by the Secretaría de Gobernación (Secretariat of the Interior) in 2001 (see Somuano 2006: 492) found that there were 2,364 NGOs in 1994, 4,246 in 1997, 4,393 in 1998 and 5,205 in 2000. The number of NGOs worldwide has increased since then. These NGOs focused their attention on issues related to such things as the environment, child care, women, health care, education and general living conditions at the local level. During the 1990s there was also an increase in the establishment of human rights organizations such as the Movimiento Ciudadana para la Democracia (MCD), the Convergencia de Organismos Civiles por la Democracia (COCD), and the Alianza Cívica (AC) (Olvera 2003b: 60). The mandate of these organizations focused on human rights and environmental issues as well as advocating democratization.

Other NGOs emerged in the mid–1990s in the wake of the Zapatista uprising, but they did so opportunistically to take advantage of the political juncture created by the uprising rather than to lend support to the EZLN. The Ciudadanas en Movimiento por la Democracia (CMD) is one such organization of women that jumped on the Zapatista bandwagon. When asked if they had any contact with the EZLN or FZLN or whether they supported the EZLN, Josefina Chavez, the general coordinator of the CMD (interview February 5, 2004), said that they did not. "What I can tell you," she said, "is that we do not exactly have a relationship with them, nor do we support them ... but in 1995 when the army invaded the communities in Chiapas ... we participated as civic observers in a human chain between the army and the indigenous people.... This was part of a national movement for peace." The CMD have worked on many projects related to women's rights, some of which were financed by the Spanish government. Recall Nagar and Raju's (2003) caution about the strings attached to such moneys. They also served as election observers, consultants for the PRD municipal government in Mexico City, members of the INMUJERES in Mexico City, and participants in the Centros Integrales de la Mujer (CIM), also in Mexico City (interview). The organization comprised approximately 280 members[14] when it was founded in 1994, but by 2004, that number had been reduced to 11 members (Chavez interview).

Chavez explains this decimation as resulting from the changing political scene. She said that when the CMD emerged it served as a coalition of women looking for camaraderie with other women searching for answers to the Zapatista uprising and their role in the then political scene. Many of these women were already politically active in more broadly based political parties of all tendencies or organizations and sought kinship with other women. By early 1996, some of these women started to return to their centers of participation and others joined organizations such as DiVersa (Diverse), a national feminist political organization. In the run-up to the 2003 elections many also left the CMD to join the "México Posible" (Possible Mexico) party that was led by Mexican feminist Dora Patricia Mercado Castro. It seems that their demise came as a direct consequence of their wedded relationship with the PRD during the height of Cuauhtémoc Cárdenas' political career and its subsequent decline. In keeping with Fernando Celis' assessment of the EZLN, Chavez also alluded to the sectarian actions of the EZLN. "They don't do outreach work with other political and social organizations," she holds. "Even the Frente Zapatista de Liberción Nacional (FZLN) is not autonomous; they are required to follow the dictates of the EZLN leadership" (interview). Chavez stated that the women's movement in Mexico was still in its very early stages. "Women, she asserted, have been active for many years but their activism has been more issue-based rather than gender-specific." The CMD, like many organizations which emerged in 1994, were somewhat opportunistic in that they took advantage of the EZLN uprising but did not have the political platform to ensure their own longevity.

Granito de Café (Grain of Coffee) is an NGO comprising employees from the UNAM who were concerned about the well-being of the indigenous people in Chiapas and sought ways to help. Maria Eugenia Santilla Ramírez, cofounder, explained (interview 2004) how the organization began in 1994 as a transmitter of information about the Zapatista movement. It was a movement she described as Marxist, akin to her own political convictions and a phenomenon that she figured had been left behind in the 1970s. It was in 1999 when Ofelia Medina, a prominent Mexican actor, attended one of their political events on women's issues that the Granito de Café began to take a different approach. Medina helped them contact the indigenous communities in Chiapas and they began to buy their coffee at a fair price, grind it, roast it, bag it and sell it. Behind their actions were benevolent motives that sought ways to improve the standard of living in the indigenous communities. Although less a political act than a business transaction, the Granito de Café would sell their coffee at political activities in solidarity with the Zapatista movement and independently of the globalized market managed by the state and the international institutions. Their actions are a small example of a parallel, grassroots, fair-trade marketing effort. Granito de Café did not aspire to grow a social movement or to effect change. Its mandate rather was to raise money to buy coffee from the Zapatistas and then sell it at the University or other public events. It was their way of helping the indigenous communities in Chiapas by providing a market, although small, for the sale of their produce. Its approach is very unifocal and escapes the transnationalized corporatist state-society relations in that it functions parallel to and on the fringes of the mainstream economic and political status quo. It asks nothing of government, nor channels anything in the line of taxes in their direction. On a very small scale, the organization's activities demonstrate a form of delinking from the Mexican economy, a concept that will be discussed in detail in chapter 6.

Finally, an example of an international organization that serves as a coalition of NGOs is that of SIPAZ. It was formed in 1995 following the Zapatista uprising by a group of pacifists from the United States who wanted to establish a permanent team of human rights observers who advocated peace. The coalition included church groups, human rights organizations and pacifists. According to the SIPAZ spokesperson (interview May 15, 2004), during the initial years people were sent to the United States for training to learn methods to transform conflict into peace. These trainees would then return to Chiapas and give workshops. Religious affiliates have worked within SIPAZ to strategize peaceful resolutions for some of the intrasocietal conflicts. For an organization to join SIPAZ there is a U.S. $200 annual fee. SIPAZ's mandate is to post bulletins about the events in Chiapas and to serve as a liaison between the indigenous communities and international organizations that want to provide support to those communities. They have also served as human shields in times of conflict. They work within the existing system as they promote peaceful solutions. They do not attempt to change either current state-society relations or social relations of production. At best their actions may be said to be anticorporatist. They take advantage of the window opened by TC to accommodate the influx of NGOs throughout the country. Like the CMD, SIPAZ's actions can best be described as opportunistic.

NGOs vary in their connection to transnationalized corporatism. They are typically tools used by concerned people who want to protect or improve the lives and living conditions of the underprivileged. It is not by chance that thousands of them emerged worldwide as neoliberalism spread around the globe. They work within existing political structures, sometimes to reform them, but more often to patch up some of the damage caused by the neoliberal policies of the capitalist state. The more grassroots the organization, the greater the ability they have to set their own agenda, including adopting an oppositional stance and supporting the political actions of other like-minded oppositional forces. In contrast, NGOs that receive funding from government sources are more unifocal, usually serve as humanitarian aid agencies, and stay clear of "politics." But that does not mean that they do not perform a latent political function. According to Veltmeyer (2007a: 39),

> NGOs for the most part have been converted into policy instruments of the government. They have become mediating agencies that in practice have not assisted capacity building and empowerment of community based organizations.... On the contrary, NGOs have generally contributed to the demobilization of these organizations, a weakening and dispersal.

The sample of NGOs examined above fits Veltmeyer's description as policy instruments of the government, if largely tacit or indirect. Furthermore, it seems quite reasonable to claim that *all* NGOs contribute to the demobilization, weakening and dispersal of the people they are working with. This outcome may be a latent, unintended outcome, rather than a policy of the government to pacify and demobilize people. If they did not have this effect, however, NGOs would be driven out of communities by the government. This is not to suggest that grassroots NGOs go into a community to undo the work that local movements themselves have done, but rather, in most cases, they go to offer their services to help rebuild destroyed communities or to offer services that the government has neglected to provide. Nevertheless, this in turn pacifies people. Few actually enter a community to help the inhabitants mobilize against the government or to participate in existing mobilizations. They usually appear after the damage is done or while it is being done.

Electoral Movements

Given that the electoral process in Mexico was riddled with corruption throughout the years of PRI one-party rule, the struggle to democratize the process has been one of the most important political struggles in recent years (see Olvera 2003a: 351). Electoral reforms have been implemented in response to widespread electoral movements.[15] The most notable of such movements have been those which arose in outraged disbelief at the official results of the 1988 and 2006 presidential elections. Both of these cases will be taken up in the course of the following historical account based on Warnock's (1995) analysis of the presidential and federal elections throughout the history of the PRI one-party state.

Warnock states that the PRI "began a process of political liberalization in 1963" (1995: 129), at which time a system of proportional representation was introduced. This was meant to give opposition parties the ability to be represented in the Chamber of Deputies, yet in practice, as he explains, most parties would have been unable to reach the 2.5 percent of the national vote required to gain representation. The biggest obstacle they encountered was corruption around the electoral process. "The main goal of liberalizing the electoral system was an attempt to preserve PRI domination and to confer some legitimacy on the one-party regime" (130). The year 1977 marked a symbolic turning point as further reforms were implemented to facilitate the participation of opposition parties in the electoral process. Prior to these reforms, it was very difficult for parties to be granted official registration. Numerous left-wing political parties had struggled to survive under PRI one-party rule. The Partido Comunista Mexicano (PCM) was the longest-standing of these opposition parties. Others included the PPS (1960), the Partido Mexicano de los Trabajadores (PMT, 1971), the Partido-Socialista de los Trabajadores (PST, 1976), and the PRT (1976). Each of these parties sought official party status at different periods in the 1970s and 1980s, so that by 1986 many such parties had become immersed in the electoral process (thereby tending to neglect their revolutionary roots!).

The opening up of the electoral system to opposition parties did not, however, signify an end to electoral fraud. In 1988, it became clear that the 1977 reforms were not enough to ensure a democratic electoral process. In preparation for the presidential elections in that year, Cuauhtémoc Cárdenas broke away from the PRI, formed the Corriente Democrática (CD) and ran for president. On election day in 1988 the computers crashed at a point in time when the Cárdenas coalition was leading in the counts. Many irregularities were reported and the ballots were subsequently burned leaving no paper trail of the actual votes.

As a result of the political unrest that followed the 1988 election, the government began working on reforming the electoral system again. Meanwhile the CD transformed itself in 1988/89 into the PRD,[16] drawing in members of many of the left-wing parties who supported Cárdenas's bold move of rejecting the PRI. Not surprisingly, the PRD immediately became the object of propaganda campaigns by the corporate and state-oriented media, and political repression by the PRI-dominated state itself. According to Zambrano Grijalva (2001: 11), "600 PRD militants died during the Salinas government" of 1988–1994. These twin developments of grudging extension of electoral democracy on the one hand, accompanied by repression of political mobilization on the other, represent the somewhat desperate strategy of velvet glove and iron hand used by corrupt, authoritarian-at-heart governments to maintain their position of power and quash opposition. Such a double-edged response is in keeping with the two-facedness of transnationalized corporatism — formal political freedom on the one hand with substantive "incorporation" of opposition, corruption, fraud, repression and ruthless economic disenfranchisement on the other.

Central to the new electoral reforms was the creation of the Instituto Federal Electoral (IFE) in 1991. The IFE was managed by the state until 1996 when it became an autonomous institution. Professional staff rather than political appointees came to manage the institution. Other advances during this period of reformation were the formal recognition of international observers, the establishment of campaign spending limits and the regulation of media time during election campaigns. The 1990 reforms also made it more difficult for parties to be granted official party status because of the new minimum number of votes needed to maintain official status. This eventually led to the demise of the PST and the weakening of the PPS.[17]

While the government was institutionalizing the regulation and monitoring of the electoral process, civil society was organizing itself in defense of political rights by organizing electoral monitoring teams of its own. The result of many small election observation teams being scattered throughout the country was the formation of the Alianza Cívica (AC) in 1994, which centralized the civic monitoring process. The alliance was a coalition of prodemocratic NGOs such as:

> Convergencia de Organismos Civiles por la Democracia, el Movimiento Ciudadano por la Democracia..., la Academia Mexicana de Derechos Humanos [AMDH]..., el Acuerdo por la Democracia [AD], el Instituto Superior de la Cultura Democrática [ISCD], la Asamblea por el Sufragio Efectivo [ASE] ... y la Fundación Arturo Rosenblueth [FAR] [Olvera 2003a: 358].

Its original objective was to monitor the 1994 presidential election campaigns and the electoral process. It also conducted election polls to determine people's expectations of the election results. For the 1994 elections it had over 12,000 legally registered observers throughout the polling stations in the country and an additional 6,000 unregistered observers (Olvera 2003a: 359–360). The association produced reports of irregularities before and during the elections. They also trained election observers before sending them out into the field. We should remember that the 1994 election was further complicated by the assassination of PRI candidate Luis Donaldo Colosio, immediately preceded by the proclamation of NAFTA and the Zapatista uprising on January 1, 1994, haunted by the residue from the 1988 electoral fiasco, and held in the wake of an economic crisis that began the decade. Salinas went to great lengths to establish a protocol prior to the 1994 elections that he hoped would prevent the uncertainty of the 1988 results. For example,

polling-booth officials would be ordinary citizens.... Electoral ballots would have numbered slips to prevent the stuffing of ballots.... Upon casting their ballots, voters would
have their fingers marked with indelible ink. Each voter would have a new voter card
with that person's name and address, voter identification number, photograph, signa-
ture, and fingerprint ... [and] no electoral lists or ballots could be destroyed during the
six months following the election [Domínguez 1999: 6].

According to Olvera (2003a: 361n), in the end the combined work of the AC and
the Unidad de Observación Electoral (UOE), a United Nations–backed initiative, succeeded in giving legitimacy to the electoral process. Fieldwork conducted by the author
in 2001 suggests that there was also a component of "fear voting" during the 1994 elections.
That is, people voted for the PRI because it presented itself as the only party capable of
maintaining stability in the country in the face of the Zapatista uprising. The AC's final
assessment of the 1994 electoral process was that it was legal yet illegitimate because of
the inequitable distribution of resources that overwhelmingly favored the PRI (Olivera
2003a: 361).

Before 1994 the PRI was the only party that had access to radio and television airtime.
In 1994 opposition parties were given 108 hours during nonpeak viewing times. This was
increased to 906 hours in 1997 (Aziz Nassif and Sánchez 2003c: 71). That said, the media
in Mexico continue to be dominated by the state apparatus and its corporate cronies who
systematically exclude the voice of oppositional forces and dissent, and serve up a steady
diet of ruling party propaganda. Nevertheless, the reforms introduced in the 1990s, while
by no means inclusive, did set the stage for greater democratization of the electoral system
in Mexico (see Domínguez and McCann 1996: 178–179). According to Aziz Nassif and
Sánchez (2003b: 50), it was not until 1997 that the electoral system could be considered
equitable. This was the first time that the three principal parties were spread around the
country; before then each of the three major parties had its greatest influence in particular
regions.

As was reported in the presidential elections in 2006 by numerous sources (see *La
Jornada, el Proceso, el Milenio*), the perceived equality in the electoral process did not
resolve the historical problem of electoral fraud. However, what is most telling about the
developments in the electoral process in Mexico is the fact that the majority of the electoral
reforms were introduced under TC. I am not suggesting that the road to democracy has
been facilitated by transnationalized corporatism, but would simply like to acknowledge
the partial historical correlation of these two processes. Some factors that would need to
be considered in order to explain fully the timing of electoral reforms include such things
as pressure coming from the United States to democratize the country in order to build
the confidence of the business sector, pressure from international institutions that required
greater transparency before handing out further economic incentives, and the government's
fear of a repeat of the social unrest following the 1988 election.

Arguably the most important political event in Mexico since 1929 was the electoral
defeat of the PRI in the presidential elections in 2000. Following over seventy years of
one-party rule, Mexicans participated in what appeared to be democratic elections. However, this did not set a precedent for the elections that followed. Subsequent municipal,
state and federal election results have been contested by many communities throughout
Mexico because of electoral fraud. Election results such as those in July 2003 in Tlalnepantla Morelos, where the population rejected the official results and created their own

parallel government, demonstrate a failed process. Similarly, in November 2004 the population rejected the election results in Paracho, Michoacán on the grounds of electoral fraud and also created a parallel government (see Chapman 2005 for both of these cases). The election of Ulises Ruiz Ortiz in Oaxaca is also questionable. Even the 2006 presidential elections were riddled with inconsistencies. It may sound harsh to refer to a "failed democratic process," but as things become more sophisticated in the Mexican electoral process, and the IFE becomes more established, so also do the criticisms. Prior to 2000, nobody could justifiably refer to the electoral process as liberal-democratic. That said, the presidential election in 2006 is widely seen as a clear example of a failed process. Failed democracy is directly reflected in and by the existing state-society relations. It should thus come as no surprise that the EZLN rejected the electoral process in a country marred by electoral fraud and political uncertainty, or that the PRD was able to draw millions of people into the streets to denounce the electoral results.

The popular response (see Tamayo 2007) to the 2006 presidential elections was unprecedented in Mexico. Equally important is the fact that such a mass movement was not repressed by the government. Again, this can best be explained under the transnationalized corporatist model where state actors become necessarily subservient to the norms of the transnational forces that have come to shape the way the state interacts with nonstate actors. López Obrador and his supporters engaged in numerous activities in their attempt to reverse the official electoral results. Although unsuccessful in this endeavor, they were successful in making it very difficult for the PAN to govern for the first year of its six-year term. Their actions forced the Tribunal Federal Electoral (TRIFE) to recount 9 percent of the polling stations. Numerous events of long-standing tradition in Mexico, such as the State of the Union speech, were interfered with. The speech is usually delivered by the president on September 1 each year, but, as mentioned in the introduction, following the 2006 presidential election the giving of the speech was blocked by PRD representatives who descended on the congressional platform and left the president with no other option than to submit a hard-copy of his report to the legislative assembly. Independence Day celebrations on September 15, which were historically presided over by the president, were also disrupted and relocated to the city center in Dolores Hidalgo from the Zócalo in Mexico City. A further disruption occurred on November 20, the day that marks the triumph of the Mexican Revolution, when commemorative events were orchestrated by community groups rather than by the state. The breaking of these traditions was a consequence of the fear of political conflict. In the streets, the PRD held many protests and set up a tent city that wove through the main streets of downtown Mexico City. The camp-in lasted for forty-nine days and stretched for about seven miles. It attracted over 2 million supporters. On September 16, a day after removing the tent city, the PRD held a Convención Nacional Democrática (CND) in the Zócalo. Although it was only symbolic in nature,[18] the convention delegates approved ten motions including one that would declare López Obrador the "legitimate president of Mexico" and another that he would be sworn in on November 20. On the twentieth, the swearing-in ceremony was held as programmed without incident but with a slightly smaller crowd witnessing the event than had participated in the previous protests. This was followed on the first of December with the official swearing in of Felipe Calderón under strong protest by the opposition forces.

The 2006–2012 sexenio could turn out to be telling for the future of Mexico. López

Obrador has been made out to be a Chavez follower by the mainstream media in an attempt to create fear in the electorate. Although he never professed to advocate a left-wing platform, and in fact wanted to reassure transnational corporations and their governing bodies that he would maintain neoliberal policies, his supporters pushed him in the opposite direction. MacDonald (2006: 24) describes the situation in the following way:

> Obrador was pushed left. The Mexican Chavez which had hitherto existed only in the imagination of the country's ruling class was taking form. By early August, Obrador was slamming Mexico's rich for fleecing the country, vowing to break neoliberalism and, later that month, to create a "cradle-to-grave" welfare state paid for by a redistribution of the country's wealth.

Electoral politics in a country with a prolonged history of fraudulent practices are not easily democratized. Although government practices have changed little, it seems that nonstate actors have a renewed sense of confidence as they take to the streets in defense of democratic electoral processes. This renewed sense of confidence cannot be explained by the electoral reforms or the "social crisis produced by neoliberalism" alone (MacDonald 2006: 25). Rather, one must take into account López Obrador's determination and willingness to be led by his supporters; the impoverishment of a large section of the population; a political platform that promised to preserve social programs, end poverty and redistribute the wealth; and the copresence of other important social movements in Mexico such as the Other Campaign and the popular struggle in Oaxaca. All of these struggles, either overtly or otherwise, are working against the consequences of neoliberalism or are seeking ways to reduce economic disparities and such problems as hunger, housing and unemployment that are pervasive throughout Mexican society. There are no guarantees that, if elected in the future, the PRD would transform state-society relations. They are not a revolutionary party but rather a coalition representing many ideological backgrounds that seek political power within the capitalist mode of production. As an oppositional force, they may appear to reject corporatist relations, but, in practice, they have been accused of having their own internal corporatist relations.

Gremial Social Movements

There have been many gremial social movements throughout Mexico since the 1970s. Such movements, including guerrilla movements, indigenous struggles for autonomy, women's rights movements and national fronts against globalization, privatization and electoral fraud all deal with matters that are specific to the membership of their group. Their mandates clearly define the particulars of their struggles, which tend to attract participants who have the same demands based on their geographical location, their identity, their economic class or their cultural background. The gremial social movements examined here have historical roots that define them and demands that identify them, yet the dialectical modifications found within each movement over time are often closely linked to political-economic changes. For example, the indigenous movement, which has historically addressed geographically defined issues related to land rights and autonomy, came to enunciate anticapitalist, anti-neoliberal slogans for the first time as it organized behind the EZLN. The antisystemic impulse of this movement is directly linked to the neoliberal political and economic policies introduced by the state.

In fact, most movements oscillate between gremial and general demands. Most of these "fronts" have been successful at building a stronger opposition and generating political awareness among the people. Gremial social movements may come to *support* antisystemic movements, as was the case with the students supporting the EZLN or the FZLN supporting the students, but the gremial movements themselves do not necessarily turn antisystemic. Under TC, gremial social movement responses are varied. There is no set pattern that all movements follow. However, none of the movements examined engage in delinking or noncorporatist strategies. Therefore, they too fall into the category of anticorporatist because, while they do not have direct corporatist relationships with the state, their actions nevertheless provide tacit support to corporatism.

Two gremial social movements worth examining are the student movement and El Barzón. Both of these movements have demands specific to their members and upon examination will help to clarify the changes in political action that have developed under TC.

The Student Movement

The student movement at UNAM is important because of its size, the size of the university and the impact that it has on other sectors of society such as the administrative staff, faculty members and the high school students who are waiting for their opportunity to enroll in a postsecondary institution. On a given day there are over 300,000 people on the campus of the UNAM in Mexico City (Ciudad Universitaria — CU), making UNAM the biggest public university in Mexico. Of concern here is how the student movement of 1968 compares to the student movement of 1999. Have their demands and actions changed under transnationalized corporatism?

1968 marked a watershed in Mexican politics (as it did in the politics of much of the rest of the world). University students from across the country took to the streets demanding "freedom for political prisoners; dismissal of the police chiefs; abolition of the Granaderos (Grenadiers)[19]; abrogation of the crime of 'social dissolution'; compensation for the families of the dead and wounded; determination of responsibility for the repression" (Hodges and Gandy 2002: 96). These slogans were used to denounce the repressive actions of the state throughout the 1960s. This was at a time when state corporatism was strong and when the state was known to use repressive actions to control sectors of society that escaped its corporatist grip. The mass protests in 1968 coincided with the "dirty war" conducted by the government of Mexico against both left-wing guerrilla and political organizations (1968–1980), and with Mexico's hosting of the Summer Olympics. The student movement quickly took on national characteristics and received support from the SME, "revolutionary organizations," taxi drivers, teachers and other groups of concerned citizens. During these months of growing mass protests, thousands of students were taken prisoner, and in the end at least two thousand students and ordinary citizens were killed. Street demonstrations grew from 15,000 participants to over 400,000 after the movement created a directive body known as the Consejo Nacional de Huelga (CNH). On October 2, 1968, one week before the Olympic Games, government forces surrounded the Tlatelolco square, where protesters had gathered in a peaceful demonstration, and began shooting. Hodges and Gandy (100) describe the scene as follows.

> The massacre was an ambush. The government carried it out in a conscious and planned manner. The agents of the police infiltrated the multitude; when the massacre began, they put a white sign around their left wrists so that they could recognize each other. The 5,000 soldiers with hundreds of tanks completely surrounded the plaza: there was no way out or around or through. A helicopter tossed out flares, and the army began shooting to kill.

On the two or three days before the protest and on the day of the massacre itself, the movement had been dwindling in numbers. It is reported that about 5,000 people attended the protest (Hodges and Gandy 2002: 100). Contrary to Tilly's assessment of social movement development, Zermeño holds that in the case of the 1968 student movement "the ruling class had not drifted into a political crisis" (see Hodges and Gandy 2002: 102). If anything, it could be argued that the students simply were not willing to be co-opted and that they took advantage of the hype around the upcoming Olympics to attract attention to their demands. Although there were some revolutionary sectors within the movement, the demands were not revolutionary, nor were they class-based demands or workers' demands but rather demands of citizens against "illegitimate" authority. Various authors (see González Casanova 1974; Cañibe in Suárez 1976) refer to the movement as one comprising middle-class discontents, an argument which may explain why the surviving protesters reverted to their gremial demands following the massacre. The student movement of the 1960s is a good example of a gremial struggle that happened to be led by students which, through a process of unification, grew into a national coalition with more generalized, although not antisystemic, demands and which in the end returned to its gremial struggles.

The student movement continued on university and high school campuses throughout the 1970s, 1980s and 1990s with a different face and under different banners. Student organizations were formed at the faculty level and attempts were made to create campus wide organizations. During this period, the demands of the struggle ranged from an end to political repression and the preservation of public education, to rejection of the imposition of one rector or another and respect for university autonomy. Throughout the 1990s, reforms to the education system were introduced which awakened a new wave of student organizing. In 1996–1997 the "direct" admission to UNAM for students who had completed their high school education at an institution that was run, authorized and affiliated with the UNAM was terminated. Admission exams came to be administered by an extra-university corporation called the Centro Nacional de Evaluaciones (CENEVAL). CENEVAL also had the power to determine who was granted a bachelor's degree (see Julieta et al. 2001). The exam it administers tests students' general academic knowledge, but it also asks personal socioeconomic questions such as How much do your parents earn? How many light bulbs are in your house? and Is the washroom inside or outside the house? (Ivonne et al. 2001: 35). This type of interrogation suggests a means of filtering out poorer students from higher education. Funding for the public universities was dramatically cut, and general maintenance deteriorated dramatically during this period. Resistance to these reforms was strongest at the high school level. Political activities on university campuses came to be restricted to auditoria and designated areas, all other activities having been forcibly prohibited.

In February 1999 the student movement took on a new dimension when it brought the university to a standstill for over ten months in response to Rector Barnes's ruling to establish fixed tuition fees (Julieta et al. 2001: 17). The students rejected the imposition of fixed rates for five reasons: (1) it violated Article 3 of the constitution which states that the government has the obligation to provide free higher education[20]; (2) it was approved in an authoritarian manner behind closed doors; (3) the proposed increase in fees would not solve the financial or academic problems of the university, implying that the rector's motives were dishonest; (4) higher education was paid for through taxes, so that charging students would set a precedent for future tuition hikes and would result in double payment for a service that is a constitutional right; (5) it was an initiative that originated with international institutions such as the World Bank and the IMF and their neoliberal, structural adjustment programs (see ibid.: 20–21).

Characteristic of the period before and during the February 1999 strike was the autonomy demanded by the many schools and faculties that participated in the political action. Activities spread from classrooms to massive university public meetings to street protests. Unlike previous student movements, parents participated alongside their children and organized their own meetings. They even had their own newsletter (Enrique et al. 2001: 44–45). The 1999 strike continued throughout the electoral campaign for the 2000 presidential elections. Although there appears to be no evidence that the student movement was connected to this process, there is testimony by some participants that they rejected the electoral process on grounds that once in office politicians sell out to the status quo (Tania et al. 2001: 50–51). Support for the student movement came from many different organizations, collectives, parties and fronts and in many different forms. As with the 1968 movement, organizations gave their support by signing petitions, publicizing the movement in their own newsletters, participating in marches and collecting money to support the movement. Neighborhood organizations, teachers, laborers, the FZLN, the Frente Popular Francisco Villa (FPFV), the POS, the Partido de la Revolución Socialista (PRS), La Guillotina, the Katrina, the Zavinos, the CNT, the SME, the SITUAM, the STUNAM and the SINTCB are just a few of the organizations mentioned in Rosas's (2001) collection that supported the student movement.

On the seventh of June the rector presented a new proposal which was to exempt any student whose family earned less than four minimum salaries (twenty dollars a day) from their proposed fixed rates. Students would have to petition for the exemption. The university hoped that this gesture would bring an end to the strike, yet many students still took exception to this proposal and the strike continued, although with less support and clearer divisions. Participants were suffering from burnout, many had lost or were losing hope, divisions grew within the movement on the issue of continuing the strike or accepting the rector's proposal, and attendance at assemblies declined. In late July, emeritus professors joined together in an unsuccessful attempt to pressure both sides to come to a negotiated agreement. It was not until mid–November that Barnes resigned and left the shattered university in the hands of his successor, Juan Ramon de la Fuente. De la Fuente was able to bring both sides to the negotiating table, and on the tenth of December a four-point agreement was signed. This marked the beginning of the end of the conflict. In January there were two plebiscites, one organized by the Comité General de Huelga (CGH) and the other one organized by Gobernación (Internal Affairs) and the general secretary of the STUNAM. On February 1, the police descended on the university and the affiliated high schools. Many students were arrested and others were attacked and released. In a community called Azcapotzalco, there were over seven hundred students arrested (Cecilia et al. 2001: 183). The end of the strike left the university community divided.

The gremial demands that began the strike showed signs of expansion when the students marched in solidarity with the antiglobalization protests that took place in Seattle in late 1999. The primary focus of the movement, however, was university based from the beginning right through to the point when a combination of negotiation and political repression ended things. The CGH rejected participation of nonstudents in the decision-making process during the strike. This excluded faculty, administration and community activists. Behind the governmental and university administrative reforms that initially sparked the movement were the interests of corporate leaders who wanted to see publicly funded education privatized. There were actually two possible outcomes to these reforms: first, by restricting enrollment in the public schools there would be greater demand for enrollment in private high schools and universities, and second, by charging tuition fees and fees for services there would be funds available to compensate for the reduction in government funding; the onus would be put on the students, thus restricting education to middle- and upper-class families. Because of the long history of publicly funded education in Mexico and the history of protest that exists, it will be difficult for the government openly to privatize education without an uprising similar to that of 1968 or 1999. However, given the transient nature of students, it is difficult to transform such a movement into an antisystemic or sustainable popular movement. The economic composition of the student body is also a factor that needs to be considered.

The student movement of 1999 emerged during a period when state-society relations were directly influenced by transnational forces. The attempt to introduce tuition fees to one of the largest publicly funded universities in Latin America is, in itself, not an unexpected move on the part of the Mexican government. As the government took to reducing public spending on all social services, education was one of the services the cost of which they were eager to pass on to, or at least share with, the "consumer." In 1968 there was no threat to the education system as a publicly funded institution, but what concerned the students during that period of state corporatism was the brutality of the state against the student population in particular. Under TC the focus changed when the students felt the public nature of the university under threat. As with the teachers' movement in Oaxaca, the students' movement quickly drew support from civil society, which is largely in favor of maintaining a publicly funded education system. The government response was very different in each of these cases. In 1968 there was direct repression when the army surrounded the square and started firing, whereas in 1999 the strike was allowed to continue for an extended period of time, shutting down the university for over ten months. This is not to suggest that there was no repression in 1999 on the part of the state, but rather that it was done more strategically. While students and young people are easily influenced and are often drawn to revolutionary parties, the general sentiment of the 1968 and 1999 student movements was not revolutionary but rather reformist. Their actions and the outcome of the movement in 1999 were in keeping with the status quo. Although the 1999 movement was drawn out, there was never an attempt to establish an independent education system run by the students for the students, for example. While students do not maintain a corporatist relationship with the state, the university administration does, as we saw when we examined the STUNAM. This reality makes it difficult for the students to go it alone.

El Barzón

The indigenous peoples and peasants have also engaged in their own gremial struggles over the years. Similar to the waves of other social movements, the peasants' movements also come in waves. The first wave ran from 1958 to 1964, and a second wave ran through 1972 and 1973. A third wave emerged in the 1990s with the most recent reforms to Article 27 of the constitution. These waves are indicative of government policies around land distribution, the willingness of governments to enforce the laws, and state-corporatist practices. So-called peasant "land invasions" are actually more properly described as the "taking back" of the lands that had been wrongly confiscated in the first place by large landowners. The first amendment to Article 27 of the constitution introduced by Miguel Alemán in 1947 provided a form of protection for the large landowners against the peasants. Under this reformed article, the peasants were not allowed to act independently by invading lands or taking them back through force. Hundreds of thousands of acres of land were nevertheless taken back in a single land invasion. Between 1940 and 1972 there were forty-one reported land occupations (see Hodges and Gandy 2002: 173). Ideally, land invasions would end with the state dividing the land among the squatters, but more often than not they ended with the state moving in and flattening the makeshift communities, and killing or disappearing the leaders and/or members of the community. These movements were driven by the right to possess land, and although they reached out to other movements, they generally remained focused on their immediate needs. Strategies changed somewhat under transnationalized corporatism as will become apparent with the examination of the Barzón movement.

In 1993 sectors of small and large agricultural enterprises joined together in El Barzón to defend their economic interests. El Barzón set a precedent for middle- and upper-class demands against the government and their economic and legal practices. This northern-based movement emerged in the state of Jalisco in 1993 with very localized demands.[21] It quickly spread to other regions of the country. According to Grammont (2001: 20), this movement of rural "*deudores*" was the first social uprising to resonate throughout the country in its disapproval of the new economic order. The participants were middle-class farmers who had benefited from the green revolution in Mexico by receiving federal funding to expand their industries. The neoliberal policies that modified land ownership rights, eliminated government subsidies and introduced commercial borrowing agencies were not welcomed by these farmers who depended on the land for their survival. Prior to the introduction of neoliberal reforms, Banrural was the primary rural financial institute. It was heavily subsidized and supported by the government, which, in a time of need, would cover the losses for unpaid debt. Under the new arrangement with commercial banks, which were often foreign-owned commercial banks, judicial measures were implemented to force partial if not full repayment. Interest rates were also much higher than the old rates managed by Banrural.

When it first emerged the movement characterized itself as apolitical, but by the end of September 1994 one part of the organization came to sympathize with the PRD and the other with the PRI. The PRD group is referred to as the Barzón-Unión and the PRI group as the Barzón-Confederación (Grammont: 20–21). Grammont (22) describes the whole movement as a struggle of middle-class agricultural workers who benefited for many years from corporatist relationships with the government but came to rebel against this arrangement when they began to feel excluded by the structural changes that were being implemented. The movement's struggle had many dimensions: it criticized the new economic model; it also fought to eliminate the divide between the rural producers and urban consumers, and between the social and the political arenas — all demands that surpassed the demand of the right to land of its predecessors.

Grammont (2001) describes the role of women fighting to defend the well-being of their families as paramount for the sustainability of the movement. The movement was by no means homogeneous. Regional groups were formed and aligned with the political party with which they felt the greatest affinity. Organizations moved in and out of El Barzón. Oaxaca in the south and Sonora in the north had differing needs and preestablished connections, both of which would dictate the actions in their own region. It would be incorrect to refer to this movement as antisystemic because it depended heavily on the capitalist system for protection, yet it rejected neoliberal policies that opened the market to transnational corporations and private financial institutions, actions that would allow us to refer to the movement as anti-neoliberal. One of El Barzón's primary strategies was to try to reopen negotiations with the government, not in the old corporatist style necessarily but through dialogue that would guarantee the basic demands of the agricultural workers and ensure reasonable repayment programs. They sought formal recognition from the state, a characteristic of corporatism. As time progressed and neoliberalism became more engrained it became harder to reestablish these relationships, and the farmers were instructed to take their concerns to the Secretaría de Hacienda y Crédito Público. Unlike the student movement, El Barzón did not draw popular support to its cause. According to Flores Benavides (1999), its successes included a debt moratorium, a judicial truce and the implementation of just payments. While the other social movements examined earlier struggled for demands that went beyond their own personal interests, middle-class movements like the Barzón focus on their members' own immediate, economic interests by engaging with the transnationalized corporatist model.

Gremial social movements can be found throughout the country and with varying agendas. They range from class-specific to cross-class, agenda-specific "interest groups." Many of them preceded the emergence of TC. Their strategies cannot be said to interfere seriously with the operation of corporatism, even though most of them engage in anticorporatist actions. As international forces have become more influential in national politics through structural adjustment programs and economic reforms, social movements have adjusted their demands to reject these extranational impositions. The primary target of political dissent continues to be the government and its institutions or a given corporation, depending on which movement organization we are talking about. As reported above, such movements hold the Mexican government responsible for repression (student movement), for the negative economic impact caused by neoliberal reforms (Barzón) and for its corrupt electoral practices (electoral movement).

In general, gremial movements can be seen to be acting in response to the economic and social inequality inherent in capitalism. The transition from state capitalism to transnationalized, neoliberal capitalism (parallel to the change from state to transnationalized corporatism) witnessed a change in political strategies by most of the organizations examined. While not all organizations identify with class politics in Marx's sense, their work does respond to the economic and political inequities that arise from capitalist relations of production. In the case of the 1999 students' movement, the transition brought new demands to the table and resulted in outreach practices that went beyond those of 1968. The Barzón is the first middle-class farmers' movement in the history of Mexico, which is indicative of the polarizing dynamics of state-society relationships under neoliberalism. The strategies adopted by the Barzón movement are very different from those practiced by the indigenous peasant movements, as we will see in chapter 5. The electoral movement is one that has emerged as electoral reforms have been introduced under TC, affording greater confidence in the electorate that organized political action in relation to elections will be effective.

Conclusions

The transition from state-corporatism to TC has brought about a wide variety of responses from nonstate actors. Here I will summarize and distill the significance of the response strategies and actions detailed in this chapter and the one preceding it. While many of the organizations and movements discussed above do not have corporatist ties with the state, and do engage in anticorporatist activities, nevertheless their actions may be interpreted theoretically as contributing to maintaining the corporatist structures that are such a cultural fixture in Mexican politics. The strongest corporatist ties continue to exist between the state and the official union leaders representing employees at state-owned and state-run services or firms. Within these official unions not all workers willingly submit to the corporatist practices of their leaderships. There are many cases, such as the SNTE, where, within the ranks of the union, members dissent and denounce the corporatist relationship. There are also cases where independent unions are established parallel to the official unions. These anticorporatist actions weaken the power of the state over the workers. Unions in general are working-class organizations that continue to advocate for the basic rights of the workers. Under TC, many have extended their focus beyond the factory floor or the workplace and formed alliances with other unions in their fight against neoliberal reforms and corporatism. The scope of their agenda and their outreach activities are what is unique to TC. Reform is nevertheless their approach. It is an approach that struggles to ensure their own survival against the will of international institutions and the Mexican government. They do not engage in delinking strategies by taking over the factories and running them themselves. That said, unions are by no means all alike. Their organizing involves a variety of activities.

Many unions have shifted from basic gremial demands to more general national and international demands. This shift coincides with TC. They have also turned to the media and the Internet as a means to disseminate their message, a new approach that was absent under state corporatism. Given the international scope of the state agenda, many unions are also reaching out to their international counterparts to create a more effective transnational response. This outreach is in a preliminary stage and still quite fragmented. While independent unions escape the grip of state corporatism, they are not immune to the political-economic developments under TC. It is not in doubt that the internal structures of many of these organizations are themselves corporatist in nature.

Opposition parties have not changed their quotidian strategies under TC. The primary change has been the willingness of most of them to unite behind a common candidate during election time. They have also formed alliances with organizations from which they had previously distanced themselves on the grounds of political differences. They can now be observed pushing to refine and defend the liberal-democratic process, which many rejected or refused to engage in under state corporatism. While some parties maintain a notably revolutionary discourse, their actions reveal reformist convictions, which confine them to the anticorporatist category. Political parties beyond the PAN and the PRI have not been put to the test of corporatism while in a position of power, and it is unlikely that they will come to hold that power through the electoral process anytime soon. One could argue that given the historical trajectory and staying power of corporatist relationships in Mexico, transnationalized corporatism will likely persist for some time into the future regardless of which party is in power.

Like unions, NGOs are not all the same, not least because of their different approaches, sources of funding and political agendas. Nevertheless, one thing they have in common is the fact that they are not accountable to the people they serve. They do not enjoy the legitimacy of the very state whose role they are fulfilling by providing services or engaging in projects that the state traditionally performed. Whether we describe them as "weapons of pacification," "an arm of the government" or a bearer of "something new and important," NGOs have flourished under TC.

NGOs are not class-based organizations and they do not engage in transformative politics; rather they engage in activities (beyond providing humanitarian aid and relief to victims of natural disasters and wars) designed to repair the tears in the social fabric of capitalist society, a practice that puts them in the anticorporatist category. Whether buying and selling coffee to benefit the indigenous people in Chiapas or organizing women to give them a voice, most of their activities seek to benefit the dispossessed sectors of society while not challenging the existing structures. NGOs are people organizing or regrouping to find solutions to the inherent inequalities or deficiencies of the capitalist mode of production. Unlike the other organizations examined here, NGOs tend to work independently of each other. This often results in the duplication of services and projects. This will become evident in the discussion about NGOs and the EZLN in chapter 5. In keeping with Veltmeyer's assessment of NGO work, it seems that while their intentions are unquestionably humanitarian, the results of their actions tend to pacify an otherwise potentially combative sector of society — the dispossessed.

In the electoral movement, where the curtailment of effective political participation is a built-in concomitant of capitalism, unrest has been exacerbated by the neoliberal reforms. While resistance to these conditions is to be expected across the conventional spectrum of social division, the magnitude of the electoral movements of 1988 and 2006 is unique to transnationalized corporatism. TC may seem on the face of it to be incompatible with the liberal democratization process. Recall Ramírez's (2003) argument that corporatist relationships create obstacles to the democratization process and undermine the creation of pluralist state-society relations. However, it turns out that one does not necessarily exclude the other, especially when corporatism of different sorts has existed in Mexico since the colonial period and has become the standard way of doing politics. In fact, corporatist relationships continue to exist at all levels of society in Mexico. Even though electoral reforms have been introduced (in fits and starts) since 1963, transparency and a clean process have not been part of them. It is difficult to celebrate the reforms when the very composition of the IFE and the appointment of its directors have been questioned. As mentioned above, political parties have united in their attempt to defend the liberal-democratic electoral process, yet internal relationships in many political parties are themselves often considered corporatist in nature. Reforms in and of themselves have not eliminated transnationalized corporatist relationships in Mexico nor have they produced reliable election results. It has been by force and fraud that the state has maintained control of the electoral process.

Like other gremial social movements, the students' movement is unifocal. This is not to suggest that it will not extend its support to other movements, but what it does mean is that as a gremial movement it has a specific agenda connected to its local sites of dispute. Once local issues are resolved, the movement tends to disappear from the political scene and to conform to the political order. As mentioned above the strategies used by the student movement are anticorporatist. The student movement is not class specific; its membership crosses over class lines.

The Barzón movement is a class-based movement with a very specific agenda. Unlike previous movements in the agricultural sector that focused on land rights and were peasant based, the Barzón is a middle-class movement confronting the economic policies of the government. Their demands are profit driven. The Barzón movement and the student movement work within the existing capitalist framework and surface when they feel a threat to their interests. This is what makes a gremial movement a gremial movement and what makes these movements anticorporatist. The Barzón movement has capitalized on its indispensable role in the Mexican economy, as representative of the national agricultural sector, to lobby the government and the financial institutions in its efforts to protect the individual interests of its members. In the end it is unclear, and may never be clear, whether the accomplishments of the movement to date have been thanks to the corporatist nature of its relationship with the state or whether it has been more a question of clientelism.

While some movements have modified their strategies to a greater degree than others have, all movements have had to adapt to the new political-economic order. There is not one sequential path followed by the different nonstate actors in Mexico. The transition from state corporatism to TC has not resulted in the implementation of the same strategies for all organizations. While not all organizations maintain direct corporatist relationships with the state, none of the organizations examined above have engaged in noncorporatist forms of resistance. In the case of those actors that have taken anticapitalist stances, it is clear that their rhetoric is rarely matched by their actions. It is fine to utter anticapitalist, anti-neoliberal slogans, but this does not result in delinking strategies. To delink or to adopt noncorporatist strategies would entail going it alone, rejecting and working outside of the existing political-organizational structures. In other words, the nonstate actors we have examined in this chapter work within the limits of liberal-capitalist democracy. They do not go beyond the corporatist–liberal-democratic conjuncture, but instead work within it. Whether intended or unintended, the consequences of their strategic responses to the changes in the state wrought by the neoliberal imperative have been to "integrate" state-society relations into the broader framework of transnationalized corporatism.

The next chapter will observe how the EZLN has attempted to step outside prevailing state-society relations by going from a noncorporatist strategy on January 1, 1994 (war of position), to immediately adopting anticorporatist methods (first declaration of the Lacandon Jungle) before returning to a partial noncorporatist approach (delinking).

5

The Zapatista Movement

Introduction

The Zapatista movement is the most important movement to emerge since the early 1980s to respond directly to the current political and economic developments in Mexico. It is the most important movement for principally three reasons. Firstly, its anticapitalist, anti-neoliberal discourse reflects a political-economic analysis that actually identifies the real structure of dominance in the country; in this regard its perspective goes far beyond the vision and goals of the other social movements.[1] Secondly, it has *acted* on this analysis in the most radical fashion by partially delinking itself, for the most part, from the governance structures of the Mexican state. Such antisystemic actions have been most clearly demonstrated with the creation of the Juntas de Buen Gobierno in 2003 and the initiation of the Other Campaign (OC) in 2006. And thirdly, it has experimented with an eclectic mix of strategies in its determination to go it alone.

In what follows, the historical developments of the Zapatista movement and its struggle to effect political change in a country immersed in the globalized market economy will be examined, a country which maintains a transnationalized corporatist model of state-society relations. It will be argued that the strategies it adopted during the uprising of January 1, 1994, were revolutionary and, while noncorporatist, quickly led to a negotiation process with the government. This resulted in an extended period of anticorporatist strategic actions which served to maintain the status quo. More recently, the movement has taken on a more noncorporatist or postcorporatist stance. These different stages of the movement demonstrate a form of radical eclecticism. Through noncorporatist actions the Zapatista movement has managed to loosen the corporatist grip of the state,[2] first by its armed uprising in 1994 and second by its partial delinking from the government. Its partial delinking strategies supplant most of the services and financial and political support which would otherwise come from the federal or state governments. In this way it is creating a new polity guided by the Sixth Declaration of the Lacandon Jungle, and undermining the conditions for corporatism in Mexico (something anticorporatism ironically fails to do).

The author disagrees with McAdam et al.'s theory (2001), which, if it were applied to the Mexican Revolution, would necessarily argue that the revolution developed as a result of the *opportunity* opened up by the centralization of the state and the democratization process that was evolving at the time. A similar dilemma surfaces when examining the political uprisings in the 1970s and 1980s throughout Latin America. As suggested in the preface (recall the case of Haiti) and argued in chapter 1, these uprisings were not conditional on the opportunities created by the nation-states or the process of democratization, but rather on the political-economic situation in the countries in question. Other issues that need to be considered when assessing the origins of a movement are its organizational abilities, the political landscape of oppositional forces throughout the country at the time, and more recently the role that nongovernmental organizations and social welfare–type policies play in pacifying otherwise combative sectors of society.

The one-party, authoritarian regime in Mexico established by the PRI did not weaken the development of social movements during their seventy-one years in power, even though these movements were repeatedly met by very violent acts of state repression. Similar acts of repression have been employed by the PAN during the current period of "democratization." If one were to consider further McAdam et al.'s (2001) theory of opportunity then one might ask why it is that the EZLN did not emerge in the early 1980s when the PRI showed signs of weakening, or following the elections of 1988 when a series of electoral reforms were introduced, or following the earthquake in 1985 when the state proved incapable of dealing with the chaotic aftermath.

At the time of the uprising on January 1, 1994, according to Higgins (2004: 2), Mexico appeared to be a very prosperous country en route to "green[er] pastures" with a strong, centralized government that maintained a close relationship with its northern neighbor, the United States. Examples of Mexico-U.S. partnerships, prevalent since the mid–1990s, include "treasury ministries, national cabinet meetings, border governors' conferences, anti-narcotics aid, NAFTA tri-national institutions, military sales and training, U.S. support for Mexico from multilateral development banks and exchanges between judicial authorities" (Fox 2004: 470). During the period of transition from state-corporatism to TC, the relationship between the two states, intensified. This followed a period of protectionism under an ISI economic model. As relations became more open between the two states, so did the relationship between the Mexican state and the IFIs and WTO. Although these connections grew, it does not follow that they signified "greener pastures" for the majority of the population. For the most part it was the elites that benefited from these relationships, while the mass of the people were faced with the task of finding effective forms of resistance to respond to economic crises and the changes in state-society relations. H. L. Williams (2001: 24–25) explains that the rapid transformation of the Mexican economy from 1982 onward dramatically altered the ways in which protest manifested itself. As the federal government retreated from direct involvement in fiscal programs, industrial production, and the regulation of prices, protesters were faced with the dilemma of deciding against whom they ought to protest.

It was clear to the Zapatistas from the beginning that their immediate enemy was the Mexican state itself, and not in the first place the U.S. state, the international institutions or the transnational corporations (see Muñoz Ramírez 2003 for a historical overview of the movement). While they denounced U.S. policies, international demands and the ease with which transnational corporations took over fertile lands, their energies were directed against the Mexican state which held the power to modify these relationships. The EZLN did not take to the street in 1994 because of a weakened state or a "democratic" opportunity, but rather because they were no longer willing to tolerate political repression, subjugation and economic devastation. They used the promulgation of NAFTA as a symbolic moment at which to emerge from the Lacandon Jungle. They feared repression and got repression, over 100 people being killed in confrontations with the Mexican army in San Cristobal de las Casas. The uprising was in response to the political-economic situation in the country at large, but especially in the region which was dominated by the national and international elites who had driven the indigenous people off their land and into mountainous jungle areas.

Olvera (2004: 416) discusses three significant changes that occurred in Mexico from 1988 to 1994, the period leading up to the Zapatista uprising. The first factor he mentions is the economic and constitutional reforms that were adopted in preparation for NAFTA. As reported in previous chapters, during this period hundreds of state corporations were privatized, and Article 27 of the constitution, which defined land ownership, was modified. The second factor he highlights is that during this period there were multiple electoral reforms which gave opposition political parties a greater chance to compete in the electoral process (as noted in chapter 4). His final observation is that "civil society" organized in defense of political, cultural and judicial rights. In addition to these points, it is important to note that under the Salinas de Gortari regime (1988–1994) there was also an opening of the border to agricultural products from Canada and the United States; the financial, credit and insurance systems were reorganized to allow for greater foreign investment; price controls were lifted off most basic agricultural crops; and many rural industries such as livestock and forestry were deregulated (see MacKinlay 2004: 301). These policies resulted in strengthened capitalist relations of production with the inclusion of the international business elites. Given the dependency on agriculture in the indigenous communities in Chiapas, it should be no surprise that there was a political uprising at a time when their basic means of subsistence were being taken away. Unlike the Barzón movement which was led by middle-class, medium- to large-sized landowners, the Zapatista movement was community based and lacked the infrastructure and financial resources enjoyed by the Barzón farmers.

When the movement emerged from the Lacandon Jungle, many referred to it as a Marxist guerrilla movement, some saw it as a "new social movement," others a class struggle, while still others described it as an indigenous movement. It is the view of the author that the initial uprising on January 1, 1994, is best described as noncorporatist, as it appeared to want to replace the existing government with its own. The characterization of the initial period of the movement may be irrelevant today, but at the time its definition would influence which organizations aligned with the movement and what the alliance amounted to. That is, for example, did they join the movement or simply support it through financial and political means?

The EZLN stated from the outset that they were not a Marxist organization but rather a group of indigenous peasants "demanding political and economic democracy in Mexico ... [In 1994 they called for] basic changes in Mexican society, including fair elections and democratic liberties for all Mexicans" (Ruggiero and Sahulka 1998)—anticorporatist demands. Although they are often referred to as a guerrilla movement, their course of action does not match the conventional definition of a movement which "engages in irregular warfare especially as ... an independent unit carrying out harassment and sabotage" (*Encyclopaedia Britannica* CD-ROM 1999).

Bruhn (1999) uses a content analysis of the early public documents of the EZLN and the Ejército Popular Revolucionario (EPR)[3] to examine the different political strategies used by each group.[4] Using Gramscian concepts she argues that the EZLN pursues a "war of position" whereas the EPR focuses on a "war of movement."[5] I will not elaborate on Bruhn's analysis of the EPR, other than to highlight her observation that the movement employs more or less conventional guerrilla movement tactics. Of greater interest for this study is Bruhn's analysis of the EZLN as a movement engaged in a Gramscian "war of position." Bruhn selectively draws from the tactical aspects of Gramsci's theory rather than the organizational aspects. That is, she emphasizes the political character of the Zapatistas' actions rather than the fact that they organized clandestinely in the Lacandon Jungle.

Adamson (1980: 225) describes Gramsci's "war of position" as a revolution that "would be an extended campaign for hegemonic influence among the population at large; once this was attained, political power would be essentially at hand and many of the conditions of socialism would already have been realized." The route to accomplishing this hegemonic influence is a cultural and social transformation of society. Boycotts, Gandhi-style resistance, peaceful demonstrations and countercultural education are examples of tactics employed in "wars of position" (226–227). They are used by opposition forces to invoke change without resorting to the physical confrontation or violence of a war of movement. They all rely on the persuasive use of language to influence the "correlation of forces" in accordance with a prevailing theme in Gramsci's theory. Adamson states that opposition movements can use combined tactics of "war of position" and "war of movement" depending on the historical conditions of the movement in relation to the state at the time (226).

According to Bruhn's assessment of the movement, the EZLN uprising on the eve of January 1, 1994, was a war of movement. Their tactics subsequently switched to those of a war of position. They ceased the armed confrontation, called for international meetings, held plebiscites and now have a strategy which has partially delinked their movement from dealings with the Mexican state.

According to Bruhn (1999: 42), "Marcos is ... the very model of a Gramscian intellectual ... whose 'social function is to serve as a transmitter of ideas within civil society and between government and civil society' (Adamson 1980: 143), [and is] 'specialized in the conceptual and philosophical elaboration of ideas' (Adamson 1980: 145)." He has filled this role by maintaining contact with the indigenous and nonindigenous sectors of society while negotiating with the government about their demands. Since the time of Bruhn's assessment of the movement, there have been new developments which shed a different light on the EZLN's relationship with the government, such as the creation of autonomous communities and the current partial delinking practices which bring the movement back to the utilization of noncorporatist strategies. While not in the form of armed confrontation, their current strategies could be considered even more radical.

Bruhn (1999) acknowledges that there are differences between Gramscian thought and the EZLN movement. As mentioned above, Gramsci saw the "war of position" as a move toward socialism, whereas the EZLN is very careful not to use the term. The importance of the pragmatic role of a political party is also different. For Gramsci the party "played a critical role not only in organizing the military side of the revolution but in preventing the masses from losing direction" (49). In contrast the EZLN denies the existence of a party of the masses and rejects the possibility that they might create such a party (49). In fact, under the Other Campaign (OC) as we will see, the EZLN rejected all three of the main political parties in Mexico.

From a more traditional Marxist perspective the Zapatista movement may be considered first and foremost a class struggle represented through the indigenous communities in Chiapas. Not all indigenous people struggle equally in Chiapas: there are those who fit into the capitalist class and those that live at the margins. Those who organize and rebel against the Mexican government are doing so in response to the capitalist social relations of production in the country. They are driven to organize in response to the exploitation and repression they suffer under neoliberalism as they seek ways to preserve their culture and to improve their political and economic position. One of their central demands was and is for land. Land had been commodified over one hundred years before, then legally stolen from the indigenous inhabitants, then only partially redistributed following the revolution (Cohen 1997: 47–49), and was now being further alienated from the indigenous people to make way for large transnational corporations. While some indigenous people have become employed by these corporations, many have been left in their misery searching for undesirable plots of land to grow enough food for their own meagre subsistence. It is in this context — that of a conflict over ownership of an essential means of production, land — that the Zapatista movement is best described as a class struggle.

This chapter, then, provides a chronological outline of the movement from 1994 to date. The best way to understand the distinctiveness of the movement and its proclivity to adopt its current strategies is to examine its chronological development. The movement began organizing during the period of transition from state corporatism to transnationalized corporatism. This origin had an impact on the strategies the movement used to respond to the state; the movement tacked from noncorporatist to anticorporatist and then again to noncorporatist actions. Much of the chapter is given over to descriptive, historical accounts of the movement, the details of which demonstrate the place of the EZLN within the transnationalized corporatist, state-society relations in Mexico. Without meaning to be dismissive of the movement and its intentions, it will be treated from a critical, Marxist perspective. The perspective is Marxist, insofar as it treats the political development of the EZLN in the context of capitalist social relations of production, where society is dominated by the owners of the means of production to the detriment of the dispossessed. It is critical, in that it exposes what are believed to be the limitations of the strategies of the movement to effect political change.

The chapter is divided into five sections. The first section traces the origins of the movement, the second discusses the "war of movement," the third the "war of position," the fourth the formation of the Caracoles, and the fifth section analyzes the Other Campaign.

Origins

The considerable volume of analysis of the Zapatista uprising from a variety of perspectives reflects the scholarly consensus that it was the most important indigenous uprising in Latin America in the 1990s because of its ability to draw on widespread international support and to diffuse its message throughout indigenous and nonindigenous communities in Latin America and beyond. Moreover, as Higgins (2004: 2) puts it, the movement remains "the most organized and convincing challenge to international neoliberalism" to date.

To understand the current Zapatista movement one needs first to understand the origins of the name, which date back to the Mexican Revolution of 1910. During the revolution, Emiliano Zapata led the Liberation Army of the south while his counterpart Pancho Villa organized in the north.[6] Following the presidential election in November of that year, Francisco I. Madero published the "Plan de San Luis Potosí" in response to the fraudulent results. He declared himself the president of the country on the grounds that General Porfirio Díaz (who had served as president for thirty years) had betrayed the people. The plan (Madero 1910) asserted that

> the legislative and judicial powers are completely subordinated to the executive; the division of powers, the sovereignty of the States, the liberty of the common councils, and the rights of the citizens exist only in writing in our great charter; but, as a fact, it may almost be said that martial law constantly exists in Mexico; the administration of justice, instead of imparting protection to the weak, merely serves to legalize the plunderings committed by the strong; the judges instead of being the representatives of justice, are the agents of the executive, whose interests they faithfully serve; the chambers of the union have no other will than that of the dictator; the governors of the States are designated by him and they in their turn designate and impose in like manner the municipal authorities.

Within a year of his self-declaration as president, Madero's reign was under scrutiny. On November 25, 1911, over a year after the 1910 uprising and a year after the Plan de San Luis Potosí was enacted, Zapata and his followers issued the "Plan de Ayala" (see appendix) in response to Madero's failure to live up to his revolutionary promises which were detailed in the Plan de San Luis Potosí. Zapata considered Madero a continuation of his predecessor, Porfirio Díaz. He considered him "inept at realizing the promises of the revolution ... [He lacked] respect for the law and justice of the pueblos, and [he was] a traitor to the fatherland" (Plan de Ayala, November 25, 1911).

The Plan de Ayala called for the replacement of Madero by General Pascual Orozco as the president of Mexico (see appendix). It also addressed the issue of land which was one of Zapata's primary concerns from the outset of the revolution. The plan called for the expropriation of one-third of the land that was in the hands of the large landowners and the return of this land to the people. If a landowner objected to these measures the other two-thirds of their land would be nationalized and transferred to the people for their use. The Plan de Ayala also set up an indemnity fund for the widowed and orphaned victims of the revolution, and created structures to realize clean local elections. This was just one segment of the long, armed, political struggle led by Zapata.

Zapata's revolutionary efforts were considered a triumph in 1917 when, six years after the issuing of the Plan de Ayala, Article 27 was introduced into the Mexican Constitution at a time when agrarian reforms were largely ignored by then president Venustiano Carranza (Cockcroft 1983: 111). It centered on "campesino" land rights. Article 27 of the 1917 constitution (Grayson 1998: 13):

- stipulated that the possession of lands and waters was vested originally in the nation, which had the right to transmit ownership to private citizens; proclaimed

that the state could restrict private property as it deemed suitable, including
expropriation with indemnification;

- authorized the division of huge estates into small holdings;
- specified that the nation owned the subsoil rights to petroleum and other mineral
  resources.

Zapata never rose to the presidency, nor was it his intention to do so. He fought for
a just system as a true revolutionary, and it was thanks to the Mexican Revolution of 1910
that the thirty-year presidency of General Porfirio Díaz was ended. Zapata was killed in
1919 after being framed by political dignitaries who wanted to terminate the obstacles
that his actions presented for the government. Gilly (1971) refers to the Mexican Revolution
as an "interrupted revolution" because of the timing of the death of Zapata, a revolution
that would have to be continued at a later date in order to fully address the class divisions
in Mexico and in order to reach socialism. It was Zapata's revolutionary legacy and his
concerns for the rural, agrarian sectors of society that led the 1994 indigenous movement
to call itself the Ejército *Zapatista* de Liberación Nacional (EZLN).

The struggle for land rights has been the central concern of the campesino/indigenous
people for centuries. More recently, they have fought incessantly for the preservation of
their "*usos y costumbres*" which are expressed in their cultural and social practices. Seekers
after "modernization" and governments at all levels have rejected these ancient ethnic,
social and cultural practices. As Díaz Polanco (2003) explains, the ethnocide campaign
dates back to the Spanish colonial period. Land and cultural preservation struggles have
led many indigenous communities to search for different degrees and forms of autonomy,
in an attempt to preserve their historical roots and political decision-making processes.

Usos y costumbres vary from community to community and can refer to political
practices or to more general cultural practices that have been upheld for centuries. "Political
practices" usually refers to the way representatives are selected. For example, in some areas
of Oaxaca, "leaders are selected through a range of processes ranging from inclusionary
community assemblies to exclusionary councils of elders meetings across four electoral
cycles" (Eisenstadt 2007: 53), each cycle lasting three years. While the institutionalization
of usos y costumbres has been criticized when used to further the agenda of a particular
political party, or when women have been excluded from the process, it is usually defended
as a grassroots, democratic, transparent process. Advocates of the preservation of usos y
costumbres consider it a process more in keeping with the will of the people than do
advocates of textbook liberal democracy. People are elected or chosen based on their community service rather than their party affiliation, and the chosen person is determined at
a general assembly. There is usually no monetary compensation attached to the position,
other than travel expenses if there is a need to travel to neighboring communities or the
capital city (58). It is the preservation of practices of this sort that drives the indigenous
movement forward.

Chiapas has one of the highest proportions of indigenous people in Mexico, approximately one quarter (INEGI, May 24, 2006: 4). The high rate of poverty in the state has
attracted left-wing organizations to the area over the years in an attempt to help organize
the population against government policies. As early as 1968, Maoist activists, many of
whom were engineers from the University of Chapingo, went to the area to help create
ejido organizations (see De Vos 2000: 36–37). The first ejido union was soon founded

under the name "Unión de Ejidos Kip." This gave the indigenous communities a foundation which provided them with the tools to hold regular assemblies, to discuss the needs of the people and to organize. The Maoist tradition also permitted them to justify the use of arms to resist the repressive actions of the "*guardias blancas*" and the army. These "tools" proved to be very useful when the government attempted to drive the people out of the jungle in 1972. A guerrilla organization called the Fuerzas de la Liberación Nacional (FLN) (thought to have originated in the north of Mexico) emerged in Chiapas in 1973 and joined forces with the more radical, organized, indigenous groups in an area know as "Las Cañadas." By 1983 this clandestine group had become more structured and established as it drew from the experiences of the existing organizations (ibid.: 38). It formed the foundations of the EZLN. What initially were defensive tactics against the aggressions of government forces and landowners' private armies soon took on the form of offensive action which was more in keeping with the tactics adopted by conventional guerrilla groups. The indigenous activists figured they had nothing to lose given that they had benefited little from their defensive approach. Their changed tactics were in response to the economic hardships they were facing.

As an oil-producing country, Mexico's economy prospered throughout the 1970s. But their luck turned in the 1980s when heavily indebted governments, including Mexico's, were forced to implement strategies to deal with the huge debt load accrued during the boom period. "At the end of 1987 the estimated total external debt [in Mexico] was 107.6 billion U.S. dollars, equivalent to 77% of gross domestic product" (Hernández-Estrada et al. 1989: 1117). As we saw in chapter 2, in response to this debt load the Mexican government introduced a program of economic austerity that included signing on to the GATT in 1986. One of the consequences of these measures was the opening of the borders to foreign investment and the end of the ISI protectionist model. It was in response to economic and political reforms such as these that the indigenous people began to organize what we know of today as the Zapatista movement. While the reforms were an attempt to improve the economy, they had a negative impact on the indigenous population which depended on agricultural production and subsidies to survive. From 1986 to 1994 the government was at the disposition of the GATT and the IFIs as it implemented structural adjustment programs to make the Mexican market more amenable to foreign investors and corporations.

Although the Zapatista movement was organizing clandestinely from the early 1980s, it is not a coincidence that it took to the streets on the day that NAFTA was proclaimed. In 1991, Article 27 had been modified to make way for transnational corporations under the (forthcoming) auspices of NAFTA (that "bill of rights for investors"). The reforms to Article 27 stripped the agrarian sector of constitutional rights to the land. The fertile land that had been handed over in small plots to Mexican farmers years before, and had been protected by constitutional law ever since, now became fair game to large agricultural processing corporations, mostly U.S.-owned. Local farmers were coerced into selling their land and giving up the only source of subsistence they knew. Subsequently, some of the indigenous people came to work the land for the new landowners for very low wages, some came to farm land many kilometers away from their home villages, and others migrated to urban areas within Mexico in search of jobs, while still others took to crossing into the United States to find work and send monthly remittances to their families back home.

The farmers who are now employed by the transnational corporations are often exposed to very toxic chemicals used in the fertilization of the crops and the spraying of pesticides on the crops. There is no job security in this type of work and there is little concern about the health of those employed. Genetically modified crops have come to replace the ancient traditions of the local peasants. A more recent development is the farming of corn for ethanol. This practice has created havoc for a population which has depended on corn to satisfy its nutritional needs since before the Spanish conquest. According to a *Washington Post* article (Roig-Franzia 2007: A1), the price of tortillas tripled and in some cases quadrupled in the six-month period from the summer of 2006 to January 2007. The price hikes are based on demand and the need to import the corn for local consumption as the fields have been taken over. Other crops have also been affected in a similar manner. Since the early 1980s foreign direct investment, privatization of state corporations and economic adjustments have all led to a greater gap between classes where fewer people have access to the means of production. As capitalism has become more neoliberal in character, this, according to Marxist economic theory, is an expected outcome.

The peasants who have opted to continue farming on distant lands have been required to plant crops that they are unfamiliar with. While at one time farming on fertile lowlands, they now travel for hours on horseback or donkey to plots of often sandy, rocky, hilly terrain. (The author witnessed this during her trip to the southern region of Chiapas in 1994.) These farmers are self-employed and depend entirely on their good health, suitable terrain and cooperative weather conditions.

The last group of farmers is made up of those who make the risky journey to the United States in search of employment. According to Papademetriou (2004: 40), "The population of unauthorized Mexican immigrants in the United States more than doubled between 1990 and 2000 ... and has continued to grow strongly in the new century." Villafuerte Solís and García Aguilar (2006: 103) argue that the changed socioeconomic conditions resulting from the crisis in production in rural areas of Chiapas from 1988 to 1994 led to an increase in migration. The problem is that migration does not address the wrongs of capitalism. It simply puts people in a position of selling their labor power abroad to foreign capitalists who jump at the opportunity to take advantage of the migrants' vulnerability. The number of people from Chiapas who have migrated to the United States since this period has continued to rise.

It is difficult to determine just how many people from Chiapas are actually working illegally in the U.S. at any given moment. One method researchers use is to determine the number of people who have either been deported back to Mexico or turned away at the border. According to a survey conducted at the U.S./Mexican border (Villafuerte Solís and García Aguilar 2006), from 1994–1995 to 1998–1999 the number of people from Chiapas that were sent back to Mexico after trying to enter the country illegally rose from 6,129 to 13,372. This increased to over 30,500 people from Chiapas who were deported in 1999–2000.

Remittances from Mexicans working in the United States have reached record highs since the turn of the century. According to figures from the Bank of Mexico (see Polaski 2004: 21), remittances in 2002 amounted to approximately 9.8 billion U.S. dollars. This figure rose to over 12 billion U.S. dollars in 2003. To Chiapas alone, remittances in 2005 amounted to over 655 million dollars (Villafuerte Solís and García Aguilar 2006: 120).

According to a Fox News (2011) article on February 2, 2011, remittances in 2010 were over 21 billion dollars. "Remittances from the United States provide more foreign funds than either foreign direct investment or tourism" (Polaski 2004: 36n19). Again, however, it needs to be said that there are no guarantees of employment with this alternative, and women and children suffer greatly as families are broken apart in this search for a better life. U.S. laws and policies are making it harder for people to cross the border as they proceed with the construction of a wall to separate the two countries. According to a *New York Times* article (Preston 2008), "302 miles of physical fence" had been completed by February 23, 2008. They are now in the process of creating a "virtual fence" which "includes ground sensors and cameras mounted on 90-foot-high towers that relay images directly to Border Patrol command centers and vehicles" (ibid.).

Needless to say the social ramifications of the constitutional reforms made to Article 27 in 1991 have had very negative consequences for the political economy of Mexico, and particularly for the farming population in areas like those inhabited by the indigenous communities in Chiapas. The majority of the indigenous population in Mexico has historically depended on the fruits of the land to provide food for the year and in some cases to provide a small income for their family. The cheap labor and cheap fertile land found in Mexico have come to be very attractive commodities for transnational corporations wanting to expand their marketable resources.

Chiapas (Sipaz 2007) is one of the poorest states in the country. While it produces 35 percent of the electrical power for the country, 34 percent of the population in Chiapas lives without electrical services. Furthermore, according to 1994 statistics (ibid.),

> In an area rich in natural resources, agriculture, and oil, nearly 60% of the population survived on the minimum wage [$5.00 per day]. 60% of school-age children were unable to attend school and the illiteracy level is 30%. Only 57% had access to potable water. Fifteen thousand indigenous people died in 1993 due to their impoverished conditions.

War of Movement

On January 1, 1994, the EZLN entered San Cristobal de Las Casas, the state capital of Chiapas, in response to these political-economic conditions. Eight hundred armed men and women ransacked the municipal archives and set them on fire while thousands of other members of the Zapatista army seized five other nearby towns. They proceeded to "[open] the food warehouses to the poor, [chase] out and in some cases [kill] the local police, [dismantle] another town hall stone by stone with sledgehammers ... axes and saws, and then [fight] the Mexican Army to a standstill for more than a week" (Cooper 1995: 127). In short, for twelve days the Zapatistas fought a Gramscian war of movement, a truly Marxist revolutionary action. At the onset the uprising appeared to be a revolutionary takeover of state infrastructure and political power. However, it became clear very soon that the movement had no real intention of holding political power in the state. Nevertheless, the noncorporatist strategy used on January 1, 1994, was welcomed by many local indigenous communities and by oppositional forces around the country who egged them on.

The uprising was staged on the day that NAFTA was proclaimed among Mexico, the United States and Canada, and about six months before the 1994 Mexican presidential elections. As evidenced in the EZLN communiqué (EZLN 2004: 643–645) of January 1, 1994, the initial demands were framed in terms of economic, political and social rights. They demanded "work, land, housing, food, health care, education, independence, freedom, democracy, justice and peace." The list of demands is comparable to articles 17, 21, 22, 23, 25, 26 and 28 of the Universal Declaration of Human Rights of 1948, articles subsequently enshrined in the International Covenant on Economic, Social and Cultural Rights of 1966 (ratified by Mexico, as noted in an earlier chapter, in 1981 and thus the law of the land). It is important to note that they were demands put on the government and not a political platform of change. This is why even though the movement began with what appeared to be a noncorporatist action it soon became clear that it in fact was following an anticorporatist strategy. Its demands conveyed the indigenous response to the changes in the national economy which endangered the livelihood and well-being of all Mexican citizens. The demands included the call for an end to the "seventy-year dictatorship" and to give the people the right to elect their own representatives. This initial call to participate in the electoral process had vanished by 2006 when the movement denounced the electoral process and the participating parties. Beyond the promulgation of NAFTA, Anguiano (1997: 150) argues that the emergence of the EZLN in 1994 was also an expression of the failure of the PRI regime to remedy the economic devastation in their communities and the inability of the PRD to provide a viable alternative to represent the subordinate classes. One could be forgiven for seeing in the EZLN's actions a return to the revolutionary left which the PRD, in particular, was ignoring.

In their Declaration of War in the First Declaration of the Lacandon Jungle (Vodovniki 2004: 644–645), the EZLN refer to themselves as the "fighting arm of [their] liberation struggle." Further on in the declaration they assert that "we will not stop fighting until the basic demands of our people have been met by forming a government of our country that is free and democratic." Although it is true that, as García de Leon (1995: 4) asserts, the EZLN does not have a "complete systematic ideology, nor the final draft of a national political and social reform project, it has generated inspiring ideas which have been projected as a new political and social order." In one way or another almost all opposition forces and intellectuals have expressed solidarity with the movement, although that support has waned in the last few years. According to Luis Vázquez of the OST and Edgard Sánchez of the PRT (interviews 2004), the leadership of the EZLN has been very sectarian and has obstructed unification efforts by other left-wing forces. They have criticized the movement because of the vagueness of its actions and the fact that during the 2006 presidential election the EZLN diverted attention away from the PRD by running a parallel campaign. However, contrary to the critique by the left-wing oppositional parties of the EZLN, it may be argued that while the EZLN comes across as sectarian its actions are actually a reflection of its unwillingness to continue engaging in the ineffective anticorporatist actions of the very parties that criticize it.

Although the First Declaration made no mention of NAFTA or neoliberalism, Subcomandante Marcos did publish articles, such as *Chiapas: el Sureste en dos Vientos, una Tormenta y una Profecía* (Chiapas: The Southeast in Two Winds, a Storm and a Prophecy) (Subcomandante Insurgente Marcos 1992), in which he denounced the political and economic strategies of the PRI. Of particular concern to Marcos, leading up to the signing of NAFTA, were those acts of the Mexican government which "ended restrictions on imports of corn and eliminated protection on the price of coffee [and] reform[ed] ... the historic Article 27 of the Mexican Constitution, which ended communal possession of agricultural property by the villagers" (Castells 1997: 74–75; see also Cleaver 1994: 151). He acknowledged and denounced the interference of imperialist powers in the oil, gas, lumber, electricity, cattle and coffee industries in Mexico. The pronouncements which emerged during the initial stage of the Zapatista movement demonstrate a clear understanding of Marxist political-economic analysis. Marcos knows what it is about the social relations of production in capitalism that alienates people from the means of production, and he knows where the dispossessed fit into this analysis.[7] Marcos's stronger anti-neoliberal, anticapitalist slogans appear in later declarations. This could be a reflection of his not wanting to come across as just another "Marxist," an appellation he disowned from the beginning.

The First Declaration of the Lacandon Jungle (General Command of the EZLN 1993, in Hayden 2002: 218) states that

> We are the product of 500 years of struggle: first against slavery, then during the War of Independence against Spain led by insurgents, then to avoid being absorbed by North American imperialism, then to promulgate our constitution and expel the French empire from our soil. Later the dictatorship of Porfirio Díaz denied us the just application of the Reform laws and the people rebelled; leaders like Villa and Zapata emerged.

In response to the historical injustices imposed on the Mexican people the Zapatistas "appeal[ed] to article 39 of the Mexican Constitution which proclaims 'the right of the people to alter or modify its form of government'" (Castells 1997: 78) and took to the streets in an armed takeover of strategic government buildings. This ambiguous call for revolutionary action against the state did not have the support of the masses to make it sustainable and effective. The government responded to these declarations and actions by reinforcing military personnel and equipment and going door to door looking for "subversives." Twelve days after the uprising the Zapatistas retreated to the jungle. The government responded to this retreat by signing a cease-fire agreement on January 27, 1994.

War of Position

From February 1994 to February 1995 the EZLN and the government were engaged in dialogue while the army continued to occupy areas surrounding the EZLN camps. This signaled an end to the initial revolutionary uprising of January 1, 1994, and the transition from a "war of movement" to a "war of position," as Gramsci would have it. In turn it signaled a move from noncorporatist to anticorporatist strategies. While not the end of the struggle, the cease-fire put a damper on the expectations of many Marxist, left-wing organizations in Mexico and abroad. The EZLN justified its actions in the Second Declaration of the Lacandon Jungle, stating that it was acting in response to the wishes of the people who told them that violence was not the desirable route to effect change. The declaration states (Hayden 2002: 221),

> The response to this call was a policy of extermination and lies; the powers of the Union ignored our just demands and let loose massacre. But this nightmare only lasted 12 days, as another force, superior to any political or military power, imposed itself upon the conflicting sides. Civil Society assumed the duty of preserving our country; it demonstrated its disagreement with the massacre and obliged a dialogue.

The Second Declaration was released in June 1994 in the period leading up to the August 21 presidential elections, in an attempt to reiterate the importance of consolidating the democratic process. The EZLN did not boycott the elections, nor did it support a particular candidate, but it did emphasize the importance of looking beyond the electoral process. The declaration called for a Convención Nacional Democrática (CND) to "organize civil expression and defend popular demands" (Almeyra and Thibaut 2006: 175). More than 6,000 people participated in the convention. People gathered in large, outdoor amphitheatres called "Aguascalientes" to discuss the political situation in Mexico and around the world. Participation ranged from indigenous people from surrounding villages to indigenous people from distant regions and political activists who supported the First Declaration of the Lacandon Jungle. It gave hope to a process of reorganization of opposition forces in Mexico acting outside of the institutional realm of the PRI, that is *outside the corporatist grip of the government*. However, their efforts proved incapable of dealing with the postelectoral period when (a) the PRI candidate Ernesto Zedillo Ponce de Leon won, and (b) the momentum from the movement did not accelerate. There were attempts to form a national opposition coalition, but to no avail. Anguiano (1997: 156) argues that the heterogeneous composition of the CND and the lack of concrete political options did not permit such a development. The call for the CND was a far cry from the revolutionary actions of two years before. It was, perhaps, a demonstration of the EZLN pushing for electoral reforms in order to be able to legitimize Mexican elections. Its actions suggested a renewed sense of confidence in the state's willingness to accommodate their demands.

The Third Declaration of the Lacandon Jungle, which was released in January 1995, denounced neoliberalism and again called for the development of a coalition force. The coalition was to be in the form of a common front to be led by Cuauhtémoc Cárdenas Solórzano and the CND. This front was to comprise teachers, students, rural and urban workers, artists and "honest" intellectuals, "consequent" religious people and militants of all organizations willing to struggle to make the PRI hand over power, the flag, the national anthem and the national shield. It also called for the rewriting of the constitution and the establishment of a transitional government of the people in search of democracy. The five demands expressed in the declaration were as follows (see declaration in Almeyra and Thibaut 2006: 182):

1. the liquidation of the state-party system and true separation of the government and the PRI;
2. that the electoral law be reformed to guarantee: transparency, credibility, equality, full participation of citizens that are not affiliated with a party or with the government, recognition of all national, regional and local political forces, and that new elections be held in the federation;
3. that a committee be assigned to draft a new constitution;
4. that the government recognize the particularities of the indigenous groups and recognize their rights to autonomy and to citizenship;
5. that the national economic plan be reoriented to favor the most dispossessed sectors of society, the workers and the farmers, who are the principal producers of the riches of this country.

In these demands we can see, perhaps, a growing distancing of the EZLN from the state. Following the publication of this declaration there were attempts by the government to capture the leadership of the Zapatista movement. This put an immediate end to the negotiations between the state and the EZLN. Although repression continued into 1996, the negotiation process resumed in March 1995. In August 1995, while negotiations were still officially taking place, the EZLN held an international plebiscite to determine the future political structure of the EZLN. Over 1 million people voted worldwide. The creation of the FZLN was one of the initiatives which stemmed from the plebiscite.

The Fourth Declaration of the Lacandon Jungle was made public in January 1996. "Democracy," it reads, "does not mean alternative power, it means government of the people, for the people and by the people" (see declaration in Almeyra and Thibaut 2006: 189).[8] It was the official call for the formation of the FZLN. The FZLN was to be open to all sectors of civil society that did not aspire to take power or to run in a federal, state or municipal election or that did not already belong to a political party. The FZLN had its central offices in Mexico City and received direct instructions from the EZLN on how to manage its affairs while serving as the liaison to nonstate actors. The internal hierarchical relationship that existed between the EZLN and the FZLN is very similar to the transnationalized corporatist relationships that exist between the Mexican state and nonstate actors in Mexico. In fact the FZLN continued to fulfill its role as liaison until the EZLN pulled the plug in 2005 and forced it to close its doors. This modeling of the corporatist relationship reinforces the assertion that corporatism is historically grounded and strongly embedded in Mexican political culture.

In an interview with Le Bot (1997: 320), Marcos stated that "the Zapatista discourse has had a great impact on the indigenous communities, teachers, intellectuals and artists, but it has not had an impact on the working class in Mexico.... This work is left up to the FZLN." It was to be a political force that would address the collective problems of the Mexican population from below. In the event the FZLN was unsuccessful at making inroads into the labor movement, this was not a reflection of labor's unwillingness to join forces with them, but rather because to be a member of the FZLN one could not belong to a union and because the support shown by the labor movement to FZLN-sponsored political events was not reciprocated.[9]

As the result of two years of negotiations, on February 16, 1996, Round One of the San Andrés Accords was signed by the government and the EZLN. This marked what many considered a monumental breakthrough for the EZLN. Round One covered indigenous rights and culture. In December of the same year it was agreed that the Comisión de Concordia y Pacificación (COCOPA)[10] would prepare a bill that would reform the constitution to cover the agreed-upon points. The next step was to initiate Round Two, which was to discuss democracy and justice. As the second round began, repression increased. In September the EZLN walked away from the negotiating table and demanded (Sipaz 2007) that the government release all Zapatista prisoners, that the government send a decision-making power to the table that was willing to respect the Zapatista delegates, that the Comisión de Seguimiento y Verificación (COSEVER) be installed, that the government bring only serious and concrete proposals to the negotiations on democracy and justice and, finally, that there be an end to the climate of military and police persecution against the indigenous communities of the region, before they would return to the negotiating table. The government refused to fully meet these conditions, and the negotiation process ended at that moment and has never resumed. This marked a more decisive distancing between the EZLN and the state.

The original agreement, or Round One as it is called, comprised the following eight points which covered basic indigenous rights (see accords in Almeyra and Thibaut 2006: 216–217): (1) Article 27 of the constitution should be reformed in keeping with the spirit of Zapata's slogans that *the land belongs to he/she who works on it* and *Land and Liberty*; (2) the indigenous people should not be held responsible for the damage to their lands or territories retroactively; (3) that given the triple oppression which indigenous women suffer as women, as indigenous people and as poor people, a new society should be built with an economic, political, social and cultural model that includes all Mexicans; (4) concrete dates should be established for the implementation of each section of the accords; (5) cultural and linguistic interpreters and translators should be available at all times for all legal issues involving indigenous people and land reforms; (6) legislation should be introduced that protects the rights of indigenous people who migrate to other regions within the country or outside of the country; (7) in order to strengthen the municipalities the government must agree to provide access to infrastructure, training and adequate economic resources; and (8) that the indigenous communities be guaranteed access to reliable, opportune and sufficient information regarding government activities, as well as access to the existing means of communication, and that the indigenous communities be allowed to have their own means of communication such as their own radio stations, television stations, telephones, newspapers, computers and satellite access. All of the demands agreed upon in Round One were reformist in nature.

Although the government had reneged on its end of the agreement, the EZLN continued to organize centers of resistance. Response to their resistance culminated in the massacre of 45 people in Acteal in 1997. The perpetrators of this massacre were unofficial, armed, paramilitary groups that had been trained in the region (Higgins 2004: 169). During this same period there were approximately 4,000 people displaced in the northern regions of the state and over 10,000 in the highlands (Sipaz 2007). When the government's position was rescinded in December of that year by President Zedillo, the Zapatistas went into a period of silence. Such a "silence" *could* be interpreted as a "revolutionary" action given that the Zapatista movement had terminated all discussion with the government, a further example of what can be referred to as eclectic radicalism. This silence would last until the presidential election in 2000.

Vicente Fox from the PAN took office on December 1, 2000, becoming the first non-PRI president of Mexico in seventy-one years. In his election campaign, Fox announced that he would resolve the Zapatista problem in fifteen minutes. Taking advantage of Fox's recent electoral victory and his campaign promises, on December 2, 2000, the EZLN (see Subcomandante Insurgente Marcos 2003: 478) announced its willingness to return to the negotiating table. The following conditions would have to be met first in order for this to happen: the realization of the agreements reached in San Andrés, liberty to all the Zapatista political prisoners, and removal of the Mexican army from 7 of the 259 positions which they occupied in the state of Chiapas.[11] These conditions were never met, but in an attempt to pursue things further the EZLN announced its intent to travel to Mexico City in February 2001 to speak to the Congress of the Union about the constitutional reforms that were proposed by the COCOPA following the *encuentro* in San Andrés, namely the San Andrés Accords.

On the twenty-fourth of February, twenty-four delegates left San Cristobal de Las Casas en route to Mexico City. The caravan was met with overwhelming support by citizens as they passed through twelve states of the republic to propagate their message. Its greatest triumph was its uncontested arrival at the Zócalo[12] on March 11, 2001, to the applause of around 200,000 people.

Caracoles: Partial Delinking

After much deliberation the EZLN was reluctantly invited into the Congress of the Union to address the government on March 28. In closing it was announced that Luis H. Álvarez, the peace commissioner, would see to it that the three demands of the EZLN were met (Muñoz Ramírez 2003: 205). While they left the meeting hopeful of a solution to their demands, it soon became clear that they were about to be betrayed again. On April 25, 2001, the Congress of the Union passed a document called Reformas Constitucionales en Materia de Derechos y Cultura Indígena (RCMDCI). This document was a modified version of the original, agreed-upon COCOPA initiative from 1996. The signing of the RCMDCI reaffirmed the EZLN disgust with the three official parties (PRI, PAN, PRD), all of which betrayed them by signing a document that undermined the San Andrés Accords.

As one might expect, the EZLN rejected the government's modified document. Marcos ended his rejection speech stating that there would be no further communications between the EZLN and the federal government or with President Fox until the agreements made in San Andrés were met. Meanwhile the EZLN would remain in a state of resistance and rebellion and engage in more radical strategies in their fight for independence from the state than they had up to that point. On January 1, 2003, Brus Li (Muñoz Ramírez 2003: 235) made a speech reflecting this new approach to autonomy and the need to act on the Acuerdos de San Andrés. He stated,

> It is now time that together we organize ourselves and that we form our autonomous municipalities. We don't need to wait until the "bad government" gives us permission. We should organize ourselves like true rebels and not wait until somebody gives us permission to become autonomous, through laws or without laws.

As the July 6, 2003, elections for deputies approached, the Zapatista communities refused to participate. They refused to allow the government to set up polling booths in their communities. This expression of discontent was in response to the manner in which the government was handling their affairs. In some cases the indigenous communities burned the electoral material (Muñoz Ramírez 2003: 241). On the nineteenth of July, in a communiqué, the EZLN announced that it was severing all relations and contact with the government and other political parties (243). This noncorporatist discourse set the movement apart from the rest of the organizations and movements that were examined in chapters 3 and 4.

On the ninth of August they shut down all of the Aguascalientes and replaced them with Caracoles.[13] This was a move to create a political and cultural space in which the Zapatistas and the non–Zapatistas of Chiapas could communicate. It was an attempt to put the decision-making powers in the hands of the communities; after all, there were many people living in the indigenous communities that were not Zapatistas, and it was difficult for the EZLN as an army to address the particular issues in each community. When the author was in La Realidad in 2004 the Zapatista supporters pointed out the road that divided them from the non–Zapatistas. It was nothing more than a narrow gravel road running through the town. As such it is symbolic of both the political divide that persists in the indigenous communities today and the current divide between the EZLN and the government.

Along with the five caracoles[14] were formed their respective new JBGs[15] (Muñoz Ramírez 2003: 245). The role of the JBG is to find peaceful solutions, through dialogue, to conflicts that arise between Zapatistas and non–Zapatistas or between the autonomous communities and the national and state governments (247–248). As autonomous bodies the Caracoles have followed the EZLN practice of rejecting most support from the Mexican government whether financial or through services. The juntas serve as a means to monitor the projects that are realized by supporting NGOs and civil associations. Representatives are elected for three-year terms in general assemblies. During that three-year period the representatives rotate responsibilities every ten days. The three areas of governance they rotate are vigilance, information and governing (see Almeyra and Thibaut 2006: 33). For the most part the indigenous communities are self-sufficient and work independently of the state by collecting taxes, planning economic strategies, maintaining basic education and health services, and building and repairing roadways in their communities. However, there is a gray area in that they maintain contact with the state government in order to transfer severely ill patients to state hospitals and to collaborate with the judicial bodies for criminal cases that reach beyond the mandate of the juntas (ibid.: 137). Otherwise they have turned inward to satisfy most of their immediate needs and have accepted the support of NGOs to complete larger projects. Such projects include constructing buildings, building electrical plants, and providing material and technical support.

The JBGs' dependency on NGOs is another gray area as far as the delinking process is concerned. While they have delinked from the state, for the most part, their interaction with NGOs demonstrates their inability to address all of the needs of the communities on their own. After all, NGO funding comes from many different sources including from governments, and the services they provide are services that would in an ideal world be provided by the government. In the case of the JBG their intentions are noncorporatist, their discourse is noncorporatist and for the most part their actions are noncorporatist, yet their use of state services in the most severe cases shows they do not conform completely to a pure noncorporatist strategy.

Historically speaking it is correct to observe that as excluded members of the political process, the indigenous people of Chiapas and throughout the country have always had to depend on their own resources to survive. The Mexican state took little interest in their well-being before January 1, 1994, and its actions since then demonstrate a continued lack of interest in addressing the needs of the indigenous people. Marx would expect nothing else from a government that is concerned about catering to the needs and interests of the capitalist class. Even with over fourteen years of NGO support being channeled into the region, the economic, political and social realities of the communities have changed little, as reflected in the repetition of the same demands in the six declarations which have been published over the period.

The whole Zapatista partial delinking model is not without its contradictions. For example, as noted in a previous chapter, there are volunteer medical practitioners who travel to the Zapatista area to provide very basic medical care and deliver medication. Contrary to Zapatista principles the medical professionals that travel from Mexico City to the Zapatista-controlled area are paid professionals mostly employed by government institutions. The support they provide to the communities is volunteer work they do in the communities on their own time. One can assume that without their regular income (which needless to say is far inferior to what a doctor of any rank makes in Canada or the United States) the doctors would not be in a position to volunteer their time to the Zapatista cause.[16] One of the grassroots health-care NGOs, COSACI, counts on general practitioners and nurses, who go to the region to give primary care for simple curable illnesses. "We usually go to the zona [area] during our vacation period" (interview, Irma de la Cruz, January 17, 2004). With the aid of these practitioners the EZLN has also trained what they call "health-care promoters." These trained volunteers include midwives, herbalists, bone doctors (hueseros) and health-care workers who reside in the communities and treat simple medical problems. The Zapatistas take great pride in pointing out that the medical services are free of charge, unlike anywhere else in Mexico.

Some teachers are also trained locally while others come from other parts of the country and volunteer their services to the community. In principle this is a very positive arrangement, but volunteers are only volunteers as long as their own financial resources allow them to provide volunteer services to others, especially in the case of the teachers who come from afar. During the author's visit to La Realidad in May 2004, the schools had been without a teacher for four months, and it was unclear when the position(s) might be refilled. The benefit to having locally trained teachers is that they are sensitive to the "*usos*" and "*costumbres*" of the communities and the ideological cast of Zapatista education. It is also a means to ensure that native languages are preserved. Health and education are just two basic services for which the Zapatistas have had to seek "extrastate" assistance. More recently, they have been soliciting national and international financial support for their communities from groups and individuals that are independent of governments. Obstacles abound for these autonomous communities and for the EZLN. One of the biggest blows came when the major Mexican bank, Bancomer, informed the EZLN that it had until the end of June 2005 to close its bank account. The bank claimed that Enlace Civil[17] was engaged in money laundering and that they did not want to be a part of it.

One cannot deny the help and steadfast support that NGOs have given to the indigenous communities in Chiapas. However, there are drawbacks to this dependency. A case in point is that although the funding may come from municipal, provincial or national sources, churches, political parties or other benefactors, in the end there are no guarantees.[18] According to a SIPAZ spokesperson (interview May 15, 2004), many international organizations have stopped supporting their center because funding has been redirected to other international projects. For example, an organization called Common Frontiers "is a [Canadian] multi-sectoral working group which confronts, and proposes ... alternative[s] to, the social, environmental and economic effects of economic integration in the Americas" (Common Frontiers 2009). It works in coordination with labor, religious and political organizations. Its initial purpose was to confront the Canada-U.S Free Trade Agreement. This was followed by its rejection of NAFTA. At the time of the Zapatista uprising it was in close contact with Mexican organizations opposed to NAFTA. It sent representatives to Chiapas in 1995 to support the Zapatista movement. Although it did not provide financial support to the Zapatista movement, it did support their cause. Its physical support and attention were soon redirected to the Free Trade Area of the Americas (FTAA) cause.

The Struggle for Mexico

Development and Peace, a Canadian NGO which channels much of its support through DESMI, provided emergency support to the Zapatista zone immediately following the uprising on January 1, 1994, in the form of human rights observers and money. Since this initial emergency support, Development and Peace has continued to provide small amounts of financial support to DESMI and to the FRAYBA. But its support in 2003 was only half that of 1994.

Regardless of the sources of their financial resources, the political autonomy of the Zapatista municipalities surpasses other similar attempts at self-governing in Mexico. As a political statement and practice the Zapatista bid for self-sufficiency has sent a clear message to the government that they are a force to be reckoned with. This is a government that has sought ways to assure the international community that everything in the region is under control and at peace. According to González Casanova (2005: 81–82),

> The caracoles give communities engaged in resistance a new way of exercising power, in which their commanders bow to the communities' authority in formulating and implementing plans for struggle and organization ... [They] express ... a culture of power that arises from 500 years of resistance ... [It is a means of] building a peaceful transition towards a viable world which is less authoritarian, less oppressive, less unjust, and which can continue to struggle for peace with democracy, justice and liberty.

These words contradict the government's propaganda of political control and tranquility.

One of the early tasks of the JBGs was to address the revived Plan Puebla Panamá (PPP). The PPP was first introduced in June 2001 by PAN president Vicente Fox. His stated objective was to increase trade in the corridor running from Puebla, Mexico, to Panama by building infrastructure to improve transportation mobility such as proper highways and airports, and by integrating electricity and communications resources (see Pickard 2004). Although put on hold for about eighteen months, the plan was relaunched in early 2004 under a more secretive agenda. The Zapatistas took great exception to the intentions of Fox's PPP and the effects it would have on indigenous lands throughout the corridor. In July 2003 the EZLN declared its opposition to the plan saying, "At least in the mountains of the Mexican Southeast, its implementation will not, for any reason, be permitted" (Subcomandante Insurgente Marcos 2004: 609). Shortly after this pronouncement the Zapatistas announced the Plan La Realidad Tijuana on August 9, 2003. This plan was to unite all of the political agents from La Realidad, Chiapas, to the border town of Tijuana that fight for democracy, liberty and justice.

The Plan La Realidad Tijuana set the conditions for the OC, which was to be a national movement reaching beyond the indigenous regions in Chiapas. The plan comprised seven common agreements and seven national demands. The seven common agreements were as follows (Brus Li 2003):

1. Reciprocal respect for the autonomy and independence of social organizations ... for their processes and decision-making methods, for their legitimate representatives, for their aspirations and demands, and for the accords which they reach with their opposition parties.
2. Promotion of forms of self-management and self-governance throughout the national territory, according to each of their means.
3. Promoting of civil and peaceful rebellion and resistance in response to the regulations of the *bad government* and the political parties.

4. Lending of total and unconditional solidarity to the one who is attacked, and not to the aggressor.
5. Forming of a network of intercommunity basic commerce and promotion of staple foods in national shops, giving preference to small and midsized business and informal commerce.
6. Joint and coordinated defense of national sovereignty and direct and radical opposition to impending privatizations of the electric industry, oil and other natural resources.
7. Forming of a network of information and culture, and the demanding of truthful, complete, timely and balanced information from the media. Creating of local media, and establishing of regional and national networks for the defense and promotion of local, regional and national culture and of universal arts and sciences.

The seven national demands were as follows (Brus Li 2003):

1. The land belongs to the one who works it. In defense of ejidal and communal ownership of the land, and the protection and defense of natural resources. Nothing without the knowledge and prior consent of the inhabitants and workers of each place.
2. Dignified work, a fair wage, for everyone.
3. Dignified housing for everyone.
4. Free public health for everyone.
5. Low cost food and clothing for everyone.
6. Free secular education for children and young people.
7. Respect for the dignity of women, children and old persons.

Although the Plan La Realidad Tijuana had noble intentions and (largely social-democratic) demands, it fell on deaf ears. Not all was lost, however, as the Zapatistas implemented the basic interconnectedness and networking structures they proposed within their own communities. They worked together within the communities to establish dignified living conditions. One of the first lessons Subcomandante Marcos (Muñoz Ramírez 2003: 284) learned about the political class was that their words did not mean anything. The second lesson was that the political class holds no political or moral principles, regardless of the political party one is talking about. The government's disregard for the Plan La Realidad Tijuana was just another reflection of this.

The Other Campaign

These lessons were also expressed in more recent developments when the Zapatistas initiated the Other Campaign (OC), a roundly noncorporatist strategy. In June of 2005, Subcomandante Marcos released a document called "La (Imposible) ¿Geometría? del Poder en México" (The [Impossible] "Geometry" of Power in Mexico) (Subcomandante Insurgente Marcos 2005a). In this document he characterizes and assesses the three primary political parties in Mexico. More specifically, he refers to the PAN as the nostalgic party — that is, they suffer from nostalgia for the democratic struggle, for political humanism, for the war of the Cristeros, and for good conscience, etc. The PRI is referred to as the stabilizer of development, the repressor, the government of devaluations and electoral fraud. He describes the PRD as the party of tactical errors. He references the "erroneous" alliances the PRD has made with the PRI and the PAN in different states, the mistake of repressing the student movement in 1999, the mistake of turning the Zócalo over to entertainment monopolies, the mistake of sending the paramilitary forces after the indigenous population of Zinacantán in Chiapas, and the mistake of introducing a zero-tolerance policy which provided a means to justify the repression of young people, gays and lesbians, etc. For many nonstate actors on the left this criticism of the PRD was not welcome.

Marcos criticized the PRD for voting in favor of the Indigenous Law and for its hostile and aggressive attitude in some of the indigenous communities in Chiapas while in office. Some (see, for example, Almeyra and Thibaut 2006: 147) argue that the image of the PRD outside of Chiapas was quite different, and that López Obrador had the support of many anticapitalist organizations. The support that he received was not necessarily support for his political positions but rather a strategic attempt to divert support away from the PRI and the PAN, the two predominant right-wing political parties in Mexico. Ornelas Delgado (2006: 124) comes down hard on the EZLN's OC stating that "it has won the support of and sparked enthusiasm from President Fox ... [who congratulated the EZLN], a political-military organization, for having chosen the political route in its struggle to improve the situation in the country." Fox guaranteed protection and safety for the OC in its anti–López Obrador tour. When the EZLN opposed the PRD it was criticized by many progressive political activists who saw the PRD candidate, Manuel López Obrador, as the strongest candidate and a viable alternative. If he were to have won the presidential elections they would have considered this the least of all evils next to the PRI and the PAN. Marcos did not consider this a good enough reason to vote for a party that had betrayed the indigenous struggle at the national and local level.

The Zapatistas' position regarding the 2006 federal elections was also hotly debated among left-wing organizations in Mexico. According to Balboa (2006), Luis Villoro, emeritus researcher at the Instituto de Investigaciones Filosóficas de la Universidad Nacional Autónoma de México (Institute of Philosophical Investigations of the National Autonomous University of Mexico), argued that supporting the Zapatistas' call to abstain would only benefit the PAN and the PRI. While he did not support the democratic process as it stood in Mexico at the time, because it did not represent the interests of the population, he nevertheless held that abstaining would only turn votes away from the PRD coalition. He did not see the Zapatistas as offering a clear alternative to the electoral process, or to the PRD for that matter.

Almeyra and Thibaut (2006: 20–21) suggest an alternative approach to understanding the Other Campaign. They hold that it is not about voting or not voting but rather about creating structures and using resources that exist to advance the political independence and political consciousness of the oppressed, and to educate and help organize the population against the repressive acts of capitalism. They call for support of the OC *and* for participation in the electoral system as another means of political expression. They argue that one does not contradict the other.

Anguiano (2006: 28) comes to the defense of the OC and points out that there are substantial historical differences between the situation in Mexico in 1988 and in 2006. In 1988 the PRD clearly represented the interests of the left, but this has changed dramatically since then. To vote for the PRD in 2006, the best of the worst, would lead to a continuation of "antidemocratic, oligarchic, and unequal" political processes. He favored unconditional support for the OC as an anticapitalist struggle that did not give false expectations to the population.

Although some would like to blame the OC for the election results, the CND, led by Manuel López Obrador of the PRD, was quick to blame the ruling party for its fraudulent acts. What appeared prima facie to be a refutation of the democratic electoral process by the OC was in fact a reflection of the rejection of the available options and an expression of distrust in the IFE and the ruling party. However, not all nonstate actors rejected the electoral process; in fact many embraced it as a tool to invoke change. While the Zapatista movement has come to articulate its anticapitalist ideology, other social movements or nonstate organizations have continued to search for ways to transform the government through reformist policies.

The disillusionment expressed by the EZLN in its analysis of the registered political parties is what initiated its call to other political and social organizations to join together in a unified struggle under the banner of the OC. The OC's approach was to consult with leftist organizations around the country and to create a "national plan of action." The EZLN organized the OC at a time when political candidates from all parties were touring the country on their election campaigns leading up to the 2006 presidential elections. Although not considered a call for abstentionism, the EZLN's position was clearly opposed to the platforms of all parties and repudiated their dishonesty around the San Andrés Accords. The strategies of the OC are much more radical than those used by the organizations that supported the PRD and those that defended the electoral process in general.

The slogans of the campaign are "democracy, liberty and justice" for those "below and to the left." It describes itself as an anticapitalist struggle, inviting all those who oppose capitalism to participate in the movement and to aid in the drafting of a new constitution. It is an attempt to unite the workers of the countryside and the city. Any organization or party that wishes to align with the OC must reject the electoral process and all other forms of political organization. While the OC has been referred to as a noncorporatist strategy, it does lack a clear vision of what would replace the current TC state-society model. However, in keeping with Amin's delinking model, the first step is to sever ties with the conventional structures so that what follows is determined by the movement itself.

The campaign began on June 19, 2005, when the EZLN declared a Red Alert. The Caracoles (autonomous communities) were shut down, and the offices of the JBG were indefinitely closed and their members put on guard to protect against a possible attack from the government.[19] The autonomous governments and all existing projects would continue to function, albeit under a different protocol. All local radio transmissions were suspended until further notice and all volunteers and NGOs that were residing in Zapatista territory were ordered to leave. There was mandatory evacuation of all minors.

The purpose of the implementation of these measures was to hold internal consultations among the Zapatista commanders and insurgents under precautionary defensive conditions. By shutting down the municipalities and setting up defense mechanisms they created a safer environment for traveling from community to community to determine their next move. After all, behind their strategies was the formation of a polity independent of the Mexican state. From the twentieth to the twenty-sixth of June they held meetings in over 1,000 communities.

The Red Alert was lifted on July 15 after the publication of the Sixth Declaration of the Lacandon Jungle (Comité Clandestino: July 2005). The Zapatistas called on people and organizations on the left to subscribe to the Sixth Declaration and to attend a series of meetings that were to be held in August and September to create the OC. The meetings were divided into areas. First, the left-wing political organizations met, followed by indigenous organizations, left-wing social organizations, NGOs and collectives, and finally individual persons or families who lacked affiliation with any organization but supported the Zapatista initiative. All of the interventions and meetings were broadcast on satellite radio. On the sixth of August, Subcomandante Marcos asserted that if you were with Andrés López Obrador, the PRD presidential candidate, then you were not welcome to participate in the EZLN initiative.

What is unique about the Sixth Declaration is that it pronounced itself anticapitalist and leftist. By declaring its anticapitalist position it is rejecting the theories of "the multitude" expressed by Hardt and Negri (2004) and Virno (2004). Almeyra and Thibaut (2006: 143–144) argue that to declare a movement anticapitalist can mean different things to different organizations, and it is in this context that they remind the EZLN that if it proposes to form a "broad social front" it will need to engage in political discussion with all leftist organizations even though they may not all agree fully with the EZLN position, its analysis of the current political situation or its tactics. It is not the same, they continue, to create a cohesive organization where all parties agree on all issues as it is to create a front where issues are discussed, and agreed-upon actions are realized as a unit. It is also not the same to declare a movement anticapitalist as it is to declare it anti-neoliberal. An anti-neoliberal movement does not necessarily reject the capitalist mode of production but seeks to work within capitalism while reforming the neoliberal economic and political order. Many would consider it a very bold move on the part of the EZLN to characterize itself as an anticapitalist movement. According to the TC model it could be argued that the organizations that are not willing to fall in line with the noncorporatist strategies of the EZLN and give up their electoral politics and union affiliations are not willing to set aside their (incorporated) anticorporatist practices and work outside the status quo. So while Almeyra and Thibault urge the EZLN to broaden its perspective, in terms of the TC thesis being advanced here this would mean calling on the other organizations to take the bold step of partially delinking from the Mexican state.

The Sixth Declaration calls for four action steps (Almeyra and Thibaut 2006: 213–214):

1. We are going to continue fighting for the indigenous peoples of Mexico, but now not just for them and not with only them, but for all the exploited and dispossessed of Mexico.
2. We are going to go to listen to, and talk directly with, without intermediaries or mediation, the simple and humble people of Mexico, and according to what we hear and learn, we are going to go about building ... a national program of struggle, but a program which will be clearly of the left, anticapitalist, anti-neoliberal, and for justice, democracy and liberty for all Mexican people.
3. We are going to build, or rebuild, another way of doing politics, one which once again has the spirit of serving others, without material interests, with sacrifice,

with dedication, with honesty, one which keeps its word, whose only payment is the satisfaction of duty performed.

4. We are also going ... to struggle ... to make a new constitution, new laws which take into account the demands of the Mexican people, which are: housing, land, work, food, health, education, information, culture, independence, democracy, justice, liberty and peace. A new constitution which recognizes the rights and liberties of the people, and which defends the weak in the face of the powerful.

In part 3 of the declaration there is a detailed definition of what it refers to as capitalism (Almeyra and Thibaut 2006: 206–206):

> In capitalism, there are some people who have money, or capital, and factories and stores and fields and many things, and there are others who have nothing but their strength and knowledge in order to work. In capitalism, those who have money and things give the orders, and those who only have their ability to work obey.
>
> Then capitalism means that there are a few who have great wealth, but they did not win a prize, or find a treasure, or inherit from a parent. They obtained that wealth, rather, by exploiting the work of the many. So capitalism is based on the exploitation of the workers, which means they exploit the workers and take out all the profits they can. This is done unjustly, because they do not pay the worker what his work is worth. Instead they give him a salary that barely allows him to eat a little and to rest for a bit, and the next day he goes back to work in exploitation, whether in the countryside or in the city.
>
> And capitalism also makes its wealth from plunder, or theft, because they take what they want from others, land, for example, and natural resources. So capitalism is a system where the robbers are free and they are admired and used as examples.
>
> And, in addition to exploiting and plundering, capitalism represses because it imprisons and kills those who rebel against injustice.
>
> Capitalism is most interested in merchandise, because when it is bought or sold, profits are made. And then capitalism turns everything into merchandise, it makes merchandise of people, of nature, of culture, of history, of conscience. According to capitalism, everything must be able to be bought and sold. And it hides everything behind the merchandise, so we don't see the exploitation that exists.

The declaration explains how capitalism benefits a select portion of the population, yet its biggest omission, some would argue, is its failure to announce what it considers a viable alternative to capitalism. It is through the exploitation of the many that a few become rich. Capitalists steal the fertile lands and the natural resources from the workers and the peasants. After stripping the dispossessed of their basic means of subsistence they repress those who denounce these injustices. Capitalists are only interested in the sale and the possession of merchandise and profit.

By the twentieth of September 2005 over 90 social organizations, over 55 left-wing political organizations, 162 social organizations, approximately 453 NGOs, 103 indigenous organizations and almost 1,600 individuals had adhered to the Sixth Declaration (Comité Clandestino Revolucionario Indígena: Sept 18, 2005). Although not all adherents participated, there were over 2,000 people who gathered in Chiapas to express their expectations and interpretation of the Sixth Declaration. The first stage of the OC, which was programmed to run from January 1, 2006, to June 18, 2006, held its first public event in San Cristobal de las Casas in Chiapas on January 1.[20] In Marcos's words,[21] "What we are going to do, together, is to shake this country from below, raise it up, turn it on its head." This stage was one of consultation and was to culminate in a summary plenary in Mexico City at the end of June 2006. The second stage was to begin in September 2006 and run until March 2007.

The OC is not a short-term project attempting to effect immediate change but rather, as Delegado Zero (occasionally "Cero") describes it, a long-term project of ten to fifteen years in duration. This brings us back to Gramsci's war of position. Delegado Zero, otherwise known as Subcomandante Insurgente Marcos (July 2006: 5), acknowledges that in keeping with political tradition, opposition groups first establish their principles, their statutes, program and action plan before taking action, whereas the OC has gone only as far as establishing general parameters and principles which will become more defined as the movement grows. He (7) also explains that to be anticapitalist does not necessarily mean to be socialist. For example, within the anticapitalist movement there are anarchists and libertarians. He considers it preemptive to determine where the movement will lead without letting the movement itself lead the way. This is his direct response to the anticapitalist, socialist organizations which are calling for the movement to clarify its anticapitalist goals.

To pave the way for the OC, the FZLN was dismantled and became an integral part of the EZLN. The OC was to replace the FZLN and become the civil branch of the EZLN with a newly defined role and agenda which was spelled out in the Sixth Declaration of the Lacandon Jungle. When the author interviewed members of the FZLN at its central office in Mexico City in 2003, there was a sense of uncertainty among the interviewees regarding the long-term goals of the organization. When asked what they saw as those goals, or how the movement might develop over the next few years, participants responded (interviews May 5, 2004), "I don't know," or "Wherever it takes us," "We are currently working on the next steps." The people that had adhered to the front were from all backgrounds; many had militated in other political organizations in the past only to end up disappointed with their sectarian ways; they saw the FZLN as more inclusive and open to discussion. Others simply wanted to focus their attention on supporting the EZLN and having their voices heard. As mentioned earlier, to adhere to the FZLN you could not belong to any other political or social organization.

There was another interruption to the OC itinerary after an orchestrated police raid in the towns of San Salvador Atenco and Texcoco in the state of Mexico, on May 3 and 4, 2006. The justification of the police raid was to remove eight flower street vendors from the city center who had set up booths in the lead-up to Mothers' Day. Hernández Castillo (2006: 42) describes the scene in the following way:

> a violent clash between 300 unarmed civilians ... and some 4,000 policemen from the state and various corporations. The police put the demonstrators down and terrorized the whole community, raiding houses, breaking down doors and arresting without warrants 207 people including children, women and the elderly.

Forty-five of the forty-seven women who were arrested have reported being sexually assaulted by police; a fourteen-year-old boy was killed and an undetermined number of people disappeared. By May 19 twenty-seven people continued to be held behind bars without the financial resources to pay for their release on bail. Delegado Zero remained in Mexico City during that time (so it is believed). "144 [of the arrestees] were charged with damage to public property ... and twenty-eight ... have been formally indicted under charges of kidnapping and damage to public property" (Herández Castillo 2006: 44). There was an international day of action, calling for the release of all the political prisoners, held on May 28 with participants from around Mexico, Europe and throughout the Americas. About a year later, on April 8, 2007, the EZLN announced that it would begin the second stage of the OC.

The second stage of the OC sent delegates to four separate regions: the north, center, south and the indigenous regions. Each region was further subdivided. The tour began in the northern region and ran from April 10, 2007, until the beginning of June, 2007. From September to December of 2007 new delegations were formed and sent to accompany the struggles in central and southern Mexico. Part of the agenda of the second stage of the campaign was to denounce the political repression suffered by campaign adherents especially in the Yucatan, Atenco and Oaxaca. It also served as a preamble to the Encuentro de Pueblos Indigenas de América (Gathering of the Indigenous People of the Americas), which was held in Sonora in mid–October 2007. All of the delegates that are traveling around the country have been appointed by the EZLN. The author had the opportunity to accompany the OC as it traveled through the state of Morelos in April 2006 and these were her observations.

The Other Campaign in the State of Morelos

The OC arrived in Cuernavaca, Morelos on April 7, 2006 at 8:30 P.M. to a crowd of approximately five hundred people bearing colorful banners and signs demonstrating support for the movement. The vehicle which was transporting Delegado Zero (Subcomandante Marcos) slowly circled the square which bears a monument of General Emiliano Zapata Salazar and which is, for many, a symbolic effigy of the Mexican Revolution. The disappointed supporters came to the quick realization that the caravan would proceed to Ocotopec, without holding a public forum, where they would spend the night. A string of cars followed the vehicles to Ocotopec as journalists and supporters, cameras in hand, strained to get a glimpse of Delegado Zero as he walked from his vehicle to a nearby house. The first public meeting was held the following day in the center of Ocotopec, just outside of Cuernavaca.

There were approximately six hundred people in attendance. This event and the subsequent forums provided a venue for representatives of different political and social struggles to make the particularities of their struggle known to Delegado Zero and to other organizations in the community. During the journey through Morelos there were presentations from different environmental groups, gay and lesbian organizations, human rights organizations, indigenous and peasant groups and other local "collectives." Some of the interventions expressed a plea for Delegado Zero to support their struggle while others used the opportunity to express their support for the OC.

On two occasions during the trip through Morelos the itinerary was modified to heed the political actions of environmentalists. On the first occasion the OC was redirected to Tetela del Monte where supporters walked for about forty-five minutes along dirt paths through a bush until arriving at a clearing where the meeting was held. The contentious issue was the building of a road and housing on the park land which had been allocated as a conservation area. In fact it is one of the few remaining park areas in Morelos. The meeting was attended by approximately sixty people, and the main focus was the pres-

ervation of the ecological area. The primary spokesperson for the environmental group
was a young woman in a wheelchair wearing a neck collar. She had been attacked in 2001
when the police went in to drive the protesters off the land.

The second deviation was on the tenth of April, the day which commemorated the
death of Zapata. On that occasion the meeting was to be held in the town of Tetelcingo.
It was suddenly moved to La Cañada de los Sauces in a residential neighborhood where
environmentalists had tied themselves to trees to protest the cutting down of the trees in
order to make way for a road. As the OC arrived, the bulldozers, police and ambulances
left the area and a sit-in was organized. One of the most organized groups that arrived
to support the effort was a group of about two hundred men and women brandishing
machetes from San Salvador Atenco.[22]

The remainder of the events were on schedule, give or take an hour or two. Delegado
Zero listened patiently to each speaker and took notes while puffing on his pipe. At the
end of each public meeting he summarized the interventions and reiterated the
anticapitalist sentiment of the OC and its purpose in touring the country. He also systematically spoke to the immediate local concerns of the people rather than speaking generally about globalization or restricting his discourse to developments in Chiapas. In all
of the speeches delivered by Delegado Zero he criticized the electoral process, the political
parties and their candidates. Security was relaxed for most events, and the majority of
the gatherings were held in obscure places rather than central squares. As a "representative
of an international media organization" the author was required to register as a journalist
for each event. There was a clear divide between those who were traveling from village
to village with the OC and the local residents who came out to support the arrival of
Delegado Zero and to be heard by him.

In the city of Cuernavaca there was a closed-door event held in a "gay" church that
proved to be a bit more difficult to enter, although the author managed to get in after
much persistence. That particular meeting was more of a discussion group attended by
about two hundred people. People were invited to comment on the OC and its developments. Critical assessments were recorded and appeared to be taken seriously. It was an
opportunity for people to complain about having been excluded or simply not taken into
account in the organizing of the tour or in the events themselves. Overall, it was a very
positive atmosphere with constructive ideas directed toward seeking means to reform the
system.

The documents which represent the movement and Delegado Zero's discourse are
all very anticapitalist and quite radical. For example, in his speech in Jojutla, Morelos,
he said,

> Here in the Other Campaign we have looked for and found that the system is responsi-
> ble [for the destruction of the land]. We have decided [that the struggle] will end when
> we finish with capitalism, when we put all corrupt politicians behind bars, when we
> drive large landowners, comerciantes and bankers out of the country.

However, the interventions made by participants at the meetings were mostly unifocal
and reformist. There seemed, then, to be a disconnect between the discourse of the movement's leader and its supporters. Most organizations reported the demands they were
making on the government, expressing thereby a desire to reform the existing structures
rather than fight against capitalism. Others recounted their role as educators or benefactors

in the impoverished regions of Morelos, again not an anticapitalist discourse. In particular, the struggles to preserve conservation areas and parks, or to fight for the right to land do not express the same anticapitalist sentiment as the leader of the movement. In the long term this could have negative consequences for the growth of the movement if people become more cognizant of the differences between their agenda and that of the OC. Put more succinctly, this disconnect between the EZLN discourse and its supporters is a reflection of different strategic approaches to effecting change. The EZLN is going down the noncorporatist road while the other organizations stick to their anticorporatist strategies. The EZLN approach is a form of radicalism that the other organizations simply do not understand.

The largest gathering during the author's one week with the OC was in the town of Tlalnepantla, Morelos, where approximately 1,000 people[23] gathered to greet Delegado Zero. Tlalnepantla had struggled with its own electoral issues over the previous three years when a significant section of the population rejected the official election results of July 2003 and formed an autonomous government parallel to the official governing body (interview Benyosef Laguna Aranda, April 24, 2004; see Chapman 2005). A confrontation with the government authorities resulted in one fatal shooting, many injured, many arrested and many inhabitants running for cover in neighboring communities. The community is still divided today, and this was reflected in a number of the interventions. One of the main attractions of the day was a "nopal[24] fair" where numerous stands were set up and women were serving free samples of their nopal dishes.

Whether the movement succeeds in its anticapitalist, noncorporatist struggle is yet to be determined (of course it is unclear what success would mean). What is most interesting about the EZLN movement are two things. One is the difference between where it began, as an armed revolutionary movement; where it is now, as an unarmed, unofficial, grassroots, traveling, partially "delinked," new polity; and the period of anticorporatist strategies that got the movement to where it is today. The second is the difference between the anticapitalist, protorevolutionary but inchoate and open-to-the-future discourse of the campaign leader, and the untheorized, gremial desires of his supplicants. Let us not forget the powerful presence of, and the authority given to, the primary spokesperson, Delegado Zero (Subcomandante Marcos), who on many occasions comes across as a somewhat authoritarian leader.[25]

Conclusions

Transnationalized corporatist state-society relations have infringed on the lives of different sectors of Mexican society in different ways. While the Mexican government has structures in place to maintain control of the indigenous communities, through the CNDPI and the military, the Zapatista movement has organized in such a way that it has managed to avoid co-optation. Its radical eclecticism, which can be traced back to when it began organizing clandestinely in the Lacandon Jungle and continues today, has given the movement a unique place in Mexican society. In its transition from clandestine organizing to a "war of movement" to a "war of position" to a bid for autonomy, it has gone from a gremial, geographically specific struggle to a campaign that reaches out to the entire Mexican society in its anticapitalist, noncorporatist struggle. Its strategies reflect this transition as it moved from using a noncorporatist strategy to an anticorporatist strategy and back again to a noncorporatist approach. It seems to be the case that its marginalization has given it greater mobility than, say, the state employees who are organized under state-run unions. Again in the case of the EZLN one sees the general need to reach out to and organize with people and organizations that it has never come in contact with before. However, only those organizations or people who are willing to set aside their anticorporatist strategies and jump on the noncorporatist bandwagon are welcome.

The noncorporatist movement is not likely to disappear in Mexico in the near future. As Subcomandante Marcos asserted, the OC is a long-term project, ten to fifteen years in expected duration. The hope is that as momentum grows, more organizations will join in the struggle. It is not tied to the state's actions (such that its own actions would be merely dictated by the opportunities that arise or the resources that become available), but rather follows its own agenda. This is manifested in its resistance to participating in the electoral movement led by López Obrador and its current partial "delinking" strategies. As the most important antisystemic movement in contemporary Mexico, the EZLN shows no sign of weakening as it consults with the population to determine its next move. It does not anticipate improvements in state-society relations in Mexico. It has used an eclectic mix of radical tactics in an attempt to provide the tools to nonstate actors to effect change. It claims not to be interested in taking power but encourages others to take power in their own hands, in a noncorporatist manner. Its approach is quite different from the antisystemic movements of the 1960s and 1970s because of this.

The Zapatista movement has responded effectively to political, economic and social developments in Mexico from the early 1980s to date. The persistence of the movement and its longevity give a clear indication that the movement is not directly tied to the "opportunities" that are created by these developments. Its actions are unique and varied. They range from armed confrontation to negotiation with political representatives, international outreach activities, silence, establishing of autonomous communities and more recently to widespread consultation. The EZLN is puzzling to many while intriguing to most. Academics, journalists and political activists have approached the movement from many different angles in attempts to understand it. As a political activist the author's biggest concern has been the noncommittal long-term goals of the movement. Similarly, Rodríguez Araujo (2002) criticizes the approach adopted by the Zapatista movement for its lack of clear objectives. He is concerned about its failure to propose an alternative mode of production to capitalism: "It is the uncertainty of a utopia without a proposal.... To oppose that which exists is not the same as creating something new" (ibid.: 195). As Almeyra and Thibaut (2006) and Subcomandante Marcos remind us, there are various understandings of what an anticapitalist movement might amount to. It would be most useful for those involved to have some sense of what they are struggling for and not just what they are struggling against. This confusion was clearly expressed by the militants of the FZLN in their interviews.

The formation of the Caracoles and the JBG marked a decisive turn in the movement. It separated the army (EZLN) from the political dealings in the communities. It gave the indigenous people a representative body, the JBG, which would manage the internal affairs of the villages. The EZLN delinked from the state and continued to be the military arm of the Zapatista communities, whereas the JBG partially delinked from the government. While the intent has been to give full power to the JBG, the EZLN continues to be involved in many decision-making processes. These newly formed, autonomous structures supersede all previous attempts at autonomy in Mexico. The many national and international NGOs which have lent their support to the indigenous communities in Chiapas have facilitated their survival as autonomous structures acting independently of the Mexican state.

The development of the OC gave the EZLN movement a renewed raison d'être as it reached out to the leftist, anticapitalist forces in Mexico. Although inconclusive during the writing of this book, the OC has provided a forum for the voiceless to be heard and a possible venue to effect radical change. The first stage of the campaign compiled many hours of feedback from the nationwide consultations. There has yet to be a published report of their findings, but the continuation of the campaign gives an indication that it has, in their minds, been a useful tool to compile information. The OC has suffered numerous political blows from the repressive forces of the government along the way and has also had to justify its every move to the socialist skeptics who criticize the movement for not taking a revolutionary lead. The Mexican government, although still engaged in repressive actions, has been far more tolerant of the Zapatista movement than would have been the case in the 1970s and 1980s.[26] That said, general repression and violence have accelerated with the war on drugs.

The OC clearly has a following, yet the big question remains: what will it amount to? Activists that approach the movement from a Marxist perspective see the EZLN as representative of the dispossessed class — the workers, the small farmers, the peasants, the unemployed, women, etc. As such, the movement has the responsibility, and what they might prefer to call the obligation, to organize Mexican nonstate actors around a concrete revolutionary agenda, a task which it refuses to do. The political-economic situation in Mexico, they would argue, is not improving, but by skirting the issue the suffering of the people and repression by the government will continue to mount. The hope generated by the January 1, 1994, uprising among the most militant of left-wing organizations was quickly lost when the movement put down its arms and proceeded with the negotiation process. Many of the organizations which initially supported the EZLN, such as the PRT, OST, and POS, have returned to their anticapitalist, revolutionary organizational discourse after feeling let down by the leadership of the Zapatista movement. Yet, under TC where noncorporatist actions involve the severing of ties with the state, it would also follow that it would seek alliances only with those organizations which are also willing to take this radical step. While some see the EZLN as sectarian, the EZLN sees the other organizations as inconsistent, which explains the guidelines it has established to determine who may adhere to the movement and who may not. Is this not a radical twist in conventional political strategizing?

6

Experiments in Delinking and Deglobalization

The expansion of the global market economy and the introduction of policies first detailed in the Washington Consensus (see Williamson 2000) have resulted in a widened gap between the rich and the poor and a decrease in the rate of economic growth in most underdeveloped countries. Latin American countries in particular experienced a lower rate of growth in per capita income in 2000 than 1970. "Per capita GDP for the entire region grew by 75 percent from 1960 to 1980 but only 7 percent in the subsequent neoliberal era, 1980–2000" (Veltmeyer 2007a: 25). These economic indicators show the failure of neoliberal policies to bring about economic growth as promised. In practical terms, "liberalization ... is a mechanism for centralization of capital on a world scale: metropolitan capital-in-production ousts third world producers, while metropolitan capital-as-finance (which is the dominant component of globalized finance) gets control over third world resources and enterprises ... at throwaway prices" (Patnaik 1999: 53). The result is the economic disparities exhibited throughout the underdeveloped countries today (not to mention the global economic meltdown of 2008–2009 and its lasting effects). In response to the hardships generated by these economic developments, people and organizations have engaged in various forms of political activity and resistance. But because of the changing role of the state and the expansion of international institutions, opposition forces engaging in resistance have had to innovate. Teeple (2004: 122) explains that

> because national states must act more or less in the interests of capital, the people of the world are increasingly left voiceless ... and defenceless.... With no political rights to speak of at the global level, non-corporate sectors in the emerging global civil society have few means of countervailing leverage. It is difficult for these same sectors to exercise national rights ... in response to the decisions at the global level. When political activity cannot find a legitimate outlet, however, it becomes extra-parliamentary or extra-legal. Given the growing nature of this predicament everywhere, resistance outside legitimate institutions can only continue to increase.

The primary purpose of this chapter is to examine three very different Latin American resistance movements that have in one way or another severed conventional relations among the usual political actors, a process that Amin (1990, 2006) refers to as "delinking" and Bello (2004) refers to as "deglobalization." While none of the examples found here are expressions of full delinking, they are all attempts at modifying hierarchical political-economic relationships to effect change. Since the theories of both authors were expounded in chapter 1, they will only be summarized here. Amin's approach calls for the delinking, rather than integration, of national governments from the international political arena. In particular he is referring to the need for underdeveloped countries to adopt new market strategies different from those of the hegemonic powers of the North. It is a proposal to turn inward and to address the popular needs of the population over the needs of multinational corporations. It intends the transfer of political hegemony to new centers. Bello's approach focuses more on the production process. He calls for underdeveloped countries to focus on producing for the needs of the local market rather than concerning itself with the needs of the international market through exportation. This includes drawing from national financial resources rather than borrowing from IFIs or foreign banks. The idea is to boost the internal economy of underdeveloped countries while servicing the needs of the people.

Despite the difference in terminology, and to some extent of focus and audience (academics for Amin, activists for Bello), their analyses and proposals are very similar. In counseling major changes in poor countries' relations to the neoliberal, international, political (more Amin) and economic (more Bello) order, both analysts recommend forms of political-economic action that go well beyond such things as standard acts of protest, coalition building and letter writing, and involve long-term commitments. Drawing from the previous chapter, the Zapatistas are an example of a movement that has stepped away from the established institutions while setting up their own internal arrangements. This case will briefly be compared with two other forms of resistance in Latin America that have adopted similar strategies of severing conventional relationships. These are the resistance to U.S. imperialism of Hugo Chavez in Venezuela in relation to the Alternativa Bolivariana para las Américas (ALBA), and the actions of workers in Argentina who have taken over factories. A further, more detailed examination of these cases would certainly be a worthwhile challenge, although it remains a task which is difficult to accomplish while the movements are still in progress.

The Zapatista movement and the factory workers in Argentina do not have state power and do not connect directly to the transnational institutions and hegemonic powers, yet the Zapatistas have adopted delinking strategies, and the factory workers in Argentina have adopted deglobalization strategies at the subnational level. The EZLN has severed virtually all political, cultural and social relations with the Mexican state and the state of Chiapas and, rather than demanding services from the government, functions as an independent polity. The Zapatista process of partial delinking does not overtly propose a transition to socialism, although many left-wing organizations would like to see it move toward that end, and, as Amin states, delinking has the potential of leading to socialism. The workers in some factories in Argentina have severed ties with their original bosses and taken the production process into their own hands; theirs is a more gremial act of delinking. Their struggle does not propose a new mode of production but continues to work within the existing market economy, yet it provides an example of workers delinking from a conventional relationship with the owners of the factories and engaging in a production process that benefits the workers and the national economy. It is only a select number of factories which have taken this route, so it would be inaccurate to conclude that the Argentinean economy has "deglobalized." The Venezuelan case is, by contrast, one of a state delinking certain aspects of its political economy from U.S.–dominated international institutions, while maintaining capitalist links within the world market.

While it is true that it has nationalized many industries and portions of others, its delinking strategies from American imperialism are most prominent in its discourse.

While the three types of resistance or transformation discussed here involve fairly radical departures from life as politically-economically usual under global capitalism, they also fall short of (or perhaps improve upon!) the classic Marxist revolutionary program, which is class based and advocates armed confrontation to terminate class divisions in a bourgeois-dominated society:

> The communist revolution is directed against the preceding mode of activity, does away with labour, and abolishes the rule of all classes with the classes themselves, because it is carried through by the class which no longer counts as a class in society, is not recognized as a class, and is in itself the expression of the dissolution of all classes, nationalities, etc.... This revolution is necessary, therefore not only because the ruling class cannot be overthrown in any other way, but also because the class overthrowing it can only in a revolution succeed in ridding itself of all the muck of ages and become fitted to found society anew [Marx and Engels 1978a (1845–1846): 193].

While they cannot be considered Marxist revolutionary movements, all three resistance movements can be said to exceed both developmental incrementalism and the standard, social-democratic, reformist approach which works within the existing political system in alliance with the state and the capitalist elites in order to effect change. It is also the case that none of the examples that will be discussed here has taken the delinking or deglobalization process as far as Amin or Bello's theories propose, but they have all taken dramatic steps on the way to disassociating themselves from the conventional social actors with whom they would customarily engage, even if their rhetoric exceeds their action. All three forms of resistance, whether approximating what is called delinking or deglobalization, may serve as useful means to address immediate needs, but because they neglect to sever *all* ties with conventional actors, and because they do not clarify the relationship between their actions and the capitalist mode of production, it is unclear what their actions ultimately portend. If the organizations in question were to delink totally, and if their goals were clearly defined, they might be at a lesser risk of being quashed; in fact their actions might make redundant the very structures and relationships they are opposing.

The most commonly theorized approaches to effecting political change are those of reform or revolution (see Bernstein 1993 [1937]); Luxembourg 2006 [1899]). Going it alone is not generally regarded as an effective option. If the EZLN, for example, is unable to conjure up more support from organizations which are also willing to delink from the government, they may find it difficult to maintain the momentum of the OC. Just as the theory of "socialism in one country" (Bukharin 1971) is unsustainable (see Trotsky 1969 [1931]), because the country in question will eventually find itself isolated and crushed, partial delinking or deglobalizing runs the risk of a similar outcome, namely isolation and annihilation. It can be argued that by clarifying the end goal, particularly in the case of the EZLN, the movement would have a better chance of enlisting support and growing the movement.

The varying degrees of delinking or deglobalization in the three cases examined here may nevertheless all be construed as positive advances toward full disconnection. Although Amin (1990: 55, 67) argues that delinking does not necessarily lead to socialism but makes such a transition more plausible, at this historical conjuncture none of the three cases appear to be heading in this direction. While the empirical data may be construed theoretically as indicative of a delinking process, the movements themselves do not refer to their actions as such. Their actions are politically driven and respond to failed relationships.

The first case study is that of the Zapatista movement, which, as discussed in the previous chapter, has partially delinked itself from government institutions and services. The second case is that of Hugo Chavez who, in the process of advancing ALBA in the company of Fidel Castro, has rejected U.S. plans for Latin America by creating an alternative trading mechanism. Although the two leaders have put in motion the process of delinking from the imperial powers of the North, their approach does not go as far as Amin would consider adequate. The third example that will be discussed here is the deglobalization strategy of the factory workers in Argentina who have taken over the factories and formed workers' cooperatives. This movement is similar to the Zapatista movement in that it takes place at the grassroots level. The Zapatista movement, Hugo Chavez and his trade initiatives and the factory takeovers in Argentina serve as examples of movements that have severed or partially severed key historical and political-economic relationships. Because the first two movements are still in progress, it will be difficult to determine fully the effectiveness or accomplishments of each. In the case of the workers in Argentina some lessons can be learned.

The Zapatista Movement

Put abstractly, delinking in the case of the Zapatistas is a matter of the disconnection of a nonstate actor from the prevailing political arrangements within a particular nation. It differs from conventional, extraparliamentary, political opposition where an organization or group protests, denounces or rebels against political authority, in that it seeks to function outside of the conventional state-society relationships altogether. Although it could be argued that opposition forces are always disconnected to some degree from the government in power, there would have to be a more radical, unconventional withdrawal to fit Amin's theoretical model. The Zapatistas' partial delinking from the Mexican state is basically a consequence of TC and failed attempts at finding a negotiated solution. The types of relationships that have been severed, and whether, as a political strategy, severance has the capacity to effect change, are the primary questions to be addressed.

After 1994, when the Zapatistas emerged from the Lacandon Jungle, and before the implementation of the partial delinking process, the movement succeeded in putting indigenous issues squarely on the Mexican political agenda at all levels. In so doing it has modified political discourse around indigenous issues, trained service providers and implemented health-care services and educational programs for indigenous communities, given indigenous women a voice, and served as a means for other organizations to be heard. Their challenge to the status quo nevertheless reached an impasse when the government showed itself unwilling to honor its side of the San Andrés Accords, which the two parties had signed in 1996. The drafting of the accords involved many people and many months of negotiating. The Mexican government breached the trust of the indigenous people in Chiapas by not keeping to the agreement but, instead, legislating its own version of an indigenous law. It was in this context that the EZLN withdrew or partially delinked from the Mexican state, including from most of its services and its institutions.

The current Zapatista approach to dealing with the Mexican government is to create its own political, economic and social structures parallel to government structures and to manage its internal affairs independently of the Mexican state. As discussed in chapter 5, the delinking strategy of the EZLN emerged after many years of negotiations and political confrontation between the EZLN and the state. The EZLN currently receives financial, material and political support from national and international NGOs and from people such as nurses, construction workers and teachers who travel to the area to volunteer their services. In this context, it is impossible to know what the delinking strategies of the EZLN would amount to if it didn't benefit from the support of the organizations and people just mentioned. In the case of the Zapatista movement this is a key component of their capacity to sever most of their relationships with the state.

There have been many indigenous struggles for autonomy over the past five hundred years in Mexico but none have gone as far as the Zapatista movement. In the 1960s and 1970s, movements seeking similar antisystemic transformations would have organized around revolutionary slogans while still working within the system. The Zapatistas do not promote conventional revolution but rather have terminated most relations with the government and developed relationships with national and international NGOs. Thus, while there is a partial delinking from the government there is a "linking up" with NGOs, a relationship that could over the long term create difficulties in the region as NGOs move out and supplies decrease. The delinking did not come about as a result of the linking up with NGOs, but rather as a consequence of years of attempts at negotiation with the government. The linking up with NGOs is something of an unexpected move on the part of the Zapatistas, given its anticapitalist discourse. Some NGOs are capitalist structures themselves, often housing themselves in large buildings and employing large numbers of personnel. In fact, many of the NGOs which have worked in the Zapatista zone emerged under neoliberalism to offer services no longer provided by the government. While it is perhaps unlikely, the relationship between NGOs and the Zapatistas could potentially undo the delinking actions of the movement from the state if most of their political and economic needs are satisfied by the NGOs.

By partially delinking, the Zapatistas have taken their own political, economic, social and cultural actions into their own hands. They have created their own government, their own health-care promoters, their own school curriculum; they train their teachers and health-care providers, they reject the presidential electoral process and they market their own goods. The delinking that they are practicing does not, however, filter down to the groups and organizations that support them. This is evident in the relationship that supporters of the OC maintain with the Mexican government and its institutions. The majority of these groups and organizations, if not all of them, continue to work within the political and economic framework set out by the Mexican government. For example, the environmental groups which met the OC while on tour through Morelos were calling for the conservation of the few remaining park areas in the state while other groups were calling for respect for human rights and land tenure. Many groups were asking Delegado Zero to negotiate their rights with the government, a request that contradicted the delinking strategies adopted by the OC. Support organizations did not adopt the anticapitalist, anti-neoliberal discourse of Delegado Zero. Likewise, the CIDHM, whose headquarters are found in Cuernavaca, Morelos, also fought for reforms within the capitalist mode of production to bring justice to different sectors of society which had suffered repression at the hands of the state. They maintained a relationship of negotiation with the state to address human rights abuses. In all of the cases mentioned above the organizations or groups benefited from services provided by the state such as health care and education. They propose reform rather than delinking. Left-wing Trotskyist and Marxist parties and organizations which support the Zapatista movement promote anticapitalist slogans and actions, yet members of these groups continue to reap the benefits of services provided by the capitalist Mexican state and have not themselves delinked. While supporting the movement, many of these organizations also criticize the EZLN for not seeking more radical socialist change. In fact it could be argued that the strategies adopted by the EZLN are more radical than its critics. It is premature to predict whether the Zapatistas' partial delinking strategies will be effective over the long term or whether they will fully delink in the future.

One observation worth noting is that by disconnecting from state services the most vulnerable often pay a steep price. The author observed this while doing fieldwork in La Realidad, Chiapas, in 2004 when she accompanied a medical doctor to the village where she gave consultation to people with medical concerns. Her stay in the village was to last six weeks. After this period, the only remaining medically trained people were the health promoters — people who took an interest in the well-being of people in the village but who had been trained to deal only with the simplest of medical cases, such as minor cuts, diarrhea, straightforward child birth and common bacterial respiratory infections. The Zapatistas use the government hospital services for the most serious cases while managing the minor cases locally. The process of assessing each case can potentially lead to undesirable consequences due to the limited training of the health-care promoters. Full delinking as promoted by Amin would mean having one's own resources to provide health-care services of all types. It would mean having the infrastructure and the personnel to work within one's means.

What is unclear at this stage of the movement is how effective its degree of disconnection from the Mexican state has been in effecting permanent change within the indigenous communities in Chiapas and throughout the country. It may well be the case that partial delinking is simply not enough in order to set the stage for Amin's possible transition to socialism. A future examination of the effects of the Zapatistas' delinking on community programs in health-care and education will provide greater insight into the effectiveness of these autonomous projects. As mentioned above, one of the primary supports of this partial delinking process is the NGOs which have been working in the area since shortly after the 1994 uprising. Without this support the communities would not have such things as the building supplies to build their schools, the school supplies for the children or the electrical plants to provide electricity to the communities. This is by no means to suggest that the indigenous people are ignorant or incapable of sustaining themselves but rather to emphasize the fact that the oppressive and repressive conditions which the communities have had to endure for many centuries, without the support of state services, have left the villages struggling to provide the most basic necessities of life.

What makes NGO support problematic is the fact that they are not permanent structures and their projects are not long term. Indeed, as argued in chapter 4, it is an unintended consequence of NGO actions that TC is actually sustained in Mexico. As new crises arise in distant lands, NGO resources are redirected (Veltmeyer 2007b). In the meantime partial delinking strategies of the EZLN serve as a political statement which denounces the state's betrayal in not fulfilling its end of the San Andrés Accords. It keeps the movement active in its pursuit of other political nonstate actors willing to organize against the government and its fraudulent practices. While from a Marxist-Leninist viewpoint, the delinking strategy falls short of the only reliable means with which to bring about socialism, namely armed revolution, for all practical purposes the EZLN has formed a new polity and new relations of production within the indigenous communities without the need for armed confrontation.

Venezuela: Chavez and ALBA

Narula and Quiles (2008) rightly describe Hugo Chavez's anti–U.S.-imperialism rhetoric as "bite" while his actions are little more than a "bark." However, while there are many ways in which Venezuela's economy is connected to the economy of the United States, Chavez has made considerable efforts to search for other Latin American governments willing to reduce these ties. One such effort is the launching of the ALBA with Fidel Castro. The ALBA emerged at a time when trade agreements of varying types were being signed throughout the American continent. It was signed in December 2004 to protest the U.S.-sponsored FTAA; this is where the delinking comes in. The U.S. government, as overseer of the world capitalist system in general and on behalf of its own multinational corporations in particular, has been the driving force behind free trade agreements throughout the Americas, yet Venezuela and Cuba have recently rejected the goals of the international elites and proposed the ALBA alternative. The ALBA is a means "to secure preferential treatment to poor countries of the region and grant financial aid to infrastructural and social investments or support local production and exports" (Herrera 2005: 42). This goes against neoliberal interests and aligns Venezuela with other countries that are also willing to disconnect from the U.S. imperialist project. This idea can only be understood if we understand the historical role that the U.S. has played in the economic and political scene in Latin America. U.S. domination and intervention has not been happenstance, a passing thing, but rather a long-standing, often crippling, imperial imposition that has interfered in the internal politics of all Latin American countries at different times virtually since the founding of the U.S. republic itself (see Blum 1998: 444–452 passim).

Regional trade blocs were in the works in Latin America as early as 1960 with the formation of the Latin American Free Trade Area, which transformed in 1969 into the Andean Community of Nations (called the Andean Pact until 1996). As Pastor (2001: 173) declares, it "was probably the most successful economic pact in the developing world in the 1960s and early 1970s." Further north the Caribbean Community (CARICOM) was founded in 1973; it currently has fifteen full members. In 1991 the Mercado Común del Sur (Mercosur or Southern Common Market) was established among Argentina, Brazil, Paraguay and Uruguay. Most recently, the U.S.–Central America Free Trade Agreement (CAFTA) was signed on May 28, 2004, by the U.S., Costa Rica, El Salvador, Guatemala, Honduras and Nicaragua (with the Dominican Republic subsequently added). The announced purpose of all of these agreements was to integrate the economies of the member states into the world economy in an attempt to reverse the process of internal economic deterioration. In preparation for this integration process, nations were expected to "restore fiscal discipline, privatize state-owned corporations, maintain a realistic exchange rate, and reduce barriers to trade and investment" (ibid.: 172). The third Summit of the Americas proposed integrating all of these smaller trade agreements into one continental agreement known as the FTAA. Since 2005 the FTAA has, however, been put on hold.

In the meantime, while in the North we discuss and promote North American integration, Venezuela and Cuba have been leading the way to a different kind of Latin American integration. What is distinctive about the ALBA initiative is that it has an anti-neoliberal, anti–U.S. agenda. It seeks to fight poverty and promote social integration through literacy, education, environmental and health-care programs. Its approach to Latin American integration is intended to fend off control of the market by transnational corporations.[1] Just as the Zapatista movement has partially disconnected from state politics and advanced the Other Campaign, so the Venezuelan and Cuban governments have advanced their proposal to create an alternative market. While the ALBA is designed to be an alternative to the role assigned to Latin America in a plan for the world economy driven by U.S. imperialism (via its transnational corporations and the international institutions it controls) from the Monroe Doctrine to the present (see Chomsky 1987: chap. 2, esp. 58–63), the historical economic ties between the United States and Venezuela are too great to sever altogether. According to Narula and Quiles (2008),

> in 2007, bilateral trade between the countries [Venezuela and the U.S.] totalled U.S. $50 billion, consisting of $10 billion in U.S. exports and $40 billion coming from Venezuela. The U.S. is Venezuela's most important trading partner, representing about 22 per cent of its imports and approximately 60 per cent of Venezuela exports. Ninety-five per cent of Venezuelan oil is exported to the U.S., establishing it as Venezuela's principal energy client. Venezuela is the U.S.'s second largest Latin American trading partner, purchasing U.S. machinery, transportation equipment, agricultural commodities, and auto parts.

Although the economic relationships are closely knit in the two countries, Chavez's discourse has led to a somewhat hostile relationship between them. On the economic front Chavez has taken some radical steps to delink from the status quo. For example, Venezuela paid off its debt to the IMF when Chavez first took office in 1999, and more recently paid off the World Bank five years ahead of schedule (see Rueda 2007). This has left Venezuela to its own financial resources and given it the ability to negotiate and manage future trade agreements with its Latin American allies independently. At an ALBA summit in Caracas on January 26, 2008, Chavez urged other Latin American countries "to begin withdrawing [their] billions of dollars in international reserves from U.S. banks" (James 2008). At the summit, Chavez also announced the launching of an ALBA development bank.

Hugo Chavez and Fidel Castro took the first steps toward the consolidation of ALBA in December 2004. At the Fifth ALBA Summit in Barquisimeto, in April 2007, Bolivia and Nicaragua signed on. Dominica signed on at the ALBA summit in January 2008. Haiti and Ecuador have expressed an interest yet they have not formalized their participation. In keeping with Amin's delinking model, Chavez has sought alternative support systems and trading partners.[2]

Shortly after the promulgation of ALBA a document was released that detailed its anti-neoliberal initiatives.

- Establish in Venezuela more than 1,000 health-care centers of various sorts that would offer services free of charge; train in Venezuela 40,000 doctors and 5,000 health technology specialists; train in Cuba, 10,000 Venezuelans in medicine and nursing;...

• Continue Cuban-Venezuelan collaboration to eliminate illiteracy in Venezuela...; work with 1,262 million Venezuelans to upgrade their studies...

• The two delegations also identified 11 projects for the establishment of joint ventures and other methods of economic complementation in Cuba and Venezuela ... including initiatives in iron and steel, railway infrastructure, maritime transport ... nickel and cobalt mining, and the repair and construction of sea vessels [Kellogg 2007: 201].

This approach to politics in Latin America and the rejection of U.S. goals for the region is not necessarily a new phenomenon, as can be recalled with the case of Salvador Allende in Chile, for example. What makes it an event worth examining is that we are not living in the 1970s, when socialism was a common goal; we are in the twenty-first century, the period of neoliberalism where the common mantra is global integration. ALBA is not an anticapitalist alternative, but rather an attempt to create a form of capitalism with a more favorable distribution of wealth and one that fulfills the basic health and educational needs of the people. Similar to the Zapatista case study, ALBA is in such a preliminary stage that it is difficult to determine the long-term ability of the program to effect change for the populations of the countries in question. If it lived up to its rhetoric to reject U.S. political and economic interference in the region, and if it totally delinked from the U.S.–backed international institutions, the Latin American landscape would be significantly modified. Of course, the question remains whether the U.S. would permit such a transformation without a military invasion.

Argentina: Factory Takeovers

The factory takeovers in Argentina provide an example of deglobalization that differs somewhat from the previous two cases. In the case of the Zapatistas, there is a partial disconnection between the communities in the southern state of Chiapas and the national and state governments and their institutions. In the case of Venezuela, there is a discourse of delinking between the Venezuelan government and the U.S. government and the international institutions which it controls. In the case of Argentina, there is a process of disconnection between the factory workers and the corporations previously dominating the market which has created a new relation of production where the workers are their own bosses. In all three cases there is a degree of severing of conventional relationships and the search for new alliances and organizational structures.

In the Argentinian case the takeover or occupation of factories by the workers and the formation of cooperatives during the economic crisis of 2001 is an example of disconnection between the workers and their bosses, the owners of the means of production. The severing of this relationship is indicative of a transformation of conventional worker-owner relations. The worker occupation of factories in 2001–2002 was just one of many strategies adopted in response to the political-economic crisis of the time. In fact, factory takeovers in Argentina date back to May–June of 1964. According to the CGT (see Cotarelo and Fernandez 1997: 7), over 3 million workers occupied around 11,000 factories during that period. Many of these occupations were short-lived and workers returned to work without resistance upon request. The more recent takeovers "reached a peak between 2001 and 2002 with over 10,000 workers operating over 100 enterprises" (Petras and Veltmeyer 2005: 50). In many cases the factory owners had declared bankruptcy and the workers then moved in and took possession of the buildings and equipment and attempted to restart production. Many of the conglomerates succeeded while others failed. Some ceased to maintain deglobalization strategies and were instead converted into profit-oriented cooperatives and were granted legal status by the government (ibid.: 51). Others were ideologically driven and went it alone. Zanon, a ceramics factory in the province of Neuquen, is the most well-known, ideologically driven, worker-run factory in Argentina today. It is one of over two hundred such cooperatives in Argentina (Dangl 2005). Zanon, which now goes by the name FaSinPat,[3] was not a cooperative recognized or registered with the state because the state rejected its internal management. To get to where they are today they had to confront the original Italian owners and defend themselves against the unions in Neuquen, the government and the police. Whereas they were successful in removing from the factories the biggest obstacles and oppressors, namely the owners up until August 2009 the workers were under constant threat from government authorities.[4] On August 13, the Neuquen provincial legislature voted in favor of legalizing the expropriation of the factory by the workers and legally recognizing it as a workers' cooperative (*El Argentino*, August 14, 2009).

The Zanon worker-run factory began in March 2002, when 220 of the 330 workers decided to take over the factory and bring it under workers' control. They agreed that everybody would receive the same income and that committees would be formed to manage sales, safety, purchasing, production and general administrative jobs, all required transformations according to Bello. In April 2002 the first lot of 20,000 square meters of ceramic products came off the assembly line. Three months later over 120,000 square meters were produced. In 2006 they were producing over 300,000 square meters and were reaching for 400,000 (see Zibechi 2006). Today, FaSinPat is the largest ceramic factory in Argentina. It has approximately 80,000 square meters of floor space and employs about 200 workers. Under its previous owners there were approximately 300 work-related accidents a year and on average one work-related death a month. Under the workers' management there are on average 33 accidents a year and there have not been any work-related deaths (ibid.).

One of the most important lessons that can be learned from the Zanon experience is that collaboration and common goals are keys to success. However, there are also unsuccessful examples where isolation led to the dismantling and demise of many worker-run factory attempts. In the case of the failed factory takeovers in Argentina, there was little support among the workers of the different factories. Full delinking on a broader level could potentially result in more generalized radical transformations of the relations of production in Argentina, a feat which has only been accomplished at particular, localized factories.

Discussion and Conclusions

Delinking and deglobalization are promoted by some as possible means by which to effect systemic change, whereas development strategies and programs are the soft-capitalist means. Social-democratic reformist strategies and armed revolution are the other standard options. The reality is that delinking and deglobalization are in the early stages of experimentation in Latin America, and where they will lead is still uncertain. The Zapatista movement is the case that best approximates Amin's theory of delinking. It has been successful in removing the state from most of its daily activities yet it has to some degree replaced its dependency on the state with a dependency on NGOs. The case of Chavez and the ALBA is a very weak example of delinking because while Venezuela claims to be opposed to U.S. imperialism, the U.S. is its biggest trading partner. If this is an attempt to advance a "war of position" in relation to the U.S. and in the eyes of its population, it could very well succeed (presuming it can find an alternative destination for its oil exports). The factory takeovers in Argentina demonstrate both the successes which are achievable by anarchist-type action, and the difficulties that arise when such actors do not have the support of other organizations to further their cause. The sustainability of these partial deglobalization actions is uncertain, but given the many factory takeovers that ended by closing their doors indefinitely it is clearly difficult to function in relative isolation in a capitalist economy driven by competition and greed.

Amin's theory of delinking and Bello's theory of deglobalization allow for a degree of uncertainty in the final outcome. This is evident in Amin's (1990: 55, 67) assertion that a state which is delinking from global governance *may* evolve into a socialist state, but that this will not always be the case. Delinking and deglobalization are seen as first steps toward a transition of some sort. In the Zapatista case the political actors rejected the status quo by forming their independent municipalities (the Caracoles) and municipal governments (Juntas de Buen Gobierno), and by acting independently of the national electoral system by establishing the OC as a parallel political process. The movement does not declare socialism as its goal but rather sees its actions as a ten- to fifteen-year project of movement building and definition. In the Chavez case, a political-economic arrangement parallel to U.S. imperialism formed among willing Latin American countries under ALBA is in the initial stages. What has been accomplished is the uniting of states that reject the FTAA and that are willing to discuss common strategies that reject American imperialism. At its sixth conference in Caracas in January 2008 the creation of a regional development bank was announced giving the member states greater independence from the IFIs. While these steps further the delinking process, they fall short of full delinking. Whether or not the latter will happen depends on the actors themselves, the confidence they have about going it alone and the willingness of others to get on board. The story to date of the factory takeovers in Argentina for the most part shows how easily deglobalization attempts can fail. While there are undoubtedly some success stories, there are also many examples of factory takeovers that were unable to survive in the current market economy.

Without question the biggest enemy of delinking and deglobalization strategies in Latin America is U.S. imperialism,[5] but lack of unity of the political left has also wrought havoc on its ability to dismantle capitalism and replace it with a political-economic system that will truly address the anti-neoliberal, anticapitalist goals as laid out by the OC, uttered by Chavez or attempted by the factory workers in Argentina. The popular uprisings in Argentina in 2001 demonstrated the divisive nature of so many Latin American political struggles. Veltmeyer (2007b: 41) holds that "the original strength of the popular uprising [in Argentina in 2001] — its spontaneous, mass, autonomous character — became its strategic weakness, the absence of a national leadership capable of unifying the diverse forces behind a coherent program aimed at taking state power." Electoral reforms have given people a greater sense of affinity with Northern democracy and a greater connection with the developed world. Elections will not, however, solve the everyday hardships of the people, nor will they lead governments or movements to delink themselves from the grip of imperialism or neoliberal capitalism. Mexico is a good example of how this is the case.

The current approaches to effecting political change have one important advantage over the revolutionary tactics of earlier times, and that is that they involve peaceful, nonviolent actions. In academia there is much controversy over what social-political change should look like and how to bring it about. One thing to keep in mind when studying developments in the South is that, in contrast to Northern academic circles, revolution and class struggle continue to be seen in the South as viable means to an end. Delinking or deglobalizing from the capitalist mode of production, with a clear vision of the future and a strong leadership, could prove to be an effective, peaceful alternative not only to "reform" and "development" but also to revolutionary violence.

Conclusions

The neoliberal hegemony that undid the North's postwar, state-welfare, capitalist consensus began in the early 1970s and took hold in Mexico in the 1980s. It has occasioned significant changes in the Mexican state and in its relations with nonstate actors. There has been an influx of new social actors and an array of new political actions. These relatively recent developments in corporate capitalism are explicable in terms of Marxist political-economic theory which avers that (a) capitalism is a system of "permanent revolution," in which (b) the owners of the means of production continue to rule the world. Never has Marx's analytic description of the development of capitalism in the *Communist Manifesto* seemed so apt.

> Modern industry has established the world market, for which the discovery of America paved the way.... The bourgeoisie has at last, since the establishment of modern industry and of the world market, conquered for itself, in a modern representative state, exclusive political sway. The executive of the modern state is but a committee for managing the common affairs of the whole bourgeoisie.... The bourgeoisie, historically, has played a most revolutionary part.... It has resolved personal worth into exchange value, and in place of the numberless indefeasible chartered freedoms, has set up that single, unconscionable freedom —FREE TRADE. In one word, for exploitation veiled by religious and political illusions it has substituted naked, shameless, direct, brutal exploitation.... **The bourgeoisie cannot exist without constantly revolutionising the instruments of production, and thereby the relations of production, and with them the whole relations of society** [Marx and Engels 1987 (1848): 23–24, emphasis added].

Mexico's capitalist class as we know it today was founded on the revolutionary actions of the PRI in the early part of the twentieth century. While the PRI lost the presidency in 2000, capitalist interests are still what drive the PAN as it continues to implement neoliberal policies to satisfy the requirements of the IFIs and the mainly international bourgeoisie. Capitalism's permanent revolutionizing of the relations of production "and with them the whole relations of society" has meant corresponding changes in Mexico's state–society relations. As neoliberal globalization took hold in the 1970s and 1980s, nation states changed their domestic political and economic structures. Global capitalist relations of production, "free trade" and transnationalized corporatist relationships are what define the Mexican state today. Marx and Engels continue,

> the need for a constantly expanding market for its products chases the bourgeoisie over the whole surface of the globe. It must nestle everywhere, settle everywhere, establish connections everywhere.... The bourgeoisie, by the rapid improvement of all instruments

of production, by the immensely facilitated means of communication, draws all, even the most barbarian, nations into civilization. The cheap prices of commodities are the heavy artillery with which it batters down all Chinese walls.... It compels all nations, on pain of extinction, to adopt the bourgeois mode of production; it compels them to introduce what it calls civilization into their midst, i.e., to become bourgeois themselves. In one word, it creates a world after its own image.... The bourgeoisie ... has agglomerated population, centralized means of production, and has concentrated property in a few hands. The necessary consequence of this was political centralization [Marx and Engels, 1987 (1848): 23–25].

As an underdeveloped country, or what some prefer to call a developing country, Mexico has fallen victim to the "constantly expanding market" that Marx refers to. While some benefit has come from being a petroleum-producing country, its national capitalist class has suffered because of its inability to compete with the multinational and transnational corporations which dominate the global economy. The general population has also suffered the consequences of industries being turned into low-paying maquila factories (assembly plants). The principal change in the relations of production under the neoliberal economic model has been a shift in power from national to international owners.

The abandoning of the gold standard and fixed exchange rates in 1971 and the consequent liberation of flows of money capital from state control meant that financial capital became the hegemonic force in the global economy, with New York as its centre (Harvey 2005: 62). The U.S.–dominated IFIs became the instruments of neoliberal hegemony, not least through the mechanism of the structural adjustment program. Countries that needed to borrow money to stay afloat had to play by the new rules, established to serve the interests of the economic superpower and its transnational corporations.[1] Promoted as a means to develop underdeveloped areas of the world by liberating the market and promoting trade, structural adjustment programs and the neoliberal policies they enforced on recipient governments have had disastrous consequences on the economic, political and social life of the people of the recipient societies. Mexico is a classic case.

The central tenets of the neoliberal dispensation for individual states are the privatization of state-owned corporations and social programs, deregulation of the private sector, downsizing of government, reduction of corporate and income taxes, paying down of the national debt, elimination of tariff barriers and an opening up to the international market economy. Underdeveloped countries like Mexico that had protectionist economies under ISI, and poorly developed social programs, have suffered greatly under neoliberalism. As industries were privatized, national revenue decreased. This lost revenue has not been made up through taxes because governments have been effectively forced to reduce taxes to attract corporations. Consequently, basic services such as health-care, education and public transportation have all suffered and the financial tab has been passed on to the consumer. As expected, the unemployed, the indigenous communities, women, factory workers and small landholding peasants are the sectors of society most affected. They are the furthest removed from ownership of the means of production and suffer the most when services are reduced or privatized.

States, then, have given in to pressure by international financial institutions to privatize their state corporations and services and to open their markets to foreign investment and trade, all in the name of so-called "development." Complying with the conditions set out by the international institutions qualifies states to receive development funds. The basis of the argument is that by putting services into private hands they will be better managed, more profitable and will employ more people. Empirical data demonstrate that it is the transnational corporations, banks, and investment and insurance companies that are the ones that benefit, not the people whose supposed welfare justified the implementation of these reforms in the first place.

The body of this study discusses how state-society relations in Mexico have been modified in response to the above changes in the global, political-economic order. The modern Mexican state, as we know it today, was reestablished following the revolution of 1910. Because of economic instability in the postrevolutionary period, Lázaro Cárdenas created the CTM in 1939 as a means to control the workers. State corporatism best describes the nature of the ensuing state-society relations. It is characterized above all by the appointing of government supporters in positions of power within the unions. These union leaders managed the membership hierarchically to keep them in line with the government's agenda.

While some argue that state corporatism ended when the PRI was defeated by the PAN in the 2000 federal elections, it is more accurate to say (as delineated in chapter 4) that state corporatism went through a gradual transformation throughout the 1980s and early 1990s, culminating in what is here called transnationalized corporatism. The electoral reforms that have accompanied its rise provide, in the view of this writer, little more than a liberal-democratic veneer, mystifying ongoing corporatist practices. TC is a continuation of the historically grounded corporatist relations first established between the inhabitants of the land and the Spanish conquerors, and cemented through the PRI years of one-party rule as state corporatism. These hierarchical structures continue to characterize state-society relations in Mexico today, albeit in transnationalized form. That is, TC names a model of state-society relations in which the state comes under the powerful constraint of the Wall Street–U.S. Treasury nexus, causing a transformation in the way the state and society interact. The state comes to operate within a power structure that represents the interests of global capital while balancing them against the interests of its own national capitalist class which in turn results in a variety of changes to state-society relations, as discussed throughout this study.

As state-society relationships have been modified under TC, nonstate political actors have sought ways to organize and respond to this new order. The paradoxical qualities of TC are manifested in the fact that corporatist relationships have become weaker and in some cases anachronistic, yet still persist. State leaders and union leaders have lost a degree of legitimacy through the transitional process. While the number of workers affiliated with official unions has decreased as state corporations have been privatized, the restructuring of the economy has led to redistribution and relocation of state-provided services and the continuation of corporatist relationships. On the surface, it may appear that little has changed in the composition of these corporatist relationships and how they are instituted, but the influence of international institutions on internal state-society relations cannot be ignored. Just as in the state-corporatist model not all actors maintained direct corporatist relationships with the state, so the same holds true under TC. In both cases the organizations that are tied most closely to the state are the unions. For the purpose of simplification and clarification, a tripartite typology of strategies was proposed and used here, in terms of which each nonstate actor has been classified. Corporate strategies apply to those unions maintaining such relationships with the government. While the state has lost some credibility within many of these unions, their leaders are still devoted to maintaining corporatist relations. Anticorporatist strategies are those adopted by nonstate actors that are manifestly opposed to corporatism but have the latent, unintended consequence of upholding TC state-society relations. Independent unions, left-wing political parties, NGOs and social movements all fall into this category. Their latent relationship with the state is one of integration; their sustaining of corporatist relationships is an unintended consequence of their oppositional strategies. In sharp contrast to the integrative oppositional strategies are the noncorporatist strategies of the EZLN and to a degree the JBG. Both have adopted delinking strategies in their attempt to create their own polity independent of the Mexican state. The utility of this typology is simply its capacity both to exhibit the fact that nonstate actors have adopted a *variety* of strategies in response to the changes in the state occasioned by the hegemonic ascent of neoliberalism, and to demonstrate the *integrative* function of oppositional groups for the system they claim to oppose.

In the corporatist category there are still many unions that continue to be affiliated with the CT and the CTM while having to adapt to the influence of supranational institutions in their dealings with the government. In many cases the old hierarchical arrangements prevail and union leaders continue to maintain close relationships with the state, as seen in the SNTE case. These unions and their leaderships are what principally sustain corporatism in Mexico. Though it has evolved from state corporatism, TC maintains such similarities to it that one can talk of corporatism as being entrenched in Mexican society. Aside from the persistent corporatist relationships between leaders of official unions and the state, many groups of union members have adopted anticorporatist strategies while working within their unions, while others have established independent unions outside of and parallel to the official unions. Many of these independent unions (for example, the SINTCB) have joined together in coalitions (the UNT) to take up common issues such as privatization. In the past, support was often extended among different unions within similar industries, but there has rarely been a common demand such as privatization or democratization capable of bringing so many organizations together in the same struggle.

Empirical evidence demonstrates that state-society relationships in official unions are corporatist whereas in independent unions, workers engage in anticorporatist strategies. However, when viewed with the interpretive lens of Marxist theory, the relations of production remain unaltered and union strategies are integrative regardless of how the workers, the owners of the means of production, and the state interact. The relations of production are such that there are owners and there are workers; the former determine the nature of the relationship and the latter are at their disposition with only their labor force to sell. The actions of official and independent unions are integrative because they do not reject capitalist relations of production but instead work within them. Therefore, even though nonofficial unions engage in anticorporatist strategies the unintended consequence of their actions is the maintaining of transnationalized corporatism.

Under TC nonstate actors of all types have been and are engaging in political coalition formation. There have been attempts by left-wing, unofficial political parties to unite; there has been a reemergence of the national front against repression; women have formed coalitions in an attempt to create a louder voice and a stronger negotiating position; and unprecedented post-electoral movements have emerged denouncing fraudulent processes. Middle-class, small farmers (Barzón), a group that would traditionally align with the state, have also organized against the economic impact of neoliberal policies. All of these actions are evidence of an incipient political change in civil society, one in which nonstate actors are organizing to denounce and act back against the transnationalized corporatist state-society relations which have come about under global, neoliberal hegemony. As was the case with unions, empirical evidence shows that the actions of nonstate actors in the aforementioned organizations are often anticorporatist, yet from a Marxist interpretive lens they remain integrated in the capitalist relations of production. Their actions uphold corporatist relationships simply by working within the existing structures rather than delinking from them.

Another expression of the changes under TC is evident in the proliferation of NGOs. NGOs have come to fulfill what were traditionally considered state responsibilities, such as the building of a school or day-care center. The current proliferation of NGOs is unprecedented in Mexico. While some NGOs predate the transnationalized corporatist period, there has been an impressive increase in the number of organizations in Mexico since the early 1990s. NGOs do not have corporatist relationships with the state because they are accountable only to their benefactors, yet, as is the case with other nonstate actors, their work remains within the parameters of TC and the prevailing capitalist relations of production. Their actions can be said to sustain the status quo rather than replacing it with a new arrangement. They do not require state approval to provide services or material goods to a particular population, and the state does not interfere with their activities because of the pacifying effect they have on the population. NGO development would not have flourished under state corporatism in the past the way it has today because of the authoritarian nature of state corporatism in Mexico, where the government employed both direct corporatist means and repressive means to control society. Under TC, as long as the NGOs do not serve as a means to organize people against the state, their presence is most welcome.

The most extreme response to TC has been the noncorporatist strategies pursued by the Zapatista movement. Its emergence on the national public stage in 1994 was in itself uncharacteristic of patterns of political action of that time. Armed confrontation was seen as a 1960s or 1970s response to political repression and injustice. The Zapatista uprising brought to the fore a renewed appreciation of the wrongs of neoliberalism. Along with its initial, unexpected uprising on January 1, 1994, its more recent strategy of almost complete delinking from the Mexican state, in line with its declared anticapitalist, noncorporatist posture, goes beyond previous indigenous struggles for autonomy. Full delinking has the potential of setting the stage for future transformative or even socialist developments.

However, while the EZLN has almost entirely delinked from the Mexican state, its dependency on NGOs creates two concerns. First, NGOs are dependent on the financial support of governing institutions from international organizations to municipal governments, and from wealthy corporations to affluent individuals in the North. This financial dependency often means that funding comes with strict guidelines and rules on how to spend the money and what qualifies as an acceptable project. The second issue of concern is that NGOs are not permanent structures. They bounce from one disaster area to another. They remain in any area only as long as it takes to reestablish some degree of stability or until a particular project is completed. They then move on to another geographical location faced with another challenge.

While NGOs have greatly benefited the indigenous communities in Chiapas, the daily lives of the inhabitants have changed little since the Zapatista uprising in 1994. This is simply because the communities lack the infrastructure needed to effect permanent change in the region and to go it alone. The lack of a clear goal, or projected end point, also jeopardizes the movement's ability to fulfill a leadership role for the rest of society. Under the OC the leadership of the Zapatista movement is attempting to reach out to the rest of civil society, to form a national, anticapitalist, anti-neoliberal coalition in order to defend basic human rights against the depredations of neoliberalism and the capitalist mode of production. For many would-be sympathizers, their efforts amount to too little, too late. They argue that the movement came on the political scene with great potential and with the backing of most, if not all, oppositional forces in Mexico, but that the current OC is a softened approach to doing politics. From a Marxist theoretical perspective one of the most important accomplishments of the EZLN has been its ability to modify local relations of production in Chiapas through its delinking advances and the creation of microcosmic communities. The political structures of the JBG and the fact that they choose not to engage in electoral politics are further examples of their delinking strategies. The Zapatista noncorporatist delinking strategy is still in the preliminary stages and it is unclear what they hope to accomplish long term and how they plan to get there. It is unclear whether it in fact has the potential to serve as an alternative to TC.

The two categories used to describe the approaches used by the different nonstate actors in Mexico are integrative and delinking. Integration results in the preservation of the existing relations of production, state-society relations and political structures whereas delinking has the potential of modifying all of these. From a Marxist point of view, on the one hand, the integrative approaches, whether corporatist or anticorporatist, are incapable of modifying the relations of production which are the backbone of capitalism; their actions are of little consequence to the staying power of TC. Indeed, anticorporatist strategies have the unintended integrative consequence of upholding TC. On the other hand, delinking or deglobalization has the potential of changing the relations of production found in capitalism. While the relations of production have been modified within the Caracoles there remain various aspects of interaction with the state that remain intact, namely the use of health-care services in emergency situations and the use of the state judiciary in extreme cases.

The Zapatistas, Chavez and the ALBA, and the factory workers in Argentina are all engaged in varying degrees of delinking, whether in action or in discourse, that call into question and act against the new world order of neoliberal capitalism. The Zapatistas have announced their delinking from the state, Chavez has declared his delinking from U.S. imperialism and the factory workers in Argentina have delinked from the owners of the factories by taking them over. In all the cases discussed above, it is clear that *partial* delinking or deglobalization strategies, their local successes and future promise notwithstanding, have to date had little impact on the staying power of capitalism. Nevertheless, since "the future is an infinite succession of presents," the (partially) changed relations of production afforded by the Zapatista, Venezuelan and Argentinean social experiments are themselves "a marvelous victory" (Zinn 2007: 270) on the way to emancipating their citizens from capitalism's "icy water of egotistical calculation."

Epilogue

I began with the Northerner's shock at encountering in Mexico the dire poverty of the South. The shock turned to outrage when I learned to connect the South's poverty to the North's wealth, each being a consequence of the other. The outrage was sharpened as I came to see the part played by states, specifically the United States of America and the United States of Mexico, and international bodies, specifically the IFIs and the GATT/WTO, in fostering and maintaining that disparity and relationship. Then, from within my own experience of trying to act back against this system of enrichment and impoverishment with its accompanying repression of opposition, I began to ask how it all worked, how it was sustained, who the relevant actors were, how they interacted, where the possibilities of change were to be found. This led me to focus my inquiry on Mexico's (traditionally state-corporatist) state-society relations with the emphasis on the role of nonstate actors, above all the startling Zapatista movement.

In an earlier incarnation I had lived for twelve years in Mexico. More recently I spent a year of research there interviewing representatives of such nonstate (and some state) actors (unions, political parties, NGOs), studying their documents and observing them in action. Subsequently I made repeated trips there to observe electoral movements, life in the Zapatista communities, and the Other Campaign.

From this ethnographic work I came to appreciate the variety of strategies being utilized by nonstate actors in trying to respond to observable and documented changes in the nature of Mexico's corporatist state. I called the changes transnationalized corporatism. These were themselves a product of neoliberal globalization's modification of capitalism's social relations of production. Marxist political economy thus afforded a means of interpreting the strategies of nonstate actors that I had come to classify as corporatist, anticorporatist and noncorporatist. In the lens of Marxist "critical functionalism" corporatist and anticorporatist strategies can be seen as integrative, noncorporatist as delinking. I finished by widening the lens to compare the Zapatista delinking strategy with related efforts to disconnect by Hugo Chavez in Venezuela and the factory takeovers in Argentina.

There are still many questions left unanswered regarding the relative efficacy of integrative versus delinking strategies. For example, it is unclear whether any of these partial delinking strategies provide a viable alternative or will eventually lead to an alternative. It is unclear whether, in the Mexican case, nonstate actors that currently engage in anticorporatist strategies will follow the lead of the Zapatistas and seek a noncorporatist strategy, or whether the "insurrectionary reformism" of APPO's Oaxaca Commune of 2006, with its combination of "revolutionary forms of struggle with goals of increasingly radical reforms" will do more than "influence the discourse and imagery of existing and emerging movements seeking to transform Mexico" (Roman and Arregui 2007: 260). It may be argued that this lack of clarity arises from just what distinguishes the Zapatista movement as an agent of change, namely its eclectic mix of tactics, its unwillingness to describe itself in terms of any grand narrative and the consequent indeterminacy of its eventual destination. In the language of contemporary social theory, such creative, indeterminate radicalism invites not only the label postcorporatist but also post–Marxist, if not post-modernist.

We should not forget, however, that what distinguishes Marxism from the post-al thread in contemporary social theory is not just its identification with a grand narrative but its insistence on the inseparability of theory and practice. In the end, then, the "undecidability" of Zapatista delinking is neither a theoretical nor an empirical question, but a practical-political one. The would-be delinkers have acted. What becomes of their actions rests in the hands of the rest of us.

Appendix: The Plan de Ayala

Liberating Plan of the sons of the State of Morelos, affiliated with the Insurgent Army which defends the fulfillment of the Plan of San Luis, with the reforms which it has believed proper to add in benefit of the Mexican Fatherland.

We who undersign, constituted in a revolutionary junta to sustain and carry out the promises which the revolution of November 20, 1910, just past, made to the country, declare solemnly before the face of the civilized world which judges us and before the nation to which we belong and which we call [*sic*; *llamamos*, misprint for *amamos*, "love"], propositions which we have formulated to end the tyranny which oppresses us and redeem the fatherland from the dictatorships which are imposed on us, which [propositions] are determined in the following plan:

1. Taking into consideration that the Mexican people led by Don Francisco I. Madero went to shed their blood to reconquer liberties and recover their rights which had been trampled on, and not for a man to take possession of power, violating the sacred principles which he took an oath to defend under the slogan "Effective Suffrage and No Reelection," outraging thus the faith, the cause, the justice, and the liberties of the people: taking into consideration that that man to whom we refer is Don Francisco I. Madero, the same who initiated the above-cited revolution, who imposed his will and influence as a governing norm on the Provisional Government of the ex–President of the Republic Attorney Francisco L. de Barra [*sic*], causing with this deed repeated sheddings of blood and multiple misfortunes for the fatherland in a manner deceitful and ridiculous, having no intentions other than satisfying his personal ambitions, his boundless instincts as a tyrant, and his profound disrespect for the fulfillment of the preexisting laws emanating from the immortal code of '57, written with the revolutionary blood of Ayutla.

    Taking into account that the so-called Chief of the Liberating Revolution of Mexico, Don Francisco I. Madero, through lack of integrity and the highest weakness, did not carry to a happy end the revolution which gloriously he initiated with the help of God and the people, since he left standing most of the governing powers and corrupted elements of oppression of the dictatorial government of Porfirio Díaz, which are not nor can in any way be the representation of National Sovereignty, and which, for being most bitter adversaries of ours and of the principles which even now we defend, are provoking the discomfort of the

179

country and opening new wounds in the bosom of the fatherland, to give it its own blood to drink; taking also into account that the aforementioned Sr. Francisco I. Madero, present President of the Republic, tries to avoid the fulfillment of the promises which he made to the Nation in the Plan of San Luis Potosí, being [*sic*, *siendo*, misprint for *ciñendo*, "restricting"] the above-cited promises to the agreements of Ciudad Juárez, by means of false promises and numerous intrigues against the Nation nullifying, pursuing, jailing, or killing revolutionary elements who helped him to occupy the high post of President of the Republic;

Taking into consideration that the so-often-repeated Francisco I. Madero has tried with the brute force of bayonets to shut up and to drown in blood the pueblos who ask, solicit, or demand from him the fulfillment of the promises of the revolution, calling them bandits and rebels, condemning them to a war of extermination without conceding or granting a single one of the guarantees which reason, justice, and the law prescribe; taking equally into consideration that the President of the Republic Francisco I. Madero has made of Effective Suffrage a bloody trick on the people, already against the will of the same people imposing Attorney José M. Pino Suárez in the Vice-Presidency of the Republic, or [imposing as] Governors of the States [men] designated by him, like the so-called General Ambrosio Figueroa, scourge and tyrant of the people of Morelos, or entering into scandalous cooperation with the científico party, feudal landlords, and oppressive bosses, enemies of the revolution proclaimed by him, so as to forge new chains and follow the pattern of a new dictatorship more shameful and more terrible than that of Porfirio Díaz, for it has been clear and patent that he has outraged the sovereignty of the States, trampling on the laws without any respect for lives or interests, as has happened in the State of Morelos, and others, leading them to the most horrendous anarchy which contemporary history registers.

For these considerations we declare the aforementioned Francisco I. Madero inept at realizing the promises of the revolution of which he was the author, because he has betrayed the principles with which he tricked the will of the people and was able to get into power: incapable of governing, because he has no respect for the law and justice of the pueblos, and a traitor to the fatherland, because he is humiliating in blood and fire Mexicans who want liberties, so as to please the científicos, landlords, and bosses who enslave us, and from today on we begin to continue the revolution begun by him, until we achieve the overthrow of the dictatorial powers which exist.

2. Recognition is withdrawn from Sr. Francisco I. Madero as Chief of the Revolution and as President of the Republic, for the reasons which before were expressed, it being attempted to overthrow this official.

3. Recognized as Chief of the Liberating Revolution is the illustrious General Pascual Orozco, the second of the Leader Don Francisco I. Madero, and in case he does not accept this delicate post, recognition as Chief of the Revolution will go to General Don Emiliano Zapata.

4. The Revolutionary Junta of the State of Morelos manifests to the Nation under formal oath: that it makes its own the plan of San Luis Potosí, with the additions which are expressed below in benefit of the oppressed pueblos, and it will make itself the defender of the principles it defends until victory or death.

5. The Revolutionary Junta of the State of Morelos will admit no transactions or compromises until it achieves the overthrow of the dictatorial elements of Porfirio Díaz and Francisco I. Madero, for the nation is tired of false men and traitors who make promises like liberators and who on arriving in power forget them and constitute themselves as tyrants.

6. As an additional part of the plan we invoke, we give notice: that [regarding] the fields, timber, and water which the landlords, científicos, or bosses have usurped, the pueblos or citizens who have the titles corresponding to those properties will immediately enter into possession of that real estate of which they have been despoiled by the bad faith of our oppressors, maintaining at any cost with arms in hand the mentioned possession; and the usurpers who consider themselves with a right to them [those properties] will deduce it before the special tribunals which will be established on the triumph of the revolution.

7. In virtue of the fact that the immense majority of Mexican pueblos and citizens are owners of no more than the land they walk on, suffering the horrors of poverty without being able to improve their social condition in any way or to dedicate themselves to Industry or Agriculture, because lands, timber, and water are monopolized in a few hands, for this cause there will be expropriated the third part of those monopolies from the powerful proprietors of them, with prior indemnization, in order that the pueblos and citizens of Mexico may obtain ejidos, colonies, and foundations for pueblos, or fields for sowing or laboring, and the Mexicans' lack of prosperity and well-being may improve in all and for all.

8. [Regarding] the landlords, científicos, or bosses who oppose the present plan directly or indirectly, their goods will be nationalized and the two-third parts which [otherwise would] belong to them will go for indemnizations of war, pensions for widows and orphans of the victims who succumb in the struggle for the present plan.

9. In order to execute the procedures regarding the properties aforementioned, the laws of disamortization and nationalization will be applied as they fit, for serving us as norm and example can be those laws put in force by the immortal Juárez on ecclesiastical properties, which punished the despots and conservatives who in every time have tried to impose on us the ignominious yoke of oppression and backwardness.

10. The insurgent military chiefs of the Republic who rose up with arms in hand at the voice of Don Francisco I. Madero to defend the plan of San Luis Potosí, and who oppose with armed force the present plan, will be judged traitors to the cause which they defended and to the fatherland, since at present many of them, to humor the tyrants, for a fistful of coins, or for bribes or connivance, are shedding the blood of their brothers who claim the fulfillment of the promises which Don Francisco I. Madero made to the nation.

11. The expenses of war will be taken in conformity with Article 2 of the Plan of San Luis Potosí, and all procedures employed in the revolution we undertake will be in conformity with the same instructions which the said plan determines.

12. Once triumphant the revolution which we carry into the path of reality, a Junta of the principal revolutionary chiefs from the different States will name or desig-

nate an interim President of the Republic, who will convoke elections for the organization of the federal powers.

13. The principal revolutionary chiefs of each State will designate in Junta the Governor of the State to which they belong, and this appointed official will convoke elections for the due organization of the public powers, the object being to avoid compulsory appointments which work the misfortune of the pueblos, like the so-well-known appointment of Ambrosio Figueroa in the State of Morelos and others who drive us to the precipice of bloody conflicts, sustained by the caprice of the dictator Madero and the circle of científicos and landlords who have influenced him.

14. If President Madero and other dictatorial elements of the present and former regime want to avoid the immense misfortunes which afflict the fatherland, and [if they] possess true sentiments of love for it, let them make immediate renunciation of the posts they occupy and with that they will with something stanch the grave wounds which they have opened in the bosom of the fatherland, since, if they do not do so, on their heads will fall the blood and the anathema of our brothers.

15. Mexicans: consider that the cunning and bad faith of one man is shedding blood in a scandalous manner, because he is incapable of governing; consider that his system of government is choking the fatherland and trampling with the brute force of bayonets on our institutions; and thus, as we raised up our weapons to elevate him to power, we again raise them up against him for defaulting on his promises to the Mexican people and for having betrayed the revolution initiated by him, we are not personalists, we are partisans of principles and not of men!

Mexican People, support this plan with arms in hand and you will make the prosperity and well-being of the fatherland.

Ayala, November 25, 1911

Liberty, Justice, and Law

Signed, General in Chief Emiliano Zapata; Generals Eufemio Zapata, Francisco Mendoza, Jesús Morales, Jesús Navarro, Otilio E. Montaño, José Trinidad Ruiz, Próculo Capistrán; Colonels Felipe Vaquero, Cesáreo Burgos, Quintín González, Pedro Salazar, Simón Rojas, Emigdio Marmolejo, José Campos, Pioquinto Galis, Felipe Tijera, Rafael Sánchez, José Pérez, Santiago Aguilar, Margarito Martínez, Feliciano Domínguez, Manuel Vergara, Cruz Salazar, Lauro Sánchez, Amador Salazar, Lorenzo Vázquez, Catarino Perdomo, Jesús Sánchez, Domingo Romero, Zacarías Torres, Bonifacio García, Daniel Andrade, Ponciano Domínguez, Jesús Capistrán; Captains Daniel Mantilla, José M. Carrillo, Francisco Alarcón, Severiano Gutiérrez; and more signatures follow. [This] is a true copy taken from the original. Camp in the Mountains of Puebla, December 11, 1911. Signed, General in Chief Emiliano Zapata [Womack 1968: 400–404].

Notes

Preface

1. Although obsolete, the word *gremial* best describes the type of movement being referred to here. According to the Oxford English Dictionary, *gremial* as an adjective is defined as "dwelling within the bosom of a university or society, resident. Also as the epithet of the ordinary or full members of a society as distinguished from honorary members ... of or pertaining to the internal affairs of a corporation or society, confined to its members." *Gremial* also refers to matters that are internal to the membership of a given group.

2. Aquirre Rojas is referring here to the presidential election in 1988 when, according to many, the PRI was defeated by the coalition of left-wing forces led by Cuauhtémoc Cárdenas despite the official result of the election, widely considered fraudulent.

3. Nevertheless, "selective" may be too kind a description of methods that have reappeared since the 2001 attacks on the World Trade Center in New York and been consolidated with the passing of Plan Mérida (The Merida Initiative) on June 10, 2008, in the U.S. House of Representatives. Plan Mérida allocates $500 million to Mexico for combating "drug trafficking, transnational crime and terrorism" (U.S. Department of State, October 22, 2007). An example of direct repression of a population is that of Xoxocotla, Morelos, where the population joined the teachers' movement to protest the opening of the education system to private funding. The government responded by sending in over 2,000 army troops and hundreds of preventative police to break up the road blockades that the people in the community had built (Morelos Cruz 2008). According to the CNTE, at least two hundred people were seriously injured and at least forty-nine arrested. Plan Mérida has given the government the tools and the license to revert to "dirty war" methods of repression and control.

Introduction

1. The CCE in Mexico is the equivalent of the Canadian Council of Chief Executives (CCCE, formerly the Business Council on National Issues) in Canada, and the Business Round Table in the United States.

2. *Sindicatos Blancos* is a term used to describe a company union which is officially recognized and led by the plant owners. The contract in these unions is often referred to as a protective contract. It is usually signed behind the workers' backs and serves as a means of control and of preventing independent union organizing.

3. To avoid possible unacknowledged bias, the author admits to having militated in the Liga Obrera Marxista (LOM) in the late 1970s and early 1980s. The LOM was the predecessor of the OST. It has gone through many changes since that period, yet two of the original founders continue to be at the forefront of the party.

4. The POS has gone through many transformations and divisions since its founding in the 1970s as an expelled faction of the PRT. It subsequently initiated talks with the LOM in an internationally driven attempt to unify the two Trotskyist groups. The unification process was short-lived and left both sides struggling to recover from losses.

5. The legitimacy of the IFE and its degree of autonomy has been questioned since the 2000 presidential elections.

6. The Grito de la Independencia is a ceremony held every September 15 to commemorate the triumph of the Mexican Revolution. The president is called on to mark the occasion at 11:00 p.m. from the National Palace. The following day the military parades through the downtown streets of Mexico City to honor the occasion.

7. Mexico has a long history of electoral corruption at all levels of government, municipal, state and federal (see Aparicio 2002). There are also many examples of government involvement in the drug-trafficking industry (see Geffray et al. 2002). The different branches of the police also have a history of corruption (see Reames 2003), which is often sustained with the support of organized paramilitary forces.

Chapter 1— Theoretical Framework

1. Marx does not explicitly integrate the peasantry into his class analysis, so Petras and Veltmeyer have introduced the idea of a reconstituted class analysis as a way to preserve the importance of a class-divided society. They do this by expanding on Marx's proletarian class category to include the peasantry and other underprivileged sectors of society.

2. In speaking of indigenous people it is referring to the communities that have been excluded from the political process since the time of the conquest. It is true that in many northern regions of the country the indigenous people have come to play an important role in productive, political and social aspects of society. However, in southern Mexico — Oaxaca, Guerrero, and Chiapas for example — the vast majority of indigenous people live on the margins. This is not to say that within communities there are not those, few in number, who are part of the political apparatus, mostly thanks to the clientelist practices of the PRI over the years.

3. By referring to Petras and Veltmeyer's definition of class as a revised definition is to refer to Marx's assessment of the peasantry in the *Communist Manifesto* (Marx and Engels 1987 [1848]) where he refers to the peasantry as a part of the "low strata of the middle class" which will eventually become integrated into the proletariat. In the *Eighteenth Brumaire* (Marx 1978c [1851]: 608) Marx states that "insofar as there is merely a local interconnection among ... small-holding peasants, and the identity of their interests forms no community, no national bond, and no political organization among them, they do not constitute a class. They are therefore incapable of asserting their class interest in their own name, whether through a parliament or a convention. They cannot represent themselves, they must be represented." However, further on in the same text Marx states that the peasantry he is referring to is the "conservative peasantry, not the peasant who strikes out beyond the conditions of his social existence, the small holding, but rather one who wants to consolidate his holding; not the countryfolk who in alliance with the towns want to overthrow the old order through their own energies, but on the contrary those who, in solid seclusion within this old order, want to see themselves and their small holdings saved.... It represents not the enlightenment but the superstition of the peasant; not his judgment but his prejudice, not his future but his past" (609). What Petras and Veltmeyer are doing is drawing from Marx's assessment of the underprivileged sections of the peasantry that struggle to overthrow the existing order and highlighting their role in contesting government policies in Latin America today. They consider the peasantry in Latin America to be one of the most consequent political actors in the current political arena. Again, be reminded that the value of a Marxist perspective lies in its methodological stance or practices rather than in its theoretical stipulations, as is evident in Marx's own analyses of particular, historical conjunctures.

4. The newness of the peasant movement is questionable. Indigenous struggles in Mexico emerged following the Spanish conquest in 1521. That said, acknowledgment and recognition of the indigenous/peasant movement could be considered relatively new because it has historically been ignored or overlooked. The demands of the movement have inevitably expanded as political and economic situations are modified; although the basic struggles for land and autonomy have existed for close to five hundred years (see Galeano 1985).

Chapter 2 — The Mexican Corporatist State

1. Zaid (1987: 12) describes the president of Mexico as "the head of state, of Mexico City state and of the 31 states; of the executive, legislative and judicial powers; of the presidential guards, the army, the air forces, the marine and the police forces, of the official party, the 'altoparlantes,' the television; the

railway and other means of communication and transportation; the currency, the budget, the creditors, wages and prices; of the land, water, the sky and the 'subsuelo'; of petroleum, electricity, minerals and chemicals; of internal and foreign commerce; of agriculture and education, healthcare and of fishing, coffee and sugar." Herzog Márquez (1999: 40) describes Mexican presidential power under the PRI in the following way: "The president says 'expropriate the banks' and the banks are expropriated. The president says 'privatize the banks' and the banks are privatized. The president says 'change the constitution' and the constitution is changed."

2. For example, the Confederación General de Trabajadores (CGT), the Confederación Sindical Unitaria de México (CSUM), the Confederación General de Obreros y Campesinos de México (CGOCM) and the Confederación Revolucionario de Obreros y Campesinos (CROC).

3. This is not to deny the fact that Cárdenas's corporatism was built on a history of corporatist practices that date back to the colonial period.

4. The PRM was preceded by the PNR, Partido Nacional Revolucionario, which was in power from 1933 to 1938. The PRI emerged from these parties following modifications in their relations with the organized sectors of society, the peasants, workers and state employees. State control over these sectors grew with the transition from one party to the next.

5. *Corporations* refers to the confederations.

6. Electoral reforms continue to be introduced in Mexico today. These reforms have not been capable of solving the issue of electoral fraud although things have certainly improved. Of concern to many is the legitimacy of the IFE. Originally designed to be an independent regulatory institution used to monitor the electoral process, and to establish and monitor the guidelines for party registration and funding, it has turned into a tool used by the government of the day to guarantee its own advantage in the electoral process. When Carlos Ugalde was appointed director of IFE in November 2003 there was an outcry from the opposition parties that considered Ugalde a PAN-PRI sympathizer. The opposition doubted the integrity and motives of the newly appointed director. The transparency of the IFE has become blurred (Garduño 2003). Ugalde was replaced by Leonardo Valdez Zurita in 2008. In March 2011, IFE came under fire for "creating a 348 million pesos fund to buy real estate instead of returning the money to the nation's treasury.... He is also under criticism for the 20% pay raise for IFE counselors" (*Mexico Perspective*, March 4, 2011).

7. Transition periods refer to the phase-out period of protectionist measures. It was to be a gradual transition over a ten- to fifteen-year period. This would allow all parties involved to adapt to the opening of the market.

8. Safeguards were introduced to ease the impact of reduced tariff rates and increased imports. These safeguards were as much in the interests of national businesses as for labor.

9. There was an attempt to hold a similar demonstration in November 1975 when over 150,000 workers were kept from entering this political space.

10. Soria (2003) examines the impact of the economic recession on the Social Security Institute of Mexico. He also explains the modifications of the Social Security Law that were implemented following a recommendation by the World Bank and the devastating consequences of these reforms for services and employment.

11. Most notable were the reforms to Article 27 that allowed for the privatization of ejido (communal) lands. This affected over 28,000 ejidos around the country occupying close to half of Mexico's agricultural land. The peasants who worked the ejido land "produced more than half of the food supply [in Mexico], and supported more than 3 million families" (Cockcroft 1998: 290–291).

12. Grupo Monterrey comprises the top twelve corporations in northern Mexico. While they have been diminished in size by globalization and the purchase by transnational corporations of national businesses, they continue to have influence over the government of the day. The PAN with its conservative ways has embraced this relationship.

13. The PAN is considered a culturally Catholic, middle-class, business party. During the 2000 electoral campaign the Mexican Catholic Church effectively endorsed Fox's candidacy via the vehicle of a pastoral letter (Blancarte 2006: 433).

14. This prediction did not anticipate the global economic crisis of 2008–2009.

15. An example of "*toma de nota*" occurred in 2006 when President Fox mounted a huge campaign against Napoleón Gómez Urrutia who had been democratically elected as leader of the miner's union (Ortega and Solís de Alba 2006: 294–297). Through his campaign, Fox managed to drive Gómez Urrutia out of the country, and since then he has been living in British Columbia, Canada, directing the union from his cell phone.

16. At the time he wrote this, Castañeda was serving as the secretary of foreign affairs under the newly

elected Fox government. In the prologue he refers to the "new relationship between Mexican society and its government, a relationship based on trust, accountability, and the rule of law" (2003: 1). He also refers to the "equitable partnership for prosperity" (3) that exists between the Mexican government and the U.S. government. These views arguably owe more to his political position than to his academic vocation.

17. See PRI (2008) at http://www.pri.org.mx/PriistasTrabajando/pri/directorios/oas.aspx for a complete list. Another example of this corporatist-like arrangement is one I experienced as a militant of the Liga Obrera Marxista (LOM) in the late 1970s and early 1980s. We had created a number of internal organizations, the political analysis and direction of which were dictated by the LOM leaders even as they tried to convince members that the organizations were autonomous. Two examples that I recall were the Alianza de Trabajadores de la Educación (ATE) and the Coordinadora de Jóvenes Socialistas (CJS). They served as a way to bring people in line with LOM principles and to try to co-opt them.

18. In Spanish, "teams" are "*equipos*," and *equipos* move with their directors. Under the PRI if a director were appointed as head of the Department of Arts and Culture, for example, he or she would move in block with the other members of the team to that department. They could have come from the Department of Agriculture or any other department for that matter. These appointments come down from the president, and the teams are handpicked by the directors. Not all directors would be reappointed when a president was replaced because new presidents would want to appoint his (all presidents in Mexico have been men) own friends.

19. The same may be said of the lists of characteristics of corporatism given by Ramírez Saiz and Córdova. As we saw in chapter 1 Ramírez Saiz (2003: 158–159) lists three conditions: the inability to liberate union associations from the regime in power, continuous state intervention in the official registration of farmer and professional associations and unions, and continued lack of transparency within the unions, with many decisions being made without the participation of the membership. Córdova (1989: 40) lists the following common characteristics of corporatist relations, most of which "Mexico fulfils": "organization of the different professions and interests; ... forced organization of those that cannot escape or decline those in power; ... always conservative, usually reactionary and frequently ... repressive and authoritarian; ... orders are imposed from above and [corporatism] is incompatible with democratic forms of organization; ... when fully developed [corporatism] is directly linked to a governing state." Since both of these lists are largely embraced by Williamson's four dimensions, they are not discussed separately here.

20. "The alleged withdrawal of states from markets amidst the globalization of capitalism was a neoliberal ideological illusion; states in the developed capitalist countries pumped more liquidity into the banks in the face of financial crises, while ensuring that crises in the developing countries were generally used to impose financial discipline. The neoliberal American state played the most active role as the imperial guarantor, coordinator and fire-fighter-in-chief for global capitalism" (Panitch and Gindin 2009: 2). See Chomsky (1996: 120) on the case of the United States.

21. When referring to authoritarian state corporatism, Williamson (1985: 11) lists the following three characteristics: "[1.] State licenses intermediaries, and intermediaries in turn license or otherwise restrict freedom of economic and social actors. This is the basis upon which the state controls societal actors and hence sustains a particular economic and social order.... [2.] It is assumed that there is limited support for the underlying values and goals of the corporatist system and that the economic and social order will have to be imposed. [3.] Corporatist structures are so established as to secure the greatest level of state control practicable."

22. A clear example of how Mexico is tied to the conditions set out by exogenous institutions was evident during the 1995 U.S./IMF bailout. The conditions on the US$20 billion package were that the Mexican government "agree to deposit the proceeds of oil export sales by PEMEX and the two export sales subsidiaries in a pass-through special account at the Federal Reserve Bank of New York ... most important ... the Mexican government committed itself to comply with the IMF program and additional requirements set by the US Treasury ... the Mexican government agreed ... to stabilize the peso through fiscal and monetary policy" (Lustig 1998: 183–184). The U.S. government also required the Mexican government to raise domestic interest rates and in 1995 established a Mexico Task Force "to monitor Mexico's economy and economic policymaking" (ibid.).

23. According to President Fox of the PAN, the INI became the CNDPI because the attention given to the indigenous communities over its fifty-four years of life had become ineffective. There was a need to change the approach to one reaching out to indigenous people and addressing their needs. The CNDPI's focus would be to create a more politically integrated response to the indigenous concerns. This federalist vision would include the participation of the legislature, the indigenous communities, civil society and local political authorities. CNDPI's objectives would be to address the issues expressed

in a national consultation with over 20,000 participants in 2002. The results of the consultation were as follows: respect for the rights and culture of the indigenous people, equal opportunities, the creation of an autonomous institution, and adequate funding to enhance the relationships between the indigenous people, the state and Mexican society. Politically, Fox's move seemed to represent a statement of renewed interest in the indigenous population in Mexico. It was an attempt to convince the different social and political actors that they would solve issues that the PRI had ignored. Gómez (*La Jornada* 2003) refers to the change as just another farce initiated by the "government of change." "It does not imply any real change," she says. She argues that if the government really wanted to effect change they would close the institution altogether and grant autonomy to the indigenous communities in Mexico. Furthermore, it is clear that the INI and the CNDPI are themselves corporatist institutions in that they serve as means to control the indigenous population.

24. Mexico is a member of the G20 for industrialized countries *and* the G20 for developing countries which was founded in August 2003 at the Fifth Ministerial WTO Conference in Cancún, México.

25. There are many international NGOs that are funded by foreign governments, whether municipal, state or federal, and then there are grassroots NGOs which receive funding from various sources. During a trip to La Realidad, Chiapas, in 2004, the author encountered a couple representing an NGO from France. The funding for their project came from their municipal government.

26. According to Article 69 of the Mexican Constitution it is the duty of the president of the Mexican republic to give an annual report (Informe) to the Congress of the Union on the first of September. The Third Informe given by President Felipe Calderón Hinojosa in 2010 can be viewed on the government website at http://tercer.informe.calderon.presidencia.gob.mx/informe. In particular the section titled "Economía Competitiva y Generadora de Empleos" highlights the economic stability and accomplishments of the PAN government during the year September 2009 to August 2010.

27. Rodríguez Alcaine (Muñoz Ríos 2003) estimates this figure at over 5 million.

28. This will be discussed further in chapter 3 in relation to the teachers' union, the SNTE, which has become decentralized.

29. Tricolour (tricolor) refers to the PRI which carries a red, white and green flag whereas blue and white (azul y blanco) refers to the flag colors of the PAN.

30. He is an investigator and coordinator of the Instituto de Estudios del Trabajo (IET) and a researcher at the UNAM.

31. There is also an "independent" teachers' union called the CNTE that was founded in 1979. The CNTE engages in mass mobilization rather than calling on government institutions to address their demands. See chapter 3 for a full account of the SNTE and CNTE.

32. In the case of the SNTE, although decentralized corporatism best describes the situation in Oaxaca, Gordillo on the national level continues to be the ultimate leader of the SNTE, and she continues to maintain a corporatist relationship with the Mexican state.

33. According to *La Jornada Observatorio Ciudadano de la Educación* (May 16, 2003), from 1980 to 2001 there was an increase of enrollment in private schools from 2.2 to 3.7 million students (a 68 percent increase). This compares with the national enrollment that increased from 10.3 percent to 12.5 percent during this period.

34. Here are three further examples of external influence. In response to the economic crisis in the early 1980s, Miguel de la Madrid "slashed government spending to comply with an IMF austerity program. This diverted funds from environmental (and other) programs, toward servicing Mexico's external debt" (M. E. Williams 2001: 138). The second example came in response to the World Bank's "green conversion" in the mid–1980s that "allocated funds specifically for 'environmental projects,' and altered its loan criteria to require environmental impact statements for all Bank-funded development projects" (163n). Thirdly, in the 1990s a task force was created to examine Mexico's environmental policy when the Secretaría de Desarrollo Urbano y Ecología (SEDUE), Mexico's first environmental agency, requested money from the World Bank. The task force would "work to harmonize Mexico's environmental policies and new market reforms, develop economic instruments to achieve environmental goals, and devise means to make the government's antipollution program self-financing" (147) in order to meet World Bank criteria.

Chapter 3 — Integrative Oppositional Strategies I

1. Independent unions are unions that are democratically organized and run and that are not affiliated with the government organizations such as the CT or the CTM.

2. The CTM official website can be found at http://ctmorganizacion.org.mx. The section titled "sindicatos afiliados" (affiliated unions) is under construction (May 17, 2011). La Botz (2011) claims there are about 10 million members in the CT, whereas the UNT and other independent unions total about 1.5 million.

3. The Ley Abascal was named after Carlos Abascal Carranza who was Fox's labor minister at the time.

4. In 2009, the PRI regained plurality control in the congress, the first time since its presidential defeat in 2000.

5. This is the clause that gives labor leaders and businesses the right to terminate the employment of a person or a group of employees who choose to withdraw from the union and form a new one. Although the clause has been deemed anticonstitutional, exclusion is still practiced.

6. During an interview on February 12, 2004, with Héctor De la Cueva from CILAS he spoke at length about the international conferences that were organized among leaders of unions representing the workers of particular industries, such as the auto industry, yet there was no mention of unified political action.

7. The SUTERM is the *official* Mexican electrical workers union. It holds direct corporatist relationships with the state. While the SME worked with the Compañia de Luz y Fuerza del Centro, the SUTERM works for the Comisión Federal de Electricidad. The consequence of having two large electrical companies has been the duplication of work. The SME was the more combative of the two unions.

8. Interestingly, it was also in 1999 that the SINTCB, a union which comprises approximately 3,000 workers, was granted legal status within Apartado A. As outlined above, Mexican unions were divided into two "apartados," A and B. Apartado A stipulates the procedures for tabling a grievance and provisions to conduct strikes, whereas Apartado B is reserved for government service workers who are not allowed to strike. While under Apartado B (as Severo Escudero Carrillo, Secretario del Trabajo, explained [interview November 14, 2003]), SINTCB engaged in violent takeovers of government offices in an effort to be heard and taken seriously. They now utilize legal channels to negotiate their demands. It is not that they have deserted the cause, but rather they have modified their approach to one of negotiation in light of their changed status from Apartado B to A. Their reformist approach to doing politics remains intact.

9. Italics are author's emphasis.

10. This is in keeping with Ramírez Saiz's characterization of corporatism in the twenty-first century, as detailed in chapter 1.

11. The university workers' union first emerged in September 1929 under the name of Unión de Empleados de la Universidad Nacional Autónoma (UEUNA). In 1933 it became the Sindicato de Empleados y Obreros de la Universidad Autónoma de México (SEOUAM). From 1945 to 1961 it was known as the first STUNAM. From 1963 to 1977 it changed its name three more times until it settled with Sindicato de Trabajadores de la Universidad Nacional Autónoma de Mexico (STUNAM) as it is known today.

12. The main planillas are: Unidad Democrática (UD), Planilla Roja Unidad Sindical (PRUS), La Planilla Democrática (PD), Movimiento Sindical Democrático (MSD), Unidad de Trabajadores por el Rescate de Nuestros Derechos (UTRND), Frente por el Cambio (FC), Alianza Democrática (AD) and El Bloque de Trabajadores Democráticos (BTD). The PRUS was in power from 1984 to 2008. Basurto (2005: 33) divides the planillas along ideological lines. He considers the PRUS as a revolutionary nationalist group. The revolutionary nationalists are considered to be "classical" groups. They are organized as a common front without political or religious affiliation, unlike the other two categories that Basurto classifies as revolutionary leftists and the radical left, which are founded on Marxist-Leninist and Trotskyist principles.

13. It is important to note that Carlos Galindo Galindo, the interviewee, became a member of the STUNAM executive for the first time in 1988. His assessment of the union could be a reflection of his inability to succeed in the electoral process prior to that date.

14. According to Salinas's speech on May 1, 1990, there were eight pillars to his "new unionism" plan. They were "1. Strong and representative unionism with an interlocutory capacity, 2. The necessity to abandon the confrontational strategy of the beginning of the century, 3. Establishment of formulas for cooperation between labor and management, 4. Preservation of the historic alliance between the labor movement and the state, 5. Respect for union autonomy as a matter of governmental policy, 6. Improvement of labor relations with obligations for both management and unions, 7. The urgency of workers' understanding and implementing efforts to increase productivity, lower costs, and cooperate to conquer markets both in and outside the country, 8. Management commitment to establishing a

culture of motivation and communication that gives incentives, encouragements, and rewards to the workforce" (Roett 1995: 19).

15. In August 2008 there was a teachers' statewide strike in Morelos, a state located southwest of Mexico City. Over 24,000 teachers went on strike for over two months. Their primary demand was the cessation of all attempts to privatize the education system. Similar to the teachers' movement in Oaxaca, the teachers in Morelos received substantial support from the communities.

16. Radio Planton is a community radio station created by the teachers of Section 22 of the SNTE and community organizations in Oaxaca. They have also worked closely with the EZLN.

17. José Basurto is currently a member of the CNTE and "subofficial mayor" of Local 19 of the SNTE. He was the founder of the Consejo Central de Lucha (CCL) of Morelos, founder of the UNT of Morelos, and ex-general secretary of the union delegations D-1-52 (special ed.) and D-1-22 (primary school).

18. In a letter addressed to the director of the Colegio de Bachilleres and signed by the general secretary of SINTCB, Arturo Hidalgo Sánchez, dated January 19, 2000, the union called for a 60 percent wage increase. These high demands are not always met, but it is common in Mexico for unions to demand comparatively high wage increases. In the same letter they argued that there had been a fall in real wages of over 47.6 percent.

Chapter 4 — Integrative Oppositional Strategies II

1. For example, the PRT, Convergencia, Fuerza Ciudadana, Partido de la Sociedad Nacionalista (PSN), PT, PNA, Partido Popular Socialist de México (PPS), PVEM, POS, OST, UNIOS, and LUS.

2. It could be argued that by joining the movement they would be truer to their principles and would be paving the way for an anticapitalist (and noncorporatist) alternative that goes beyond mere rhetoric.

3. An exception to this is the Frente Nacional Contra la Represíon that has served as a broad front or organization ideologically friendly to all.

4. That is, the everyday problems of living in the street or in poverty.

5. Rosario Ibarra de Piedra is very familiar with party politics as she became the first female presidential candidate in Mexico when she ran for the PRT, a Trotskyist party, in 1982. She was slated to run again in 1988 but ceded her candidacy to Cuauhtémoc Cárdenas. She was a federal deputy from 1985 to 1988 and then again from 1994 to 1997. She became a senator in 2006.

6. An example of the government's dislike for human rights defenders concerns the death of Digna Ochoa, a human rights lawyer who many believe was assassinated by government officials in 2001 (see Diebel 2005). Of course these things are very hard to prove in a corrupt judicial system that protects the interests of the state.

7. Samuel Ruiz was the bishop of the Diocese of San Cristóbal de las Casas in Chiapas from 1959 to 2000. He received many awards during his life and died on January 24, 2011. The author helped bring Samuel Ruiz to give a talk in Waterloo, Ontario, in 2009 and had the opportunity to spend the day with him.

8. Alejandro Aldana, the spokesperson for the center, explained (interview on May 25, 2004) that the *caciques* had greater power than the municipal, state and federal governments.

9. These assertions predate the Other Campaign of 2006 when the Zapatistas left their communities to travel around the country to see what the demands of the people were.

10. Recall that the UNT emerged following the death of Fidel Velázquez, the leader of the CTM since its founding in 1936. The founder of the UNT, Hernandez Juarez, "led 160 federations and unions in forming the UNT as a reform alternative to the PRI-affiliated [CTM]" (see Preston and Dillon 2004: 475). Garza Toledo (2004: 118) criticizes the UNT for "the authoritarian attitudes of the leaders ... and the top-down attitudes of their intellectual advisers."

11. On June 9, 2009, Nellys Paloma died of unknown causes. Her sudden death signified a great loss to the indigenous women's movement in Chiapas and around Mexico.

12. At that time it was called Comal Citlalmina.

13. According to Hoddersen (2006: 54–55) "it is estimated that most of the world's current 37,000 non-government organizations (NGOs), which deal with social problems around the world, came into existence during the 1980s and 1990s."

14. Though this is a rather small membership given the political euphoria of the time as people took to the street in solidarity with the Zapatista movement, it is significant in that it comprised some of the most radical feminists in Mexico City.

15. The push for electoral democracy in Mexico has also come from its Northern neighbors who seek to create in Mexico a liberal-democratic polity modeled on their own. It is glaringly obvious, however, that what is missing in the transfer of this model from North to South are the civil and political rights (never mind the admittedly attenuated economic, social and cultural ones) enjoyed in the North. That there have, nevertheless, been reforms also reflects the fact that the Mexican state is not immune to democratization. It is a process, however, which is far from completion.

16. The PRD was not founded on a left-wing platform, but rather advocated a more nationalist approach to capitalism than its PRI and PAN counterparts. The diversity that characterized the founding of the PRD is now manifested in the divisions within the party. Valdés (1994: 74) argues that "the PRD is a federated party made up of political groups which makes it difficult to define a clear identity over and above the various factions. The interests of each group tend to have such importance that, on key issues such as the party program, the leaders have to resist the appearance that any one faction is seeking to impose its views."

17. On September 1, 2003, at a demonstration in Mexico City, the PPS distributed its first newspaper since the mid-nineties.

18. As one who attended the CND on the sixteenth of September the author considered the event symbolic for three reasons. First, anyone who arrived at the event and wanted to register as a delegate was able to do so. Second, the voting was realized with a show of hands, many of which were not visible from the main stage in the center square. Third, there was no room for proposals or discussion from the floor.

19. The granaderos in Mexico are a heavily armed group of antiriot police. They are commonly dispatched for demonstrations and large political gatherings. They are known to be ruthless. They arrive in buses or on horseback and don shields, guns and bayonets.

20. Although public education is officially free there are many ancillary services that students are required to pay for (just as in Canada). Ivonne et al. (2001: 28) explain that tuition is 350 pesos, a computer account costs another 350 pesos, a student card costs 50 pesos, administrative fees are 50 pesos each and uniforms can cost as much as 550 pesos. Keep in mind that the minimum wage in Mexico is 50 pesos a day and that over 60 percent of the population lives in poverty. At the time of writing, the U.S. dollar was approximately equivalent to 10 pesos.

21. The farming communities in northern Mexico are known for their large wealthy ranches that contrast with the impoverished indigenous farming communities in southern Mexico.

Chapter 5 — The Zapatista Movement

1. This is not to undervalue the existence of anticapitalist political parties, whether Maoist, Trotskyist or Marxist-Leninist, which were prevalent in the 1960s and 1970s and continue to linger in the background of the political arena today, as discussed in chapter 4.

2. "In the Mexican countryside, corporatism means compulsory participation in local branches of the official peasants' union and state government co-optation of rural squatters by offers of land, but only if negotiations are conducted through the official peasants' union" (Eisenstadt 2007: 54). Many rural communities in Mexico continue to follow this corporatist model.

3. The EPR is an armed guerrilla movement that emerged on the public scene in Aguas Blancas in the state of Guerrero in June 1996. It identified itself as the culmination of thirty years of armed revolutionary activity in the southern regions of Mexico. Their struggle is against exploitation, oppression, misery, marginalization and repression, among other things. They denounce neoliberal reforms, globalization and state corruption. They call on the Mexican population to join with them in a revolutionary struggle to replace the current political economic order with a transitional governing body representative of the oppressed sectors of society (Partido Democrático Popular Revolucionario–Ejército Popular Revolucionario [PDPR-EPR] 1996).

4. The value of this comparison is that both movements were active in the same period (EZLN in 1994; EPR in 1996) and within the same cultural, political and social setting. Bruhn (1999: 30) does not claim to represent the "true" goals of either movement but simply their public images and influence in society.

5. The "war of movement" refers to the Marxist/Leninist idea of the proletariat taking over the state.

6. Gilly (1997: 24–25) reminds us that before 1910 there were numerous "indigenas" rebellions — for example, the Tzeltal rebellion in 1712, the Caste War in Chiapas in 1869 and the Caste War in

Yucatan. See also Eduardo Galeano's astounding *Memory of Fire* (1985), for comparable episodes in the entire history of resistance to Spanish rule from 1492 on.

7. Compare David Harvey's Marxist concept of "accumulation by dispossession" (Harvey 2005: 137–182).

8. The Fourth Declaration calls for the establishment of something "new and good"; this something new and good is to be formed through the FZLN. As many authors have pointed out, the vagueness of such assertions has come to distance people rather than attract them. This is a population that has mobilized on concrete demands and slogans over its more than five hundred years of repression, invasion and dominance from afar. Demands for autonomy, land rights and democratic inclusion have been a constant theme of popular resistance in Mexico since the conquest. To suggest that the FZLN will lead the struggle for something "new and good" was heard as not saying much of anything.

9. The author attended numerous antiprivatization protests in Mexico City in 2003–2004 and saw no sign of the FZLN at any of them. However, during this same period they held their own events independently of other calls to action.

10. The COCOPA is a body created to mediate the dialogue between the EZLN and the government.

11. According to Venegas (2001), Fox announced at a dinner party with Canadian NGOs that all of these conditions had been met and that he hoped to return to the negotiating table with the EZLN. The EZLN rejected this assertion.

12. The Zócalo is the central square in Mexico City. It is the political center of the country and has served as both an area to validate PRI legitimacy and more recently as a gathering point to denounce PRI/PAN policies. The Presidential Palace and the treasury line two sides of the square.

13. These are groupings of autonomous indigenous communities in what we might refer to as regions.

14. The five caracoles are La Garrucha, Oventic, La Realidad, Morelia and Roberto Barrios.

15. Autonomous municipal indigenous governments.

16. Is this not in fact indirect government support?

17. The bank account is actually that of Enlace Civil, a civil organization, which functions as a liaison between the EZLN and civil society.

18. There have been no guarantees of sustained support from the Mexican government either, but in theory the state is held accountable by the electorate, whereas NGOs are accountable only to their funding agencies.

19. In February 1995 when the EZLN held an internal consultation the Mexican army moved in and attacked the communities. The issuing of the most recent Red Alert followed an announcement that the government had found marijuana fields in Zapatista territory. The Zapatistas also received notice of military maneuvering in the area.

20. On January 6, 2006, Comandanta Ramona died. She had been fighting cancer of the kidney for over a decade. Ramona's role in the EZLN ranged from advocating women's rights, to leading the speeches during the negotiations with the government, to leading the military action on January 1, 1994, in San Cristóbal. Her death is a reminder of the deficiencies in the health-care services in the indigenous communities. It marks a great loss both to the EZLN and to sympathetic struggles throughout the world. Her death resulted in a minor delay in the Other Campaign and a modification to the original schedule.

21. These words were spoken by Subcomandante Insurgente Marcos (2005b) in a speech he made in the Caracol La Garrucha. In this speech he also made public the initial itinerary of the Other Campaign. The itinerary was modified in January after the death of Ramona and again after the repressive attacks on the town of Atenco in early May.

22. The community of Atenco was successful in stopping the construction of an international airport in their community in 2002. It would have meant the expropriation of over 5,000 hectares of farming land. The peasants in this community have reached out to support many political struggles around Mexico, and their trademark has come to be the machete.

23. This included alternative press journalists and foreign observers.

24. Nopales are a cactus leaf that has been eaten by indigenous people for centuries. Tlalnepantla is one of Mexico's primary nopal producers.

25. The author attended the Coloquio Aubry in the Universidad de la Tierra just outside of San Cristóbal de las Casas in December 2007, where Delegado Zero (DZ) invited intellectuals and political activists to discuss anticapitalist movements and the direction they were taking. DZ's authoritarian ways were again revealed when he gave the closing remarks to each discussion group and refused to allow a

question-answer period at the end of each session. Canadian Naomi Klein was the only participant who willingly addressed the audience in a press conference arrangement following her section of the colloquium.

26. Ramos and Méndez (July 2006: 35) remind us of the massacres in Guerrero and Chiapas, the harassment of entire populations through the closing of highways, low-flying helicopters, the confiscation of food and medication, kidnappings, disappearances, incarcerations, persecutions, illegal detention, and physical and psychological torture. All of these measures continue to be employed by the local, state and federal governments throughout the country. They refer to it as the criminalization of social movements.

Chapter 6 — Experiments in Delinking and Deglobalization

1. Light (2007: 238–240) discusses how the globalization of market segments leads to control of many industries by transnational corporations. He uses the example of patented drugs in the CAFTA agreement.

2. Global Exchange (2007) describes ALBA as "a project to strengthen alliances among southern countries, to redraw the political map, and end U.S. domination in the hemisphere. Venezuela is promoting concrete programs of regional integration that are real alternatives to the failed model of corporate globalization. These projects appear threatening to the Bush administration, because they aim to reduce Latin America countries' dependence on the U.S." (http://www.globalexchange.org/countries/americas/venezuela/VZneoliberalismALBA.pdf).

3. Fábrica Sin Patrones — factory without bosses.

4. See Rosa Luxemburg (2006 [1937]) for a critical assessment of cooperatives.

5. Veltmeyer (2007b: 22) holds U.S. imperialism responsible for the "40 to 60 percent [of the population which] ... is mired in poverty." This percentage is as high as 80 percent in many rural areas. In fact "thirty nine percent of the extremely poor, those who have to survive with less than a dollar a day, are found in Mexico and Brazil, both regional champions of neoliberalism" (31).

Conclusions

1. Or, alternatively, the trilateral world of three economic power blocs (USA, Europe, and Southeast Asia).

Bibliography

Adamson, Walter L. 1980. *Hegemony and Revolution: A Study of Antonio Gramsci's Political and Cultural Theory.* Berkeley: University of California Press.

Aguilar, Luis E. 1978. *Marxism in Latin America.* Philadelphia: Temple University Press.

Aguilar García, Javier. 1990. "Relaciones Estado-Sindicatos: 1982–1990." *Productividad y Salarios,* November-December, 38.

_____. 2006. "La Representatividad en el Sindicalismo Mexicano." In *El Sindicalismo en México: Historia, Crisis y Perspectiva,* ed. José Merced González Guerra and Antonio Gutiérrez Castro, 65–89. México: Plaza y Valdés.

Aguirre Rojas, Carlos Antonio. 2005. *América Latina en la Encrucijada: Los Movimientos Sociales y la Muerte de la Política Moderna.* México: Editorial Contrahistorias.

Albo, Greg, Sam Gindin, and Leo Panitch. 2010. *In and Out of Crisis: The Global Financial Meltdown and Left Alternatives.* Oakland, CA: PM Press.

Alcalde Justiniano, Arturo. 2006a. "Balance Sindical del Gobierno de Transición: Promesas Incumplidos." In *Los Sindicatos en la Encrucijada del Siglo XXI,* ed. Inés González Nicolás, 39–60. México: Fundación Friedrich Ebert.

_____. 2006b. "El Sindicalismo, La Democracia y la Libertad Sindical." In *El Sindicalismo en México: Historia, Crisis y Perspectivas,* ed. José Merced González Guerra and Antonio Gutiérrez Castro, 161–202. México: Plaza y Valdés S.A. de C.V.

Alexander, Robin, and Dan LaBotz. 2003. "México's Labour Law Reform." *Mexican Labor News and Analysis* 8. http://www.ueinternational.org/Mexico_info/mlna_articles.php?id-40#99.

Almeyra, Guillermo, and Emiliano Thibaut. 2006. *Zapatistas: Un Nuevo Mundo en Construcción.* Buenas Aires: Editorial Maipue.

Álvarez, Sonia E., Evelina Dagnino, and Arturo Escobar. 1998. *Culture of Politics, Politics of Culture: Re-visioning Latin American Social Movements.* Boulder, CO: Westview Press.

Álvarez Béjar, Alejandro. 2006. "Mexico's 2006 Elections: The Rise of Populism and the End of Neoliberalism." *Latin American Perspectives* 33 (2): 17–32.

Amadeo, Javier. 2006. "Mapeando el Marxismo." In *La Teoría Marxista Hoy: Problemas y Perspectivas,* ed. Atilio Boron, Javier Amadeo, and Sabrina González, 53–105. Buenas Aires: Clacso.

Americas Program Citizen Action Profile. 2005. "Cross-Border Campaign Wins Maquila Union Demands." February. http://americas.irc-online.org/am/813.

Amin, Samir. 1990. *Delinking: Towards a Polycentric World.* London: Zed Books.

_____. 2003. "Confronting the Empire." *Monthly Review* 55 (3): 15–22.

_____. 2006. *Beyond US Hegemony? Assessing the Prospects for a Multipolar World.* London: Zed Books.

Ángel Barrios, Miguel, and Abelardo Mariña Flores. 2003. "Empleo, Remuneraciones y Productividad en la Industria Manufacturera Mexicana." In *Globalización: Reforma Neoliberal del Estado y Movimientos Sociales,* ed. Ana Alicia Solís de Alba, Max Ortega, Abelardo Mariña Flores, and Nina Torres, 31–44. México: Editorial Itaca.

Anguiano, Arturo. 1975. *El Estado y La Política Obrera Del Cardenismo.* México D.F.: Ediciones Era.

_____. 1997. *Entre el Pasado y el Futuro: La Izquierda en México, 1969–1995.* México D.F.: Universidad Autónoma Metropolitana.

_____. 2006a. "La Sexta Declaración, La Irrupción de la Otra Campana y el Medio de la Clase Política." *Bajo el Volcán: Revista del Posgrado de Sociología, Universidad Autónoma de Puebla* 6 (10): 23–30.

_____. 2006b. "Política del Oprimido y Estrategia Anticapitalista." In *Imperio y Resistencia: Dominación,*

193

Migración, Resistencias y Alternativas, Memorias del Coloquio Internacional, ed. Arturo Anguiano. México: Universidad Autónoma Metropolitana, Xochimilco.

_____. 2010. *El Ocaso Interminable: Política y Sociedad en el México de los Cambios Rotos*. México: Ediciones Era.

Aparicio, Ricardo. 2002. "La Magnitud de la Manipulación del Voto en las Elecciones Federales de Año 2000." *Perfiles Latinoamericanos* 20 (June–July): 79–99. http://redalyc.uaemex.mx/redalyc/src/inicio/ArtPdfRed.jsp?iCve=11502005&iCveNum=2221.

Aristotle. 1981. *The Politics*. Harmondsworth: Penguin.

Aspe, Pedro, and Paul E. Sigmund. 1984. *The Political Economy of Income Distribution in Mexico*. New York: Holmes and Meier.

Aziz Nassif, Alberto. 2003. Introduction to *México al Inicio del Siglo XXI: Democracia, Ciudadanía y Desarrollo*, ed. Alberto Aziz Nassif, 3–23. México D.F.: Centro de Investigaciones y Estudios Superiores en Antropología Social.

Aziz Nassif, Alberto, and Jorge Alonso Sánchez. 2003a. "Los Poderes y las Instituciones." In *México al Inicio del Siglo XXI: Democracia, Ciudadanía y Desarrollo*, ed. Alberto Aziz Nassif, 27–37. México D.F.: Centro de Investigaciones y Estudios Superiores en Antropología Social.

_____. 2003b. "Las Primeras Experiencias de Alternancia." In *México al Inicio del Siglo XXI: Democracia, Ciudadanía y Desarrollo*, ed. Alberto Aziz Nassif, 47–64. México D.F.: Centro de Investigaciones y Estudios Superiores en Antropología Social.

_____. 2003c. "Votos, Reglas y Partidos." In *México al Inicio del Siglo XXI: Democracia, Ciudadanía y Desarrollo*, ed. Alberto Aziz Nassif, 65–96. México D.F.: Centro de Investigaciones y Estudios Superiores en Antropología Social.

Azul, Rafael. 2007. "Mexican Government Steps Up Repression in Oaxaca." *Socialist Viewpoint* 7 (1). http://www.socialistviewpoint.org/janfeb_07/janfeb_07_14.html.

Balboa, Juan. 2006. "Divide llamado del EZLN a no votar por AMLO." *La Jornada*, March 18. http://www.jornada.unam.mx/2006/03/18/013n1pol.php.

Basurto, Jorge. 1997. *Los Movimientos Sindicales en la UNAM*. México: Instituto de Investigaciones Sociales, Universidad Nacional Autónoma de México.

_____. 2006. *La Vida Política del Sindicato de Trabajadores de la UNAM*. México: Instituto de Investigaciones Sociales, Universidad Nacional Autónoma de México.

Bedford, David. 1994. "Marxism and the Aboriginal Question: The Tragedy of Progress." *Canadian Journal of Native Studies* 14 (1): 101–117.

Bello, Walden. 2004. *Deglobalization: Ideas for a New World Economy*. Updated edition. Black Point, NS: Fernwood.

Benavides, M.E. and G. Velasco. 1993. *Sindicato Magisterial en México*. Mexico City: IPE.

Bennett, Viviente. 1995. *The Politics of Water: Urban Protest, Gender, and Power in Monterrey, México*. Pittsburgh: University of Pittsburgh Press.

Bensusán, Graciela. 2005. "El Sindicato Mexicano de Electricistas y la Reestructuración Laboral de Luz y Fuerza del Centro." *Revista Mexicana de Sociología* 67 (3): 543–591.

Berg, Bruce L. 1998. *Qualitative Research Methods for the Social Sciences*. 3rd ed. Boston: Allyn and Bacon.

Bergsman, Joel. 1980. "Income Distribution and Poverty in Mexico." World Bank Staff Working Paper No. 395. Washington: World Bank. http://www-wds.worldbank.org/external/default/WDSContentServer/WDSP/IB/2003/07/26/000178830_98101903404647/Rendered/PDF/multi0page.pdf.

Bernstein, Eduard. 1993 [1937]. *The Precondition of Socialism*. Cambridge, UK: Cambridge University Press.

Bizberg, Ilan. 2003. "Estado, Organizaciones Corporativas y Democracia." In *México al Inicio del Siglo XXI: Democracia, Ciudadanía y Desarrollo*, ed. Alberto Aziz Nassif, 183–229. México D.F.: Centro de Investigaciones y Estudios Superiores en Antropología Social.

Blancarte, Roberto. 2006. "Religion, Church, and State in Contemporary Mexico." In *Changing Structures of Mexico: Political, Economic and Social Perspectives*, 2nd ed., ed. Laura Randall. Armonk: M. E. Sharpe.

Blum, William. 1998. *Killing Hope: U.S. Military and CIA Interventions Since World War II*. Montreal: Black Rose Books.

Bond, Patrick. 2005. "Strategies for Social Justice Movements from Southern Africa to the United States." *Foreign Policy in Focus*, January 20. http://www.fpif.org.

Boron, Atilio. 1995. *State, Capitalism, and Democracy in Latin America*. Boulder, CO: Lynne Rienner Publishers.

_____. 2003. *Tras el Búho de Minerva*. La Habana: Editorial de Ciencias Sociales.

_____. 2006. "Por el Necesario (y Demorado) Retorno al Marxismo." In *La Teoría Marxista Hoy: Problemas y Perspectivas*, ed. Atilio Boron, Javier Amadeo, and Sabrina González, 35–52. Buenas Aires: Clacso.

Brachet-Márquez, Viviane. 2007. "The Democratization of State Corporatism: Mexico, Portugal and Brazil in Historical Perspective." Latin American Studies Association. Montreal, September 5–8.

Breceda-Lapeyre, Miguel G. 2002. "Private Investment in Mexico's Electricity Sector." Commission for Environmental Cooperation, Environment, Economy and Trade Program. Mexico, November. http://cec.org/files/pdf/ECONOMY/mbinvest_en.pdf.

Brickner, Rachel K. 2006. "Mexican Union Women and the Social Construction of Women's Labor Rights." *Latin American Perspectives* 33 (6): 55–74.

Bruhn, Kathleen. 1999. "Antonio Gramsci and the Palabra Verdadera: The Political Discourse of Mexico's Guerrilla Forces." *Journal of Interamerican Studies and World Affairs* 41 (2): 29–56.

Brus Li. 2003. "Comandante Brus Li's Words in Oventik." *Centro de Medios Independientes*, August 9. http://chiapas.mediosindependientes.org/display.php3?article_id=105793.

Brysk, Allison. 2000. *From Tribal Village to Global Village: Indian Rights and International Relations in Latin America*. Stanford, CA: Stanford University Press.

Bukharin, Nikolai. 1971. *The Economics of the Transformation Period*. New York: Bergman.

Calderón Hinojosa, Felipe. 2007. "Message to the Nation from Mexican President Felipe Calderón." *Presidencia de la República*, March 28. http://quetzalcoatl.presidencia.gob.mx/en/press/?contenido=29660.

_____. 2010. "Tercer Informe de Gobierno." *Presidencia de la República Mexicana*, September 1. http://tercer.informe.calderon.presidencia.gob.mx/informe.

Cammack, Paul, David Poll, and William Tordoff. 1993. *Third World Politics: A Comparative Introduction*. 2nd ed. Baltimore: Johns Hopkins University Press.

Carlsen, Laura. 2009. "El Gobierno de Calderón Usa la Policía para Tomar Compañía Eléctrica y Desmantelar Sindicato." *America's Program*, October 14. http://www.cipamericas.org/es/archives/1877.

Castañeda, Jorge G. 1994. *Sorpresa Te Da La Vida*. México: Aguilar.

_____. 2003. "Prologue: Toward a New Bilateral Relationship." In *Mexico's Politics and Society in Transition*, ed. Joseph S. Tulchin and Andrew D. Selee, 1–4. Boulder, CO: Lynne Rienner Publishers.

Castells, Manuel. 1997. *The Power of Identity*. Malden, MA: Blackwell.

Cecilia, Argelia, Evelia, Ileana, Paty, Leticia, Tania Jimena, Tania Paloma, Julieta, and Rosa Maria. 2001. "En Ausencia de la Banda." In *Plebeyas Batallas: La Huelga en la Universidad*, ed. Maria Rosas, 183–187. México D.F.: Ediciones Era.

Centeno, Miguel Ángel. 1997. *Democracy within Reason: Technocratic Revolution in Mexico*. 2nd ed. University Park: Pennsylvania State University Press.

_____. 2002. "The Centre Did Not Hold: War in Latin America." In *Studies in the Formation of the Nation State in Latin America*, ed. James Dunkerley, 54–76. London: ILAS.

Chapman, Debra D. 2005. "Strategic, Opportunistic and Post-Electoral Autonomy: A Comparative Analysis of Three Cases from Mexico." In "Special Issue on Social Movements in Latin America." *Journal for the Critique of Science, Imagination and New Anthropology* [Slovenia] 33 (222): 200–217.

Chilcote, Ronald H. 2000. *Theories of Comparative Political Economy*. Boulder, CO: Westview Press.

_____. 2003. "Post-Marxism: The Retreat from Class in Latin America." In *Development in Theory and Practice: Latin American Perspectives in the Classroom*, ed. Ronald H. Chilcote. Boulder, CO: Rowman and Littlefield, 84–186.

Chomsky, Noam. 1987. *Turning the Tide: The U.S. and Latin America*. 2nd ed. Montreal: Black Rose.

_____. 1993. *The Prosperous Few and the Restless Many*. Interviewed by David Barsamian. Berkeley, CA: Odonian Press.

_____. 1996. *Class Warfare: Interviews with David Barsamian*. Monroe, ME: Common Courage Press.

_____. 2000. *Rogue States: The Rule of Force in World Affairs*. Cambridge, MA: South End Press.

Christie, Nils. 1994. *Crime Control as Industry: Towards Gulags, Western Style*. 2nd ed. London: Routledge.

Cleaver, Harry M. 1994. "The Chiapas Uprising." *Studies of Political Economy* 44:141–157.

CNDPI. 2000a. "Cuadro 1. Población Total, Población Indígena y Sus Características. Población Total e Indígena de 5 años y mas, Total y Hablantes de Lengua Indígena, Según Condición de Habla Española, Leguas Predominantes y Tipo de Municipio, México 2000." CNDPI. http://www.cdi.gob.mx/indicadores/em_cuadro01_oax.pdf.

CNDPI. 2000b. "Cuadro 8. Ingresos. Población Indígena Ocupada, Según Nivel de Ingresos en Salarios Mínimos Mensuales Por Municipio Indígena o Con Presencia de Población Indígena, México." CNDPI. http://www.cdi.gob.mx/indicadores/em_cuadro08_oax.pdf.

Cockcroft, James D. 1983. *Mexico: Class Formation, Capital Accumulation, and the State.* New York: Monthly Review Press.

_____. 1998. *Mexico's Hope: An Encounter with Politics and History.* New York: Monthly Review Press.

Cohen, Leah. 1997. *Glass Paper Beans: Revelations on the Nature and Value of Ordinary Things.* New York: Doubleday.

Comité Clandestino Revolucionario Indígena. "Primera Sesión Plenaria del 16 de Septiembre de 2005." In *Revista Rebeldía.* México, September 18, 2005. http://www.revistarebeldia.org/revistas/numero 35/07primerareunionplenariayresumenesdedsicusion.pdf.

Common Frontier. "About Us." http://www.commonfrontiers.ca/aboutus.html (accessed February 16, 2009).

Consejo Nacional de Población. 2005. La Desigualdad en la Distribución del Ingreso Monetario en México. México D.F. http://www.conapo.gob.mx/publicaciones/desigualdad_%20ingreso/desigual dad.pdf.

Cook, Maria Lorena. 1996. *Organizing Dissent: Unions, the State, and the Democratic Teacher's Movement in Mexico.* University Park: Pennsylvania State University Press.

Cooper, Marc. 1995. "Starting from Chiapas: The Zapatistas Fire the Shot Heard Around the World." In *The New American Crisis: Radical Analyses of the Problems Facing America Today,* ed. Greg Ruggiero and Stuart Sahulka, 126–138. New York: New Press.

Córdova, Arnaldo. 1974. *La Política de Masas del Cardenismo.* México D.F.: Ediciones Era.

_____. 1979. *La Política de Masas y el Futuro de la Izquierda en México.* México D.F.: Ediciones Era.

_____. 1989. "El Corporativismo Mexicano Hoy." In *Sociedad, Desarrollo y Sistema Política en México,* ed. Francisco López Cámara, 39–46. México D.F.: Universidad Nacional Autónoma de México.

Coser, Lewis. 1964. *The Functions of Social Conflict.* 2nd ed. New York: Free Press.

Cotarelo, Maria Celia, and Fabián Fernández. 1997. "La Toma de Fabricas: Argentina, 1964." *Razón y Revolución* 3. http://www.razonyrevolucion.org.ar/textos/revryr/prodetrab/ryr3Cotarelo.pdf.

Cuevas Fuentes, Rogelio, and Lindsay Windhager. 2006. "Oaxaca: The Popular Uprising Escalates." *Relay: A Socialist Project Review* 14 (November/December): 22–24.

D'Aliesio, Renata. 2011. "Canadians Can't Complain: Better Life Index." *Globe and Mail,* May 24, A6.

Dangl, Benjamin. 2005. "Member of Worker-Run Factory in Argentina Was Kidnapped, Tortured." *Znet,* March 9. http://www.zmag.org/content/showarticle.cfm?ItemID=7403.

Delgado, Álvaro, and Verónica Espinosa. March 31, 2002. "En Guanajuato, Corporativismo Panista." *Proceso # 1326.*

Department of Finance, Canada. 2002. "G-20 Backgrounder." Government of Canada, January 9. http://www.fin.gc.ca/g20/docs/bkgrnd-e.html.

DESMI. 2007. "Contexto Político, Económico y Social de la Región en Donde DESMI Interviene." http://www.laneta.org/desmiac/Contexto_Pol_Econ.htm (accessed May 22).

Devlin, Robert, and Ricardo Ffrench-Davis. 1999. "Towards an Evaluation of Regional Integration in Latin American in the 1990s." *World Economy* 22 (2): 261–290.

De Vos, Jan. 2000. "Raíces Históricas de la Crisis Chiapaneca." In *Chiapas: Los Desafíos de la Paz,* ed. Cynthia Arnson and Raúl Benítez Manaut, 29–40. México: Miguel Ángel Porrua.

Díaz Polanco, Héctor. 2003. *Autonomía Regional: La Autodeterminación de los Pueblos Indios.* 4th ed. México: Siglo XXI.

Diebel, Linda. 2005. *Betrayed: The Assassination of Digna Ochoa.* Toronto: HarperCollins.

Domínguez, Jorge. 1999. "The Transformation of Mexico's Electoral and Party Systems, 1988–1997: An Introduction." In *Toward Mexico's Democratization: Parties, Campaigns, Elections, and Public Opinion,* ed. Jorge Domínguez and Alejandro Poiré, 1–23. New York: Routledge.

Domínguez, Jorge I., and James A. McCann. 1996. *Democratizing Mexico: Public Opinion and Electoral Choices.* Baltimore: Johns Hopkins University Press.

Edwards, Sebastian. 1995. *Crisis and Reform in Latin América: From Despair to Hope.* New York: Oxford University Press.

Eisenstadt, Todd A. 2007. "Usos y Costumbres and Post Electoral Conflicts in Oaxaca, México, 1995–2004: An Empirical Normative Assessment." *Latin American Research Review* 42 (1): 52–77.

El Argentino. 2009. "Expropiaron Zanon a Favor de Los Trabajadores." *El Argentino.com,* August 14. http://www.elargentino.com/Content.aspx?Id=53803.

Elizondo, Carlos. 2003. "After the Second of July: Challenges and Opportunities for the Fox Administration." In *Mexico's Politics and Society in Transition*, ed. Joseph S. Tulchin and Andrew D. Selee, 29–53. Boulder, CO: Lynne Rienner Publishers.

Enrique, Ileana, Ivonne, Julieta, Javier, Tania Paloma, Tania Jimena, Cristina, Olga, Javier, and Alonso. 2001. "Las Mamas y los Papas." In *Plebeyas Batallas: La Huelga en la Universidad*, ed. Maria Rosas, 41–56. México D.F.: Ediciones Era.

European Industrial Relations Observatory On-line. 2001. "CBI and TUC Issue Joint Report on Productivity." October. http://www.eurofound.europa.eu/eiro/2001/11/inbrief/uk0111104n.htm.

Evers, Tilman. 1985. "Identity: The Hidden Side of New Social Movements in Latin America." In *New Social Movements and the State in Latin America*, ed. David Slater, 43–71. Dordrecht: Foris Publications/CEDLA.

EZLN. 2004. "First Declaration from the Lacandon Jungle." In *Ya Basta! Ten Years of the Zapatista Uprising*, ed. Ziga Vodovnik, 643–645. Oakland, CA: AK Press.

Fernández Nadal, Estela, and Gustavo David Silnik. 2001. "Humanismo y Desalineación: El Aporte Teórico de Ernesto Che Guevara al Pensamiento Marxista Contemporáneo." In *Itinerarios Socialistas en América Latina*, ed. Estela Fernández Nadal, 127–148. Co_rdoba, Argentina: Alcio_n Editora.

Flores Benavides, Liliana. 1999. "Rumbo al 2000 ... y El *Barzón* no se Revienta. ¿Y Después de seis años de lucha que?" *El Barzón*, July 10. http://www.elbarzon.org/quien/historicos_iicongreso.shtml.

Foweraker, Joe, Todd Landman, and Neil Harvey. 2003. *Governing Latin America*. Cambridge, UK: Polity Press.

Fox, Jonathan. 2004. "Assessing Binational Civil Society Coalitions: Lessons from the México-US Experience." In *Dilemmas of Political Change in México*, ed. Kevin J. Middlebrook, 466–522. London: Institute of Latin American Studies.

Fox, Vicente. 2003. "Vicente Fox durante la ceremonia de firma del decreto por el que se expide la Ley que crea la Comisión Nacional para el Desarrollo de los Pueblos Indígenas." Comisión Nacional para el Desarrollo de los Pueblos Indígenas, May 19. http://www.cdi.gob.mx/ini/eventos/firmadecreto.html.

Fox News: Latino. 2011. "Remittances to Mexico up Marginally in 2010." Fox News: Latino, February 2. http://latino.foxnews.com/latino/money/2011/02/02/remittances-mexico-marginally.

Fuentes, O. 1983. *Política y Educación en México*. Mexico City: Nueva Imagen.

Fukuyama, Francis. 1992. *The End of History and the Last Man*. New York: Free Press.

Gaceta Académica. 2001. *Publicación mensual del SINTCB de los maestros para los maestros del Colegio de Bachilleres*. January. Nueva Época.

Galeano, Eduardo H. 1985. *Memory of Fire*. New York: Pantheon Books.

García de León, Antonio. 1995. "Chiapas: Los Saldos de un Año de Rebeldía." *La Jornada* (Perfil), January 2, 4.

Garduño, Roberto. 2003. "Impone PRI y PAN el Nuevo Consejo del IFE." *La Jornada*, November 1. http://www.jornada.unam.mx/2003/11/01/003n3pol.php?origen=index.html&fly=1.

Garza Toledo, Enrique de la. N.d. "El Sindicalismo Mexicano Frente a Transición Política." *Consejo Latinoamericano de Ciencias Sociales (CLACSCO)* Colección: División de Ciencias Sociales y Humanidades. Universidad Autónoma Metropolitana, Iztapalapa. http://www.biblioteca.clacso.edu.ar.

_____. 1994. "The Restructuring of State-Labor Relations in México." In *The Politics of Economic Restructuring: State-Society Relations and Regime Change in Mexico*, ed. Maria Lorena Cook, Kevin J. Middlebrook, and Juan Molinar Horcasitas, 195–217. San Diego: Center for U.S.-Mexican Studies. University of California.

_____. 2004. "Manufacturing Neoliberalism: Industrial Relations, Trade Union Corporatism and Politics." In *Mexico in Transition: Neoliberal Globalization, the State and Civil Society*, ed. Gerardo Otero, 104–120. Nova Scotia: Fernwood; London, New Cork: Zed Books.

Gates, Leslie. 1994. "Organized Labour Under Attack in México." *Znet*. http://zena.secureforum.com/Znet/ZMag/articles/may94gates.htm.

Gatica Lara, Ignacio. 2007. "El Corporativismo Sincial Mexicano en su Encrucijada." *El Cotidiana*, May-June, 71–79.

Geddes, Barbara. 1991. "Paradigms and Sand Castles in Comparative Politics of Development Areas." In *Political Science: Looking toward the Future*, vol. 2, *Comparative Politics, Policy and International Relations*, ed. William Crotty, 15–75. Evanston, IL: Northwestern University Press.

Geffray, Christian, Guilhem Fabre, and Michel Schiray. 2002. "Globalisation, Drugs and Criminalisation: Final Research Report on Brazil, China, India and Mexico." United Nations Educational, Scientific and Cultural Organization. http://unesdoc.unesco.org/images/0012/001276/127644e.pdf.

Giddens, Anthony. 1971. *Capitalism and Modern Social Theory: An Analysis of the Writings of Marx, Durkheim and Max Weber*. Cambridge, UK: Cambridge University Press.

Gilly, Adolfo. 1971. *La Revolución Interrumpida: México, 1910–1920; Una Guerra Campesina por la Tierra y el Poder*. México: Ediciones Caballito.

_____. 1997. *Chiapas: La Razón Ardiente; Ensayo Sobre la Rebelión del Mundo Encantado*. México: Ediciones Era.

Girón González, Alicia. 2001. "Inestabilidad y Fragilidad Financiera del Pesos Mexicano." *Problemas del Desarrollo*, January–March, 33–54.

Global Exchange. 2007. "Alternatives to Corporate Globalization: Venezuela's ALBA." June 11. http://www.globalexchange.org/countries/americas/venezuela/VZneoliberalismALBA.pdf.

Globe and Mail. 2011. "Drug Wars: The Soul of Mexico." Editorial. *Globe and Mail*, May 16, A12.

Gobeyn, M. J. 1993. "Explaining the Decline of Macro-corporatist Political Bargaining Structures in Advanced Capitalist Societies." *Governance* 6 (1): 3–22.

Gómez, Magdalena. 2003. "¿Indigenismo del Cambio?" *La Jornada*, May 20. http://www.jornada.unam.mx/2003/05/20/017a2pol.php?origen=index.html&fly=1.

Góngora, Soberanes, Janette, Javier Rodríguez Lagunes, and Marco Antonio Leyva Piña. 2005. "Corporativismo y Democracia Sindical: Paradojas del Sindicato Nacional de Trabajadores de la Educación." In *Veredas: Revista del Pensamiento Sociológico* 6 (11): 93–131.

Gonzáles Casanova, Pablo. 1974. *La Democracia en México*. Mexico City: Era.

_____. 1993. "The State and Politics in Latin America." In *Latin America Today*, ed. Pablo González Casanova, 54–126. Tokyo: United Nations University Press.

_____. 2000. "La Nueva Izquierda." *La Jornada*, March 9. http://www.jornada.unam.mx/2000/03/09/gonzalez.html.

_____. 2005. "The Zapatista 'Caracoles': Networks of Resistance and Autonomy." *Socialism and Democracy* 19 (3): 79–92.

González Figueroa, Gerardo Alberto. 2004. "Organismos Civiles en Chiapas: Entre el Conflicto y la Democracia." El Colegio Mexiquense. http://www.cmq.edu.mx/docinvest/document/DD30335.pdf.

Grahl, J., and P. Teague. 1997. "Is the European Social Model Fragmenting?" *New Political Economy* 2 (3): 405–426.

Grammont, Hubert C. 2001. *El Barzón: Clase Media, Ciudadanía y Democracia*. México: Editorial Plaza y Valdés.

Grayson, George W. 1998. *Mexico: From Corporatism to Pluralism?* Fort Worth, TX: Harcourt Brace College Publishers.

_____. 2004. "Mexico's Semicorporatist Regime." In *Authoritarianism and Corporatism in Latin America — Revisited*, ed. Howard J. Wiarda, 242–255. Gainesville: University Press of Florida.

_____. 2007. "Mexico, the PRI, and López Obrador: The Legacy of Corporatism." *Foreign Policy Research Institute*, Spring, 279–297.

_____. 2010. *Mexico: Narco-Violence and a Failed State?* New Brunswick: Transaction Publishers.

Guerrero Santos, Esteban. 2007. "Porque nos Amparamos." *Sindicato de Trabajadores de la Universidad Nacional Autónoma de México*, April 24. http://www.stunam.org/30actividades/30act07/amparacontralissste07.htm.

Guevara Niebla, Gilberto. 2002. "El Final de un Ciclo." *Proceso*, September 28, 1352.

Gutiérrez Castro, Antonio. 2006. "Breve Recorrido Histórico del Sindicalismo Mexicano." In *El Sindicalismo en México: Historia, Crisis y Perspectivas*, ed. José Merced González Guerra and Antonio Gutiérrez Castro, 17–42. México: Plaza y Valdés S.A. de C.V.

Hannerz, U. 1996. *Transnational Connections: Culture, People, Places*. London: Routledge.

Hardt, Michael, and Antonio Negri. 2000. *Empire*. Cambridge, MA: Harvard University Press.

_____. 2004. *Multitude: War and Democracy in the Age of Empire*. New York: Penguin.

Harvey, David. 2005. *The New Imperialism*. Oxford: Oxford University Press.

_____. 2007. *A Brief History of Neoliberalism*. New York: Oxford University Press.

Hathaway, Dale. 2000. *Allies across the Border: Mexico's "Authentic Labor Front" and Global Solidarity*. Cambridge, MA: South End Press.

Hayden, Tom. 2002. *The Zapatista Reader*. New York: Thunder's Mouth Press.

Hermanson, Jeff, and Enrique de la Garza Toledo. 2005. "El Corporativismo y Las Nuevas Luchas en las Maquilas de México: El Papel de las Redes Internacionales de Apoyo." In *Sindicatos y Nuevos Movimientos Sociales en América Latina*, ed. Enrique de la Garza Toledo, 181–213. Argentina: CLACSO.

Hernández Castillo, Aída. 2006. "State Violence and Gender in San Salvador Atenco, Mexico." *Relay: A Socialist Project Review* 12 (July/August): 42–45.

Hernández Estrada, Julio, Manuel R. Villa-Issa, and Adán Quintana Loya. 1989. "Mexican External Debt and Its Effects on U.S.-Mexico Agricultural Trade." *American Journal of Agricultural Economics* 71 (5): 1117–1122.

Herrera, Remy. 2005. "If I Had a Hammer: Hugo Chávez and the Bolivarian Revolution." *Political Affairs* 84 (11): 36–43.

Herzog Márquez, Jesús Silva. 1999. *El Antigua Régimen y la Transición en México.* México: Editorial Planeta Mexicana.

Higgins, Nicholas P. 2004. *Understanding the Chiapas Rebellion: Modernist Visions and the Invisible Indian.* Austin: University of Texas Press.

Hoddersen, Guerry. 2006. *One Hemisphere Indivisible: Permanent Revolution and Neoliberalism in the Americas.* Seattle: Red Letter Press.

Hodges, Donald, and Ross Gandy. 2002. *Mexico Under Siege: Popular Resistance to Presidential Despotism.* London: Zed Books.

Holloway, John. 2002. *Changing the World Without Taking Power: The Meaning of Revolution Today.* London: Pluto Press.

Hopkins, Terence K., and Immanuel Maurice Wallerstein. 1996. *The Age of Transition: Trajectory of the World System: 1945–2025.* London: Zed Books.

Hyman, Richard. 1971. *Marxism and the Sociology of Trade Unionism.* London: Pluto Press.

INEGI. 2006. "Resultados Definitivos del II Conteo de Población y Vivienda 2005 Para el Estado de Chiapas." May 24. http://www.inegi.gob.mx/inegi/contenidos/espanol/prensa/Boletines/Boletin/Comunicados/Especiales/2006/Mayo/comunica11.pdf.

_____. 2007. "Employed Population According to Economic Activity." August 9. http://www.inegi.gob.mx/est/contenidos/espanol/rutinas/ept.asp?t=enoet3&c=6266.

International Federation of Chemical, Energy, Mine and General Workers' Union. 2011. "Unions Join Forces to Demand Trade Union Rights in Mexico." ICEM, March 28. http://www.icem.org/en/27-North-America/4326-Unions-Join-Forces-to-Demand-Trade-Union-Rights-in-Mexico.

Ivonne, Ingrid, Andrea, Alfredo, Cristina, Alonso Argelia, Guadalupe, and Pedro. 2001. "El Pliego." In *Plebeyas Batallas: La Huelga en la Universidad,* ed. Maria Rosas, 28–35. México D.F.: Ediciones Era.

James, Ian. 2008. "Chávez Urges Withdrawals from U.S. Banks." *USA Today,* January 26. http://www.usatoday.com/money/economy/2008-01-26-516177978_x.htm.

Julieta, Norma, Alonso, Berenice, Evelia, and Alejandro. 2001. "Extramuros en Cardiología." In *Plebeyas Batallas: La Huelga en la Universidad,* ed. Maria Rosas, 18–21. México D.F.: Ediciones Era.

Justo, Juan B. 1978. "Argentina and the Problems of Socialism." In *Marxism in Latin America,* ed. Luís E. Aguilar. Philadelphia: Temple University Press.

_____. 1984. "Argentina and the Problems of Socialism." In *Marxist Thought in Latin America,* ed. Sheldon B. Liss, 112–119. Berkeley: University of California Press.

Kamat, Sangeeta. 2003. "NGOs and the New Democracy: The False Saviors of International Development." *Harvard International Review* 25 (1): 65–69.

Katz, Claudio. 2007. "Socialist Strategies in Latin America." *Monthly Review* 59 (4). http://www.monthlyreview.org/0907katz.php.

Keck, Margaret, and Kathryn Sikkink. 1998. *Activists beyond Borders: Advocacy Networks in International Politics.* Ithaca, NY: Cornell University Press.

Kellogg, Paul. 2007. "Regional Integration in Latin America: Dawn of an Alternative to Neoliberalism?" *New Political Science: A Journal of Politics and Culture* 29 (2): 187–209.

Kohout, Michal. 2008. "The New Labor Culture and Labor Law Reform in Mexico." *Latin American Perspectives* 35:135–150.

Le Bot, Yvon. 1997. *Subcomandante Marcos: El Sueño Zapatista.* Barcelona: Plaza and Janes.

La Botz, Dan. 2005. "Mexico's Labour Movement in Transition," *Monthly Review* 57 (2). http://www.monthlyreview.org/0605labotz.htm.

_____. 2006. "Mexican Police Kill Two Workers, Injure Dozens at Steel Plant; Conflict Between Mine Workers Union and Government Spreads." *United Electrical International,* April. http://www.ueinternational.org/Mexico_info/mlna_articles.php?id=101#540.

_____. 2009. "Mexican Government Seizes Power Plants, Liquidates Dissident Union." *Labor Notes,* October 13. http://labornotes.org/node/2496.

_____. 2011. "Union-Busting Bill Stopped by Union Action—In Mexico." *Labor Notes,* April 25. http://www.labornotes.org/print/2011/04/union-busting-bill-stopped-union-action-mexico.

Laclau, Ernesto. 1985. "New Social Movements and the Plurality of the Social." In *New Social Movements and the State in Latin America*, ed. David Slater, 27–42. Dordrecht: Foris Publications/CEDLA.
_____. 1990. *New Reflections on the Revolution of Our Time*. London: Verso.
Laclau, Ernesto, and Chantal Mouffe. 1985. *Hegemony and Socialist Strategy: Towards a Radical Democratic Politics*. London: Verso.
_____. 1987. "Post-Marxism without Apologies." *New Left Review* 1 (166): 79–106.
La Jornada. 2003. "Observatorio Ciudadano de la Educación: Comunicado #99. Educación Privada." *La Jornada*, May 16. http://www.jornada.unam.mx/2003/05/16/046n1soc.php?origen=soc-jus.php&fly=2.
_____. 2009. "Corporativismo Refrendado." Editorial, February 2. http://www.jornada.unam.mx/2009/02/21/index.php?section=edito.
Lehmbruch, Gerhard. 1979. "Liberal Corporatism and Party Government." In *Trends toward Corporatist Intermediation*, ed. Philippe C. Schmitter and Gerhard Lehmbruch, 147–183. Beverly Hills, CA: Sage Publications.
Leyva Piña, Marco Antonio. 2006. "Los Sindicatos Ante el Conflicto Sociolaboral." In *El Sindicalismo en México: Historia, Crisis y Perspectivas*, ed. José Merced González Guerra and Antonio Gutiérrez Castro, 131–160. México: Plaza y Valdés S.A. de C.V.
_____. 2007. "El Sindicato Nacional de Trabajadores de la Educación: Del Corporativismo a la Política como Cinismo." In *2000–2006: Reflexiones Acerca de un Sexenio Conflictivo*, ed. Luis H. Méndez B. and Marco Antonio Leyva P, 3:79–104. México: Universidad Autónoma Metropolitana Unidad Azcapotzalco.
Light, Donald W. March 2007. "Globalizing Restricted and Segmented Markets: Challenges to Theory and Values in Economic Sociology." In *The Annals of the American Academy of Political and Social Science: NAFTA and Beyond; Alternative Perspectives in the Study of Global Trade and Development* 610(1), 232–245.
Liss, Sheldon B. 1984. *Marxist Thought in Latin America*. Berkeley: University of California Press.
Loaeza, Soledad. 2008. *Entre lo Posible y lo Probable: La Experiencia de la Transición en México*. México: Editorial Planeta Mexicana.
Lombardo Toledano, Vicente. 1967. Colección de los Mensajes. *Vicente Lombardo Toledano: A Un Joven Socialista Mexicano*. México Empresas Editoriales.
López Monjardin, Adriana, and Rafael Sandoval Álvarez. 2003. "Las Amables Telarañas del Poder." *Rebeldía* 3:36–46.
Lowy, Michael. 1992. *Marxism in Latin America from 1909 to the Present: An Anthology*. New York: Humanity Books.
Lustig, Nora. 1998. *Mexico: The Making of an Economy*. 2nd ed. Washington, DC: Brookings Institution Press.
LUX: La Revista de los Trabajadores (SME official newspaper/magazine). February-March 1991; October–December 1997; January-February 2002; 1997: IV.
Luxemburg, Rosa. 2006 [1899]. *Reform or Revolution*. New York: Dover.
MacDonald, Ian. 2006. "Mexico's Class Struggle for Democracy." *Relay: A Socialist Project Review* 14 (November/December): 24–27.
MacKinlay, Horacio. 2004. "Rural Producers' Organizations and the State in México: The Political Consequences of Economic Restructuring." In *Dilemmas of Political Change in Mexico*, ed. Kevin J. Middlebrook, 286–331. London: Institute of Latin American Studies.
Madero, Francisco I. 1910. Plan de San Luís Potosí. November 10. http://www.latinamericanstudies.org/mexican-revolution/potosi-plan.htm.
Magazine, Roger. 2003. "An Innovative Combination of Neoliberalism and State Corporatism: The Case of a Locally Based NGO in Mexico City." *American Academy of Political and Social Science* 590:243–256.
Mandel, Ernest. 1994. *The Place of Marxism in History*. Atlantic Highlands, NJ: Humanities Press International.
Mariña Flores, Abelardo. 2003. "La Recesión Mundial Capitalista: Naturaleza y Alcances." In *Globalización: Reforma Neoliberal del Estado y Movimientos Sociales*, ed. Ana Alicia Solís de Alba, Max Ortega, Abelardo Mariña Flores, and Nina Torres, 17–29. México: Editorial Itaca.
Martens, Kerstin. 2001. "Non-governmental Organizations as Corporatist Mediator? An Analysis of NGOs in the UNESCO System." *Global Society* 15 (4): 387–404.
Martín Cypher, James. 2010. "Mexico's Economic Collapse." *Nacla Report on the Americas*, July/August, 51–52.

Martínez, Fabiola. 2006. "Acepta el TEPJF Recurso 'Madre.'" *La Jornada*, July 30. http://www.jornada. unam.mx/2006/07/30.

Martínez, Fabiola, and Antonio Vázquez. 1997. "Facturada, Comienza Hoy la Asamblea Nacional Convocada por el Foro." *La Jornada*, August 22. http://www.jornada.unam.mx/1997/08/22/facturada.html.

Martínez Heredia, Fernando. 2006. *Socialismo, Liberación y Democracia: En el Horno de los Noventa.* Melbourne: Ocean Sur.

Marx, Karl. 1978a [1844]. "Economic and Philosophic Manuscripts of 1844." In *The Marx-Engels Reader*, 2nd ed., ed. Robert C. Tucker, 66–125. New York: Norton.

_____. 1978b [1859]. "A Contribution to the Critique of Political Economy: Preface." *The Marx-Engels Reader*, 2nd ed., ed. Robert C. Tucker, 3–6. New York: Norton.

_____. 1978c [1851]. "The Eighteenth Brumaire of Louis Bonaparte." *The Marx-Engels Reader*, 2nd ed., ed. Robert C. Tucker, 594–617. New York: Norton.

Marx, Karl, and Frederick Engels. 1970 [1845/46]. *The German Ideology: Part 1.* Ed. C.J. Arthur. New York: International Publishers.

_____. 1978 [1845–1846]. "The German Ideology." *The Marx-Engels Reader*, 2nd ed., ed. Robert C. Tucker, 146–200. New York: Norton.

_____. 1978b [1848]. "Manifesto of the Communist Party." *The Marx-Engles Reader*, 2nd ed., ed. Robert C. Tucker. New York: Norton, 469–500.

_____. 1987 [1848]. *The Communist Manifesto.* Ed. Jack Wayne. Toronto: Canadian Scholars' Press.

McAdam, Doug, Sidney Tarrow, and Charles Tilly. 2001. *Dynamics of Contention.* New York: Cambridge University Press.

McGinn, N., and S. Street. 1986. "Educational Decentralization: Weak State or Strong State?" *Comparative Education Review* 30 (4): 471–490.

Melucci, Alberto. 1989. *Nomads of the Present: Social Movements and Individual Needs in Contemporary Society.* Philadelphia: Temple University Press.

_____. 1996. *Challenging Codes: Collective Action in the Information Age.* Cambridge: Cambridge University Press.

Méndez, Alfredo, Alma E. Muñoz, and Octavio Vélez. 2006. "Detienen a Flavio Sosa antes de Contactar al Gobierno de Calderón." *La Jornada*, December 5. http://www.jornada.unam.mx/2006/12/05/index.php?section=politica.

Méndez, Enrique. 2003. "Gordillo, Colaboracionista Obsequiosa, Acusa Palacios." *La Jornada*, July 17. http://www.jornada.unam.mx/2003/07/17/003n1pol.php?origen=politica.php&fly=1.

Merton, Robert K. 1967. "Manifest and Latent Functions." In *On Theoretical Sociology*, 73–138. New York: Free Press.

Mexico Perspective. 2011. "IFE President Comes Under Fire from Mexican Congress, Media." March 4. http://mexicoperspective.com/2011-02-28-ife-absentee-voting-valdes-zurita.html.

Meyer, John W. 1999. "The Changing Cultural Content of the Nation State: A World Society Perspective." In *State/Culture: State-Formation After the Cultural Turn*, ed. George Steinmetz, 123–144. Ithaca, NY: Cornell University Press.

Middlebrook, Kevin J. 1995. *The Paradox of Revolution: Labor, the State, and Authoritarianism in Mexico.* Baltimore: Johns Hopkins University Press.

_____. 2004. "Mexico's Democratic Transitions: Dynamics and Prospects." In *Dilemmas of Political Change in Mexico*, ed. Kevin Middlebrook, 1–56. London: Institute of Latin American Studies.

Migdal, Joel S. 1988. *Strong Societies and Weak States: State-Society Relations and State Capabilities in the Third World.* Princeton, NJ: Princeton University Press.

Migdal, Joel S., Atul Kohi, and Vivienne Shue. 1994. *State Power and Social Forces: Domination and Transformation in the Third World.* Cambridge: Cambridge University Press.

Miliband, Ralph. 1969. *The State of Capitalist Society.* London: Weiderfeld and Nicholson.

Millar, Michael. 2005. "Government, CBI, TUC Spell Out How Immigration Will Help UK." *Personnel Today*, September 5. http://www.personneltoday.com/articles/2005/09/05/31483/government-cbi-and-tuc-spell-out-how-immigration-will-help.html.

Mojab, Shahrzad. 2007. "Women's NGOs Under Conditions of Occupation and War: Problematic Feminism." *Against the Current*, July–August, 14–18.

Molina, Oscar, and Martin Rhodes. 2002. "Corporatism: The Past, Present and Future of a Concept." *Annual Review in Political Science* 5:305–331.

Montalvo Ortega, Enrique. 2003. "Reforma Neoliberal del Estado y Transición Conservadora." In *Globalización Reforma Neoliberal del Estado y Movimientos Sociales*, ed. Ana Alicia Solís de Alba, Max Ortega, Abelardo Marina Flores, and Nina Torres, 113–132. México: Editorial Itaca.

Morales Cruz, Rubicela. 2008. "Otro Desalojo Violento en Morelos; Enfrentamiento Deja 10 Heridos." *La Jornada*, October 10. http://www.jornada.unam.mx/2008/10/10/index.php?section=sociedad& article=049n1soc.

Morales-Moreno, Isidro. N.d. "Mexico's Agricultural Trade Policies: International Commitments and Domestic Pressure." *WTO: Managing the Challenges of the WTO Participation*. http://www.wto.org/english/res_e/booksp_e/casestudies_e/case28_e.htm.

Morton, Adam David. 2003. "Structural Change and Neoliberalism in Mexico: 'Passive Revolution' in the Global Political Economy." *Third World Quarterly* 24 (4): 631–653.

Moulian, Tomas. 1981. "Por un Marxismo Secularizado." *Chile-Argentina* 72–73:100–104.

Muga, David A. 1988. "Native Americans and the Nationalities Question: Premises for a Marxist Approach to Ethnicity and Self-Determination." *Journal of Ethnic Studies* 16 (1): 31–51.

Munck, Ronaldo. 2007. "Marxism in Latin American/Latin American Marxism?" In *Twentieth Century Marxism*, ed. Daryl Glaser and David Martin Walker, 154–175. London: Routledge.

Muñoz, Alma E. 2007. "Retroceso Educativo, por la Gran Mafia del SNTE: Fuentes Molinar." *La Jornada*, September 4. http://www.jornada.unam.mx/2007/09/04/index.php?section=sociedad&article=041n2soc.

Muñoz Ramírez, Gloria. 2003. *EZLN: 20 y 10 El Fuego y la Palabra*. México: Revista Rebeldía, *La Jornada*.

Muñoz Ríos, Patricia. 2003. "Estúpida Mentira, que la CTM Vaya a Colapsarse." *La Jornada*, February 24. http://www.jornada.unam.mx/2003/02/24/003n1pol.php?origen=index.html.

Nagar, Richa, and Saraswati Raju. 2003. "Women, NGOs and the Contradictions of Empowerment and Disempowerment: A Conversation." *Antipode* 35:1–13.

Narula, Monica, and Michelle Quiles. 2008. "The United States and Venezuela: More Than Just a Gun Show." COHA Research Associates. August 12. http://www.coha.org/2008/08/the-united-states-and-venezuela-the-gun-show.

Nedelmann, Birgitta, and Kurt G. Meier. 1979. "Theories of Contemporary Corporatism: Static or Dynamic?" In *Trends toward Corporatist Intermediation*, ed. Philippe C. Schmitter and Gerhard Lehmbruch. Beverly Hills, CA: Sage, 95–118.

Nolan, James L. 1994. *Mexico Business: The Portable Encyclopedia for Doing Business with Mexico*. 2nd ed. San Rafael, CA: World Trade Press.

Nun, José. 1981. "La rebelión del coro." *Nexos* 146:19–26.

Ochoa Camposeco, Víctor Manuel. 2003. *Análisis del "Proyecto Abascal" de Reforma de la Ley Federal de Trabajo*. México: Grupo Parlamentario del PRD en la Camera de Diputados, LVIII Legislatura/Congreso de la Unión.

O'Donnell, Guillermo. 1993. "On the State, Democratization and Some Conceptual Problems: A Latin American View with Glances at Some Postcommunist Countries." *World Development* 21:1355–1369.

O'Donnell, Guillermo, and Philippe C. Schmitter. 1986. *Transitions from Authoritarian Rule: Tentative Conclusions about Uncertain Democracies*. Baltimore: Johns Hopkins University Press.

Olvera, Alberto J. 2003a. "Movimientos Sociales Prodemocráticos, Democratización y Esfera Publica en México: El Caso de Alianza Cívica." In *Sociedad Civil, Esfera Publica y Democratización en América Latina: México*, ed. Alberto J. Olvera, 351–409. México: Fondo de Cultura Económica.

_____. 2003b. "Las Tendencias Generales de Desarrollo de la Sociedad Civil en México." In *Sociedad Civil, Esfera Publica y Democratización en América Latina: México*, ed. Alberto J. Olvera, 42–70. México: Fondo de Cultura Económica.

_____. 2004. "Civil Society in Mexico at Century's End." In *Dilemmas of Political Change in Mexico*, ed. Kevin J. Middlebrook, 403–439. London: Institute of Latin American Studies.

Ornelas, Carlos. 2000. "The Politics of the Educational Decentralization in Mexico." *Journal of Educational Administration* 38 (5): 425–441.

Ornelas Delgado, Jaime. 2006. "Dejemos el Pesimismo Para Tiempos Mejores." *Bajo El Volcán* 6(1): 117–126.

Ortega, Max, and Ana Alicia Solís de Alba. 2006. "Las Luchas Sindicales mas Importantes del Sexenio Foxista." In *El Sindicalismo en México: Historia, Crisis y Perspectivas*, ed. José Merced González Guerra and Antonio Gutiérrez Castro, 283–304. México: Plaza y Valdés S.A. de C.V.

Ortiz Mena, A., and R. Rodríguez. 2005. "Mexico's International Telecommunications Policy: Origins, the WTO Dispute and Future Challenges." *Telecommunications Policy* 29 (5–6): 429–448.

Oszlak, Oscar. 1981. "The Historical Formation of the State in Latin America: Some Theoretical and Methodological Guidelines for Its Study." *Latin American Research Review* 16 (2): 3–32.

Otero, Gerardo. 2004. "Mexico's Double Movement: Neoliberal Globalism, the State and Civil Society." In *Mexico in Transition: Neoliberal Globalism, the State and Civil Society*, ed. Gerardo Otero. Nova Scotia: Fernwood.

Panitch, Leo. 1979. "The Development of Corporatism in Liberal Democracies." *Trends toward Corporatist Intermediation*, ed. Philippe C. Schmitter and Gerhard Lehmbruch, 119–146. Beverly Hills, CA: Sage.

_____. 1980. "Recent Theorization of Corporatism: Reflections on a Growth Industry." *British Journal of Sociology* 31:161–187.

Panitch, Leo, and Sam Gindin. 2009. "From Global Finance to the Nationalization of the Banks: Eight Theses on the Economic Crisis." *The Bullet*, February 25. http://www.socialistproject.ca/bullet/bullet189.html.

Papademetriou, Demetrios G. 2004. "The Shifting Expectations of Free Trade and Migration." In *NAFTA's Promise and Reality: Lesson from Mexico for the Hemisphere*, ed. John J. Audley, Demetrios G. Papademetriou, Sandra Polaski, and Scott Vaughan, 39–59. Washington, DC: Carnegie Endowment for International Peace.

Parsons, T., and N. Smelser. 1956. *Economy and Society*. Glencoe, IL: Free Press.

Pastor, Robert A. 2001. *Toward a North American Community: Lessons from the Old World for the New.* Washington, DC: Institute for International Economics.

Patnaik, Prabhat. 1999. "Capitalism in Asia at the End of the Millennium." *Monthly Review* 51 (3). http://www.monthlyreview.org/799pat.htm.

Patroni, Viviana. 2001. "The Decline and Fall of Corporatism? Labour Legislation Reform in Mexico and Argentina during the 1990s." *Canadian Journal of Political Science* 34 (2): 249–274.

Peláez Ramos, Gerardo. 1999. *Diez Años de Luchas Magisteriales (1979–1989)*. México: Ediciones del STUNAM.

Pérez-Silva, Ciro. 2005. "Deja Gordillo la Secretaría General del PRI: Podrá Postularse a 2006." *La Jornada*, September 20. http://www.jornada.unam.mx/2005/09/20/003n1pol.php.

Petras, James. 1999. *The Left Strikes Back: Class Conflict in the Age of Neoliberalism*. Boulder, CO: Westview Press.

Petras, James, and Henry Veltmeyer. 2001. "Are Latin American Peasant Movements Still a Force for Change? Some New Paradigms Revisited." *Journal of Peasant Studies* 28 (2): 83–118.

_____. 2002. "The Peasantry and the State in Latin America: A Troubled Past, an Uncertain Future." *Latin American Peasants* 29 (3–4): 41–82.

_____. 2003. *System in Crisis: The Dynamics of Free Market Capitalism*. Black Point, Winnipeg: Fernwood.

_____. 2005. *Social Movements and State Power: Argentina, Brazil, Bolivia, Ecuador*. London: Pluto Press.

Pickard, Miguel. 2004. "The Plan Puebla Panama Revived: Looking Back to See What's Ahead." *Observatoire Des Ameriques*, April. 12. www.er.uqam.ca/nobel/oda/pdf/chro_0413_ppp-en.pdf.

Polaski, Sandra. 2004. "Job, Wages, and Household Income." *NAFTA's Promise and Reality: Lesson from Mexico for the Hemisphere*, ed. John J. Audley, Demetrios G. Papademetriou, Sandra Polaski, and Scott Vaughan, 11–38. Washington, DC: Carnegie Endowment for International Peace.

Poulantzas, Nicos. 1975. *Political Power and Social Classes*. London: New Left Books.

Preston, Julia. 2008. "New Tactics to Control Immigration Are Unveiled." *New York Times*, February 23. http://select.nytimes.com/mem/tnt.html?_r=2&emc=tnt&tntget=2008/02/23/washington/23immig.html&tntemail0=y&oref=slogin&oref=login.

Preston, Julia, and Samuel Dillon. 2004. *Opening Mexico: The Making of a Democracy*. New York: Farrar, Straus and Giroux.

PRI (Partido Revolucionario Institucional). 2008. "Organizaciones Adherentes al PRI con Registro Nacional." *PRI*, October 26. http://www.pri.org.mx/PriistasTrabajando/pri/directorios/oas.aspx.

Quiroz Trejo, José Othón. 2004. "Sindicalismo, Núcleos de Agregación Obrera y Corporativismo en México: Inercias, Cambios y Reacomodos." *Cotidiano* 20 (128): 7–17.

_____. 2007. "Un Sexenio Gatopardesco: Del Corporativismo Obrero al Empresarial." In *El Impreciso Espacio de la Sociedad Civil*, ed. Luís H. Méndez B. and Marco Antonio Leyva P., 37–56. México: Universidad Autónoma Metropolitana Unidad Azcapotzalco División de Ciencias Sociales y Humanidades, Coordinación de Difusión y Publicaciones.

Ramírez, Miguel D. 1989. *Mexico's Economic Crisis: Its Origins and Consequences*. New York: Praeger.

Ramírez Saiz, Juan Manuel. 2003. "Organizaciones Cívicas, Democracia y Sistema Político." In *México al Inicio del Siglo XXI: Democracia, Ciudadanía y Desarrollo*, ed. Alberto Aziz Nassif, 133–181. México D.F.: Centro de Investigaciones y Estudios Superiores en Antropología Social.

Ramos, Armando, and Francisco Méndez. 2006. "Levantar una Bandera Común." *Rebeldía* 44 (July): 32–39.

Ramos Sánchez, J. Daniel. 2000. *La Ilusión del Crecimiento de la Economía Mexicana*. México City: Universidad Nacional Autónoma de México.

Reames, Benjamin. 2003. "Police Forces in Mexico: A Profile." Center for U.S.-Mexican Studies, San Diego. http://repositories.cdlib.org/cgi/viewcontent.cgi?article=1025&context=usmex.

Reveles, José. 2006. *Las Manos Sucias del PAN: Historia de un Atraco Multimillonario a los Más Pobres*. Mexico: Editorial Planta Mexicana.

Reyes-Heroles, J. 1985. *Educar para Construir una Sociedad Mejor*. Mexico City: SEP.

Reyna, José Luis, and Richard S. Wienert. 1977. *Authoritarianism in Mexico*. Philadelphia: Institute for the Study of Human Issues.

Riddell, John. 2008. "From Marx to Morales: Indigenous Socialism and the Latin Americanisation of Marxism." *Links: International Journal of Socialist Renewal*, June 16. http://links.org.au/node/478.

Rist, Gilbert. 1997. *The History of Development: From Western Origins to Global Faith*. London: Zed Books.

Robles, Jorge, Luis Ángel Gómez, and Araceli Álvarez. 2007. "El Sexenio en el que Vivimos en Peligro: Una Visión Desde el Mundo Laboral." In *2000–2006: Reflexiones Acerca de un Sexenio Conflictivo*, ed. Luis H. Méndez B. and Marco Antonio Leyva P., 3:105–126. México: Universidad Autónoma Metropolitana Unidad Azcapotzalco.

Rodríguez Araujo, Octavio. 2002. *Izquierdas e Izquierdismo*. Mexico: Siglo Veintiuno Editores.

Roett, Riordan. 1995. *The Challenge of Institutional Reform in México*. Boulder, CO: Lynne Reinner.

Roig-Franzia, Manuel. 2007. "A Culinary and Cultural Staple in Crisis: Mexico Grapples with Soaring Prices for Corn — and Tortillas." *Washington Post*, January 27, A1. http://www.washingtonpost. com/wp-dyn/content/article/2007/01/26/AR2007012601896_pf.html.

Roman, Richard, and Edur Velasco Arregui. 2001. "Neoliberalism, Labour Market Transformation, and Working-Class Responses: Social and Historical Roots of Accommodation and Protest." *Latin American Perspectives* 28:52–71.

_____. 2006. "The State, the Bourgeoisie, and Unions: The Recycling of Mexico's System of Labor Control." *Latin American Perspectives* 33 (2): 95–103.

_____. 2007. "Mexico's Oaxaca Commune." In *Socialist Register 2008: Global Flashpoints; Reactions to Imperialism and Neoliberalism*, ed. Leo Panitch and Colin Leys, 248–264. Monmouth, Wales: Merlin Press.

Romero, Jorge Javier. 2008. "El Corporativismo Inmorible." *Crónica de Hoy*, May 12. http://www.cron ica.com.mx/imprimir.php?id_nota=363013.

Rosas, Maria. 2001. *Plebeyas Batallas: La Huelga en la Universidad*. México D.F.: Ediciones Era.

Rueda, Jorge. 2007. "Venezuela Pulling Out of IMF, World Bank." *Boston Globe*, May 1. http://www. boston.com/news/world/latinamerica/articles/2007/05/01/venezuela_pulling_out_of_imf_world_ bank.

Ruggiero, Greg, and Stuart Sahulka. 1998. *Zapatista Encuentro: Documents from the 1996 Encounter for Humanity and against Neoliberalism*. New York: Seven Stories Press.

Samstad, James G. 2002. "Corporatism and Democratic Transition: State and Labor during the Salinas and Zedillo Administrations." *Latin American Politics and Society* 44 (4): 1–28.

Sánchez Fernández, Rebeca. 2004. "Segundo Aire Del Corporativismo Sindical." *La Jornada*, October 4.

Sánchez Sánchez, Víctor Manuel. 1989. "Alcances de la Democracia en el Sindicato Mexicano de Electricistas." In *Democracia y Sindicatos*, ed. Victoria Novelo, 109–163. Mexico: Centro de Investigaciones y Estudios Superiores.

Sandbrook, Richard, Marc Edelman, Patrick Heller, and Judith Teichman. 2006. "Can Social Democracies Survive in the Global South?" *Dissent* 53 (2): 76–83.

Schmitter, Philippe. 1979. "Still the Century of Corporatism?" In *Trends toward Corporatist Intermediation*, ed. Philippe C. Schmitter and Gerhard Lehmbruch, 7–52. Beverly Hills: Sage.

Schmitter, Philippe, and W. Streeck. 1991. "From National Corporatism to Transnational Pluralism." *Political Sociology* 19 (2): 133–164.

Shefner, Jon. 2007. "Rethinking Civil Society in the Age of NAFTA: The Case of Mexico." *Annals of the American Academy of Political and Social Science* 610:182–200.

Sipaz (International Services for Peace). 2007. "The Conflict: Peace Process, War Process; Brief History of the Conflict in Chiapas, 1994–2005." *Sipaz*, January 8. http://www.sipaz.org/crono/proceng. htm.

Smillie, Ian, and John Hailey. 2001. *Managing for Change: Leadership, Strategy and Management in Asian NGOs*. London: Earthscan.

Solidaridad. 1972. Editorial. August 31.

Somuano, Fernanda. 2006. "Nongovernmental Organizations and the Changing Structure of Mexican Politics: The Cases of Environmental and Human Rights Policy." In *Changing Structure of Mexico: Political, Social and Economic Prospects*, 2nd ed., ed. Laura Randall, 489–500. New York: M. E. Sharpe.

Soria, Víctor M. 2003. "Recesión Económica, Política Social y Reforma del Estado: Su impacto en el Instituto Mexicano del Seguro Social." In *Globalización: Reforma Neoliberal del Estado y Movimientos Sociales*, ed. Ana Alicia Solís de Alba, Max Ortega, Abelardo Mariña Flores, and Nina Torres, 45–72. México: Editorial Itaca.

Spook World Independent News. 2011. "Mexico: Labour Legislation Reform without Consultation." *Spook News*, April 7. http://www.scoop.co.nz/stories/WO1104/S00165/mexico-labour-legislation-reform-without-consultation.htm.

Suárez, Luís. 1976. *Lucio Cabañas, El Guerrillero sin Esperanza*. Mexico City: Roca Publishing.

Subcomandante Insurgente Marcos. 1992. "Chiapas: el Sureste en dos Vientos, una Tormenta y una Profecía." http://ujs-pr.tripod.com/herramientas/textos/chiapas.htm.

_____. 2003. "Carta a Vicente Fox como nuevo Presidente, 2 de Diciembre de 2000." *EZLN: Documentos y Comunicados*, 4:474–480. Mexico: Ediciones Era.

_____. 2004. "We Are Mexicans ... but We Are Also Indigenous: Chiapas; the Thirteenth Stele, Part Four; a Plan." In *Ya Basta! Ten Years of the Zapatista Uprising*, ed. Ziga Vodovnik, 606–611. Oakland, CA: AK Press.

_____. 2005a. "La (imposible) ¿geometría? del Poder en México." *La Jornada*, June 20. http://www.jornada.unam.mx/2005/06/20/008n1pol.php.

_____. 2005b. "La Otra Campana." *Revista Rebeldía*, September, 3–65. http://www.revistarebeldia.org/html/descargas/rebeldia_35.pdf.

_____. 2006. "Aprender a Decir Nosotr@s." *Rebeldía* 44 (July): 3–10.

Tamayo, Sergio. 2007. "Dinámica de la Movilización: Movimiento Poselectoral y por la Democracia." In *2000–2006: Reflexiones Acerca de un Sexenio Conflictivo*, ed. Luis H. Méndez B. and Marco Antonio Leyva P., 3:155–186. México: Universidad Autónoma Metropolitana Unidad Azcapotzalco.

Tania Paloma, Enriqueta, Julieta, Alejandro, Ileana, Evelia, Cecilia, Guadalupe, Fernando, Ingrid, and Andrea. 2001. *Plebeyas Batallas: La Huelga en la Universidad*, ed. María Rosas, 49–56. México D.F.: Ediciones Era.

Te Brake, Wayne. 1998. *Shaping History: Ordinary People in European Politics, 1500–1700*. Berkeley: University of California Press.

Teeple, Gary. 2004. *The Riddle of Human Rights*. Aurora: Garamond.

Tilly, Charles. 1995. *Popular Contention in Great Britain, 1758–1834*. Cambridge, MA: Harvard University Press.

_____. 2004. *Social Movements, 1768–2004*. Boulder, CO: Paradigm.

Torres, Carlos Alberto. 1995. *Education and Social Change in Latin America*. South Melbourne: James Nicholas Publishers. http://books.google.ca/books?id=iKI7-wb7IWsC&pg=PA1&source=gbs_selected_pages&cad=0_1&sig=wsnNDtyNrnY-kRZ1kVC83NLZddQ#PPA3-IA2,M1.

Touraine, Alain. 1971. *The Post Industrial Society, Tomorrow's Social History: Classes, Conflicts and Culture in the Programmed Society*. New York: Random House.

_____. 2002. "The Importance of Social Movements." *Social Movement Studies* 1 (1): 89–95.

Trochim, William M. K. 2006. "Purposive Sampling." *Research Methods Knowledge Base*. http://www.socialresearchmethods.net/kb/sampnon.php.

Trotsky, Leon. 1969 [1931]. *The Permanent Revolution and Results and Prospects*. New York: Merit Publishers.

United Electrical International. 2007. "Miners' Union Leader Reinstalled; Partial Victory for Union." *Mexican Labor News and Analysis*, April. http://www.ueinternational.org/Mexico_info/mlna_articles.php?id=116#679.

United Nations. 2006. *Human Development Index*. http://hdr.undp.org/hdr2006/pdfs/report/HDR06-complete.pdf (accessed May 31, 2007).

_____. 1990. *Human Development Report, 1990: United Nations Development Program*. New York: Oxford University Press.

U.S. Department of State. 2007. "The Mérida Initiative: United States–Mexico–Central America Security Cooperation." October 22. http://www.state.gov/r/pa/prs/ps/2007/oct/93800.htm.

Valdés, Leonardo. 1994. "Partido de la Revolución Democrática: The Third Option in Mexico." In *Party Politics in "An Uncommon Democracy": Political Parties and Elections in Mexico*, ed. Neil Harvey and Monica Serrano, 61–75. London: Institute of Latin American Studies.

Valdez Ugalde, Francisco. 1994. "From Bank Nationalization to State Reform: Business and the New México Order." In *The Politics of Economic Restructuring: State-Society Relations and Regime Change in Mexico*, ed. Maria Lorena Cook, Kevin J. Middlebrook, and Juan Molinar Horcasitas, 219–241. San Diego: Center for U.S.-Mexican Studies, University of California.

Vargas, Rosa Elvira. 2008. "Intacto, el Corporativismo de Regimenes del PRI." *La Jornada*, August 6. http://www.jornada.unam.mx/2008/06/08/index.php?section=politica&article=010elpol.

Vasconi, Thomas A. 1990. "Democracy and Socialism in South America." *Latin American Perspectives* 17 (2): 25–38.

Velasco, Andrés. 2002. "Dependency Theory." *Foreign Policy* 133 (November-December): 44–45.

Velasco Arregui, Edur, and Adolfo Morales Valladares. 2005. "Mercado Laboral, Crisis del Corporativismo y Resistencia Sindical: La Coordinadora Intersindical Primer de Mayo en el Fin de Siglo Mexicano." In *Confederaciones Obreras y Sindicatos Nacionales en Mexico*, ed. Luís H. Méndez B., Carlos García, and Marco Antonio Leyva, 53–86. Mexico D.F.: Ediciones y Gráficos Eón and UAM Azcapotzalco.

Veltmeyer, Henry. 1997. "New Social Movements in Latin America: The Dynamics of Class and Identity." *Journal of Peasant Studies* 25 (1): 139–169.

_____. 2007a. *Illusion or Opportunity: Civil Society and the Quest for Social Change*. Halifax: Fernwood.

_____. 2007b. *On the Move: The Politics of Social Change in Latin America*. Peterborough: Broadview Press.

Venegas, Juan Manuel. 2001. "En Chiapas se cambian las armas por servicios de salud y educación: Fox." *La Jornada*, April 20. http://www.jornada.unam.mx/2001/04/20/003n1pol.html.

Vergara, Rosalía. 2005. "Charrísimo Intacto." *Proceso*, November 6, 1514.

_____. 2006. "Corporativismo Azul." *Proceso*, July 23, 1551.

Villafuerte Solís, Daniel, and Maria del Carmen García Aguilar. 2006. "Crisis Rural y Migraciones en Chiapas." *Migración y Desarrollo* 1:102–130.

Villegas Rojas, Pedro. 2006. "Los Proyectos de Reforma a la Ley Federal del Trabajo." In *El Sindicalismo en Mexico: Historia, Crisis y Perspectivas*, ed. José Merced González Guerra and Antonio Gutiérrez Castro, 331–350. México D.F.: Konrad-Adenauer-Stiftung: Centro Nacional de Promoción Social: Plaza y Valdés.

Virno, Paolo. 2004. *Grammar of the Multitude: For an Analysis of Contemporary Forms of Life*. Los Angeles: Semiotext.

Vite Pérez, Miguel Ángel. 2002. "México Entre lo Legal y lo Ilegal." *Revista Mexicana de Sociología* 64 (1): 207–227.

Vodovnik, Žiga. 2004. *Ya Basta! Ten Years of the Zapatista Uprising*. Oakland, CA: AK Press.

Wallerstein, Immanuel Maurice. 1987. *Historical Capitalism*. London: Verso.

Warnock, John. 1995. *The Other Mexico: The North American Triangle Completed*. Montreal: Black Rose Books.

Weisbrot, Mark, and Luis Sandoval. 2006. "Mexico's Presidential Election: Background on Economic Issues." Center for Economic and Policy Research. June. http://www.cpr.net/publications/mexico_background_2006.pdf.

Wiarda, Howard J. 1997. *Corporatism and Comparative Politics: The Other Great Ism*. London: M. E. Sharpe.

_____. 2004. *Authoritarianism and Corporatism in Latin America — Revisited*. Gainesville: University Press of Florida.

Williams, Heather L. 2001. *Social Movements and Economic Transition: Markets and Distributive Conflict in Mexico*. Cambridge, UK: Cambridge University Press.

Williams, Mark Eric. 2001. *Market Reforms in Mexico: Coalitions, Institutions, and the Politics of Policy Change*. Lanham, MD: Rowman and Littlefield.

Williamson, John. 2000. "What Should the World Bank Think about the Washington Consensus?" *World Bank Research Observer* 15 (2): 251–264.

Williamson, Peter J. 1985. *Varieties of Corporatism: A Conceptual Discussion*. London: Cambridge University Press.

_____. 1989. *Corporatism in Perspective: An Introductory Guide to Corporatist Theory*. London: Sage.

Womack, John, Jr. 1968. *Zapata and the Mexican Revolution*. New York: Vintage.

Wood, Ellen Meiksins. 1995. *Democracy against Capitalism: Renewed Historical Materialism*. Cambridge, UK: Cambridge University Press.

_____. 2003. *Empire of Capital*. London: Verso.

Woods, Ngaire, and Amrita Narlikar. 2001. "Governance and the Limits of Accountability: The WTO, the IMF and the World Bank." *International Social Science Journal* 53 (170): 569–583.

Xelhuantzi López, Maria. 2004. "El Sindicalismo Mexicano: Entre La Coyuntura y la Historia." *El Cotidiano* 128 (November-December): 18–24.

Yashar, Deborah J. 1999. "Democracy, Indigenous Movements, and the Postliberal Challenge in Latin America." *World Politics* 52:76–104.

_____. 2007. "Resistance and Identity Politics in an Age of Globalization." In *The Annals of the American Academy of Political and Social Science: NAFTA and Beyond; Alternative Perspectives in the Study of Global Trade and Development*, special editors, Patricia Fernandez-Kelly and Jon Shefner, 160–181.

Zaid, Gabriel. 1987. *La Economía Presidencial*. México: Editorial Vuelta.

Zambrano-Grijalva, Jesús. 2001. "Los Saldos del 2 de Julio: La Transición al Día." In *Después del 2 de Julio: Dónde Quedó la Transición? Una Visión Desde la Izquierda*, ed. Arturo Anguiano, 9–20. México: Universidad Autónoma Metropolitana.

Zapata, Francisco. 2006. "Mexican Labor in a Context of Political, Social, and Economic Change, 1982–2002." In *Changing Structure of Mexico: Political, Social and Economic Prospects*, 2nd ed., ed. Laura Randall, 438–453. London: M. E. Sharpe.

Zeigler, Harmon. 1988. *Pluralism, Corporatism and Confucianism: Political Association and Conflict Regulation in the United States, Europe and Taiwan*. Philadelphia: Temple University Press.

Zibechi, Raúl. 2006. "Argentina: Otro Mundo es Posible; Cerámicas Zanon." *Programa de las Americas: International Relations Centre*, January 14. http://www.ircamericas.org/esp/3012.

Zinn, Howard. 2007. *A Power Governments Cannot Suppress*. San Francisco: City Lights Books.

Index

www.ingramcontent.com/pod-product-compliance
Lightning Source LLC
Chambersburg PA
CBHW080553270326
41929CB00019B/3283